Praise for *Memoir of Moses*

"Deuteronomy is a book in which memory plays a central role, particularly as it seeks to shape Israel's corporate life. Drawing on the insights of developments in memory theory and using this in close and careful readings of the text, Culp helps us realize why and how this important aspect of the book can be recovered while also noting the different ways Deuteronomy draws on memory in shaping the commitments of its audience. Culp has not only reminded us of the importance of this motif for the book, he has creatively shown us how this continues to be important for those of us who read this book as Scripture."

—**David G. Firth**, Trinity College Bristol/University of the Free State

"Culp guides us beyond the method of memory as a source behind Deuteronomy to the manner in which the book creates memory for future generations. Essential reading for memory studies and Deuteronomy research."

—**Richard S. Hess**, Denver Seminary

"Culp's *Memoir of Moses*, at once a formidable piece of sophisticated scholarship and highly accessible, brings important developments in memory theory into an immensely engaging and fruitful conversation with the biblical book of Deuteronomy. He demonstrates how the book's persistent invitation to remember the central acts of God in salvation history shapes its readers, ancient Israelites as well as modern Jews and Christians, into faithfully virtuous communities of faith who find their identity in a personal relationship with God. I highly recommend this well-written volume to scholars interested in memory theory and the book of Deuteronomy. Beyond this, the work rewards careful study also for biblical scholars in other fields, as its creative combination of memory theory and biblical study promises much fruit for almost all other parts of Scripture."

—**Knut M. Heim**, Denver Seminary

Memoir of Moses

Memoir of Moses

The Literary Creation of Covenantal Memory in Deuteronomy

A.J. Culp

LEXINGTON BOOKS/FORTRESS ACADEMIC
Lanham • Boulder • New York • London

Published by Lexington Books/Fortress Academic
Lexington Books is an imprint of The Rowman & Littlefield Publishing Group, Inc.
4501 Forbes Boulevard, Suite 200, Lanham, Maryland 20706
www.rowman.com

Unit A, Whitacre Mews, 26-34 Stannary Street, London SE11 4AB

Copyright © 2020 The Rowman & Littlefield Publishing Group, Inc.

All rights reserved. No part of this book may be reproduced in any form or by any electronic or mechanical means, including information storage and retrieval systems, without written permission from the publisher, except by a reviewer who may quote passages in a review.

British Library Cataloguing in Publication Information Available

Library of Congress Cataloging-in-Publication Data Available

ISBN 978-1-9787-0692-7 (cloth)
ISBN 978-1-9787-0691-0 (electronic)

For Andie
 My own Eärendil Star
 Little prism of pure light

Contents

Acknowledgments	xi
Introduction	1
1 A Path Overgrown: Scripture as a Memory Producer	7
2 What Your Eyes Have (Not) Seen: Deuteronomy as Collective Memory	33
3 You Who Stand Here Today: From Collective Memory to Autobiography	63
4 Making Memories: Identifying Deuteronomy's Memory Vectors	99
5 Emplotting Memory: Story as Memory Vector	117
6 Sedimenting Memory: Ritual as Memory Vector	141
7 Emoting Memory: Song as Memory Vector	175
Conclusion: A Wrinkle in Time: Memory as Portal into the Divine Presence	191
Bibliography	201
Index	223
About the Author	233

Acknowledgments

I am grateful to Gordon Wenham for his insights and comments on my work, which always felt more like friendship than oversight. Whatever virtues this present book possesses, they are in no small part because of him. I am also thankful for Gordon McConville, who offered important feedback on a central chapter. Finally, I wish to thank my friends from Trinity College, Bristol, and Christ Church, Clifton Down. Your community and conversation have shaped me indelibly.

Introduction

This book began in a Narnian land, or at least its idea did. When I was completing my seminary studies I would read fiction in the evenings, and at one point I returned to an old favorite: C. S. Lewis's *The Chronicles of Narnia*. As I came to the sixth book, *The Silver Chair*,[1] something caught my attention for the first time: the scene from which the story unfolds has deep echoes of the Bible. In that scene Jill receives instruction from Aslan about her mission, to rescue her companion Eustace and to find the lost Prince Rilian. Aslan has given Jill four signs to guide her journey but suspects she has not grasped them:

> "Child," said Aslan, in a gentler voice than he had yet used, "perhaps you do not see quite as well as you think. But the first step is to remember . . . remember, remember, remember the signs. Say them to yourself when you wake in the morning and when you lie down at night, and when you wake in the middle of the night. And whatever strange things may happen to you, let nothing turn your mind from following the signs. And secondly, I give you a warning. Here on the mountain I have spoken to you clearly: I will not often do so down in Narnia. Here on the mountain, the air is clear and your mind is clear; as you drop down into Narnia, the air will thicken. Take great care that it does not confuse your mind. And the signs which you have learned here will not look at all as you expect them to look, when you meet them there. That is why it is so important to know them by heart and pay no attention to appearances. Remember the signs and believe the signs. Nothing else matters."[2]

I soon discovered this echoed Deuteronomy, where Moses prepares Israel to live without him in the promised land. Time and again he calls the people to remember what Yahweh had done in Egypt and the wilderness so that they might live rightly in the land. It was interesting to me that Deuteronomy, like *The Silver Chair*, cast memory as a vital guide for the people and portrayed its preservation therefore as a chief calling of the people.

I was fascinated by Lewis's use of Deuteronomy in the book and wondered how it compared to the perspective of biblical scholars. But when I went searching, I was surprised by what I found: very little. There was, to be sure, a growing interest in memory theory among biblical scholars, an interest that followed on from the boom in memory research in the 1980s. But these interests were mostly married to existing concerns within biblical studies, namely, uncovering the world behind the text. Memory theory had become a new tool for understanding how texts, as we now have them, came to look like they do.

Yet the most basic question of how Deuteronomy used memory to shape community was left largely untouched. This struck me as odd considering the great importance that the book attaches to memory. It was not just that Deuteronomy emphasizes memory like in Isaiah or the Psalms, but that it pins the future of the people on that memory. If Israel remembered, they would enjoy life in the land under Yahweh's special care; but if they forgot, Yahweh's punishment would fall upon them and they would be banished. For this reason, Deuteronomy went to great lengths to set in place mechanisms of memory, which would ingrain in each new generation the all-important covenantal memory.

All this happened in 2006, when I had already made plans to move to England to study under Gordon Wenham. Upon arrival, I asked what Gordon thought of my new proposal (I had been accepted for study for another proposal). As it turned out, Gordon had been doing some translation work in Deuteronomy and was struck by the book's concern with memory. So, with his approval I set to work, finishing in 2012. In some ways, biblical studies has moved on since then, but in others it remains the same. Most importantly for this study, there continues to be little interest in the question of how Deuteronomy meant to use memory to shape the community of Israel. I have wanted to return to this vital question, drawing together other areas of scholarship and making the discussion available to wider audiences. Thus the book that sits before you.

Chapter 1 sketches a history of how biblical studies came to its current situation and why the present work is needed. It draws attention, in the first place, to what I call the overgrown path: how the study of biblical texts as memory producers fell out of favor and was lost to time. I suggest this came from a combination of scholarly trends and timing. At the time when scholars were studying texts as memory producers, they did not possess the theoretical tools to develop their work further; and by the time these tools came available, biblical studies had moved on. By then it had become preoccupied with the forces that lay behind the text. Memory theory, as such, became the latest tool for exploring those forces, for studying texts as memory products. Whatever the value of this pursuit, it is still only one side of the memory coin; we must also study texts as memory-producing agents. Equipped now with a multitude of tools, the time is ripe to return to this.

Chapter 2 addresses the why question: Why is it that Deuteronomy not only emphasizes memory but also commands it? To examine why Deuteronomy turns remembering into the very heart of covenantal life, the "fulcrum" for loving Yahweh and listening to his voice, I draw on the field of collective memory and its conceptualizing of texts as agents of cultural memory making. This is not entirely novel, as others have looked at Deuteronomy in a similar light. But what I find is that other studies have not paid enough attention to key elements of the text itself and brought these into conversation with memory theory. Most striking in this regard is Deuteronomy's generation conflation, that is, its use of rhetoric to cause each new generation to feel as if they were the exodus generation. Within this, I find two elements especially central: the use of the "eyes" motif and of highly visual language. What I discover is that while Deuteronomy does bear the marks of collective memory texts—to cause new generations to identify with the group's defining generation—it does so in service to Israel's unique theology. Through use of highly visual language, the book causes people to "see" themselves as participants in Israel's original journey, and this "seeing," in turn, motivates them to "listen" to Yahweh's voice. Contrary to much of scholarship, then, this chapter finds that Deuteronomy does not subordinate the visual to the aural in Israel's worship, but rather puts them in complementary relationship. In order for Israel to go on "hearing" Yahweh's voice, Israel must continue "seeing" him in memory.

Chapter 3 addresses the what question: What kind of memory does Deuteronomy cultivate in order to accomplish its purposes? Since form follows function, it is important to follow up on the previous chapter, on memory's function, with a discussion of its form. Unfortunately, however, there is a marked shortage of resources for answering this question, both in regard to Deuteronomy and memory theory more broadly. What I set to do, therefore, is begin by building a model that bridges the two key areas of memory theory, collective memory and individual memory, to show how frameworks of social memory become structures of personal identity. To do this, I especially leverage research on the psychology of memory and autobiographical memory. Once the model is established, I apply it to memory in Deuteronomy. What I discover is that, on the surface, memory is comprised of the common parts of salvation history: patriarchal promises, promised land, exodus, Mt Horeb, and wilderness. But beneath the surface, under the gaze of memory theory, there is much more going on. I lay out the subtle and finely tuned way in which Deuteronomy constructs a memory for motivating obedience to Israel's God Yahweh.

Chapters 4–7 address the how question: How, then, does Deuteronomy cultivate this memory in Israel? The first step is to discern what is and is not a conduit of cultural memory, that is, a memory "vector." Leveraging memory theory again, I take up this issue in chapter 4 and suggest that true memory vectors are those things that are intentional, performative, and programmed. This sets commemorative practices apart from things that create memory accidentally or irregularly. Such things are not unimportant mnemonically, but they lie outside of what the text is trying to cultivate in the community. In regard to Deuteronomy's true memory vectors, I suggest that three elements meet the criteria: song, story, and ritual. I devote a chapter to each, analyzing it exegetically and then mnemonically.

Chapter 5 explores the role of story as a memory vector. It especially analyzes Deut 6, which encapsulates the workings of memory in Deuteronomy: it calls Israel to love Yahweh and to listen to his word (6:4–5), ingrains this call in children through religious habits (6:6–9), and motivates obedience to it through remembering Yahweh's exodus deeds (6:20–25). Here storytelling is the chief memory vector, the one that encompasses the other practices and achieves the twin dynamics of generational identification and autobiographical transformation. Story, along with ritual, plays a key role in helping new generations to "see" themselves as participants in the exodus journey. In order to illumine how it does so, I leverage key elements of memory theory, especially the notions of "emplotment" and "sociomental topography." These allow us to pinpoint the power of story and its unique role in memory-making.

Chapter 6 explores the role of ritual as a memory vector. Focusing on the festive calendar in Deut 16, it builds on the idea that Deuteronomy organizes its pilgrimage feasts as a mnemonic device for community life. Over the course of the year, the three feasts take worshippers on a symbolic journey from Egypt to the promised land: Passover–Unleavened Bread commemorates the exodus and wilderness experiences, and Weeks and Booths commemorate the promised land. They accomplish this especially through elements of calendrical and gestural repetition, performing the ritual in such a way as to mimic the circumstances of the original event. In this way, Israel's pilgrimage feasts take the core elements of covenantal memory and ingrain them in a unique manner: by "sedimenting" them into the very bodies of the people. My own work advances previous studies in a number of ways, especially by showing that there is another form of repetition at work, which I call "emotive" repetition: the feasts create "mood congruency" by taking worshippers from the bitterness of Egypt (Passover-Unleavened Bread) to the joy of the promised land (Weeks and Booths).

Chapter 7 explores the role of song as a memory vector. It focuses on the Song of Moses in Deut 32, a text that echoes throughout the Old and New Testaments but which at times gets overlooked in scholarship. The song makes for an interesting study, because its substance and nature are quite different from the other memory vectors. While story and ritual focus on the events of the exodus generation, the song's focus is more universal: it characterizes Israel's relationship with Yahweh in more general terms and as something from an indeterminate primeval time. Furthermore, the song functions explicitly as a warning, as something that stands as a reminder of the dangers of disloyalty. As such, the song also facilitates a different kind of identification: it draws people exclusively into the Moab event, where the song was first sung. Whenever people sing it anew, therefore, they are brought back to the Moab moment and its solemn warning. Here, I leverage memory theory to uncover song's most distinctive quality: its transportive power. Unlike anything else, song has the ability to move people, to sweep them up in emotive states, and transform their understanding of the world. That is what I explore in regard to the Song of Moses.

Last section concludes the work by returning to the original issue: understanding Deuteronomy as a memory-producing agent. But rather than provide just a summary of my study, I bring its findings into conversation with contemporary biblical interpretation. I suggest, in particular, that the study helps accomplish what Luke Timothy Johnson says is the key to faithful interpretation:

> If Scripture is ever again to be a living source for theology, those who practice theology must become less preoccupied with the world that produced Scripture and learn again how to live in the world Scripture produces.[3]

I draw, on the one hand, from Paul Ricoeur and his notion of texts as world-projecting agents. But where he is often criticized, on his overly general view of how texts transform people, I suggest that memory theory is helpful. My own study has especially labored to show how Deuteronomy, through memory-making, projects a *particular* kind of world that creates a *particular* kind of encounter. And I draw, on the other hand, from theological hermeneutics. While I agree with those that see Scripture as a place where we are summoned before God to listen to his voice, my study suggests that there is more to it. Scripture is not merely a listening exercise, but also a seeing exercise; before we can "hear" God's voice we must "see" his work through memory. When we do so, Scripture becomes like Lewis's wardrobe, which draws us into its world and then returns us back to our own, transformed.

NOTES

1. C. S. Lewis, *The Silver Chair* (New York: HarperTrophy, 1953).
2. Lewis, *The Silver Chair*, 25–26.
3. Luke Timothy Johnson, "Imagining the World Scripture Imagines," in *Theology and Scriptural Imagination*, ed. L. Gregory Jones and James J. Buckley (Oxford: Blackwell, 1998), 3.

Chapter 1

A Path Overgrown

Scripture as a Memory Producer

In biblical studies, we find ourselves in a somewhat ironic situation: we have amnesia *about* memory. At one time, half a century ago, scholars were exploring how memory worked in the life of ancient Israel and how Scripture served within this. There came a point, though, when the exploration had gone as far as it could with the tools of the day, and that path of study was left alone. Gradually, it became overgrown. Several decades later, around the turn of the millennium, there would be a boom in memory study arising from the social sciences and eventually spilling into biblical studies. But by then scholarship had forgotten the old path and become preoccupied with a new one. Its new interest was in the DNA of community memory. This aligned well with existing interests in biblical studies, and the blazing of a new trail had begun: exploring Scripture as a *product* of community memory rather than a *producer* of it.

To this day, the old path remains relatively unknown and unexplored, and we are the poorer for it. We are poorer methodologically, for the study of community memory is a two-sided coin: it includes both memory products *and* memory producers. Whatever the value of the one, it is incomplete without the other. This is true for both the social sciences and for biblical studies. And we are poorer theologically, for it has caused us to overlook the very purpose of Scripture: to produce a "world" for the faithful to "live in." This is especially true when it comes to Deuteronomy, which stands alone in making memory a covenantal obligation and in seeking to install an ongoing memory program in Israel.[1] In the present chapter, therefore, I aim to show how concern for Deuteronomy as a memory maker was lost, and why it should be found again.

AN OVERGROWN PATH

In Old Testament studies, memory rose to prominence in the 1960s. Yet memory itself was not the primary focus. The primary focus was on a popular topic of the time: "actualization," the way in which Israel brought its historic moments to life in each new generation. Scholars were especially interested in how the main conduits of Israel's religion—namely, its rituals and texts—served in this actualizing of the past, so they analyzed the associated bodies of literature—the priestly (ritual) and the Deuteronomic (textual)—to find answers. What they realized was that while ritual and text accomplished actualization differently, they had the same basic purpose: to maintain Israel's covenant with God. Since memory was seen as a key part of actualization, it was understood through this lens.

For the role of memory in Deuteronomy, two works were particularly influential and still stand as watershed publications: Brevard Childs's *Memory and Tradition in Ancient Israel* and Willy Schottroff's *Gedenken im Alten Orient und im Alten Testament*.[2] Interestingly, they wrote their works simultaneously, each without knowing about the other. There is, as such, a fair bit of overlap between their works, but there is also in each much that is unique.

Childs pursued the question of how memory helped form Old Testament tradition. He saw Deuteronomy reflecting a key stage in this formation of tradition, suggesting that its use of memory grew out of Israel's great crisis, the exile. Along with most of scholarship then, Childs believed that the cult was the original conduit through which Israel contemporized its past events. So, when the exile ceased the cult as Israel had known it, there was a crisis: how now would the people encounter Yahweh as they had before? This, Childs argues, was the question that Deuteronomy sought to answer.

The task of Deuteronomy, then, was to translate the cultic into the common, to provide a new means for revitalizing the message of Yahweh to each new generation.[3] The way in which it did so, according to Childs, was through a new form of theological memory. He identified two main strands. First, there is remembering that roots the covenant relationship, including the commands, in the historical reality of Yahweh's acts on Israel's behalf.[4] He argues that this is the case for Deut 7:18; 8:2; 9:7; 24:9; 25:17.[5] By way of example, consider Deut 7:18: "But do not be afraid of them; remember well what the Lord your God did to Pharaoh and to all Egypt." The idea is that memory establishes "the continuity between the past covenantal history and the present," so as to show that the mighty God of the past is still working on Israel's behalf at present.[6] Not only this, but according to Childs it also reminds Israel of "her own covenantal pledge."[7] Therefore, this kind of remembering does not so much renew the past, but "serves in making Israel noetically aware of a history which is ontologically a unity."[8]

Second, Childs argues for a type of remembering that, in some sense, is meant to renew the past. Passages in which this is present, he avers, include Deut 5:15; 15:15; 16:12; 24:18, 22.[9] He uses 5:15 as a test case: "Remember that you were slaves in Egypt and that the Lord your God brought you out of there with a mighty hand and an outstretched arm. Therefore the Lord your God has commanded you to observe the Sabbath day." Now, Childs disagrees with the argument that the underlying dynamic of the Sabbath is to arouse empathy for slaves. Rather, he says "quite the reverse is true": Israel is to observe "the Sabbath *in order to* remember her slavery and deliverance."[10] The difference between these two ideas is the former sees the Sabbath command as primarily humanitarian, the latter as primarily theological. What is more, the latter implies that certain rituals, such as the Sabbath, are employed in the service of remembering. That is, the chief function of some rituals is to produce theological memory, to renew a past event in the present.[11]

But how exactly did Childs see theological memory linking present Israel to its past events? For his first function (establishing continuity), Childs did not make clear the process; perhaps it is through simple recall of information. For his second function (event renewal), however, Childs offered a fuller account. He maintained the standard idea that events were renewed through *Vergegenwärtigung* (actualization), though he offered his own nuanced view. Deuteronomy certainly did not fit the common ancient Near Eastern view, where ritual reenactment was used to materialize a past event in the present. Rather, it better fit with the view that saw renewal coming through the recitation, not dramatization, of Yahweh's great deeds.

Yet Childs still felt that this latter view needed nuancing. He retained two points as his foundation: that Israel saw the past as historical and that its actualization was, in some sense, an *identification with* and *participation in* past events.[12] But he takes issue with the notion of how the elements of the event and participation relate. Childs's main critique is that those who emphasize the historical character of actualization fail to recognize the dynamic quality of past events. For while an episode in the redemptive story "enters the world of time and space at a given moment," he says it also "causes a continued reverberation beyond its original entry."[13] The events are never entirely bound in time and context, but "continue to meet and are contemporary with each new generation."[14]

I think Childs is right in his basic evaluation, navigating between the cyclical nature of myth and the pointal nature of a fixed historical event. Yet to me his understanding of memory and its role in covenant life suffers on a couple of fronts. First, his use of the concept of actualization is perhaps not as helpful as it might seem. Although Deuteronomy does employ memory in this way, it is both infrequent (only in Passover-Unleavened Bread) and ultimately subservient to the larger mnemonic program. And second, Childs's division of memory's roles into identification and actualization, while analytically helpful, obscures the larger *telos* of memory. In Deuteronomy, these roles serve together under the governing aim of memory having an ongoing impact in the daily lives of the people. Gerhard von Rad suggested this years ago,[15] though his view has been largely overlooked in memory studies. To me this is precisely the reason that we need to employ memory research, for it allows us to lift the lid on Deuteronomy's memory program and peer inside to see how it all works. Such an option was simply not available to Childs, so he was forced to observe things from the outside.

Schottroff, however, saw things differently. Whereas Childs found the basic idea of actualization helpful, Schottroff did not. He suggested instead that memory served as an agent of covenant inculcation, not so much reviving the past but leveraging it to inculcate covenantal devotion. Thus, Schottroff argued that the primary sphere of memory is not cultic covenant renewal ceremonies, but the reading of the Torah at Tabernacles.[16]

In this way, Schottroff cast Deuteronomy's use of memory in the mold of the Hittite vassal treaties of the ANE.[17] He focused in particular on benevolence, a feature that sets the Hittite treaties apart from the Assyrian.[18] Because Hittite treaties aimed to motivate loyalty through devotion rather than fear, they made the favors of the overlord central. They structured the text so that the sovereign's goodness was what drove the vassal's obedience to the requirements and stipulations.[19] The idea was for the vassal to view the contract obligations through a lens of gratitude rather than blind surrender. Memory played a vital role, as such, for it was the thing that kept the sovereign's benevolence before the vassal's eyes.

Schottroff saw a similar dynamic at work in Deuteronomy, both at the level of individual passages and the book's larger framework. For individual passages, he points to a certain pattern.[20] One version of it was quite rigid, comprised of: command > exhortation to remember > re-inculcation of command:[21]

> Observe the Sabbath day by keeping it holy, as the Lord your God has commanded you. . . . Remember that you were slaves in Egypt and that the Lord your God brought you out of there with a mighty hand and an outstretched arm. Therefore the Lord your God has commanded you to observe the Sabbath day. (Deut 5:12–15)

Another version, however, was more open. It used any number of events from the exodus journey, not just the exodus itself, to motivate obedience to a particular command, though not necessarily one connected to the legal material.[22] The basic feature of this pattern, therefore, was the pairing of "command admonition" (*Gebotsmahnung*) with "memory admonition"

(*Erinnerungsmahnung*). To Schottroff this showed, at the micro level, that memory is an essential element of command obedience: it makes the command intelligible and motivates obedience to it.

At the macro level, Schottroff pointed to the book's framework, seeing Deut 6–11 as a homiletic application of the ensuing laws of chapters 12–26.[23] This means that material contained in chapters 6–11 is best understood as exhortational, as a sermon meant to motivate obedience to the legal stipulations. Such a function gains clarity in light of Deut 31:10–13:

> Then Moses commanded them: "At the end of every seven years, in the year for cancelling debts, during the Feast of Tabernacles, when all Israel comes to appear before the Lord your God at the place he will choose, you shall read this Torah before them in their hearing."

When the people assembled every seven years, therefore, they would hear more than just a litany of laws and the command to obey them; they would also hear the *reason* for obeying—because the Torah arises from the Lord's deliverance of and covenant with Israel.

The role of memory, too, gains clarity here. If Deut 6–11 establishes that memory is the central engine of covenantal obedience, then Deut 31:10–13 outlines how this memory was to be inculcated in the people—through public reading of the Torah.[24] In the sanctuary and at regular intervals, the treaties were read aloud in the treaty tradition. A vassal would stand in the presence of superiors and, as the treaty was read, the vassal would be reminded afresh both of his obligations to the overlord and of the overlord's deeds that initiated their contractual relationship. Subsequently, both the stipulations of the contract and the motivation for their obedience were inculcated into the vassal. And so it is with Deuteronomy, Schottroff argues: every seven years at the Feast of Tabernacles, the Torah was to be read aloud.

Since Schottroff was swimming against the current of opinion,[25] it is understandable that he would kick so strongly. He was right to locate Deuteronomy's use of memory squarely in the idea of covenant, and right, in my opinion, to do so in light of the ancient convention of vassal treaties (especially Hittite). Yet he went too far in rejecting actualization outright. That Deuteronomy used memory to inculcate devotion is undeniable. But it does not mean that the process excludes aspects typically associated with actualization. In particular, it seems to me that the components Childs highlights—identification and encounter—are part of the larger process leading to covenantal devotion, which Schottroff highlights.

To me, Schottroff's and Childs's difficulties in pinning down the role of memory simply illustrates the problem: they did not have available to them the tools to properly unpack the phenomenon. Their guiding questions, however, were on point, seeking how Scripture uses memory to create faithful followers in each generation. In a sense, the works of Schottroff and Childs were fruit that could only ripen with the growth of memory studies. But that is not what happened.

TWO PATHS OF SOCIAL MEMORY

As is sometimes the case, Schottroff's and Childs's conclusions were remembered, but their original questions were not. As these questions fell into disuse, they, like an unused path, became overgrown and largely forgotten. Biblical studies moved on to blaze new paths, and it did not return again to the old ones.

In the meanwhile, the field of memory research had been growing and took on such a life that was impossible to ignore. One branch in particular attracted a lot of attention: collective memory. This notion was much discussed because it unsettled long-held assumptions about how memory worked. In short, it challenged the idea that memory is the province of the individual.

Today, we regard French sociologist Maurice Halbwachs as the father of collective memory. He was the one who coined the term *mémoire collective* ("collective memory") in 1925.[26] Of course, it is now widely known that the notion of group memory had been in circulation for quite some time, perhaps even since the ancient Greeks.[27] But the title is still fitting for Halbwachs, as he played a key role in catalyzing the field. In particular, he brought the notion of collective memory to the forefront of scholarly discourse and, as such, his views have served a "generative" role for other studies.[28]

Collective memory studies have mushroomed since Halbwachs, and while some scholars are now seemingly ambivalent to his work,[29] his ideas are still a good point of departure. What, then, are the central parts of Halbwachs's view? To begin with, Halbwachs gave prominence to the idea that memory is not *merely* an individual phenomenon. He set out to show that individual memory is bound up with, and dependent upon, the surrounding culture. This includes the variety of a person's overlapping communities, such as family, religion, and society. So much is this the case that one cannot conceive of individual memory apart from its social environment.

Halbwachs explains:

> To be sure, everyone has a capacity for memory [*mémoire*] that is unlike that of anyone else, given the variety of temperaments and life circumstances. But individual memory is nevertheless a part or an aspect of group memory, since each impression and each fact . . . is connected with the thoughts that come to us from the social milieu.[30]

Halbwachs, of course, is not denying that memories are ultimately stored in an individual's mind or that each possesses contours unique to that person. Rather, he is saying that memories are at every turn socially conditioned. The very mind in which they are stored, and the mediums by which they are transmitted are culturally formed: from the basic elements of language to conceptualizations of the world. That is why one can say that even when a person remembers something he experienced alone, the recollection is still social in nature.[31]

Beyond memory being inherently social in nature, Halbwachs also argues that it serves an essential role within society.[32] Chiefly, it establishes the core identity of a group and thereby functions as the hub that connects individuals.[33] In order for individuals, who carry with them a host of different memories, to become members of a group, it is necessary to have a defining essence that may be shared.[34] It does not matter whether every individual has experienced the events that comprise this essence; rather, it is only important that each individual sees these events as definitive for his own identity.[35] Once this takes root, the collective memory serves as an identity framework (*cadre*) for the person; it becomes a template for self-understanding. This template, in turn, calibrates the person's identity. Incoming information and experiences are filtered and organized accordingly. Some things are highlighted, while others are de-emphasized and thus forgotten.

Halbwachs develops things further when it comes to religious groups.[36] Like all groups, religious communities tend to form collective memory around foundational events and in times of transition. But what is unique to religious groups is their emphasis on tradition, that is, the perpetuation of ideas generationally.[37] It is crucial for them that their defining events remain central to the community in every generation. For Christianity, Halbwachs notes, one observes this in the church's rite of Eucharist, which perpetuates the remembrance of Christ's crucifixion.[38] And, as we shall see, this is also the case with Deuteronomy's use of the exodus generation. Religious collective memory is therefore characterized not only by a horizontal dynamic, dispersing memory among the present generation but also by a vertical one, carrying memory from the past into the future generations.[39] In her study on religion and secularism in Europe, Danièle Hervieu-Léger aptly calls this dynamic the "chain of memory."[40]

One of the central features of Halbwachs's view, then, is how groups use memory to make the past relevant to the present. For this reason, his approach is often called "presentist."[41] Indeed, such a focus is what, he says, distinguishes memory from history.[42] History, he argues, is a relatively fixed framework aiming to construct a thorough and, as far as possible, objective view of the past. Memory contrasts this, however, for it is an elastic framework that views past events in reference to their significance to present issues concerning the group.[43] As such, memory is intentionally selective and subjective. We should note, though, that for Halbwachs, this does not mean memory is necessarily untrustworthy when it comes to historical events.[44] It means instead that memory is simply concerned with interpreting their significance for the present.

The focus of Halbwachs's work—how groups use memory to enliven the past in the present—would seem to speak directly to the questions of Schottroff and Childs. So why did they not employ him? Although Halbwachs began developing his ideas in 1925, the sands of time covered them until much later. The main reason for this was that Halbwachs, upon protesting the arrest of his Jewish father-in-law, was himself arrested by the Gestapo and put in Buchenwald, where he died in 1945. As such, significant parts of Halbwachs's work were not published until after he had died. When they were finally published, his writings did not garner a whole lot of attention. In fact, it was not until the so-called "memory boom" in the late 1970s that Halbwachs's ideas gained prominence. This was, of course, well after Schottroff and Childs wrote, meaning the work was unknowable to them.

So, it is understandable that Schottroff and Childs did not use Halbwachs, but what about biblical scholars since them? Why have they not revisited the question of actualization in light of memory research? Undoubtedly, one of the main reasons is that memory research itself has moved away from Halbwachs. Instead of focusing on how memory is meant to function in the present, scholarship tends now to focus on the dynamics behind memory—its history of use and underlying motivations. In this school of thought, the governing metaphor for memory is a palimpsest—a manuscript whose surface has been written over many times, still evidencing, however slight, different layers from different hands. The focus of memory studies has therefore shifted toward discovering the subterranean world beneath memories.

In one sense, it is not entirely true to say the field has moved away from where it started. For in the 1920s, Aby Warburg, a German art historian, was already working in that area that has become prominent. In perhaps his best-known work, an unfinished project now called the Mnemosyne Atlas, Warburg used screens of images to explore the survival and reemergence of ideas throughout history. His aim was to trace how various cultural activities, such as festivals and art, witnessed to this process. While Warburg's work was not identical to the kind common today, it does share the same basic focus: seeking to analyze the genetics of memories. Considering that Halbwachs and Warburg were contemporaries, it is fair to see them as forefathers of the two common threads of memory research today: presentist and diachronic, respectively.[45]

In another sense, however, it is perfectly fitting to see the current trend as a departure. While Warburg stands as an early example of the now common approach, few would trace their lineage to him. More common is for scholars to see their work as an intentional departure from Halbwachs. A central reason for the departure stems from an important critique. It concerns Halbwachs's understanding of how events are assigned meaning in group remembering.

The critique is that Halbwachs portrays the process in a rather "singular," seamless, and idyllic manner.[46] It is as if collective memory comes about innocuously, with everyone agreeing on key events and their meaning. The reality is that memory is often contested, sometimes fiercely. And because those who control memory control the present, memory is the battleground for ideologies.[47] Groups from different perspectives vie for their own to be central within the community, nation, etc.

But the view that prevails today is not one that simply sees group memory as contested. Rather, it is one that sees power as the primary motivator of such contestation. This idea may have existed before, but it became central when the field of political science began using the concept of collective memory. In line with the assumptions of that field, collective memory took on a hegemonic bent: collective memory, it was argued, is a tool that groups use to exercise control over the beliefs and values of the people.[48] Eventually, this view became commonplace, and ever since then it has served as the baseline assumption for what motivates group remembering.

It is important to note the effect that this has had on the field. By seeing power struggles as inherent to collective memory, the field has assumed a hermeneutics of suspicion. "Things are not as they seem" is the theme, and every memory is suspect. Consider an archive, which, to many, is a rather inert and mundane item. When viewed as part of cultural memory, however, it becomes a power-wielding agent.[49]

> [P]ostmodern reflections in the past two decades have made it manifestly clear that archives—as institutions—wield power over the administrative, legal, and fiscal accountability of governments, corporations, and individuals . . . Archives—as records—wield power over the shape and direction of historical scholarship, collective memory, and national identity, over how we know ourselves as individuals, groups, and societies—archivists—as keepers of archives—wield power over those very records central to memory and identity formation through active management of records.[50]

Following this paragraph, the authors then chide archivists for their "on-going denial . . . of their power over memory," a denial that is deemed "dangerous."

What we find, then, is two paths in approaching collective memory.[51] The one is the presentist path, which Halbwachs popularized; it focuses on the way in which groups make the past relevant to the present. The other is the diachronic path, which focuses not on memory in the present but on the world behind memory. Typically, this translates into scholars seeking to uncover perceived layers of power struggles and contestation. While the former path is, I suggest, valuable for understanding Scripture as an actualizing agent, the latter is what has dominated in memory research and in biblical studies.

THE PATH TAKEN BY BIBLICAL SCHOLARS

It is not surprising that biblical scholarship has largely followed the diachronic approach to memory. Not only is the approach dominant in its own field, and thus a natural starting point for interdisciplinary crossover, but it also aligns well with a prevailing ideology in biblical studies. Here, I mean the longstanding interest in the world behind the text—the discussion of sources, redaction, and the like. Undoubtedly, this emphasis of memory theory provides an attractive new tool for exploring old questions. What is surprising, though, is that biblical studies have followed this path so exclusively. From looking at the field, one might conclude that there is only one way to employ memory theory.

A case in point is a project at the University of Copenhagen called The Centre for Bible and Cultural Memory (BiCuM). A flagship project for the use of memory theory in biblical studies, BiCuM articulates its vision in language reminiscent of Halbwachs:[52]

> The notion of cultural memory is the decisive factor in a society's reconstruction of the past through a number of media. BiCuM investigates how memory is a fundamental instrument in the formation of cultural, religious, ethnic, and national identity in the Old Testament. . . . The past as constituted in memory through the presence of the collective frames of memory is the subject to the Centre's investigation.

The website goes on to identify four particular forms of media of interest in the ancient world—place, objects, narrative, and ritual—and three axes at which these operate: local/global, center/margin, and private/official.[53]

At first glance, it would appear that the center's work is an extension of Halbwachs. The focus on frames of social memory, of course, was a hallmark of his approach, and the center's application of it to specific media and social spheres is a helpful development. Further, the center extends another aspect of Halbwachs by analyzing the role of collective memory in religious life, in this case that of ancient Israel.

But as one reads on, it becomes clear that for all of the affinity, and perhaps indebtedness, to Halbwachs, the center's approach is ultimately diachronic. It seeks to understand the text not as a memory producer but as a memory product. Thus, the center's interest is "in the Old Testament as a *religious product* of the process of memorization," which "appears as *overwriting* (palimpsests) and reuse of material artifacts, such as buildings, monuments, and texts, and of ritual practice".[54] Driving home my point further, the website says that the "common memory perspective directs our reading strategy and interpretation to developing models of analysis based on modern ideas of adequate cultural and memory studies." The implication here is that there is one legitimate way to appropriate memory theory in biblical studies—the diachronic way.

The center's approach is not unique, and to confirm this one only needs to peruse some recent publications from Old Testament scholars, such as Adriane Leveen, *Memory and Tradition in the Book of Numbers*; Mark Smith, *The Memoirs of God*; and Ronald Hendel, *Remembering Abraham* and *Reading Genesis*.[55] Each of these has its own emphasis and makes a unique contribution, but all of them are ultimately built on the foundation of a diachronic reading.

Take Leveen's work. Her thesis is that Numbers revolves around opposite views of memory. The first part, chapters 1–10, casts memory as a constructive aspect of community. From this perspective, memory is a stabilizing force that ought to center on YHWH's gracious acts. By remembering these acts, Israel continues to shape itself into a thankful and obedient people. For Leveen, a key component of obedience in Numbers is recognition of and subservience to priestly authority. But the second part of Numbers, chapters 11–25, espouses another view of memory—that it is subversive and dangerous. From this perspective, memory is capricious and unpredictable in the life of the community. If not used properly, memory can unravel the fabric of the group by undermining priestly authority. Leveen argues that the point at which these two ideologies meet, chapters 10–11, therefore poses a central question: What will the people choose to remember? If they choose to remember Egypt as a place of slavery, then Israel will remain committed to YHWH; but if they choose instead to recall Egypt as a place of comfort, then they will only see obedience to YHWH as an obstacle to the good life.

For Leveen, these opposing ideologies do not divide the message of the text but rather create a unifying theme. Through careful editing and arranging, Numbers uses the two views to highlight a central call on Israel's life— the need to remember rightly. It seems, also, that Leveen sees this dynamic as witnessing to the "social drama that lies behind the text." By social drama she means the process by which cultures, in this case Israel, resolve social conflict by dramatizing it. Leveen particularly finds evidence for this in Num 15–17 where tassels, the altar plating, and Aaron's flowering staff serve as reminders for episodes of schism from the wilderness. Now crystallized in the text, these items continue to attest to the dangers of misremembering.

To be sure, Leveen's work moves beyond a purely diachronic approach. She offers a helpful reading of how Numbers exhorts Israel to remember rightly, and presumably she sees the text somehow perpetuating this call in its audiences. But to me that is the problem: one is left to presume the role of the text in memory formation. For all of the discussion of memory theory, the work still is ultimately focused on the world behind the text. Although interesting, the proposed scenario—of rival views of memory and their intentional juxtaposition in the text—does not appear to offer a significant development on what one can learn from the text itself. Certainly, there are good and bad examples of remembering, and Numbers leverages these to issue a warning. But whether it can be said that the two views are juxtaposed and represent an organizing feature of the text is far from certain.[56]

In addition to the above realms of academia, we find the same tendencies in workshops and conferences as well. One in particular serves as a good example: a collaborative workshop between Ludwig Maximilians University and the University of Alberta convened in Munich, Germany, in 2011. The substance of the workshop now appears in the book *Remembering and Forgetting in Early Second Temple Judah*.[57]

The book breaks down into two basic parts: essays on methodology or theory and essays on applied issues in the text. There are only two essays of the former kind, and they bookend the larger work;[58] the rest are of the applied variety. What is instructive, I think, is comparing the proposed method and theory in the bookend chapters to the actual approach employed.

In the opening essay, Ben Zvi sets out the purpose of the work: to examine the prophetic books as sites of memory. The significance of doing so, he says, is that

> the prophetic books were . . . meant to socialize their intended readers into a general, shared mindscape. One of the main ways in which they did so was to shape and evoke social memory. This shared social memory contributed much to the process of constant formation of communal identity. At the same time the particular shared social memory instilled in the remembering group ways of thinking, organizing knowledge, construing questions and ways to address them—in other words, an ideological, comprehensive viewpoint that we may call social mindscape.[59]

Ben Zvi's aim would appear similar to what I am advocating—to shift toward viewing Scripture as a memory agent.[60] Sadly, the rest of the essay indicates otherwise. That the world behind the text is still the focus is clear. One finds familiar talk of "social processes of remembering and forgetting" and "matters of power . . . always involved in the production" of memory.[61] Like Leveen, then, there is an acknowledgment of the text as a memory producer, but little analysis on *how* exactly it functioned in that capacity.

The ensuing essays reveal a similar ambiguity between method and application. Indeed, many of them identify important questions about memory that arise from the text. For instance, Friedhelm Hartenstein and Christoph Levin tackle the tension between the text's exhortation to remember and not remember; William Morrow seeks to clarify the enigmatic "book of remembrance" in Mal 3:16; and Diana Edelman pursues the mnemonic relationship between Pesach-Massot and the exodus.[62] But here again one struggles to find sustained application of memory theory to the biblical text, especially in regard to its role as a site of memory.[63] The majority of the essays instead betray the assumption that memory study means diachronic study. And in some essays, it is not clear that the notion of memory features at all.[64]

The book's concluding essay, by Francis Landy, bookends the work by taking up the idea that Ben Zvi forwarded in the beginning: Scripture as a site of memory. Landy particularly focuses on developing a "poetics of memory." By this, he means elucidating key issues of text and memory, namely: the thematics of memory (when it is spoken of and why); the techniques of memorizing forwarded by the text; the relationship between semantic and episodic memory; the role of sensory and emotive elements; and the interface between individual and collective memories.[65] Like Ben Zvi, then, Landy makes overtures that would seem to move us toward the project of understand Scripture as a memory producer.

From my perspective, Landy has hit the nail on the head. The proposal for a poetics of memory is very much needed, and the types of things he identifies are key components. Yet Landy, like Ben Zvi, still seems to operate out of diachronic assumptions. In one sense, this is expected, for Landy speaks of memory studies from the perspective of a "historian of memory."[66] Undoubtedly, such a perspective would attend more to diachronic things. But it becomes confusing when, in the same breath, Landy compares the historian to the literary critic in the aim of studying the "intentions of the communities that created and were created by these texts."[67] Do we not need different tools for this task?

DEUTERONOMY OVERGROWN

Research on memory in the book of Deuteronomy has followed predictably in these trends. One vein has focused on the text's diachronics and another on memory as rhetorical feature. The former pursuit proceeds along a well-trod path. The latter arises out of the "text immanent" approach and takes a variety of tacks, but rarely does this include memory as a formative agent for the community.

Probably, the most visible work in the diachronic vein is Mark Smith's *The Memoirs of God*.[68] His study centers on how the Bible betrays Israel's developing perceptions of itself and its representations of the past. In Smith's view, it is possible to discern from the text both Israel's historical crises and its responses to them. This is to say that one can identify Israel's shifts in self-perceptions as it attempts to make sense of particular crises. This is important, in Smith's view, because it illumines the background of theological tenets within the text. One tenet in particular is of interest to Smith: monotheism.

To understand biblical monotheism, Smith employs the tool of collective memory. He says, "I examine the double role that collective memory plays in the formation of Israelite monotheism."[69] What Smith means by "double role" are the twin dynamics—remembering and forgetting—that Israel used to create its collective identity. That is, he looks to explicate how Israel, by remembering one thing and forgetting another, forged its identity as a monotheistic people.

How, then, does such remembering or forgetting come to form monotheism? To answer this, it is necessary first to understand Smith's earlier work on monotheism.[70] In general, Smith argues that biblical monotheism arose from a long process of religious convergence, differentiation, and reinterpretation. The cultural trajectory that this took may be expressed as follows: from polytheistic Ugarit to polytheistic Israel to monotheistic Israel. Collective memory becomes helpful because, for Smith, it speaks to the last point of this process: reinterpretation. In particular, collective memory illumines how cultures continually reinterpret past events to make them meaningful for the present. But as this reinterpretation happens, things important to previous generations fade into the periphery as things important to the present one take center stage. In Smith's reading of monotheism, then, this means that at some point, Israel began to remember itself as a monotheistic people. As the monotheistic memory came to be central, Israel's polytheistic history was pushed to the periphery. And, ultimately, this polytheism became intentionally unremembered, that is, cast in a different light: not as Israel's orthodox past but as its chasings after foreign gods.

This very process, Smith says, is illustrated in the Old Testament's diverse representations of one event: Mount Sinai. He finds at least four different reinterpretations of that single event,[71] two of which are instructive. On the one hand is Exodus 24:9–11, which portrays the Sinai event as a time when the elders of Israel saw the very form of God. Further, this passage describes God in quite corporeal terms: "his feet," "his hand," etc. Smith sees this portrait as an older, primordial representation of Israel's God. Deuteronomy 4:10–14, on the other hand, is rather different. It depicts the Sinai experience as one in which the people "saw no form," but heard only Yahweh's voice. That voice is now captured in the Torah, which the people are commanded to obey. For

Smith, this is a newer version of the Sinai event. And its differences are due to the fact that Deuteronomy wants to emphasize the relationship between the Sinai revelation and the book of Torah. In Smith's understanding, therefore, Deuteronomy is a prime example of the diachronics of memory: the text reframes earlier memories of Sinai in a very different way.

As for the rhetorical vein of memory studies, it has a number of strands. There is one idea, though, that is common across the spectrum: that Deuteronomy portrays memory as vital for the life of the community. Yet what is also common is the absence of scholars taking the next step, that is, asking how the text meant for memory to function in that role.

Often these take a canonical approach, seeing Deuteronomy as the capstone of the Pentateuch and the transition into the Former Prophets. Two issues that have been emphasized in this regard are the imminent death of Moses and Israel's coming into the promised land. Thomas Mann, for example, sees in Deuteronomy an important shift concerning the accompaniment of YHWH's presence with his word.[72]

> In the context of the wider Pentateuchal narrative the emphasis on Yahweh's words rather than on a visible form takes on a greater significance. From the moment Israel left Egypt until the end of the book of Deuteronomy (31:15), Yahweh's guidance has been marked by the visible phenomena of cloud and fire. But those phenomena will cease when Israel crosses the Jordan. Then there will be only the ark of the covenant, the ark that contains Yahweh's words.[73]

Here Mann argues that the authenticity of YHWH's word and, subsequently, the motivation to obey it were initially rooted in visible proof (divine deeds). But from Deuteronomy onward there will be no signs of that kind, for the word will be captured in the text.

So a question naturally arises: what now will motivate Israel to obey YHWH's words? Mann's answer is narrative. Through rooting the demands of the Torah in the redemption by YHWH, Israel will recall that its life is borne not out of imposition of divine will, but out of loving relationship. Mann rightly notes that Deuteronomy exemplifies this fact by grounding the *Shema* (Deut 6:4–5), "the heart of *torah*," in narrative.[74] Moses exhorts parents to use the story of Israel's redemption to explain to children the meaning of the commands (Deut 6:20–25). In addition to its role in orientating theology, the story of redemption also plays a key part in motivating Israel's ethics. "Israel cannot genuinely love Yahweh without also loving the widow, the orphan, the resident non-Israelite, the poor, and the hired servant"—"indeed, helping the helpless is the ethical form of memory."[75] And finally, the redemptive story plays a key role in Israel's worship as well. Analyzing Deut 26, Mann suggests that the integration of ritual action and narrative recital in the feasts betrays the centrality of Israel's story to its worship. He says, "the *ritual action* commanded for the celebration of the first harvest (vss. 1–4) is supplemented by another commandment, that the participants recite the *narrative* which provides their identity as the covenant people (vss. 5–10a)."[76]

It appears that Mann more or less equates Israel's memory with its story: "the connection between law and motivation is the connection between *torah* and narrative," that is, between the Torah and "remembering the story."[77] The function of memory, then, is to provide the central engine in Deuteronomy's so-called "theology of the heart,"[78] preventing the "petrification" of Israel's exodus story. Mann summarizes well when he says that in Deuteronomy "memory is the fulcrum for theology (chaps. 1–11), for ethics (chaps. 12–25), and for worship (chap. 26)."[79]

Mann's understanding of memory in Deuteronomy is apt, and he offers some helpful developments on Schottroff and Childs. In particular, Mann locates the text's use of memory in canonical context: Israel's transition into the promised land and the parallel waning of YHWH's visible presence. The resulting issues with the authentication of his word and the motivation to obey it, suggest the context for viewing memory. In the promised land (and beyond), memory will accompany the words of the Torah with Yahweh's presence and motivate obedience to it. These two ideas, that memory replaces the visible signs and thus motivates obedience, shall become important in later chapters.

For all of its virtues, though, Mann's work leaves some important things untouched. To begin with, the way in which he seems to equate memory and story needs fleshing out. Certainly, story plays a pivotal role, but there is so much more to it than that. If we truly want to understand memory's role in the life of Israel, we would be wise to employ contemporary findings on the nature of human memory. And second, Mann appears to assume that the role of the text in memory-making is obvious. Apart from brief mentioning of things such as parents teaching children and men's recitations in ritual, he says little about the actual inculcation of memory into the community.

Others have similarly addressed the aspects articulated by Mann. Peter Craigie has flagged up the issue of memory's unique role in Israel's aniconic worship.[80] So while Mann's view revolved around canonical context, Craigie's is more theologically bent. He poses the problem:

> The abstract nature of God in the Israelite religion, and the absence of any physical representation of him, imposed great difficulties for a people living in a world where all other men represented their gods in visual, physical form . . . They had never literally seen their God, but they had seen what God had done . . . Their "seeing" was that of religious experience . . . [and] for a people who knew their God through experience, the memory of that experience became a vital part of the religious life.[81]

Craigie intuits what, in my opinion, is a key function of memory in aniconic worship: to allow a kind of "seeing" of YHWH. As with Mann, however, Craigie does not develop the nature of such seeing or offer how it might work.

Ryan O'Dowd has also taken up the question of memory in relation to Israel's transition.[82] For him, the central question is epistemological: How will YHWH be *known* once Moses his mediator is dead? Deuteronomy, he believes, answers this with a dual solution: Torah and memory. These two are meant to serve together to make YHWH known throughout the generations. Torah, on the one hand, is the ongoing mediation of YHWH's will for the community. And memory, on the other, is meant to root the Torah in a particular moment in time, the revelation at Mount Horeb.

In O'Dowd's view, the chief role of memory would seem to be the fostering of a relational epistemology. The view has much in common with a traditional view of actualization, in which memory facilitates an ongoing encounter with YHWH at Horeb. But O'Dowd focuses less on the experiential side of the encounter and more on its ability to create relational knowledge. The idea, then, is that by knowing the Lord of the covenant in this way, Israel will better understand itself and its call to a particular way of life. But while I appreciate O'Dowd's work, I do not find its premise all that convincing. There is no doubt that this relational knowledge plays some role, but to me it does not represent the central aim of memory.

In developing his idea, O'Dowd raises two other points that are worth mentioning. First, he argues that Deuteronomy uses a certain kind of rhetoric, which he calls "Horeb-actualizing imagery," to facilitate Israel's encounter with YHWH.[83] A key feature of this rhetoric is its sensory elements, particularly its use of highly visual language in describing what Israel "saw" with its very own "eyes" (4:9; 6:23; 11:2–7). Like Craigie, therefore, O'Dowd sees the visual rhetoric of Deuteronomy playing an important role. Neither scholar offers an account of *how* such rhetoric actually served mnemonically, but I agree that it is an important point and will take it up in later chapters. Second, O'Dowd proposes the mechanisms by which Deuteronomy seeks to inculcate memory: domestic education; civil structures and rituals; and ceremonies. According to this model, actualization occurs through interrelated contexts built into the various levels of community: family teaching in the home (Deut 4, 6, 11); public worship at the chosen place (Deut 16); and covenant ceremonies (Deut 27–34). O'Dowd is right to try to identify such mechanisms, and I would agree with him on many points. But what weakens his work is the lack of rigor associated with the mechanisms. Questions concerning why some things have been chosen and others omitted and how each may function in regard to memory are largely overlooked.

Jerry Hwang's work, *The Rhetoric of Remembrance*,[84] is something of a halfway point between purely textual approaches and ones that employ memory theory. He explores Deuteronomy as an actualizing text, focusing on its use of "fathers" and associated rhetoric to fuse all generations of Israel into one. This rhetoric, he suggests, is meant to create in each audience a sense that they are one with the past generations and now stand before Yahweh at Moab at a key moment of covenant renewal. This idea is not new. What is new, however, is Hwang's use of speech act theory. As he rightly notes, most studies stop after identifying the purpose of Deuteronomy's rhetoric and never go on to investigate *how* it produces this effect. Speech act theory, then, is a tool suited to just such a task, for it has "potential for exploring the intrinsic 'hermeneutics of self-involvement' in Deuteronomic covenant theology."[85]

Hwang especially uses the concept of "imaginative speech-acts." This appears to be his own creation, in an effort to provide a more helpful version of Searle's "assertive" speech act.[86] Hwang wants to show that language accomplishes things not only by invoking propositions but also by conjuring up experiences. The power of Deuteronomy, for instance, is not in its rehearsal of historical facts, but in its drawing of "audiences into the narrative world of Deuteronomy by whisking them to the plains of Moab and pointing to an even more remote past with the 'fathers.'"[87] And this is where memory comes in, for Hwang suggests that the imaginative experience is synonymous with, or closely related to, collective memory: it is the "'imaginative recovery of the root of memory,' thus binding together all generations of God's people in 'a regular and periodic *liturgic processing of the normative memory.*'"[88] Here Hwang offers what, in my opinion, is the most significant contribution of his work: connecting speech act theory with collective memory. The problem, though, is that his own work leaves a lot to explore. For one, his application of speech act theory to Deuteronomy is rather uneven, only introducing it toward the end of his work and in select ways. And for another, while the title and theme of his book is memory, he never actually engages memory theory. Like so many studies, his presumes that the meaning and workings of memory are transparent. As we shall see, I seek to bridge speech act theory with memory studies in the concluding chapter of this book.

Now, while most textual approaches have not used memory theory in a significant way, there are a couple of notable exceptions. Michael Carasik has approached memory in Deuteronomy from a psychological perspective.[89] His larger study looks at how the Hebrew Bible, particularly Proverbs and Deuteronomy, conceptualizes the idea of the mind. Ultimately, Carasik perceives in Deuteronomy a deep fear of the mind, which it seeks to control with memory. The function of memory, in this view, is to take away "the role of creative thought."[90] Instead of encouraging freethinking, as Proverbs does, Deuteronomy seeks to fill up the mind with the Torah.[91] I find this conclusion flawed for a number of reasons, not least of which because Carasik's psychological framework forces too modern a notion of the mind upon the text. But

Carasik's work does broach noteworthy topics. While most have followed Childs in seeing memory as actualization, Carasik portrays it instead as an efficacious reminder. The effect is that it moves memory out of the realm of experiential encounter and relocates it to that of self-understanding. Further, Carasik sees the text's visual imagery playing an important part in that process. In this way, he is similar to Mann and Craigie.

In addition to Carasik, Nathan MacDonald has also analyzed Deuteronomy through a mnemonic lens. Of particular interest here is an essay from his book *Not Bread Alone*,[92] but it is important to understand the essay against his earlier work in *Deuteronomy and the Meaning of "Monotheism."*[93] In this earlier work, MacDonald makes a case for Israel's monotheistic worship being an exclusive devotion to and not just an enumeration of the person of YHWH. While YHWH may be one in number, the point is that he is *the one* for Israel; he alone is the one to whom Israel owes allegiance, loyalty, and love. Monotheistic worship is therefore "an obligation that is all consuming and incomparably demanding"[94] and requires a potent engine for motivation. That engine, MacDonald rightly argues, is memory. Thus by "constant vigilance," by which he means the deployment of mnemonic devices (e.g., inscribing, teaching, singing), the Israelites mold their hearts to the demands of being YHWH's people.

In his essay "Chewing the Cud," then, MacDonald examines one of Deuteronomy's mnemonic devices further: food consumption. Leveraging the work of David Sutton and Paul Connerton,[95] MacDonald introduces the notions of "inscribed" and "incorporated" memory. Inscribed memory is the kind stored and retrieved by means of inscription, such as writing on stone tablets or papyrus scrolls. Incorporated memory is embodied, like the ability to ride a bicycle. While MacDonald finds the distinction helpful, he points out that it is also somewhat artificial to Deuteronomy, which portrays the two as "mutually supportive."[96] One only need look at Deut 6:4–9 to see this. The inscribing practices in verses 6–9 are clearly meant to cause the incorporation of the Shema of verses 4–5 into the lives of the Israelites.

The same is true of food consumption. In its festive calendar (16:1–17), "communal meals are the basic means by which Deuteronomy establishes its particular memory of the past amongst the Israelites."[97] *Mazzot* bread and roasted meat incorporate memories of Egypt and the exodus at Passover-Unleavened Bread, as does the cornucopia of the promised land at Weeks and Tabernacles. But at the same time, the very acts of feasting are supported by the inscribed memory of Deuteronomy. It provides not only the impetus and nature for the feasts but also undergirds them with narration and substance. MacDonald rightly concludes, therefore, that the goal of Deuteronomy's memory mechanisms, not least festive eating, is to ensure that Israel's remembering goes beyond inscription to incorporation.

CLEARING THE PATH

MacDonald's work is helpful and points us in the right direction, but it is only a beginning. He has returned to the path that Halbwachs pioneered, now long overgrown, and has begun to clear it, but it will take more workers with tools to open the path properly. In what follows, I hope to do just that—to help clear the path a little more.

My own work will address issues in both methodology and theology. Methodologically, it is not enough to point out the path and begin to stumble down it; we must first consider which tools will help us best open up and explore the path. And these tools must be fit for purpose. While there will be some overlap, the tools used for exploring texts as memory producers are not the same as those used for exploring them as memory products. I have found certain elements from the psychology and sociology of memory especially helpful in this regard, and I shall introduce these in due course.

Theologically, we must discern how memory serves the theology and purposes of the text itself. We must ask, in other words, *what*, *why*, and *how*: why does the text use memory in the first place, what kind of memory does it seek to cultivate, and how does it do so? These questions are especially important for Deuteronomy, a text that is peerless in its focus on memory.

NOTES

1. Consider a couple of quotes: "Only in Israel and nowhere else is the injunction to remember felt as a religious imperative to an entire people. Its reverberations are everywhere, but they reach a crescendo in the Deuteronomic history and the prophets . . . And with hammering insistence: Remember," Yosef Yerushalmi, *Zakhor: Jewish History and Jewish Memory* (Seattle: University of Washington Press, 1982), 9; "Here, if anywhere in world literature, we have a text whose theme is 'making memory,'" Jan Assmann, *Religion and Cultural Memory*, trans. Rodney Livingstone (Stanford: Stanford University Press, 2006), 17.

2. Brevard Childs, *Memory and Tradition in Israel* (London: SCM, 1962) and Willy Schottroff, *Gedenken im Alten Orient und im Alten Testament* (Neukirchen-Vluyn:Neukirchener Verlag, 1967). I should mention that there was another study done at the same time: P. A. H. de Boer, *Gedenken und Gedachtnis in der Welt des Alten Testament* (Stuttgart: W. Kohlhammer, 1962). Though significant in its own right, I do not discuss this study here for two reasons: (1) its helpful material is already covered in either Childs or Schottroff or (2) its unique contributions are not of help in the present study.

3. On this Childs follows Gerhard von Rad. See, for example, von Rad, *Studies in Deuteronomy*, trans. D. Stalker (London: SCM Press, 1953). Childs also assumed that in Deuteronomy, we find a shift from sacred to secular, though as we shall see later, this is not the best understanding of things.

4. Rad, *Studies in Deuteronomy*, 51.
5. Rad, *Studies in Deuteronomy*, 51.
6. Rad, *Studies in Deuteronomy*, 51.
7. Rad, *Studies in Deuteronomy*, 51.
8. Rad, *Studies in Deuteronomy*, 52.
9. Rad, *Studies in Deuteronomy*, 52.
10. Rad, *Studies in Deuteronomy*, 53.
11. Childs, *Memory*, 74–80, holds that older strands of the OT see the cult as the means by which Israel's tradition is actualized. Deuteronomy (and others), however, portrays memory as the way to actualize the past, and so relativizes the cult. Now, it is not exactly clear how Childs sees Deuteronomy and the cult interacting regarding actualization. But it seems that ritual, being subsumed under theological memory, becomes a mechanism of actualization not in itself but, rather, as that which supports memory.
12. Childs, *Memory*, 82.
13. Childs, *Memory*, 83.
14. Childs, *Memory*, 83.
15. For a helpful distillation of von Rad's views on this, see Joseph Groves, *Actualization and Interpretation in the Old Testament* (Scholars Press, 1987), 7–62.
16. This does not mean Schottroff denies *zkr*'s associations with either the cult generally or covenant renewal specifically. Rather, his argument is that *zkr*'s *main* sphere of provenance needs to be understood as Yahweh's covenant with Israel (*Gedenken*, 339).
17. Schottroff, *Gedenken*, 122. The relationship between Deuteronomy and ANE vassal treaties has been much discussed, especially in regard to the Assyrian and Hittite forms.
18. It is true that both treaty forms characterize obedience in terms of "love," but the substance of this love is rather different. The Assyrian treaties rely heavily on warnings about the consequence of disobedience, thus motivating loyalty through fear. The Hittite treaties, however, prefer to motivate loyalty through recalling the overlord's benevolence to the vassal. They therefore lean more on devotion.
19. Here he follows Viktor *Korošec*, *Hethitische Staatsverträge* (Leipziger rechtswissenschaftlicher Studien, 1931) and G. E. Mendenhall, *Law and Covenant in Israel and the Ancient Near East* (Biblical Colloquium, 1955).
20. Schottroff, *Gedenken*, 118–19.
21. Schottroff, *Gedenken*, 118. See also Deut 15:12–15; 16:12; 24:17, 21.
22. Cf. 7:18; 8:2, 18; 9:7; 16:3; 24:9; 25:17.
23. Schottroff, *Gedenken*, 120–21. He follows here Gerhard von Rad, *Deuteronomium-Studien* (Vandenhoeck & Ruprecht, 1948), 36.
24. Schottroff, *Gedenken*, 122–23.
25. Schottroff is especially reacting against Sigmund Mowinckel (*Gedenken*, 123).
26. In *Les cadres sociaux de la mémoire* (Paris: Librairie Félix Alcan), which is now available in a more recent version by the same title from the publisher Albin Michel (1994). His ideas were developed further in *La topographie légendaire des Évangiles en Terre Sainte* in 1941 (Paris: Presses Universitaires de France) and posthumously in *The Collective Memory* (New York: Harper & Row, 1980). The

distillation of *Les cadres sociaux and La topographie* is found in English in *On Collective Memory*, ed., trans., and with an introduction by Lewis Coser (Chicago, IL: University of Chicago Press, 1992).

27. The concept of group memory had been around for quite some time, possibly even dating back to ancient Greece. See Nicolas Russell, "Collective Memory Before and After Halbwachs," *The French Review* 79, no. 4 (2006): 792–804.

28. Jeffrey Olick, Vered Vinitzky-Seroussi, and Daniel Levy, eds., *The Collective Memory Reader* (Oxford: Oxford University, 2011), 16.

29. This is true at least of the English-speaking world. In France, however, there has since the 1990s been a renaissance of interest in Halbwachs. See Gérôme Truc, "Memory of Places and Places of Memory: For a Halbwachsian Socio-ethnography of Collective Memory," *International Social Science Journal* 62 (2012): 147–159.

30. Maurice Halbwachs, *The Collective Memory* (New York: Harper & Row, 1980), 53.

31. Of course, there is still much debate today on this issue. For a discussion on the widespread acceptance across disciplines of social memory, see James Fentress and Chris Wickham, *Social Memory* (Oxford: Blackwell, 1992), 7. For a forceful critique of the idea, see Noa Gedi and Yigal Elam, "Collective Memory—What is it?" *History and Memory* 8, no. 1 (1996): 30–50.

32. Esp. see Halbwachs, "Individual and Collective Memory," 22–49, in *On Collective Memory*.

33. How exactly this happens is a diverse and complicated issue. We shall look at this issue in Deuteronomy in the final chapter. For now, it is important to note that collective memory can be transmitted both intentionally, through purposeful programs, and unintentionally, through the various media and social interactions of life.

34. In this Halbwachs is extending the basic idea of the sociologist Emile Durkheim, his mentor, that societies require a sense of solidarity and continuity.

35. This does not mean that all individuals in a group have only one identity. Rather, each person has a host of concentric circles of identity, such as family, religion, and nation. What Halbwachs is speaking of, then, is how each of these form frameworks to belong to the particular groups. How these relate and are prioritized is a much more complicated question.

36. See "Religious Collective Memory," 84–119, in *On Collective Memory*.

37. This is especially true of Judaism and Christianity.

38. Halbwachs, *On Collective Memory*, 93.

39. We note that Halbwachs (*On Collective Memory*, 178–179) argues that another dynamic accompanies the vertical axis of religious collective memory: a tension between dogmatic and mystic currents. The dogmatic, on the one hand, is concerned with preserving doctrines and symbols according to tradition. This kind of memory, it is believed, allows the present community to live in line with the historic one. The way in which the system is preserved is by authority figures. The mystic, on the other hand, is concerned with reviving the vibrant aspects of the faith. As such, it is less concerned with remembering the system of doctrine than with remembering, and so experiencing, the living deity behind it. Individuals who are not part of the authority typically facilitate this.

40. Hervieu-Léger, *Religion as a Chain of Memory*, trans. Simon Lee (New Brunswick, NJ: Rutgers University Press, 2000).

41. See Lewis Coser's introduction in *On Collective Memory*, esp. 25–28.

42. Halbwachs, *The Collective Memory*, 78–87.

43. Overall, this is a helpful distinction. But for a subtle and penetrating exploration of the issue, see Paul Ricoeur, *Memory, History, Forgetting*, trans. Kathleen Blamey and David Pellauer (Chicago, IL: University of Chicago Press, 2004), 133–279.

44. The general reliability of memory has been confirmed by research as of late. See leading researcher Daniel Schacter, *Searching for Memory* (New York: Basic Books, 1996), 3–11.

45. Ronald Hendel, *Reading Genesis*, ed. R. Hendel (Cambridge, UK: Cambridge University Press, 2010), 31. For a broader picture of others working in related areas at the time, see Olick, Vinitzky-Seroussi, and Levy, eds., *The Collective Memory Reader*, 63–176.

46. See Kader Asmal, Louise Asmal, and Ronald Roberts, *Reconciliation Through Truth* (Cape Town: David Philip, 1996), 9.

47. For a good discussion on this with many examples, see Katharine Hodgkin and Susannah Radstone, eds., *Memory, History, Nation* (Brunswick, NJ: Transaction Publisher, 2006). Interestingly, Hodgkin and Radstone (p. 1) say that the contestation is usually not over which events are central to memory, but how these should be interpreted and represented. The debate, as such, typically centers on a particular representation: a narrative, a monument, etc.

48. See, for example, Eric Hobsbawm and Terence Ranger, eds. *The Invention of Tradition* (Cambridge, UK: Cambridge University Press, 1992).

49. Joan M. Schwartz and Terry Cook, "Archives, Records, and Power: The Making of Modern Memory," *Archival Science* 2 (2002): 1–19.

50. Schwartz and Cook, "Archives, Records, and Power," 2.

51. Hendel, *Reading Genesis*, 31. We note, too, that the diachronic and presentist notions reflect the distinction that Jan Assmann in *Moses the Egyptian: The Memory of Egypt in Western Monotheism* (Cambridge, MA: Harvard University Press, 1997) calls "mnemohistory" and "memory of conversion," respectively.

52. "BiCuM: The Centre for Bible and Cultural Memory," accessed January 13, 2014, http://www.teol.ku.dk/english/dept/bicum/hoejrebokse/bicum/.

53. University of Copenhagen, Faculty of Theology, "The Dissemination of the Centre," accessed January 13, 2014, http://www.teol.ku.dk/english/dept/bicum/projects/.

54. Emphasis mine. University of Copenhagen, "The Dissemination of the Centre," http://www.teol.ku.dk/english/dept/bicum/projects/.

55. Adriane Leveen, *Memory and Tradition in the Book of Numbers* (Cambridge, UK: Cambridge University Press, 2008); Mark S. Smith, *The Memoirs of God: History, Memory, and the Experience of the Divine in Ancient Israel* (Minneapolis, MN: Fortress, 2004); Hendel, "Cultural Memory," 28–46, in *Reading Genesis*, ed. R. Hendel (Cambridge, UK: Cambridge University Press, 2010) and *Remembering Abraham* (Oxford: Oxford University Press, 2005).

56. For a brief discussion of Leveen's work, see my review in *Anvil: Journal of Theology and Mission* 26 (2009): 293–94.

57. Ehud Ben Zvi and Christoph Levin, eds., *FAT 85* (Tübingen: Mohr Siebeck, 2012).

58. The essays on method and theory, respectively: Ehud Ben Zvi, "Remembering the Prophets through the Reading and Rereading of a Collection of Prophetic Books in Yehud: Methodological Considerations and Explorations," 17–44; and Francis Landy, "Notes Towards a Poetics of Memory in Ancient Israel," 331–45.

59. Ben Zvi, "Remembering the Prophets," 18.

60. This is reinforced by the language he uses discussing the notion of sites of memory as "a mechanism for socialization and social reproduction" (p. 40.).

61. See pp. 29 and 40, respectively.

62. Respectively: Hartenstein, "YHWH's Ways and New Creation in Deutero-Isaiah," 73–89; Levin, "'Days are Coming, When It Shall No Longer Be Said' Remembering and Forgetting in the Book of Jeremiah," 105–24; Morrow, "Memory and Socialization in Malachi 2:17–3:5 and 3:13–21," 125–42; Edelman, "Exodus and Pesach-Massot as Evolving Social Memory," 161–93.

63. There are a couple of notable exceptions: Sonya Kostamo, "Remembering Interactions Between Ahaz and Isaiah," 55–72 and Kåre Berge, "The Anti-Hero as a Figure of Memory and Didacticism in Exodus: The Case of Pharaoh and Moses," 145–60.

64. See Christina Ehring, "YHWH's Return in Isaiah 40:1–11* and 52:7–10: Pre-exilic Cultic Traditions of Jerusalem and Babylonian Influence," 91–104.

65. Landy, "Poetics of Memory," 342.

66. See, for instance, pp. 336–37.

67. Landy, "Poetics of Memory," 337.

68. Smith, *Memoirs*.

69. Smith, *Memoirs*, 3. He does so primarily in chapter 4: "The Formation of Israel's Concept of God: Collective Memory and Amnesia in the Bible," 124–58.

70. See Mark S. Smith, *The Origins of Biblical Monotheism* (Oxford: Oxford University Press, 2001) and *The Early History of God*, 2nd ed. (Grand Rapids, MI: Eerdmans, 2002).

71. Smith, *Memoirs*, 140–48.

72. Thomas W. Mann, *The Book of the Torah* (Louisville, KY: Westminster John Knox, 1988).

73. Mann, *Torah*, 144.

74. Mann, *Torah*, 150.

75. Mann, *Torah*, 153.

76. Mann, *Torah*, 155.

77. Mann, *Torah*, 153.

78. Mann acknowledges that Deuteronomy uses other motivational tools, which he details as sanctions (24:7), blessings and curses (Chs. 27–28), holiness (14:1–2), and humanitarianism (24:6) (p. 153).

79. Mann, *Torah*, 156.

80. Peter Craigie, *The Book of Deuteronomy*, NICOT (Grand Rapids, MI: Eerdmans, 1976).

81. Craigie, *The Book of Deuteronomy*, 132–33.

82. Ryan O'Dowd, "Memory on the Boundary: Epistemology in Deuteronomy," in *The Bible and Epistemology: Biblical Soundings on the Knowledge of God*, ed. Mary Healy and Robin Parry (Milton Keynes: Paternoster, 2007); and Ryan O'Dowd, *The Wisdom of Torah: Epistemology in Deuteronomy and the Wisdom Literature* (Göttingen: Vandenhoeck & Ruprecht, 2009), 25–52.

83. O'Dowd, "Memory on the Boundary," 7.

84. Jerry Hwang, *The Rhetoric of Remembrance: An Investigation of the "Fathers" in Deuteronomy* (Winona Lake, IN: Eisenbrauns, 2012).

85. Hwang, *Rhetoric of Remembrance*, 169, quoting the phrase coined by Anthony Thiselton. Hwang rightly notes that speech act theory has had surprisingly little impact on Deuteronomy studies, an area where it would be most natural.

86. Hwang, *Rhetoric of Remembrance*, 175.

87. Hwang, *Rhetoric of Remembrance*, 175.

88. Hwang, *Rhetoric of Remembrance*, 175, quoting Walter Bruggemann. Also, see p. 8 where Hwang labels this same dynamic "collective memory."

89. Michael Carasik, *Theologies of the Mind in Biblical Israel* (New York: Peter Lang, 2006). See especially "Deuteronomy and the Control of the Mind," 177–217.

90. Carasik, *Theologies of the Mind*, 214.

91. For more on Carasik's understanding of Proverbs and Deuteronomy in this regard, see his article "To See a Sound: A Deuteronomic Rereading of Exodus 20:15," *Prooftexts* 19, no. 3 (1999): 257–76.

92. Nathan MacDonald, "Chewing the Cud: Food and Memory in Deuteronomy," in *Not Bread Alone*, 70–99 (Oxford University Press, 2009).

93. Nathan MacDonald, "Recite Them: Remembering 'Monotheism,'" in *Deuteronomy and the Meaning of "Monotheism"*, 124–50 (Mohr Siebeck, 2003).

94. MacDonald, *Monotheism*, 210.

95. David E. Sutton, *Remembrance of Repasts*, 2nd ed. (Oxford: Berg, 2001) and Paul Connerton, *How Societies Remember* (Cambridge, UK: Cambridge University Press, 1989).

96. MacDonald, "Chewing the Cud," 96.

97. MacDonald, "Chewing the Cud," 96.

Chapter 2

What Your Eyes Have (Not) Seen

Deuteronomy as Collective Memory

Deuteronomy focuses on memory, but this in itself is not unique, for other Old Testament books do so as well (e.g., Isaiah, Ezekiel, Psalms). What makes Deuteronomy unique is not that it emphasizes memory, but that it *commands* it. That Deuteronomy turns remembering into a covenantal duty is what sets it apart from other books. So the question, then, is *why*? Why of all the biblical books is it that Deuteronomy sees memory as so important and puts it at the center of covenantal life? Or in Thomas Mann's words, why does memory become here "the fulcrum for theology (Chaps. 1–11), for ethics (Chaps. 12–25), and for worship (chap. 26)"?[1] That is what I seek to answer in this chapter.

DEUTERONOMY AS MEMORY MAKER

Jan Assmann offers a good point of departure when he says the following about memory in Deuteronomy:[2]

> We undoubtedly can speak here of a cultural, ritual memory technique that stands in the service of bonding memory and has the purpose of bringing to life and stabilizing a collective identity through a process of symbolic dramatization . . . Here, if anywhere in world literature, we have a text whose theme is "making memory."[3]

In this way, Assmann marks Deuteronomy as a collective memory text[4] in the tradition of Maurice Halbwachs.[5] That is, he sees the book as having "presentist" concerns and using memory to address those concerns.

To Assmann, the overarching concern that Deuteronomy addresses is Israel's "liminal situation."[6] The people face a great transition from life under Moses in the wilderness to life in the promised land without him. Assmann sees the text anticipating challenges in three areas in particular: spatial, lifestyle, and temporal.

Spatially and lifestyle-wise the people are crossing the Jordan and so face the transition from desert to fertile land, from nomadism to settled life. The transition itself will not be difficult, for a multitude of blessings will accompany it. Israel will enter "a good land, a land of brooks of water, of fountains and springs, flowing out in the valleys and hills, a land of wheat and barley, of vines and fig trees and pomegranates, a land of olive trees and honey," where they "will eat bread without scarcity . . . [and] lack nothing" and in which they will find plentiful iron and copper (Deut 8:7–9). But in Deuteronomy's view, the plenty is the problem, for it will cause the people to grow satiated and proud. As such, Moses exhorts Israel to remember the wilderness (8:2–5, 11–16), in order to maintain the fear of the Lord (v. 6) and humility (v. 3).

In this capacity, memory is functioning as what Assmann calls a "counterfactual agent":[7]

> The people are expected to master the trick of remembering privation in the midst of abundance, and to recollect their nomadic lifestyle while living a settled existence in towns or in the fields. In short, they must recollect a way of life that is not confirmed by any "framework" of their present reality . . . [counterfactual memory] keeps present to the mind a yesterday that conflicts with every today.[8]

Assmann's premise here is helpful: that memory is meant to reinforce a reality key to Israel's identity, but which finds no reminders in daily life.[9]

Beyond serving as a counterfactual against culture, Assmann sees memory also as one against religion. He calls this aspect "extraterritoriality."[10]

> The extraterritorial nature of memory seems to me to be closely linked with the positioning of revelation outside the worldly reality . . . The people had to leave Egypt in order to be able to enter into the new world of the Law and of monotheism, and now, everything depends on them being able to remain in this new world . . . This means that the laws that they are to remember and abide by are not the laws of the land, but the extraterritorial laws from Mount Sinai. By obeying these laws the people live as strangers on this earth.[11]

Israel was brought out of Egypt and is coming into the promised land, but in between it was in the wilderness. And in the wilderness—the extra territory—Yahweh revealed and covenanted himself to Israel. Therefore, Assmann argues that Israel's normative memory is meant for more than establishing

Israel's identity; it is the reminder that inherent in this identity is a certain otherness or set-apartness.

And temporally, the people are entering a new era, one without the eyewitnesses to Yahweh's mighty deeds.

> These things have been experienced by the generation of contemporary witnesses who now, after forty years in the wilderness, are about to die. To make sure that this memory does not die with them, it has to be transmuted into tradition, into the symbolic forms of cultural memory . . . [This] salvages memory from oblivion and elevates the experiences of the exodus, the revelation, and the wilderness to the status of a normative past for all future generations.[12]

The memories of the eyewitnesses must be preserved before the exodus generation dies out so that their memories might be told in each new generation. In this way, Deuteronomy seeks to establish a "chain of memory."[13]

THE BLURRING OF GENERATIONS

Assmann's approach is generally helpful, especially in how it highlights Deuteronomy's aim to consolidate and perpetuate defining memories. But there are also some weaknesses. Most notably, his approach appears to lean more on memory theory than Deuteronomy scholarship, which means he overlooks key elements of the book's rhetoric and theology. This is unfortunate, for some of these are vital for understanding memory and would further unlock the questions he asks. One element is particularly important, and we turn to it now: Deuteronomy's collectivizing of Israel.

In Assmann's view, the audience of Deuteronomy is the exodus generation, and the book's aim is to capture their eyewitness testimony before the generation dies out.[14] The difficulty with this, however, is that it overlooks a defining feature of the text: the so-called "problem of the generations." By this we mean the way in which Deuteronomy portrays the exodus generation as dead and gone but then speaks to its audience as if they were that generation. The book begins, for example, by saying this:[15]

> And the time from our leaving Kadesh-Barnea until we crossed the brook Zered was thirty-eight years, until the entire generation, that is, the men of war, had perished from the camp, as the Lord had sworn to them. For indeed the hand of the Lord was against them, to destroy them from the camp, until they had perished. (Deut 2:14–15)

After saying this, however, the book goes on to speak to the people as if they were the exodus generation. And the language is not ambiguous, with Moses even commanding the people to remember what they had seen with their own eyes!¹⁶ Why would Deuteronomy do this?

Gerhard von Rad was one of the first to explore this as an intentional part of Deuteronomy's rhetoric.¹⁷ He noted that the blatant contradiction between two emphases—that the exodus generation is now dead (2:14–15) but that the present generation is treated as it were the one from the exodus—was too obvious and consistent to be accidental. And he pointed out further that it connected to other rhetorical features such as the repeated use of "today" and "you" in addressing the Moab generation.¹⁸ These, he argued, suggest a larger rhetorical goal: to contemporize and collectivize. The rhetoric seeks to create in the present generation the feeling that they are one with the exodus generation. And in so doing, it brings the ancient promises to bear upon the current people and enlivens their commitment to the covenant.¹⁹

Von Rad came to refer to this "emphatic contemporaneity" as *Vergegenwärtigung*.²⁰ But his usage deviated from the then common Old Testament parlance.²¹ It was then typical, following Mowinckel, to differentiate between the *Vergegenwärtigung* and the *Wiederholung*, the latter being a general, spiritual contemporizing and the former a cultic revivification of particular events.²² As Groves says, von Rad's notion intentionally straddled the two:

> Von Rad creates an ambiguous situation by applying *Vergegenwärtigung* to both the literary device of giving material contemporary relevance to its readers and to the re-experiencing of the event through the cult.²³

Besides straddling the means of contemporizing, von Rad's notion also straddled their effects. Not only does *Vergegenwärtigung* enliven past events, but it inscribes them in the audience in order to make the events "alive and relevant" and to create a "deep identification" with them; it "takes older material and makes it religiously significant—indeed religiously determinative" for the present.²⁴ It seems that these two effects, the present experience and the ongoing identification, can be construed as horizontal and vertical axes of the contemporizing process. The practice of reading (and hearing) Deuteronomy and participating in its ritual spreads the experience across the community in the present (horizontal plane), while the ongoing effects continue in the people long after the experience itself is over (vertical plane). Groves rightly notes, however, that a key unresolved issue in von Rad's view is that, for the vertical component, the "mechanics of that process are unclear."²⁵ This is important, and I return to it shortly.

Now, von Rad's view that Deuteronomy uses rhetoric to create an "emphatic contemporaneity" is generally well accepted.²⁶ But some have helped tighten his idea in regard to the "problem of the generations." Von Rad himself emphasized the rhetoric as a means of collapsing the generational time gap. In doing so, however, he deemphasized another important aspect: Deuteronomy also seeks to contrast the exodus and Moab generations. Indeed, Israel is to identify continually with the redemption and revelation of the exodus generation; but it is also to learn from, and eschew, its failures. This "dialectic negation" is evident both in particular texts (e.g., 4:3–4; 6:16; 9:7–8; 11:6–7) and in the way the whole oratory at Moab is set against the failure of the previous generation (1:14–15).[27] It results in a necessary tension: the Horeb generation stands, on the one hand, as a warning of the consequences of disobedience and, on the other, as the core identity of Israel.

A corollary of this is the question of which generations are being conflated, that is, who is bridged to whom? For von Rad, Deuteronomy seeks to bridge the generation of Moab with that of Horeb; and by extension, to bridge each new audience with the generation of Horeb.[28] Here, too, scholars have tended to follow von Rad.[29] There are some notable exceptions, however, such as Lohfink. He argues that the present generation is portrayed as that of exodus-Horeb-Moab, which then bridges to "alle Vorfahren aller denkbaren Generationen," with "all conceivable generations" referring to whoever came before being biblically linked to Israel.[30] As Deurloo points out, though, this obscures the fundamental distinctions and trajectories of the contemporization.[31] I shall argue that the contemporizing program aims to bridge Horeb and Moab, with ongoing relevance for the present audience, and while this is rooted in the patriarchs, they are not actually part of the contemporizing itself.

Von Rad, therefore, provides the groundwork for understanding Deuteronomy as collective memory. His work is especially helpful in highlighting how the defining feature of the text itself, the contemporizing rhetoric, echoes the impulse of social remembering: to make past events matter in the present. That von Rad calls the process *Vergegenwärtigung* and says its purpose is to create a "chain of witnesses" drives home the point even further.[32] Yet now we need to develop things further. While von Rad helps us address a weakness in Assmann's approach, namely the lack of textual grounding, he has not helped with the larger issue: how memory is transmitted vertically. Like Schottroff and Childs, von Rad explores the horizontal plane without doing the same for the vertical. In the words of Groves, he leaves the "mechanics" of the process unexplored.[33] This is what I turn to now, focusing on two types of contemporizing techniques: the moments of decision and the "eyes" motif.

DRAWN INTO THE JOURNEY

The first feature, moments of decision, has been expounded by J. G. Millar and merits some attention.[34] Millar's basic argument is that Deuteronomy is written in such a way so as to create in its audience a sense of journey.

That journey is through significant places of covenantal decision—positive and negative, and past, present, and future: Mount Horeb, Kadesh Barnea, Moab, Shechem, the "chosen place," exile, and back into the land. The effect is that the audience feels grafted into Israel's journey from place to place and, in turn, at each place is confronted anew with the call at Mount Horeb: to choose covenantal loyalty before Yahweh. J. G. McConville summarizes the idea well: "The heart of this journey narrative is in the capacity of Horeb, the archetypal place of decision, to be recreated in new places of encounter."[35]

According to Millar, the way in which Deuteronomy accomplishes this is by using temporal and spatial rhetoric to frame the book (Chs. 1–11 and 27–34).[36] He examines this more closely by looking at how Chapters 1–3, 4, 5–11, and 27–34 develop the ideas of time and space. In analyzing Chapters 1–3, Millar acknowledges scholarship's long held view that these chapters are different from the larger book in language, tone, and emphases.[37] But he argues that there is a connection: "the categories of 'Time' and 'Place' are introduced as the bedrock of the parenetic material which follows."[38] In this view, Chapters 1–3 highlight two ways taken by Israel: "places of failure" and "the road to success."[39]

Chapter 1 revolves around places of failure, opening and closing with the pivotal one: Kadesh Barnea (1:2, 46). There the Israelites, on hearing the spies' report, choose to disobey Yahweh. So instead of a short journey to the promised land, they are punished with a generation of wilderness wandering. Chapters 2–3, Millar suggests, develop the movement resulting from Israel's decision at Kadesh.[40] In 2:1 the people begin moving again, not toward the land but simply wandering. After thirty-eight years, once the present generation dies, they begin a new movement again toward the land (2:16). Deut 2:16—3:20 is characterized by progress toward the promised land and success in various battles along the way. Here the response at Kadesh of doubting and fear is replaced with obedience. Yahweh issues orders and Israel follows them, and for this reason, the movement becomes one of progress toward the land. Deut 3 then closes with the people at Beth Peor, on the plains of Moab looking at the border of the promised land. Thus Moab stands against the backdrop of Kadesh, the "archetypal place of failure, and presents the 'time and place of Israel's second chance.'"[41]

Deut 4, Millar says, develops the notion of time and place found in Chapters 1–3. While Chapters 1–3 link Kadesh and Moab, Chapter 4 links Moab and Horeb.[42] For Millar, this signals that Deuteronomy portrays Moab not only as a place of decision but also as the place of Yahweh's revelation. Thus, its purpose is "to relate the theophany at Horeb to the Mosaic preaching of 'law' at Moab"; to conflate the forty years between Horeb and Moab into one moment, the present, in which Israel again encounters its covenant Lord.[43]

Millar argues that this dynamic is noticeable in number of ways. First, we see it in the use of החקים והמשפטים ("the statutes and the ordinances") as a *Struktursignal*. In the larger book, the word pair appears at critical junctures: it frames Chapter 4, the paranesis in Chapters 5–11, and the law code in Chapters 12–26. Millar follows Georg Braulik, understanding החקים והמשפטים as referring not to the law code alone (Chs. 12–26), but to the teaching of the whole book.[44] For Millar, this means the purpose of the word pair is to "unite the Decalogue, the Mosaic preaching and the Lawcode under a single rubric."[45] In Deut 4, a similar situation is present. The word pair frames Chapter 4 (vv. 1, 45) and links it to the opening of Chapter 5; and throughout Chapter 4 the Mosaic preaching, the revelation at Horeb, and the Decalogue are interwoven.[46] Most pertinent to Millar is the way in which 4:9–14 fuses the revelation at Horeb with the voice of Moses. It establishes Moses's voice, heard at Moab and contained in the Book of Deuteronomy, as the ongoing revelation of Yahweh.[47]

Millar argues that a second way Deut 4 links Moab with Horeb is through its use of "today" (היום).[48] The book of Deuteronomy uses "today" no less than sixty-two times, with Chapter 4 featuring seven examples.[49] The general view, as we already noted, is that the motif's purpose is to create "emphatic contemporaneity."[50] That is, Moses repeatedly says "today" in order to drive home the reality of the decision now facing Israel. The setting of the book is Moab, of course, but Millar argues that "today" occurs in such a way as to "harness the past, present and future in all manner of places to the decision faced by Israel today at Moab."[51] Thus the "today" of Moab becomes the "today" of the present, always presenting its audience with the challenge to covenant loyalty.

Third, related to the last point, Millar suggests that Deut 4 seeks to further conflate Moab and Horeb by blurring their distinction. We notice this in the puzzling verse of 4:10: Moses commands the people to "remember the day you stood before Yahweh your God at Horeb."[52] The problem, of course, is that the present generation was not actually at Horeb! Just a few chapters earlier, Deut 1:35 and 2:14 make clear that all of the previous generation, those present at the Kadesh rebellion, have died; those now standing before Moses are a different generation. Why, then, does he issue the command to remember something they never experienced in the first place?

In Millar's view, this further evidences Deut 4's aim to consolidate Horeb and Moab into one moment. He draws attention to the use of "you" and of the fire and cloud motif.[53] Recounting the Horeb experience, Moses continually uses "you": "you stood before Yahweh" (v. 10); "you came near and stood at the foot of the mountain" (v. 11); "he declared his covenant to you" (v. 13); "you saw no form that day" (v. 15); "you were shown these things" (v. 35); "he made you hear his voice . . . showed you his great fire, and you heard his words" (v. 36) (emphases mine). Knowing that the "you" in view did not experience these things, it seems clear that Moses is intentionally blurring the generational gap. The current audience did not actually encounter Yahweh at Horeb, but Moses wants them to feel as if they did and to identify themselves with it.[54]

Now, Deuteronomy's use of "you" is connected to the wider issue of the *Numeruswechsel* or "number change." This term refers to the fact that when addressing Israel, Deuteronomy varies in employing the singular and plural forms of verbs and pronominal suffixes. There have been mainly two resulting scholarly trajectories to it as a textual feature. One looks at the *Numeruswechsel* as evidencing editorial work, using it to further analyze and tease apart these strands.[55] The other sees it as a rhetorical feature to be studied as part of Deuteronomy's literary purposes.[56] Lohfink, a proponent of the latter position, first argued that the rhetorical aim of the *Numeruswechsel* is basically twofold: to get the audience's attention and to solidify the people.[57] Scholars in this camp have, more or less, continued to understand the number change along these lines.[58]

Thomas Römer has taken up the second idea, that of solidifying the people, and developed it further.[59] He says this:

> [The *Numeruswechsel*] expresses the fact that the community can be spoken to as an individual and that, consequently, each individual ("thou") represents the community ("you"). In this way, the responsibility of each individual to the instructions . . . is stressed. This responsibility is linked to a decision.[60]

Römer echoes Millar's thesis that Deuteronomy seeks to create generational solidarity, bringing Israel to a perpetual point of decision. But here Römer highlights something that, while certainly present, is only latent in Millar: that the *Numeruswechsel* rhetoric is meant to help Israel conceptualize itself as a unity.[61] It is intended not only to collapse the generations but also to shape the very Israelite psyche: namely, so as to see the individual as the whole and the whole as the individual. This is important to note because it adds yet another connection to collective memory: the *Numeruswechsel* betrays an ambition to fuse the collective and the individual.[62]

Returning to Millar, we note an important connection to memory. Millar rightly says that memory plays a key, albeit curious, part in Deuteronomy's generational bridging.[63] Memory is key in that it allows people perpetually to experience the revelation and the covenant making; this in turn allows them to identify with and pledge loyalty to Yahweh's covenant. But memory is curious in that it is required of people who have never experienced the events in the first place. How does this work? What Millar says is that remembering here is "an act of corporate, imaginative remembrance."[64] Although he does not expound on this, we may consider it along the lines of collective memory: the memories provide frameworks and the people fill them in with imagination. But I suggest, and shall discuss later, that Deuteronomy has in mind something more. Its aim is for Israel to transmit the Horeb memory not just as a framework, but as a visual and lifelike recollection. It is not unimportant, then, that Römer flags up that Deuteronomy's contemporizing intends to bridge not only generation to generation but also community to individual.

As for Deut 5–11, Millar sees the ideas of time and place playing a lesser role. Rather than serving as "controlling concepts," they instead "provide a thread which runs throughout."[65] That being said, they do reveal a shift in emphasis, too. Whereas Chapters 1–4 present Moab as the place of recapitulation, Chapters 5–11 show it as a place of anticipation.[66] Chapters 1–4 establish the critical moments in Israel's past and their significance to the present; Chapters 5–11, however, show how the events impact the future. This is evidenced, he says, by a shift in emphasis concerning Yahweh's revelation: from manner of revelation to content of revelation, from visible phenomena (fire and clouds) to the audible (voice).[67] Indeed, he is right to highlight the auditory aspect in Chapter 5, in that the voice of Yahweh is fused with the voice of Moses. But it is perhaps reductionistic to do so at the expense of the visible phenomena. After all, the mention of the fire on the mountain occurs liberally and frames the Decalogue itself in Chapter 5: verses 4–5 (two times) and 22–27 (five times). Perhaps, then, it is better to say that the visible phenomena form the backdrop of the fusing of Yahweh and Moses's voice: "At that time I [Moses] stood between the Lord and you to declare to you the word of the Lord, *because you were afraid of the fire*" (5:5, emphasis mine).

With this said, I agree with Millar's overall view that Deut 5–11 changes its gaze toward the future.[68] As a place of recapitulation, which Deut 1–4 emphasizes, Moab is the archetypal "place of revelation" and "place of action [or decision]." As a place of anticipation, which Deut 6–11 emphasizes, the bent is future-oriented: it focuses on Moab as a "place of entry," "place of occupation," and "place of return." The success of Israel in the land, this section makes clear, depends on its ability to recapture the revelation at Horeb and respond appropriately.

The final section, Deut 27–34, Millar sees as employing the temporal and spatial references to show the journey as ongoing.[69] After the legal material in Deut 12–26, Chapters 27–28 renew the journey motif with Mounts Ebal and Gerizim, the first places of significance upon entering the promised land.[70] The ceremonies to be carried out here, Millar argues, show these mountains as the next places of significance in Israel's journey.[71] It is no coincidence, he says, that with these there is an echoing of Horeb and Moab, the foundational places of the covenant, and a foreshadowing of Shechem, the first place of covenant renewal in the land (Josh 24). Deut 29 shifts again from the near future of Mounts Ebal and Gerizim to the present of Moab. What is implicit throughout Deuteronomy becomes explicit here: that this itself is a moment of covenant renewal. "These are the words of the covenant the Lord commanded Moses to make with the Israelites in Moab, besides the covenant he had made with them at Horeb" (29:1 [28:69 MT]). The covenant at hand, then, is not replacing that of Horeb but is "augmenting and updating it for the new conditions of life in the land of Canaan."[72] Viewed through Millar's journey theme, the functions of Moses's preaching extends beyond the present at Moab into the future in the land.

That Moses's preaching has ongoing significance is highlighted by Deut 30. This chapter, which Millar sees as the denouement of Deuteronomy, hinges on interplay of שׁוב ("to turn, return").[73] In particular, the interplay connects two kinds of returning: when Israel in exile "return" to Yahweh, Yahweh will "return" Israel to the land (vv. 2–3). For Israel to return to the land, then, it must again come under the instruction of this Torah which, it is clear, refers to Moses's preaching at Moab. As such, Deut 30 highlights the importance of the Mosaic teaching in Israel's journey, a journey that extends beyond Moab and the promised land into exile and back. Having reached the climax of Moses's teaching, Millar understands Deut 31:9–13 offering not further instruction but the practical implementation of that instruction.[74] Millar summarizes:

> Moses' instruction to write down the law and read it to the nation en masse at regular intervals coheres neatly with much of what we have seen. It supports the repeated injunctions to remember what Yahweh has done and what Israel has learned at every stage of her journey, and in turn the accompanying necessity that Israel re-enact the decision at Horeb, Moab and Shechem at each and every moment of their national existence.

Moses's preaching at Horeb, captured in written form, shall go with Israel on its journey of faith, perpetually instructing it in covenantal life and calling it to choose covenant loyalty.

While Millar's understanding of Deut 27–34 is helpful indeed, I think there is one significant aspect that he overlooks: the Song of Moses (32:1–43). In his conception, the sense of journey through moments of decision is instilled mainly through the rhetoric of the text, which the people would be exposed to in full only once every seven years at the Feast of Booths. For Deuteronomy, which aims to transmute the sacral into daily life, it would be surprising for such an important dynamic to be left to such an infrequent rite. I suggest Deuteronomy does not do this, but in fact uses the song as the way in which moments of decision are perpetuated domestically.[75] This is discussed at length in a later chapter.

The value of Millar's views for the present study, then, is in two areas. First, it fleshes out von Rad's notion of "emphatic contemporaneity." In particular, the motif of journey through moments of decision adds depth to our understanding of the generational dialectic. The present audience is indeed meant to feel at one with the redemption and revelation of the exodus generation, but so is it meant to heed the mistakes of that generation and decide accordingly. Second, Millar's work confirms that memory is integral to the contemporizing process of Deuteronomy. But like others before him, his generic construal of it shows that more work needs to be done here.

REMEMBERING WHAT YOU HAVE (NOT) SEEN

Having considered the contemporizing effects of Deuteronomy's rhetoric of moments of decision, we now turn to our second aspect: the "eyes" motif. By this, I mean the instances in which the present generation is portrayed as having seen with its own "eyes" (עינים) the events of the exodus generation. It occurs numerous times and in key places.[76]

Scholars typically understand this use of "eyes" as part of Deuteronomy's contemporizing rhetoric. Moshe Weinfeld expresses it thus:[77]

> The deuteronomic orator often employs [these] rhetorical phrases . . . to implant in his listeners the feeling that they themselves have experienced the awe-inspiring events of the Exodus; and he repeats these phrases again and again as if to hypnotize his audience.[78]

The conclusion is perhaps obvious, for the "eyes" motif is found working in concert with the other contemporizing features. For instance, the *Numeruswechsel* is interwoven into the motif itself, evidenced by Deut 29:2–3: "You have seen all that the Lord did before your eyes in the land of Egypt . . . the great trials that *thy eyes* saw" (emphasis mine). Here we also see the link with the moments of decision, for the "eyes" motif introduces what is the covenant ceremony at Moab. And the "fathers" are also closely associated with the motif: "The Lord set signs and wonders before our eyes . . . and brought us out from there to give us the land that he swore to our fathers" (Deut 6:22–23).

Deuteronomy 4

The question, then, is what specific role the "eyes" motif plays in Deuteronomy's contemporizing. Deut 4 perhaps best illumines this role. In its canonical form, Chapter 4 can be seen as a bridge between Chapters 1–3 and 5–11.[79] In particular, it builds on the material of Chapters 1–3, the review of Yahweh's judgment and mercy, in order to motivate obedience to the covenant, the material of Chapters 5–11.[80] Or as Patrick Miller says it, "Obedience to the instruction of God is both the implication of their past history with God and the necessity for their future life with God."[81] Of course, the idea that Deut 4 is integrally connected to what comes before and after is not universally held.[82] But there are enough linkages structurally, linguistically, and conceptually to justify this view.[83]

One concept that is especially central to Deut 4 is the law.[84] What defines the chapter, however, is not the fact that it focuses on the law, but the way in which it does so. Thomas Mann says it well:[85]

> The scope of the sermon is enormous . . . But the central focus of the sermon is on the giving of the covenant at Horeb (Sinai), and the implication of how the covenant was given—that is, by sound, not by sight. While Moses appeals to what Israel saw (4:3, 9, 11, 34, 36b), the thrust of the sermon is on what Israel heard—or more specifically, that Israel heard. What Israel heard will be reiterated in Deuteronomy 5—the "ten words" or commandments. Here the focus is on the medium of the message.[86]

Thus, this chapter itself becomes an exposition of the second commandment (5:8–10),[87] a sermon explaining and exhorting Israel's imageless worship.[88]

A look at Deut 4's structure illumines how this idea develops. In general, the chapter breaks down as follows: verses 1–8, 9–40, 41–49.[89] The first two sections, verses 1–8 and 9–40, which form the main body of the chapter, are further framed by the call to "listen" (שׁמע) to the "statutes and laws" (חקים ומשׁפטים) (4:1) and to "keep" (שׁמר) the "statutes and commands" (חקים ומצות) (4:40).[90] In each case, the significance of "listening" and "keeping" is tied to the goal of taking the land and thriving in it. If this bracketing establishes the focus on the law and its telos generally, its internal workings illumine the ban on images specifically. But while it seems clear that verses 9–40 give a rationale for aniconic worship,[91] there is little consensus on what this rationale is.[92] Perhaps the most common idea among exegetes is that aniconism is a means of preserving the unique nature of Yahweh, namely, his transcendence.[93] This is problematic, however, for at least a couple of reasons. First, transcendence is hardly unique to Yahweh, and other cultures balance ideas of transcendent gods with imagistic worship perfectly well.[94] Second, this view relies too much on the scholarly tendency to see Deuteronomy as emphasizing Yahweh's transcendence over his immanence.[95] A helpful idea, though, has been proposed by Nathan MacDonald.[96] He argues that the rationale for aniconic worship lies in the reality of Yahweh's ubiquitous presence. Such is evident by the way in which Deut 4 holds the two in parallel, crystallized in the confession of verse 39: "Acknowledge and take to heart this day that the Lord is God in heaven above and on the earth below; there is no other." The problem with images, then, is that they violate this credo by limiting Yahweh "to one sphere only."[97] This explains the concrete expression of aniconism in verses 15–19, which prohibits worship using images of earthly creatures or celestial bodies.[98]

An important corollary of this is how Deut 4 addresses "the continued presence of YHWH [to Israel] in the post-Horeb period, and the presence of YHWH to the nations."[99] In regard to the nations, it is through Israel's obedience to the commands that it bears witness to Yahweh. MacDonald rightly points out, moreover, that in verse 6 "the wisdom and discernment of Israel are manifest in the eyes of the nations, and it is YHWH's statutes that they hear."[100] This pairing of "seeing" and "hearing" also plays an important role in regard to Yahweh's ongoing presence in Israel. MacDonald does not develop what that role is, but says that the two are inextricably bound and that "both are necessary in order to draw the appropriate conclusion from YHWH's revelation at Horeb."[101]

"Seeing" in Deuteronomy 4

While MacDonald is right to argue for the connection between "seeing" and "hearing," this is not the scholarly consensus.[102] The common opinion instead is that Deut 4 juxtaposes the two senses. That is, in portraying the Horeb revelation as one of word and not sight, Deut 4 dispatches (or at least subordinates) the latter.[103] There are a variety of permutations of this view. Deurloo, on one side of the spectrum, offers a more subtle dichotomy that portrays the relationship as one of transition: the seeing of the fire and the hearing of the voice at Horeb gives way to just the hearing of that voice in Torah.[104] Geller, on the other side, argues for a strong opposition between seeing and hearing:

> Deuteronomy 4 has established a context in which "seeing" and "hearing" are contrasted rather than combined in the common hendiadys. Not only does [the writer] oppose the terms to each other, but also orders them religiously: hearing is promoted, seeing is demoted in significance as regards revelation, and, by extension, all religious experience . . . what has been "heard from heaven" stands over and above what was "seen on earth." The former is the true core of revelation, the latter secondary and subsidiary.[105]

But while I acknowledge that the revelation itself is portrayed as one of voice and not form, and that this voice at Horeb becomes the words of the Decalogue (in 4:9–14, from Ch 4 to Ch 5), I suggest that the above thinking is not an accurate depiction of the relationship between "seeing" and "hearing" in Deut 4.

What, then, is the relationship? A couple of scholars have been particularly helpful on this question. Michael Carasik speaks to the issue perhaps most directly.[106] To begin with, Carasik disputes what Stephen Geller identifies as the core issue between seeing and hearing in Deut 4. In Geller's view, Deut 4 seeks to confront, and reverse, the wisdom notion that seeing is superior to hearing as a means of knowledge. Because hearing is the conduit of the commandments, it must be elevated to a higher epistemological status than seeing. Against this,[107] Carasik argues there is another issue at center: "How were the commandments, received by ear and transmitted by speech, to be infused with the immediacy and power of the historical events that shaped Israel, perceived by the eye?"[108] In his opinion, then,

> [T]he difficulty facing the author of Deuteronomy 4 was not an imbalance between the eye and the ear; rather, it was their estrangement. The problem was not to make hearing superior to sight, but to make it the equivalent of sight, to make the commandments that each generation was to teach to the next as immediate a part of the Israelites' experience as the mighty deeds that God had performed "before your eyes."[109]

So, in Carasik's view, the problem of Deut 4 is not how to phase out or subordinate sight, but how to bind it to hearing in a way that motivates obedience and that is commensurate with Yahwistic worship.

In a more recent work, Carasik has developed this idea further.[110] His larger study seeks to illumine the working of the mind in biblical Israel. Carasik begins by arguing that the view that "seeing" is subordinated to "hearing" is, in a large part, a vestige of a now defunct idea. That idea held that the Israelites had a distinct mentality, in which "it was hearing, not sight, that was the crucial sense through which one learned about the world."[111] While the view itself has been dismissed, Carasik sees its premise as the root from which the subordination of "seeing" still grows. Whether a straightforward correspondence can be deduced from this, instead of from, say, Deut 4's strong aniconism, is not clear; but even if Carasik is partly right, his point is insightful. To demonstrate that such an idea of distinct mentalities is in fact baseless, Carasik employs contemporary research from the social sciences. He says,

> In fact, it is physical . . . anthropology that provides a definitive argument against overemphasis on the oral nature of Israel's culture; all human cultures are primarily visual, for the primacy of sight as a means of understanding the world is not a cultural phenomenon at all, but a biological one.[112]

That the sense of sight is generally primary in the human person is commonly accepted. Carasik's study goes beyond this, however. He seems to assume that all of the various biblical texts can be understood in light of this principle.¹¹³ There are a couple of problems with this. First, even if sight is the primary sense in general, research shows that different senses become primary in different contexts. Sight may be the default, but that does not exclude the others from coming to the fore as situations demand. Second, related to the first point, it cannot be presumed therefore that all texts work on the primacy of sight. The situations and purposes of particular texts may in fact mean that they seek to emphasize other senses.

Having said this, I think Carasik is right that Deut 4 is one such case in which "seeing" is of utmost importance. Returning to his previous point, how then does Deuteronomy seek to bind seeing to hearing in a way that motivates obedience? Carasik discerns in Deut 4 an all-important triad of eyes–ears–heart (esp. 4:9; 29:1–2).¹¹⁴ For the people to "hear" and obey the substance of the Horeb revelation, they must take it to heart; to take it to heart they must in some sense "see" the events surrounding it.

> the experience of having seen something with one's own eyes was all-important for Deuteronomy . . . But direct visual experience could not be transmitted. This aspect of the perpetuation of the wilderness experience was filled, for Deuteronomy, by זכר. When later generations remembered God's deeds, they would be aware of the same events which their ancestors . . . saw with their own eyes.¹¹⁵

Here Carasik says not only that the senses of seeing and hearing are an ongoing necessity in Israel's affections but also that memory is the way in which the "visual experience" is transmitted.¹¹⁶ It is also noteworthy that he identifies story as the primary conduit by which Deuteronomy portrays the visual experience being generationally transmitted.¹¹⁷

Steven Weitzman has recently engaged this same issue from a somewhat different angle.¹¹⁸ His main contention is that Deuteronomy reflects an early program of "self-reform," aiming especially, "to reform [the self] through . . . a 'regiment of perception'—a set of practices by which to discipline, train, and refocus Israel's senses."¹¹⁹ The goal of the refocusing is to teach Israel to perceive things rightly and thereby live obediently.¹²⁰ Weitzman argues that the notion of sense reform is ubiquitous in Deuteronomy, both in its reuse of older stories (Chs. 1–11) and reformulation of older laws (Chs. 12–26). In fact, for him sensory reform stands over and above the centralization of worship as Deuteronomy's distinguishing feature.¹²¹

It remains to be seen whether the sensory aspect of Deuteronomy is as central as Weitzman argues. Still his construal of the role of seeing in Chapter 4 specifically and Deuteronomy generally is insightful. As it regards Deut 4, he says,

> The ban against idols in Deuteronomy's retelling is an attempt, not simply to prevent Israel from worshipping other gods as in Exodus, but to preserve the

sensory character of the Horeb theophany . . . Deuteronomy looks to Israel's memory to transmit the sensory experience of seeing God's power and hearing his voice.[122]

And as it regards Deuteronomy generally, he argues that the book attempts to implement "a regimen of ritual behaviors" whose purpose is to

> screen out certain perceptions (visually manifest gods); sharpen the memory of other perceptions (the sight of God's miracles, the sound of his voice); and even generate a kind of virtual sensory experience to be shared with those not present to see and hear for themselves.[123]

Like Carasik, Weitzman argues that "seeing" plays an important ongoing role in Israel's life of faith and that it is generationally transmitted through memory. Moreover, both of these scholars aver that a key role of memory is to transmit Israel's events in vivid, visual images.

Having discussed these views, though, the question arises as to whether the text itself, particularly Deut 4, supports them. We consider this briefly now. Earlier I argued that Deut 4 is framed by "hearing" (שמע) and "keeping" (שמר) the "statutes and laws" (חקים ומצות). Weinfeld has shown that within this there is a further framing: the pairing of "seeing" and "hearing."[124] Verses 1–8: Moses exhorts Israel to "hear (שמע) the statutes and laws that I am teaching you" (v. 1); and he says, "See (ראה), I have taught you the statutes and laws" (v. 5). Verses 32–40: Moses asks the question, "Has a people ever heard (שמע) a voice of a god speaking from the midst of a fire, as you yourself heard (שמע), and lived? (v. 33)"; and he asks further, "Or has a god tried to come and take a nation . . . like all that the Lord your God did for you in Egypt before your eyes?' (v. 34). While Weinfeld sees these pairings as antithetical, as shifting from the visual to the aural,[125] it is more natural to understand them as complementary.[126] For one thing, consider verses 35–36:

> You yourselves were shown (ראה) [these things] in order to know that the Lord, he is your God; there is no other like him. From heaven he caused you to hear (שמע) his voice to instruct you. On earth he caused you to see (ראה) his great fire; and his words you heard (שמע) from the midst of the fire.

Verse 35 indicates that "seeing" is necessary to comprehend the person and uniqueness of Yahweh;[127] and verse 36 interweaves the elements together: seeing–hearing–seeing–hearing. Nothing here suggests that the two senses ought to be separated; if anything, it shows them to be inextricably bound in perceiving Yahweh's uniqueness and obeying his "statutes and laws."

Some may still argue that, from the evidence above, we can only be sure that the binding of "seeing" and "hearing" is descriptive of Horeb but not prescriptive for Israel's ongoing worship. In Deut 4:9–10a, however, that option evaporates:

> Except guard yourself and guard your soul closely, lest you forget the things that your eyes saw and they depart from your heart all the days of your life. And you shall make them known to your children and to your children's children—the day that you stood before the Lord your God at Horeb.

Here what might have been merely descriptive of the Horeb encounter is made prescriptive for the generations of Israel: that "seeing" should accompany "hearing." In opening the central section of Deut 4 (vv. 9–31), the section rooting the second commandment in the Horeb event, verse 9 sets out Israel's duty strongly. In fact, though this language of "guarding" (שמר) is characteristic of Deuteronomy,[128] the construction here is especially strong. The sentence begins with "except," the emphatic use of the particle רק,[129] which is meant to flag up that what comes next is "the most important thing."[130] Following רק is the exhortation to "guard," given twice in short order, the second of which is intensified with מאד.[131] The object of this careful guarding, then, is no less than "your soul" (נפשך)[132] and the stakes are the affections and loyalty of Israel's "heart" (לבב). Undoubtedly, Moses is trying to make crystal clear that the duty he is setting out here is of utmost importance to the nation.

So, what is this duty? The duty is to remember "the things that your eyes have seen"[133] and to pass this memory onto "your children and your children's children." Granted, in keeping with the serious tone of Deut 4:9, the duty is expressed negatively: "lest you forget" (פן־תשכח). But שכח and זכר are twin elements of memory. What in this context is Israel to remember? At first it would seem to refer to Yahweh's judgment at Baal-Peor, the previous command to remember (v. 3). However, the ensuing verse makes clear that Horeb is in view.[134] Israel is to remember the "day that you stood before the Lord your God at Horeb." The passage then launches into the visual nature of that experience, elucidating what Israel did or did not see. What Israel did not see, of course, was a "form" (תמונה), but what it did see is much more the substance of verses 10–12. "The mountain burned with fire to the heart of the heavens—darkness (חשך), clouds (ענן), and thick cloud (ערפל)" (v. 11). It was from the "midst of the fire" that the Lord spoke (v. 12). And from verse 11 onward, the motif of "fire" (אש) is used to evoke the Horeb imagery (vv. 11, 12, 15, 24, 33, 36 [2 times]).[135]

We notice something here in Chapter 4 that is true elsewhere in Deuteronomy: that where Moses exhorts remembrance and the transmission of what "your eyes have seen" there is also an increase in visual language.[136] As a general rule, the book of Deuteronomy recounts past events in language more vivid than that of the rest of the Pentateuch. Weinfeld argues that this is because of Deuteronomy's sermonic style:

> The author of Deuteronomy has endowed the book with the typical features of an oration . . . As is expected of a good orator the author directs his message to the heart and emotions of his audience, enlivening and variegating the ancient traditions by retelling them in such a manner as to capture and maintain the interest of his listeners.[137]

To the purposes of capturing attention and moving the audience, we may add making the content memorable—an aim inherent in any oration. But beyond making Israel's past memorable in general, it seems that Deuteronomy aims in particular to emblazon images of events in people's minds. It is noteworthy that contexts featuring the "eyes" motif, the exhortation to remember, and the command to transmit these things generationally also feature vivid language (e.g., Deut 4:9–12; 8:2–18; 9:7–29; 11:2–7 and 6:20–25).

This brings us back to the guiding question of this section: What role does the "eyes" motif play in Deuteronomy's contemporizing? The previous evidence suggests that "seeing" plays a central and ongoing role in Israel's religious life. Namely, it is meant to motivate Israel's "hearing," that is, love for Yahweh and Torah obedience. The "eyes" motif taps into this "seeing" when Moses commands Israel to remember what "your eyes have seen" and pass this memory onto the children.

On the one hand, then, the "eyes" motif plays a similar role to the other contemporizing rhetoric of Deuteronomy. Current Israel did not in fact see the original events, but is spoken to as if it did; the rhetoric is meant to create a kind of generational solidarity, to cause the present people to feel at one with the past.[138] On the other hand, and more importantly, the "eyes" motif reveals a larger mnemonic program: Israel is, in some sense, meant to "see" something it never saw. Moses commands it. It seems each generation is to preserve and transmit, through memory, the visual phenomena of Israel's founding events.[139] As seen in Deut 4, the visual phenomena of the Horeb theophany play a key role in Israel's aniconic worship: just as at Horeb there was no form but only a voice from the fire, so there shall never be a form in worship but only Torah motivated by memory.

CONCLUSION

Deuteronomy is unique among the biblical books in its aim to cultivate memory in the community. For this reason, it may be understood generally as a text of religious collective remembering, that is, as a text aiming to create a "chain of witnesses." Yet those who have recognized this have not adequately accounted for Deuteronomy's distinctives. What I have sought to do here, therefore, is explore why exactly Deuteronomy seeks to cultivate memory.

It is true, as Jan Assmann says, that the need for memory arises from Deuteronomy's "liminal situation," though perhaps not in the way he suggests. For Assmann, the transition from wilderness to promised land looms large in Deuteronomy, and memory is key to a successful transition. Its purpose is to capture for posterity Israel's defining encounter with Yahweh. But the impetus is not the death of the exodus generation and the fear of losing their eyewitness memories. The impetus, instead, is the desire to crystalize the Moab experience as Israel's enduring experience so that each generation may stand again before Yahweh at a moment of decision.

Deuteronomy does this by using its rhetoric to create, in Gerhard von Rad's words, "emphatic contemporaneity" which has the purpose of both collectivizing and contemporizing. The rhetoric collectivizes by speaking to the Moab generation as if they were the exodus generation, fusing the two together. In this way, the people at Moab—and, by extension, each generation to follow—feel as if they themselves were participants in Israel's defining experience—the exodus journey. Yet Deuteronomy's rhetoric also aims to contemporize its message, making each new audience feel as if they were standing before Moses at Moab and faced with the charge "Now choose life!" (Deut 30:19). As such, the goal of Deuteronomy's memory making is perhaps not so much to create a "chain of witnesses" (Danièle Hervieu–Léger) as a journey through moments of decisions (Gary Millar). The point is for each new audience to become participants in some sense, feeling as if they had experienced the exodus and now stand before Moses at Moab.[140]

Yet it was also noted that one of Deuteronomy's distinct features, its highly visual language, has been largely overlooked in the discussion. This, I suggested, is a significant oversight, for visual language is at the center of Deuteronomy's memory program. I shall discuss how this works mnemonically in the next chapter; in this chapter, I highlighted its importance theologically. What we found was that the scholarly tendency to see Deuteronomy, due to its strong aniconism, as transitioning away from all things visual, was not supported by the text itself. In fact, the text would seem to suggest precisely the opposite. Rather than moving away from visual things, it seeks to put a certain kind of image at the center of Israel's worship: the mental image of Yahweh's deeds. We find this even in Deut 4, a *locus classicus* of aniconism. There the text seems to pair, rather than contrast, "hearing" and "seeing": if Israel is to fulfill the call of "hearing" Yahweh's voice, it must continue "seeing" his past deeds. This seeing, according to Deuteronomy, comes through memory, and that is why Deuteronomy places such weight on it.

NOTES

1. Thomas W. Mann, *The Book of the Torah* (Louisville, KY: Westminster John Knox, 1988), 156.
2. Jan Assmann, *Religion and Cultural Memory: Ten Studies*, trans. Rodney Livingstone (Stanford: Stanford University Press, 2006).
3. Assmann, *Religion*, 16–17.
4. I use the term "collective memory" interchangeably with "social memory" and "cultural memory." Indeed, at times scholars have used each as a technical term set off against the others. But it is common to use the terms interchangeably, and biblical scholarship has tended to follow this practice, e.g., John Rogerson, "History and Cultural Memory," in his work *A Theology of the Old Testament* (Minneapolis, MN: Fortress Press, 2010), 13–40.
5. I should note that Assmann's own work employs both approaches of studying texts as memory products and as memory producers—called by him "mnemohistory" and "memory of conversion," respectively—and at points these two are interwoven in his approach. See Jan Assmann, *Moses the Egyptian: The Memory of Egypt in Western Monotheism* (Cambridge, MA: Harvard University Press, 1997).
6. Assmann, *Religion*, 17. It should be noted that Assmann himself sees Deuteronomy, as we now have it, reflecting a 7th–5th century BCE background (p. 16). So the concerns of the text stem from the threat of Assyria and its form reflects the vassal treaty tradition of Esarhaddon. Yet his understanding of the deeper DNA of the text is much more complicated. It includes not only Assmann's reading of how the text surface presents memory, but also his theory on the subterranean memory running beneath the text (one could divide these, respectively, into conscious and unconscious memory, but even these do not fully account for the subtleties of Assmann's argument). That reading is particularly rooted in Freudian ideas of repressed memory. In brief, Assmann suggests that Akhenaten, the Egyptian ruler who initiated the heretical concept of monotheism, was such an anathema that his memory survived in repressed form. This "terrifying vision" of Akhenaten passed along, somehow, through many generations and cultures until it finally reemerged with the Jews in the Hellenistic period. There it came to life as a man called Moses, who was said to have founded monotheism. Thus, the ancient repression of Akhenaten and his Amarna religion emerged with fervency in the figure of Moses and his biblical monotheism, especially in the book of Deuteronomy (pp. 59–60). Or to say it differently, what finally comes to the surface in Deuteronomy had a long, labyrinthine gestation in the Israelite subconscious. We see that in Assmann's study of memory in Deuteronomy he reifies Freud's original thesis from *Moses and Monotheism*.
7. Assmann, *Religion*, 16. This is to be distinguished from the notion of "counter-memory" as used by Michael Foucault (*Language, Counter-Memory, Practice*, ed. D. F. Bouchard [Ithaca, NY: Cornell University Press, 1977]) and followed by Ronald Hendel (*Remembering Abraham* [Oxford: Oxford University Press], 41–43). In that sense, counter-memory is an intracultural act challenging the status quo by re-remembering it. For Hendel, it means finding voices in the text that purposely counteract previous ones.

8. Assmann, *Religion*, 54.

9. Georg Braulik agrees with Assmann here, too ("Deuteronomy and the Commemorative Culture," in *The Theology of Deuteronomy*, 190–91, translated by Ulrika Lindblad [North Richland Hills, TX: BiBAL Press, 1994], 183).

10. Assmann, *Religion*, 54.

11. Assmann, Religion, 53.

12. Assmann, Religion, 17–18.

13. Danièle Hervieu-Léger, *Religion as a Chain of Memory*, trans. Simon Lee (New Brunswick, NJ: Rutgers University Press, 2000).
See Lewis Coser's introduction in *On Collective Memory*.

14. At this point it may be asked what, then, I see as the intended audience of Deuteronomy. As will become clear, my view is that Deuteronomy has as its permanent goal the creation of memory in each new generation, and, as such, that it has no one audience in mind. The message is inherently universal and enduring. It seems a similar view is adopted by James Robson in *Honey from the Rock: Deuteronomy for the People of God* (Nottingham: Apollos, 2013). For more on how texts served enduring roles in cultural formation in the ancient world, see David Carr, *Writing on the Tablet of the Heart: Origins of Scripture and Literature* (Oxford: Oxford University Press, 2005) and *The Formation of the Hebrew Bible* (Oxford: Oxford University Press, 2011).

15. Literarily, we may understand Deut 2:14–15 as playing a role similar to the opening of Charles Dickens's *A Christmas Carol* (1843): "Marley was dead, to begin with. There is no doubt about that . . . Old Marley was dead as a doornail . . . This must be distinctly understood, or nothing wonderful can come of the story I am going to relate."

16. For example, Deut 4:9–12; 8:2–18; 9:7–29; 11:2–7, and 6:20–25.

17. In English, Gerhard von Rad addressed this in *Old Testament Theology*, vol. 1, trans. D. M. G Stalker (Harper & Row, 1962), 225. His first engagement with the issue, however, is found earlier in his *Das Gottesvolk im Deuteronomium* (Stuttgart: Kohlhammer, 1929).

18. Gerhard von Rad, *The Problem of the Hexateuch and Other Essays* (New York: McGraw Hill, 1966), 28–30.

19. Rad, *Das Gottesvolk*, 23–24.

20. Rad, *Hexateuch*, 28.

21. For a good study on the notion of actualization, see Joseph Groves, *Actualization and Interpretation in the Old Testament* (Atlanta: Scholars Press, 1987); he examines von Rad's view on pp. 7–62.

22. Sigmund Mowinckel, *Psalmenstudien* (1921–24; repr. P. Schippers, 1961), 16–43.

23. Groves, *Actualization and Interpretation*, 9.

24. Groves, *Actualization and Interpretation*, 10. See also von Rad, *Hexateuch*, 33.

25. Groves, *Actualization and Interpretation*, 12.

26. E.g., Moshe Weinfeld, *Deuteronomy 1–11: A New Translation with Introduction and Commentary* (New York: Doubleday, 1991), 203, says this: the use in Deut 4:10 of "'standing before the Lord' at Sinai is the origin of the existentialistic

concept in Judaism . . . [of] 'the scene of Mount Sinai,' which was understood as a collective experience of Israel bequeathed to all coming generations." Jeffrey Tigay, *Deuteronomy* (Philadelphia, PA: The Jewish Publication Society, 1996), 46, says that Deuteronomy "conceives of all generations of Israelites as a single corporate personality, so that later generations can be addressed as if they were part of earlier events, particularly the great formative events whose effects lasted ever afterwards." Patrick D. Miller, *Deuteronomy* (Louisville, KY: Westminster John Knox, 1990), 67, calls Deuteronomy's rhetoric of contemporaneity a key "hermeneutical formula" of the book. See also Norbert Lohfink, *Die Väter Israels im Deuteronomium* (Freiburg, Switzerland: Universitätsverlag, 1991), 23. For a discussion of the contemporizing rhetoric not only in the paranesis but also in the legal material, see Dale Patrick, "The Rhetoric of Collective Responsibility in Deuteronomic Law," in *Pomegranates and Golden Bells*, eds. David Wright, David Noel Freedman, and Avi Hurvits (Eisenbrauns, 1995), 421–36.

27. Karel Deurloo, "The One God and all Israel in its Generations," *Studies in Deuteronomy*, eds. F. García Martínez et al. (Brill, 1994), 43. He is following C. J. Labuschagne, *Deuteronomium*, vol. 1 (Callenbach, 1987), 24.

28. Rad, *Hexateuch*, 28–30.

29. Brevard Childs, *Introduction to the Old Testament as Scripture* (Minneapolis, MN: Fortress Press, 1979), 215; Deurloo, "The One God," 43; Tigay, *Deuteronomy*, 46; J. Gordon McConville, *Deuteronomy* (Westmont, IL: InterVarsity Press, 2002), 36–38; Weinfeld, *Deuteronomy*, 203.

30. Lohfink, *Die Väter*, 23.

31. Deurloo, "The One God," 43. Jerry Hwang suggests something similar in *The Rhetoric of Remembrance: An Investigation of the "Fathers" in Deuteronomy* (Winona Lake, IN: Eisenbrauns, 2012). Hwang's work provides a helpful compendium of scholarship on the "fathers" in Deuteronomy.

32. Rad, *Hexateuch*, 100. Here von Rad, though approaching it from a different angle, sounds very similar to Hervieu-Léger's aforementioned notion of religion as a "chain of memory."

33. For a good critique of the concept of historical actualization, as held by von Rad and Childs, see Groves, *Actualization and Interpretation*, 103–63. Michael Carasik has also recently critiqued Childs's view of memory as actualization (*Theologies of the Mind* [New York: Peter Lang, 2006]). We shall discuss his view later, but note for now that, along with von Rad, he is unable to elucidate the mechanics of memory's ongoing impact.

34. J. G. Millar, "Living at the Place of Decision," in *Time and Place in Deuteronomy*, eds. J. G. Millar and J. G. McConville (Sheffield: Sheffield Academic Press, 1994), 15–88 and J. G. Millar, "Ethics and Journey," in *Now Choose Life* (Leicester: Apollos, 1998), 67–98. We note that a more recent study along these lines exists: Randall Pannell, *Those Alive Here Today* (Longwood, FL: Xulon Press, 2004). The problem, however, is that Pannell's study is the published version of his doctoral work from 1979 and it does not incorporate newer scholarship (including Millar's). As such, the work is relatively unhelpful in this regard.

35. McConville, *Deuteronomy*, 36.

36. Millar, *Time and Place*, 15–16. As should become clear, Millar's understanding of contemporization is akin to that of Groves (*Actualization and Interpretation*, 166–79), not those such as von Rad and Childs who hold to historical actualization.

37. Millar, *Time and Place*, 16–17. Earlier theories held that Deuteronomy had a kind of double introduction with Chs. 1–3 and 5–11 (e.g., H. W. P. Kleinert, *Untersuchungen zur alttestamentlichen Rechts—und Literaturgeschichte*, vol. 1 [Bielefeld: Verlhagen & Klasing, 1872]). But beginning with Martin Noth (*Überlieferungsgeschichtliche Studien*, vol. 1, [Halle an der Saale: Niemayer Verlag, 1943]; English translation, *The Deuteronomistic History*, 2nd ed. [Sheffield: JSOT Press, 1991]) it became common, and remains so, to see Chs. 1–3 not as an introduction to Deuteronomy but to that of the larger Deuteronomistic history.

38. Millar, *Time and Place*, 17.

39. Millar, *Time and Place*, 23.

40. Millar, *Time and Place*, 27.

41. Millar, *Time and Place*, 23.

42. Here we mostly just consider Millar's view. Below we shall engage Deut 4 and its scholarship in more detail.

43. Millar, *Time and Place*, 36.

44. See Braulik, "Die Ausdrücke für 'Gesetz' im Buch Deuteronomium," *Biblica* 51 (1970): 39–66. For a different view, see Norbert Lohfink, "Die '*huqqim umispatim*' im Buch Deuteronoium und ihre Neubegrenzung durch Dtn. 12.1," *Biblica* 70 (1989): 1–27.

45. Millar, *Time and Place*, 37.

46. Millar, 36–41. For a discussion of work on Deut 4, see Dietrich Knapp, *Deuteronomium 4* (Göttingen: Vandenhoeck & Ruprecht, 1987).

47. For more on the idea that the revelation at Horeb is fused into Moses's sermon at Moab, see Jean-Pierre Sonnet, *The Book Within the Book* (Leiden: Brill, 1997).

48. Millar, *Time and Place*, 41–48.

49. Deut 4:4, 8, 20, 26, 38, 39, 40.

50. For a study on the use of "day" in Deuteronomy, see Simon DeVries, *Yesterday, Today and Tomorrow* (Grand Rapids, MI: Eerdmans, 1975), 164–86. DeVries commends von Rad's view that "today" plays a vital role in Deuteronomy's program of generation conflation.

51. Millar, *Time and Place*, 43.

52. Millar, *Time and Place*, 42.

53. Millar, *Time and Place*, 41–48.

54. Weinfeld, *Deuteronomy*, 203, says this: the use in Deut 4:10 of "'standing before the Lord' at Sinai is the origin of the existentialistic concept in Judaism... [of] 'the scene of Mount Sinai,' which was understood as a collective experience of Israel bequeathed to all coming generations." Miller, *Deuteronomy*, 67, calls Deuteronomy's rhetoric of contemporaneity a key "hermeneutical formula" of the book. See also McConville, *Deuteronomy*, 105–7.

55. For example, Willy Staerk, *Beiträge* zur Kritik des Deuteronomiums (Leipzig: A. Pries, 1894), 1–2, 97–98; G. Minette de Tillesse, "Sections 'Tu' et

Sections 'Vous' dans le *Deutéronome*," *Vetus Testamentum* 12 (1962): 29–87; H. D. Preuss, *Deuteronomium* (Darmstadt: Wissenschaftliche Buchgesellschaft, 1982), 95, 103. However, for the view that *Numeruswechsel* results not from editing but from source dependency, see Jeffrey Stackert, *Rewriting the Torah* (Heidelberg: Mohr Siebeck, 2007), 128–29, n. 42 and 180, n.35.

56. Norbert Lohfink (*Das Hauptgebot* [Rome: Pontifical Biblical Institute, 1963]) and his student Georg Braulik (*Die Mittel deuteronomischer Rhetorik erhoben aus Deuteronomium 4.1–40* [Rome: Pontifical Biblical Institute, 1978]) initiated this in regard to Deut 5–11 and Deut 4, respectively. (But for a critique of Lohfink, see Yuichi Osumi, *Die Kompositionsgeschichte des Bundesbuch Exod 20, 22b–23, 23* [Göttingen: Vandenhoek & Ruprecht, 1991], 38–44, 50–52.) Further, such number changes have been identified within other parts of the OT (Exod 21 and Lev 19) and in the broader ANE (A. D. H Mayes, *Deuteronomy* [London: Oliphants, 1979], 35–37; Klaus Baltzer, *The Covenant Formulary in Old Testament, Jewish and Early Christian Writings* [Oxford: Blackwell, 1971], 33, 71).

57. Lohfink, *Das Hauptgebot*, 239.

58. Though, of course, there are exceptions. See also Duane Christensen, "The Numeruswechsel in Deuteronomy 12," in *A Song of Power and the Power of Song*, ed. Duane Christensen (University Park, PA: Eisenbrauns, 1993), 394–402. Christensen argues that the *Numeruswechsel* is an integral part of Deuteronomy's metrical structure.

59. Thomas Römer, "Deuteronomy in Search of Origins," in *Reconsidering Israel and Judah*, ed. Gary Knoppers & J. G. McConville (University Park, PA: Eisenbrauns, 2000), 112–138.

60. Römer, "Deuteronomy," 118–19.

61. See also J. G. McConville, *Grace in the End* (Grand Rapids, MI: Zondervan, 1993), 38.

62. We should note that Römer connects his understanding of the *Numeruswechsel* to Deuteronomy's use of the "fathers" (אבות). Against the traditional view that "fathers" refers to the patriarchs, Römer argues the term also has the exodus generation in view. His argument is subtle and detailed, but mainly it conceives of the exodus generation as the original reference of "fathers," with the notion of the patriarchs being fused to it by later redactors (mostly through appositional modifiers; see also Deut 1:8; 6:10; 9:6, 27; 29:13; 30:20). Practically speaking, Römer's view results in a kind of double reference to the "fathers" in the present text (see also Konrad Schmid, *Erzväter und Exodus* [Neukirchen-Vluyn: Neukirchener Verlag, 1999]); but while the exodus generation plays a part, the patriarchs are still the focus. For his fullest articulation, along with Norbert Lohfink's rebuttal, see Thomas Römer, *Israels Väter* (Göttingen: Vandenhoeck & Ruprecht, 1990). See also Lohfink, Die Väter, esp. 27–47.

63. Millar, *Time and Place*, 42.

64. Millar, *Time and Place*, 42. He attributes the core of his idea to Walter Brueggemann, "Imagination as a Mode of Fidelity," in *Understanding the Word*, eds. J. T. Butler, E. W. Conrad, and C. B. Ollenburger (Sheffield: JSOT Press, 1985), 1–27.

65. Millar, *Time and Place*, 51.

66. See Millar's helpful graphic, *Time and Place*, 61. For a detailed study of Deut 5–11, see Lohfink, *Das Hauptgebot*.

67. Millar, *Time and Place*, 53.

68. See also McConville, *Deuteronomy*, 138.

69. For discussions on the issues of Deut 27, see Moshe Anbar, "The Story of the Building of an Altar on Mount Ebal," in *Das Deuteronomium*, 304–10; Paul Barker, "The Theology of Deuteronomy 27," *Tyndale Bulletin* 49, no. 2 (1998): 277–303.

70. For how Deut 27–34 connects to 12–26, see Peter Craigie, *The Book of Deuteronomy* (Grand Rapids, MI: Eerdmans, 1976), 212, and Lohfink, *Das Hauptgebot*, 233–34, though modified in "Moab oder Sichem—Wo Wurde Dtn 28 nach der Fabel das Deuteronomiums Proklamiert?," in *Studies in Deuteronomy in Honour of C. J. Labuschagne on the Occasion of his 65th Birthday*, F. García Martínez et al. (Brill, 1994), 139–153.

71. Millar, *Time and Place*, 69–77.

72. Millar, *Time and Place*, 78–79. There has been much discussion on the relationship between this so-called "Moab covenant" and that of Horeb. The prevailing view is that this Moab covenant of Deut 29 is, in some sense, connected to the Horeb one. That said, some see it as an entirely different covenant. R. N. Whybray (*Introduction to the Pentateuch* [Eerdmans, 1995], 97–98), for example, sees these as two separate covenants, a fact that he says is overlooked by scholars. Taking up Whybray's idea, Dennis Olson ("How Does Deuteronomy Do Theology? Literary Juxtaposition and Paradox in the New Moab Covenant in Deuteronomy 29–32," in *A God So Near*, eds. Brent Strawn and Nancy Bowen [Eisenbrauns, 2003], 201–13) offers a theological reading of Deuteronomy's juxtaposition of the two covenants (though see his misreading of Millar, 205, n. 8). Even for those who see some level of continuity between Horeb and Moab, there is a question of extent. Typically, one sees the extent of the relationship as indicated by Deut 29:1 (MT 28:69). To what does "these are the words of the covenant" refer? If it refers to the previous material (see also H. F. von Rooy, "Deuteronomy 28:69—Superscript or Subscript?" *Journal of Northwest Semitic Languages* 14 [1988]: 215–22; also, see the Masoretic chapter divisions), then one would see more continuity between the Horeb and Moab covenants. But if it refers to the upcoming material (see also Lohfink, "Dtn 28,69—*Überschrift* oder Kolophon?" *Biblische Notizen* 64 [1992]: 44; also, see the Septuagint and Vulgate divisions), then one would see less overlap. Lohfink's argument is more convincing and scholarship has tended to follow it (but see McConville, *Deuteronomy*, 413–14). In light of Deuteronomy's emphatic contemporaneity, though, one does not have to cede continuity if one agrees with Lohfink. The overarching point remains that these are a series of covenantal moments all of which are collapsed into one ever-present "today."

73. Millar, *Time and Place*, 80–83. We recall that Millar views Deut 4 as overture, which introduces the pivotal themes, and as such he sees Deut 30 as offering their resolution. Together, then, Deut 4 and 30 form an inclusio.

74. Millar, *Time and Place*, 84.

75. It is curious that Millar barely discusses the role of the song (*Time and Place*, 86).

76. Deut 1:30; 4:3, 9, 34; 6:22; 7:19; 9:17; 10:21; 11:7; 29:2, 3. We should note a couple of things. First, the motif occurs exclusively in Deuteronomy's framework. And second, the objects of the eyes include both positive and negative things from the previous generation: Yahweh's mighty deeds (1:30; 4:34; 6:22; 7:19; 10:21; 11:7; 29:2, 3); Horeb revelation (4:9); punishment at Baal-Peor (4:3); Moses's breaking of the tablets (9:17); judgment on Dathan and Abiram (11:7).

77. Moshe Weinfeld, *Deuteronomy and the Deuteronomic School* (Oxford: Oxford University Press, 1972). See also McConville, *Deuteronomy*, 104; Craigie, *Deuteronomy*, 125. Weinfeld rightly sees the "eyes" motif as part of the larger idea of "seeing," even when "eyes" is not present. We restrict ourselves to "eyes" because it is a narrower focus that better accomplishes our purposes.

78. Weinfeld, *Deuteronomic School*, 173.

79. Brevard Childs, *Introduction to the Old Testament as Scripture* (Fortress Press, 1979), 213–15. Also, see T. C. Vriezen and A. S. van der Woude, *Ancient Israelite and Early Jewish Literature*, trans. Brian Doyle (Brill, 2005), 257; Robert Polzin, *Moses and the Deuteronomist* (New York: The Seabury Press, 1980), 36–43.

80. Childs, *Scripture*, 215.

81. Miller, *Deuteronomy*, 53.

82. For example, see S. Mittmann, *Deuteronomium 1, 1–6, 3: literarkritsch und traditionsgeschichtlich Untersucht* (Berlin: Alfred Töpelman, 1975). But see also the devastating critique of Mittmann by Georg Braulik, "Literarkritische und archaeologische Stratigraphie: Zu S Mittmanns Analyse von Deuteronomium 4, 1–40," *Biblica* 59 (1978): 351–83. Also, see A. D. H. Mayes who argues for discontinuity between Deut 1–3 and 4 ("Deuteronomy 4 and the Literary Criticism of Deuteronomy," *Journal of Biblical Literature* 100, no. 1 [1981]: 23–51). With that said, Mayes (p. 48) does argue for many connections, albeit by a redactor's hand, that link 4:1–40 with much of Deuteronomy's framework: 6:10–19; 7:4–5, 7–15, 25–26; 8:1–6, 14b–16, 18b–20; 10:12—11:32; and also 26:16–19; 27:9–10; 28:1–6, 15–19; 29:1—30:20; 32:45–47.

83. Structurally and linguistically, Braulik has shown the most interconnections. In addition to the above work, *Die Mittel deuteronomischer Rhetorik*, also see "Das Deuteronomium und die Menschenrechte," *Theologische Quartalschrift 166* (1986): 15–16 and the aforementioned "Die Ausdrücke für 'Gesetz' im Buch Deuteronomium." Respectively, these argue that Deut 4 foreshadows the following law code in structure and, in its use of "the statutes and the ordinances," ties it to the rest of the Mosaic preaching (which starts in 1:1). Conceptually, there are a couple of key features. First, Mayes has argued that the central theme of Deut 4 is the law, which is immediately developed then in Chapter 5 with the Decalogue (and throughout Deuteronomy) ("Deuteronomy 4," 26). And second, as already discussed, Millar demonstrates that the motif of journey and moments of decision form a key thread, beginning in Deut 1–3, running through 4, and then being developed in 5–11 (Millar, *Time and Place*, 17). See also McConville who notes also the mention of "Beth-Peor" (3:29; 4:3–4) and the ban on Moses's entry into the land (3:23–28; 4:21–22) (*Deuteronomy*, 100–101); and Norbert Lohfink, "Verkündigung des Hauptgebots in der jüngsten Schicht des Deuteronomiums (Deut. 4, 1–40)" in *Höre Israel!* (Düsseldorf:

Patmos Verlag, 1965), 82–120. For an analysis of the issues underlying the relationship between Deut 1–3 and 4, see the article by Nathan MacDonald, "The Literary Criticism and Rhetorical Logic of Deuteronomy i–iv," *Vetus Testamentum* 56 (2006): 203–24. While MacDonald does not find many of the above arguments for coherence convincing—for they tend "to do no more than redescribe the problem" (p. 212)—he himself argues for important, though subtle, interconnections between the chapters in the themes of divine presence, human obedience, election, and the land.

84. It is important here to note a subtle but foundational point about memory and law in Deuteronomy: unlike in Exodus and other Pentateuchal passages in Deuteronomy Israel does not remember the law itself. Rather, Israel remembers things *in order to* obey the law. This point was made by Brevard Childs quite some time back in *Memory and Tradition in Israel* (London: SCM Press, 1962), yet people continue to speak as if law were the object of memory. For example, see Assmann, *Religion*, 53, and Barat Ellman, *Memory and Covenant: The Role of Israel's and God's Memory in Sustaining the Deuteronomic and Priestly Covenants* (Minneapolis, MN: Fortress, 2013), 103–4. For a fuller discussion and critique of Ellman's views, see my review in *Journal of Hebrew Scriptures* 14 (2014), http://www.jhsonline.org/reviews/reviews_new/review723.htm.

85. Thomas W. Mann, *Deuteronomy* (Louisville, KY: Westminster John Knox Press, 1995).

86. Mann, *Deuteronomy*, 37.

87. This is considered the second commandment in all circles except Roman Catholic and Lutheran, where it is part of the first commandment.

88. For a good monograph on this, see Knut Holter, *Deuteronomy 4 and the Second Commandment* (New York: Peter Lang, 2003).

89. I follow McConville in seeing vv. 41–49 as part of the chapter's integral structure. He offers a number of reasons, two of which seem most pertinent. First, he points out, following Millar's view, that these verses, "though they fall outside Moses's first speech, bind the chapter into the themes of history and journey" (*Deuteronomy*, 101). He also shows that the language seems to mirror 1:1–5 and thereby forms an inclusio framing Deut 1–4. For more on this, see Jack R. Lundbom, "The Inclusio and Other Framing Devices in Deuteronomy," *Vetus Testamentum* 46 (1996): 302–4.

90. Holter, *Second Commandment*, 106–7. For arguments on the fuller framework: Holter, *Second Commandment*, 101–7; Braulik, *Die Mittel*, 64, 86–87; Weinfeld, *Deuteronomy 1–11*, 199. For a critical view of the framework, see Dietrich Knapp, *Deuteronomium 4*, 110.

91. Gerhard von Rad, however, argues that that it is a historical justification, not a theological explanation (*Old Testament Theology*, 217). Silvia Schroer has taken up this idea and nuanced it in terms of *Begründung* ("substantiation") and *Erklärung* ("explanation") (*In Israel gab es Bilder* [Freiburg, 1987], 7).

92. For a good classification and summary of the views of aniconism's rationale, see Nathan MacDonald, "Aniconism in the Old Testament," in *The God of Israel*, ed. Robert Gordon (Cambridge, UK: University of Cambridge Press, 2007), 20–34. It should be noted that MacDonald disagrees with von Rad's notion of historical

justification, finding Schroer's *Begründung* more helpful. See also the discussion of aniconism by Carl Evans, "Cult Images, Royal Policies and the Origins of Aniconism," in *The Pitcher Is Broken*, eds. Steven Holloway and Lowell Handy (Sheffield: Sheffield Academic Press, 1995) 192–212.

93. E.g., Samuel Rolles Driver, *Deuteronomy* (Edinburgh: T. & T. Clark, 1902), 65; Von Rad, *Theology*, vol. 1, 217–18; Craigie, *Deuteronomy*, 135.

94. Ronald Hendel, "Social Origins of the Aniconic Tradition," *Catholic Biblical Quarterly* 50 (1988): 365–82; 371.

95. For a good argument against this notion, see Ian Wilson, *Out of the Midst of the Fire* (Atlanta, GA: Society of Biblical Literature, 1995). Also, see Sandra Richter, *The Deuteronomistic History and the Name Theology* (Berlin: De Gruyter, 2002).

96. MacDonald, "Aniconism." See also MacDonald, "Deuteronomy i–iv," 214–18.

97. MacDonald, "Aniconism," 33.

98. We note that what follows does not depend on MacDonald's view of aniconism in Deut 4. His view does, however, provide further grounding of what we argue below is the purpose of "seeing" and "hearing."

99. MacDonald, "Aniconism," 33.

100. MacDonald, "Aniconism," 33.

101. MacDonald, "Aniconism," 32–33.

102. A fact that he himself points out ("Aniconism," 32).

103. See Holter, *Deuteronomy 4*, 22–27; Samuel Terrien, *The Elusive Presence* (Eugene, OR: Wipf & Stock, 2000), 202; Ryan O'Dowd, *The Wisdom of Torah* (Göttingen: Vandenhoek & Ruprecht, 2009), 93–94; Stephen A. Geller, "Fiery Wisdom: Logos and Lexis in Deuteronomy 4," Prooftexts 14 (1994): 103–39 and *Sacred Enigmas* (London: Routledge, 1996), 39; Deurloo, "The One God," 44.

104. Deurloo, "All Israel," 44.

105. Geller, "Fiery Wisdom," 113. See also Geller, *Sacred Enigmas*, 39. Note that Geller ties his opposition of "heard from heaven" and "seen on earth" to the classic notion that Deuteronomy emphasizes Yahweh's transcendence over his immanence ("Fiery Wisdom," 116).

106. Carasik, "To See a Sound: A Deuteronomic Rereading of Exodus 20:15," *Prooftexts* 19, no. 3 (1999): 257–76.

107. Carasik does not ignore the question of the relationship between the epistemology of Proverbs and Deuteronomy but says the following: "The eye plays a minor role in the epistemology of proverbs, the ear a major one. In Deuteronomy, however, the eye plays not merely an equal but a complementary role, since remembering the historical events that the eyes saw is supposed to provide the motivation for performing the commandments . . . Thus the wisdom tradition was not so much the origin of Deuteronomic ideology as its jumping-off point" ("To See a Sound," 259).

108. Carasik, "To See a Sound," 261.

109. Carasik, "To See a Sound," 261.

110. Carasik, *Theologies of the Mind*, esp. "Deuteronomy and the Control of the Mind," 177–217.

111. Carasik, *Theologies of the Mind*, 33–43.

112. Carasik, *Theologies of the Mind*, 33.
113. Carasik, *Theologies of the* Mind, 186–94.
114. Carasik, *Theologies of the* Mind, 185.
115. Carasik, *Theologies of the Mind*, 214. It is curious that, like Assmann, Carasik takes Moses's audience to be that of the exodus generation, and so assumes that the transmission of visual features is the transmuting of the eyewitnesses' experience into memory.
116. "The link and the hinge between the visual and the aural, between זכר and שמר, lies in the one great experience of seeing God's fire and hearing his word at Mount Horeb" (Carasik, *Theologies of the Mind*, 195–96). Carasik helpfully points out that in Deuteronomy the commands are learned and obeyed, but never "remembered"; what are remembered are the great acts of Yahweh, which motivate obedience to the commands.
117. Carasik, *Theologies of the Mind*, 195.
118. Steven Weitzman, "Sensory Reform in Deuteronomy," in *Religion and the Self in Antiquity*, eds. David Brakke, Michael L. Satlow, and Steven Weitzman (Bloomington, IN: Indiana University Press, 2005), 123–39.
119. Weitzman, "Sensory Reform," 124.
120. Notice, though, that Weitzman forwards a different triad from Carasik: eyes–ears–mouth (*Religion and the Self*). While Weitzman is right that taste does feature as a sense in Deuteronomy, Carasik's triad is better because sight/sound are of central importance to the loyalty of Israel's heart.
121. Weitzman, *Religion and the Self*, 125. He explains it like this: Deuteronomy aims "not merely to resituate religious experience in a new setting but to intervene in the nature of religious experience itself by reorienting the sensory self through which it is filtered" (p. 136).
122. Weitzman, *Religion and the Self*, 128, 132.
123. Weitzman, *Religion and the Self*, 133–34.
124. Moshe Weinfeld, *Deuteronomy*, 201.
125. Weinfeld, *The Deuteronomic School*, 207.
126. For a good critique of Weinfeld on his visual/aural distinction, see Wilson, *Midst of the Fire*, 89–97.
127. See also Macdonald, "Aniconism," 33; "Deuteronomy i–iv," 221–22.
128. McConville, *Deuteronomy*, 105. In Deut 4, it appears also in vv. 2, 6, 15, 23, 40. That fact that in these other cases the duty of "keeping" often refers to the statutes and laws, coupled with v. 9 where it refers most directly to remembering what "your eyes have seen," is another indication that "seeing" and "hearing" are inextricably bound.
129. Takamitsu Muraoka, *Emphatic Words and Structures in Biblical Hebrew* (Leiden: Brill, 1985), 131, n. 66.
130. Bruce Waltke and M. O'Connor, *An Introduction to Biblical Hebrew Syntax* (University Park, PA: Eisenbrauns, 1990), 669.
131. Note also that the first use of שמר appears in the niphal and with לך, which in itself is emphatic in its repetitiveness: lit. "guard yourself for yourself." See also Waltke and O'Connor, *Hebrew Syntax*, 388.

132. I have translated נפש as "soul" here to preserve the severity of what Deuteronomy portrays as at stake. It is understood that the biblical notion of נפש is rather broad (see H. W. Wolf, *Anthropology of the Old Testament* [Westminster, 1974], 10–25).

133. It is interesting that here Deuteronomy uses דברים for the object of "your eyes have seen." Perhaps it is that the term, which can mean "things" or "words," is employed with intentional ambiguity here, again fusing the relationship between "seeing" and "hearing." For more in this vein, see Carasik, "To See a Sound."

134. Jeffrey Tigay, *Deuteronomy* (Philadelphia, PA: The Jewish Publication Society, 1996), 46; Craigie, *Deuteronomy*, 132–33; Weinfeld, 203; Mayes, 151; Christensen, 81; McConville, 105.

135. See Patrick Miller on the motif of fire in Deut 4 (*Deuteronomy*, 59; "Fire in the Mythology of Canaan and Israel," *Catholic Biblical Quarterly* 27 [1965]: 256–61).

136. For a good discussion on the usual reticence of biblical description, see Robert Alter, *The Art of Biblical Narrative*, rev. ed. (New York: Basic Books, 2011), 143–62.

137. Weinfeld, *The Deuteronomic School*, 171–72.

138. Here Hwang's concept of "imaginative speech-acts" is nearer to what I envision (*The Rhetoric of Remembrance*, 187–89).

139. It curious to note that a goodly amount of scholars, despite positing some sort of opposition between "seeing"and "hearing" in Deut 4, still see memory as playing an ongoing role in Israel. See also Terrien, *The Elusive Presence*, 202; O'Dowd, *The Wisdom of Torah*, 93–94; Geller, "*Fiery Wisdom*," 121; Deurloo, "The One God," 44; Weinfeld, *Deuteronomy*, 203.

140. As Sarah Sentilles says, "the theologian constructs a picture of the world. But the theologian's finished product is not something to hang on a wall. It is a work of art to be lived in." See Sarah Sentilles, *Draw Your Weapons* (London: The Text Publishing Company, 2017), 247. Here Sentilles is paraphrasing the ideas of Gordon Kaufman.

Chapter 3

You Who Stand Here Today

From Collective Memory to Autobiography

Having looked at why Deuteronomy cultivates memory, we now turn to the what question: What kind of memory does it cultivate? Since form follows function, it is important to consider how Deuteronomy's particular form (what) of memory accomplishes its function (why) for memory. What we are asking, in essence, is how a certain kind of social memory creates a certain kind of individual, how social frameworks are realized in personal identity. This, however, is a more difficult question than it would appear. Not only is it severely underexplored in biblical studies[1] but also in memory scholarship.[2] In order to answer this question for Deuteronomy, therefore, I must first build my own theoretical scaffolding. I do this by drawing together two fields of research on individual memory: the psychology of memory and autobiographical memory. Having done this, I return to Deuteronomy.

THE NATURE OF PERSONAL MEMORY

In recent times, one of the most important developments has come from the field of psychology and its reconceptualizing of human memory. Before this, from at least the time of Plato, the prevailing idea of memory was as a wax tablet, a thesaurus, or a treasury room.[3] This is still the common view in popular culture. The idea is that memory is a recollection of an event that is stored whole in the filing cabinet of the individual's mind. When a person remembers, he locates the file, brings it to the forefront of the mind, and views it like one would a snapshot or a movie clip. The memory is more or less identical each time and is stored and accessed as a whole item.

According to contemporary research, however, this view greatly misrepresents the nature of memory. Daniel Schacter is a leading voice in the psychology of memory and provides a helpful overview.[4]

> [M]emory is not a single or unitary faculty of the mind . . . [but] is composed of a variety of distinct and dissociable processes and systems, each system depends on a particular constellation of the networks in the brain that involve different neural structures, each of which plays a highly specialized role within the system.[5]

Memory, therefore, is neither a repository of whole experiences nor stems from a single aspect of the mind.[6]

How then does human remembering work and what, in fact, is *a* memory? Schacter says that memory can be understood as existing in three interrelated parts: engram, engraphy, and ecphory.[7] As for the engram, it is the basic substance of a memory—the neural network of experience fragments that compose a memory.[8] We should be clear that the engram itself is not "a memory"; it is the constituent raw material, so to speak, engrained into the brain. Morris Moscovitch describes it like this: The engram "is not yet a memory, but provides the necessary . . . condition for memories to emerge . . . A memory emerges when the engram interacts with retrieval cues."[9] Karl Pribram offers a helpful analogy for understanding this phenomenon: the hologram.[10] A hologram arises as a life-like image from a host of light rays cast in a certain way; it cannot be limited to a particular light ray or located in one particular area. Analogously, a memory is not an item that can be traced to one engram or to one area of the brain. It is, like a hologram, a representation that arises from the complex interaction of many memory fragments from many areas of the mind.

Engraphy, the second aspect, is the process of receiving, ordering, and storing information. Essentially, it is the transforming of experience—ideas, sights, sounds, smells, thoughts, or feelings—into memory.[11] Engraphy is of central importance because it determines how well an item is encoded which, in turn, determines how enduring and meaningful it will be as a memory.[12] If something does not receive deep encoding, it enters a short-term system called short-term or "working memory."[13] Here material lasts a brief time, just long enough for a person to use it in daily life. However, if the material receives "elaborative encoding," it will enter long-term memory where it can last up to a lifetime.[14] Elaborative encoding can occur in a host of ways, from simple mnemonic devices such as rhyming to more in-depth knowledge associations. Whatever the form, the efficacy of encoding depends on the "levels-of-processing effect."[15] That is to say, the deeper and more thoroughly a concept is understood and interconnected with other information, the more enduring its memory will be.[16] Ultimately, the mind flags up the repeated "attention" given to the item and its many associations as indicating meaningfulness and significance.[17] This process of moving a recollection from one memory system to a deeper one is called "consolidation."[18] The result is that deeply encoded aspects are not only remembered, but they also take up governing places in memory's knowledge and interpretive frameworks (more on this below).

The last element of the memory triad, ecphory, is the process of activating or triggering memories.[19] It is the mechanism of awakening those elements of stored experience that lie dispersed throughout the vast complexes of the mind. But while this is indeed the mechanism that retrieves memories, we must understand what "retrieve" means here. Schacter says that "one critically important idea is that the brain engages in an act of 'construction' during the retrieval process."[20] That is, there is no one part of the brain that contains the whole memory; rather, some parts contain fragments of sensory experience and others "contain codes that bind sensory fragments to one another and to preexisting knowledge, thereby constituting complex records of the past encodings."[21] One corollary is that no memory is recalled in the same way twice. Certainly, patterns can be entrenched, through encoding, that establish a more or less stable representation, but like a hologram, the representation itself will change according to the perspective from which it is activated.

That leads to another corollary: the triggers of a memory are of absolute importance. Research has shown that regardless of how well an item is encoded, it cannot be activated unless properly cued.[22] Tulving and Thomson elucidated this dynamic as the "encoding specificity principle."[23] In brief, the idea is that memory is more accessible when information from its encoding is also available at retrieval.[24] Or to say it differently, a memory's retrieval cues must be interwoven with, and so tap into its encoding to be readily reached. Other than knowledge interconnections, two other factors in this are the mental state of the person and the environment in which the remembering occurs.[25] Mental states, especially moods, lead to congruent remembering: the mood a person was in when encoding a memory is the mood that it is best retrieved in. Here one thinks of the prescribed solemnity or joy of Israelite feasts. Features of an environment are just as important: if a person can go back to the place where the memory was encoded, or reproduce some of its features, retrieval is much more likely.[26] Here one thinks of what Assmann calls Deuteronomy's counterfactual memory program, that is, the ambition to construct in a foreign world an environment that conjures up Israel's defining memory.

From this brief summary of individual memory, we note two things: memory is *constructive* and *selective*. Far from the classic conception of a storehouse in which memories are stored and recalled, human remembering is much more dynamic. For one thing, an individual's recollecting is constructive: each memory it produces is a unique representation arising from the combination of memory traces (engrams), encoding (engraphy), and retrieval (ecphory). Practically, this means that though memory is a generally reliable representation of the past, it is also one shaped by the concerns of the present context. And for another thing, an individual's memory is constantly in flux: it adapts and molds according to the incoming stimuli and how much encoding that stimuli receives. The significance of this is that memory is always reshuffling itself in order to select the ideas and episodes most salient to its context. The items that receive the most encoding are consequently given prominent features in the memory framework.

HOW GROUP MEMORIES BECOME PERSONAL IDENTITY

Yet how do these various workings of memory become personal identity or autobiography? This brings us to the two systems of long-term memory that undergird autobiography: semantic and episodic memory.[27] Semantic memory, on the one hand, is traditionally understood as conceptual or abstract knowledge that exists independent of particular events. This includes things such as meanings, categories, facts, and propositions. Remembering a phone number, for example, is the province of semantic memory. But while it has been called a person's "sum total of knowledge,"[28] semantic memory is much more than information storage. It may be understood instead as a network of associations and concepts underlying our knowledge of the world.[29] These networks, then, serve the vital function of forming frameworks of meaning, which filter, categorize, and integrate incoming information.[30] Semantic memory, therefore, provides the interpretive lens through which we interpret the world and our place within it.

Episodic memory, on the other hand, is the recollection of experiences and the events, objects, and people that comprise them.[31] Further, the experiences and their constituent parts are recalled in reference to particular times and spaces. For example, the memory of one's wedding would include specific experiences and the times and places in which they occurred. These aspects, we note, refer to the substance of recollection. And while such substance remains a defining aspect of episodic memory, recent scholarship has emphasized an additional feature: "autonoetic consciousness."[32] This refers to the fact that people remember episodes in relation to themselves, from their own perspective. More specifically, it means that to remember experiences is to be "there" yourself—"mental time travel" in which the traveler re-experiences the event.[33] The experience, though, is "subjective," meaning the traveler understands it is not real time.[34]

How, then, does autobiographical memory (AM) relate to these two systems? In general, we can understand AM as the sense of self, or personal identity, that arises from the interrelations of semantic and episodic memory.[35] But as to the specifics of the process, we note this:

> This undertaking has been fraught with difficulty because of the great quantity and variability of the data. It is a daunting task to try to discover the general principles that govern the encoding, storage, and retrieval of personal experiences accumulated over their lifetimes by different individuals with different personal histories.[36]

That being said, the authors do forward a handful of commonly accepted ideas.[37] From these, I draw two that are pertinent. First, like individual memory in general AM is dynamic and constructive. It continues to refigure itself according to incoming information. This is why, for example, a person who never actually experienced the September 11 incident but saw the images on television may still identify with the event. Second, developing on the first point, AM is rooted in particular episodes but modulated by semantic memory.

The second point requires explanation. It is generally accepted that particular episodes of memory form the foundation of one's AM, and that from these the mind extracts semantic information through "a process of abstraction and generalization."[38] The matrices of meaning that result interconnect with each other at common points, and they form frameworks of worldview and meaning in the individual's mind. Exactly how these aspects of AM align to create self-identity, however, remains under discussion. The chief issue seems to concern where self-identity taps into AM.[39] In general, there are two different perspectives.[40] The one focuses on personal narrative as the entry point of identity, and so it emphasizes semantic memory: self-identity is rooted not in particular episodes, but in general events. Thus, the storylines that govern general events are the veins from which identity flows.[41] The other one focuses on particular episodes, seeing specific situations as then giving rise to the personal narratives.[42] Here vivid memories form the spine of one's self-identity. While both perspectives are valid, for me, the latter offers a more convincing view of the way in which self-identity taps into AM.

How, then, does the mind construct self-identity from memory? Martin Conway and Christopher Pleydell-Pearce have forwarded an influential model called the "self-memory system."[43] It is not necessary for us to engage all of its aspects, which are complex, but only enough to establish the main contours so to employ the model later. At its foundation, the self-memory system is composed of two elements: the autobiographical knowledge base (AKB) and the working self.

The AKB provides the material—the informational lumber, fasteners, and girders—from which an individual's identity is built. This material is comprised of three kinds of data: that concerning (1) lifetime periods, (2) general events, and (3) event-specific aspects.[44] Lifetime periods, first, are represented by thoughts such as, "when I was at university." These are distinct periods of time that, more or less, have identifiable beginnings and ends. Each represents general knowledge that typifies the period: relationships, locales, activities, plans, goals, etc. More specifically in regard to content, lifetime periods represent *temporal* and *thematic* knowledge of that time. Temporal knowledge relates to the duration of the period. It might be that the university period lasted five years. Thematic knowledge concerns features that are characteristic of a period. One may remember the university period as a time full of activities and friends, relatively carefree and liberating. For both of these, there is often overlapping of different spheres of knowledge. It should be said, too, that such knowledge also carries attitudes related to the information.

The second kind of AKB knowledge, general events, is more specific than lifetime periods.[45] These represent items such as "my morning runs," "my first times," etc. We notice, as such, that general events knowledge encompasses both *generalizations of repeated events* and *sets of related events*. A generalization of repeated events, on the one hand, is a single representation of a constellation of the same kind of event. For example, "my morning runs" will be a rather generic memory of daily jogs, even though the jogs themselves may have been quite different in route, weather conditions, time of year, etc. Sets of related events, on the other hand, are events linked by a *common theme*. For example, the above category "my first times" would group first-time events from disparate areas: first time going to a cinema, flying, driving on your own, etc. There are two further features of first-time memories that are noteworthy. First, these memories tend to be vivid: they include increased visualized details of the events. Second, and most significantly, first-time memories are laden with information about goal attainment. That is, when one remembers, say, driving alone, he may recall it either as an event that he competently navigated or one that he struggled to cope with. Whichever the case, the person's assessment of goal attainment will color the rest of his self-memory.

The third and final category of AKB is event-specific knowledge.[46] What distinguishes this from the other two types of knowledge is not only its focus on specific events but also its vivid nature. In particular, it is typically comprised of *sensory imagery* (sights, sounds, smells, and touch). Take, for example, an incident of being almost run over by a car while bicycling. One is likely to recall such an event in vivid detail, seeing it replay in the mind like a movie clip: the car hurtling forward, then swerving, tires squealing, and lurching to a halt only inches from the bicycle. For the most part, these memories lose their vividness quickly and are subsumed within the general events category. That is why we are not, except in cases of extreme trauma, forever haunted by such incidents. But there are also constructive life memories that maintain their lucidity. Specific events fall into four categories: originating events, turning points, anchoring events, and analogous events.[47]

If particular events are key to shaping identity, as we argued previously, then it is important to understand how they work. Let us briefly consider these four types. Originating events, to begin with, are those defining moments from which a new life path or period begins.[48] For example, the legendary basketball player Michael Jordan attributes the beginning of his path toward greatness to a single event: when he was cut from his high school basketball team. This further illustrates the function of originating events: to imbue purposes and goals into self-identity. The memory of originating events, therefore, provides the motivation to attain long-term goals. The second kind, turning points, is slightly different. Instead of serving as a point of departure, these stand as moments of redirection.[49] For example, in the well-known example of C. S. Lewis, he recalls a particular moment in his study at Magdalen College when he converted to Christianity.[50] In his own self-understanding, he sees that moment as the turning point of his new life of faith. Turning points are closely related to originating events and share most of the same features. We observe, too, that both of these are seen as causal events: they cause the resulting life trajectory.[51]

The third and fourth kinds, anchoring and analogous events, have similar roles. Anchoring events are episodes that provide the foundation of belief systems.[52] By "belief systems" we do not necessarily mean religious belief systems, but rather particular beliefs gathered from life situations. The memory of a professor telling a student that she is capable of nearly anything might embolden and encourage her for the rest of her life. Analogous events, then, serve as models for later experiences. A student caught cutting corners on an assignment and deeply embarrassed might, as a result, remember the experience and always do things thoroughly. How, then, do anchoring and analogous events differ? Pillemer does not make this clear, but it seems thus: an anchoring event *roots* a belief in a concrete memory, and so provides grounding for something that can be applied across a spectrum of situations. An analogous event, however, *models* a circumstance (and its lessons) that is instructive in other instances.

If the AKB is the material from which autobiography is built, then the working self is the builder. It is the organizing force that structures the materials of memory into a matrix of meaning and self-identity. While the actual workings of this are quite complex, it seems they can be summarized thus: schematic and goal-oriented.[53] The working self is schematic in that it exists in "abstracted knowledge structures" arising from concrete memories.[54]

These structures help organize memory into meaningful frameworks, that is, they "provide an evaluative and interpretive context for the current view of self."[55] Arising from such schemas is the second piece of the working self: goal-orientation.[56] While schemas give knowledge coherence and meaning, goal-orientation gives them a *telos*. That is, the theme undergirding a schema also fuels a related goal-orientation. So, for the common schema of religion, there might be a goal such as *honor God by helping the poor*. The resulting piece of memory, as such, is not some static image of oneself, but rather a purpose-laden self-portrait.[57] Contained in the self-portrait is both *who I am* and *who I ought to be*. These goal structures are important for our study of Deuteronomy, therefore, in that they further illumine the dynamics underlying Israel's autobiographical memory.

Conway and Pleydell-Pearce offer their own summary of the interaction between AKB and the working self:

> The formation of a distinct and stable pattern [of memory] is . . . briefly: ESK [event-specific knowledge] representations have mappings to one general event . . . general events have a *main* mapping to one lifetime period . . . Activation spreading from an item of ESK activates a single general event that in turn activates a single lifetime period forming a focused and stable representation, and all that is then required is a linking of this pattern to the goal structure of the Working Self and a memory will be formed.[58]

Beyond explicating how self-identity stems from AM, I suggest that this model has yet another important implication for Deuteronomy: it provides a method for analytically mapping Israel's autobiography. Such mapping would help answer one of our main questions in this chapter: How does collective memory translate into individual memory? That is, what are the major episodes and ideas and what is their purpose regarding identity?

Before turning to Deuteronomy, however, I must address something that thus far has remained implicit. If collective memory aims to shape Israel's identity, and identity grows out of personal episodic memories, then somehow the collective must instil such memories in the individual.[59] But how? How does one acquire memories of an experience that one never experienced? Though the issue is present in any approach that ultimately roots identity in episodes instead of storylines, there is a remarkable paucity of discussion on the topic. It is assumed that it happens without being elucidated how.

With that being said, I think there is an area of memory research that offers a theoretical bridge: "imagination inflation." Imagination inflation occurs when a person holds as true a memory that is either an exaggerated version of a true event or an entirely fictional one.[60] Also called false memory, this especially came to light in the 1980s when there arose a spate of instances in which adults, typically from the guidance of therapists, "recovered" memories of childhood sexual abuse.[61] It was later discovered that these many of these so-called "recoveries" were in fact created through suggestion; that is, through their suggestion therapists were accidentally "inducing autobiographical memories" in clients.[62] The clients came to remember, in very vivid images, episodes of abuse that never happened.

This understandably led to an increase in scholarly research to uncover why such misremembering happens. What scholars generally have come to believe is that this is an issue of "source monitoring."[63] Because memory is inherently constructive—arising from engram, encoding, and retrieval—there is a fine line between what is imagined and what is remembered. The mind typically distinguishes between the two by identifying the correct source of each: imagination or perception. Issues come up, however, when the mind views episodes from imagination as deriving from perception instead; this is when imagination becomes "inflated" and registers as a memory.[64] This brings us to the pertinent question for our own study: how exactly does such source confusion occur?

Research suggests that imagined events come to be seen as memories when they are encoded with memory-like features.[65] What makes an imagination memory-like is an increase in "qualitative characteristics," namely "perceptual" and "contextual" aspects.[66] This is to say that true memories betray a deeper familiarity with the event experience, both in what it was like and where it occurred; so the more an imagined item reflects this the more likely it will register as a true memory. Scholars further identify perceptual and contextual aspects, respectively, as sensory (sights, sounds, etc.) and temporal/spatial.[67] But while an increase in sensory features in general causes an imagined item to be seen as a real memory, there is one aspect that is especially influential: sight.[68] Arising from the "Picture-Superiority Effect," the idea that images are the most potent mnemonic,[69] research has shown that visual features are what transform imagined events into memories.[70] The preponderance of visual detail causes a person to hold the event not as something imagined, but as something perceived. This idea has been helpfully developed by Goff and Roediger, who show that the dynamic is heightened further when the rememberer envisions himself as a participant in the scene.[71] The rehearsal of events in vivid visual detail and with oneself as a participant, therefore, causes a person to see the events not as imagined but as perceived; the person sees the events as part of his own autobiography.[72] We suggest that this is how collectives transmit key memories to individuals, a point that has great significance for Deuteronomy.[73]

It is not incidental, I suggest, that Deuteronomy's emphasis on visual phenomena aligns with that of autobiographical memory. Deuteronomy 4 makes clear that for Israel to "hear" Yahweh's words, it must continue to "see" the theophany at Horeb; the visual phenomena is of chief importance in motivating obedience. But, as I have noted, the seeing is both broader and deeper than just this. It is broader in that the same language of seeing with "your eyes" and "remembering" includes other events of the exodus generation. It is deeper in that it is meant to be transmitted generationally through remembering; more than just the fleeting experience of ritual actualization, the seeing is to endure moment by moment in Israel's daily life. Assmann rightly connects this to the construction of collective memory but, as is typical of sociological approaches, he neglects the individual side of memory. Our own study has shown not only how individual memory works, but how the collective shapes the individual's autobiography. This happens, I proposed, through a point of exchange at which the collective induces its defining episodes in the individual: visually detailed episodes of particular times and places. By rehearsing events in visual detail, the collective constructs in the individual a synthetic personal memory; it is as if each new generation actually experienced the defining events for itself. It is therefore reasonable, I think, to understand Deuteronomy's visual emphasis as betraying a similar aim.[74]

DEUTERONOMY AND THE SHAPE OF COVENANTAL MEMORY

What, then, is the nature and shape of Israel's autobiography in Deuteronomy? That is what we turn to now. In order to do so, we seek to do two things: (1) to identify the constituent pieces of Israel's defining memory and (2) to analyze that substance in light of autobiographical memory as outlined above. The point here is to sketch Israel's autobiography, as presented by Deuteronomy, so ultimately to root collective memory in individual identity. I note that the aim here is not exegetical, which might rather obscure our bird's-eye view, but topographical; exegesis of pertinent passages will be executed in the next chapter.

Jan Assmann has suggested three memories as the nucleus of Israel's identity: the exodus, the revelation at Horeb, and the wilderness experience.[75] But there are a couple of fundamental issues with this. First, he never articulates his selection criteria. Other than the obvious issue methodologically, this is problematic because of scholarly disagreement as to what might be considered central events in Deuteronomy. Von Rad would disagree with at least one of the above three, for he sees Israel's *Heilsgeschichte* in Deuteronomy as originally excluding the Horeb event.[76] Nearly oppositely, Lohfink focuses on Horeb over and above the other events, saying that compared to Horeb they are just the "portico and the vestibule."[77] More in line with Assmann is MacDonald, who following classic construals of the *Heilsgeschichte* situates the exodus, Horeb, and wilderness between the patriarchal promises and the conquest of the land.[78] The question is which of these, if any, is correct? And how do we distinguish which events comprise Israel's defining identity?

Although Assmann does not discuss criteria, it seems that three particularly guide his choices: space allocation, frequency of use, and memorization command. That is, the memories that occupy the most space, occur the most often, and are commanded for remembering must be of central importance to Deuteronomy. These appear to be reliable criteria, but in light of our previous discussion, we should like to add one more: visual emphasis. Such emphasis might surface in a variety of ways, but we have in mind two: as the object of the "eyes" motif or as a visually detailed account of an event. If Deuteronomy does in fact aim to induce episodes of memory, then this is of crucial importance in identifying those memories. Beyond mere identification, however, the imagery is also key to elucidating the *workings* of memory. We recall that visual aspects, or event-specific knowledge (ESK), are both the porthole through which collective memory becomes individual and the foundation for autobiographical memory. After identifying the pertinent imagery, therefore, we analyze its shaping of Israel's identity.

The second major problem with Assmann's proposal is that it fails to account for aspects of memory other than episodes. We have seen that episodic memory is indeed important, but that it is by no means the whole of one's autobiography. There are a host of other parts necessary to situate and orient those episodes. What, then, might these pieces be in Israel's memory? I suggest that they are the patriarchal promises and the promised land.

The Patriarchal Promises and the Promised Land

For the patriarchal promises and promised land, there is an important shared feature: though both are ubiquitous in Deuteronomy's message, neither is the object of the "eyes" motif or the memory command. Rather than indicating their absence from Deuteronomy's construal of memory, however, I suggest that this fact directs us to their true roles. Deuteronomy 7:8–13 exemplifies these well:

> But it was because the Lord loved you and kept the oath he swore to your forefathers that he brought you out with a mighty hand and redeemed you from the land of slavery, from the power of Pharaoh king of Egypt. Know therefore that the Lord your God, he is God, the God who is faithful, keeping his covenant of love to a thousand generations of those who love him and keep his commands . . . If you pay attention to these laws and are careful to follow them, then the Lord your God will keep his covenant of love with you, as he swore to your forefathers. He will love you and bless you . . . in the land that he swore to your forefathers to give you.

Perhaps better than any other passage, this shows that the promises and the land situate the events of the exodus generation by giving them continuity and trajectory.

Regarding the promises as continuity, J. D. W. Watts says it well: Yahweh's "oath to Abraham is the basis of his love and concern for Israel."[79]

> Thus God's constancy in dealing with Israel and the steadfastness of his will for salvation and fellowship are confirmed . . . [the oath] also ties the doctrine of Deuteronomy into a fundamental whole. Not only is God identified in this way, but the election which is the basis of covenant and the holy land of Canaan are Israel's because of the promises made to Abraham. So the relation to Abraham holds the structure together and provides its unity.[80]

The promises therefore establish a silver thread that runs from the patriarchs, through the Mosaic period and material, and into life in the land.[81]

In mnemonic terms, then, the promises motif does not have episodic features but is purely semantic.[82] What this means is that it serves as a governing framework, or schema, that orientates the key episodes of the exodus generation, "blend[ing] perceptual imagery with narrative, inference, and interpretation."[83] Perceptual imagery, we have argued, comes especially from the exodus, Mount Horeb, and wilderness events. The promises then provide these with a plotline, namely, that of the previous Pentateuch material: Yahweh's promise for land, seed, blessing, and divine presence.[84] We shall engage in this more shortly, but for now mention the basics. Viewed through the lens of the exodus generation, the promises take on a more concrete expression. The seed is not just a bloodline, but further a people redeemed by and covenanted to Yahweh. Their obedience to the covenant stipulations, Torah, in turn determines the level of blessing and divine presence the people will experience in the land. We notice, then, that beyond giving the core memories coherence and trajectory, the promises also provide Israel important self-concepts. Through the promises, the people come to understand themselves as part of an ongoing program under a faithful Lord (Deut 7:9). So, if in the exodus, Mount Horeb, and wilderness episodes Israel is to *see* itself as part of the defining events, then in the patriarchal promises it is to *understand* how the events grow out of the promises and *conceive* of itself as part of that growth.

Regarding the land as trajectory, Deuteronomy "stresses the common Pentateuchal theme that [the land] is the goal of Israel's journey."[85] But to portray it as just a goal is to do the land a great injustice as the object of Israel's longing. Since Gen 17:8, Israel has yearned for the land. As von Rad says,

> The life of the chosen people in the "pleasant land" at rest from all enemies round about, the people owning their love for God and God blessing his

people—this is the epitome of the state of the redeemed nation as Deuteronomy sees it.[86]

No doubt this is why it is portrayed as a kind of paradise.[87] And with that land now in view, Deuteronomy sets out how Israel may gain and retain it and enjoy a blessed life within it.[88]

> [T]he land plays a significant role . . . On the one hand the land is the place where the law is to be obeyed; but on the other, it also appears as the place which Israel cannot possess unless she obeys the law.[89]

Millar insightfully summarizes the land as a "context for decision," "motivation for decision," and "measure of decision."[90] Ultimately, the fulfillment of that ancient promise of the land of Canaan depends on Israel's ability to embody the lessons and instruction of the exodus generation.

Here we should highlight something that sets the land apart from the promises in its depiction in Deuteronomy: visual description. While the patriarchal promises appear frequently and are important to Israel's memory, visual features never accompany them.[91] The promised land, however, is frequently portrayed in visual imagery. The typical description of the land is "good" (טוב).[92] This sets the overarching theme within which we locate the imagery. By far the commonest image of the land, both in Deuteronomy and elsewhere, is that of one "flowing with milk and honey" (זבת חלב ודבש).[93] Whatever connection the description has to agricultural possibilities in the land,[94] the obvious point is to depict "the ideal land filled in abundance . . . a kind of paradise."[95] It has been shown further by P. D. Stern that this, too, is imagery from the ANE environment, namely, that which is found in descriptions of the storm god Baal from Ugarit.[96] If he is right that the description serves as a "Yahwistic counter-slogan,"[97] by which Deuteronomy leverages ballistic ideas to elevate Yahweh, then the imagery takes on even more import. The visualization of the land becomes a fulcrum for cultural contestation, where Israel pictures its Lord as the true owner and itself as the true heir of it.

Apart from the "milk and honey" imagery, the land receives other picturesque descriptions. In Deut 6:8–12, the land is portrayed as a place of abundance:

> a land with great and goodly cities that you did not build, houses filled with every good thing that you did not fill up, wells you did not dig, and vineyards and olive groves you did not plant.[98]

Deut 11:9–11, in contrasting the land to Egypt, says it is "a land of mountains and valleys that drinks rain from heaven." And in Deut 8:7–9, we find the most picturesque one of all:

a land with streams and pools of water, with springs flowing in the valleys and hills; a land with wheat and barley, vines and fig trees, pomegranates, olive oil, and honey; a land where bread will not be scarce and you will lack nothing; a land where the rocks are iron and you can dig copper out of the hills.

Of this passage, McConville says it is the land's "most vivid portrayal, picturing its natural richness with an *accumulation of its features*."[99] It should be clear by now that the land imagery aims to establish an idealized vision of Canaan in Israel's mind. But it should be noted, too, that like the other pieces of memory there is another side. In both Deut 6:8–12 and 8:7–9, what follows the gushing portraits of the land is a sober warning not to "forget" (שׁכח) the Lord. The land is indeed a great blessing, but as with all such things, it carries the danger of satiety and complacency. Israel must be vigilant to remember the giver (6:12; 8:11–18). It seems, therefore, that the writer wants to emblazon in Israel a visual portrait of the land, to fuel its longings and motivate obedience; but he also wants to interweave temperance into this vision, to warn of its inherent dangers.

What, then, does this mean in mnemonic terms? From Deuteronomy's perspective, these images are not meant to build episodic memories of Israel's past, but to construct a portrait of its goal. This is what scholars of autobiographical memory call a *directive* function:[100] it establishes the aims that govern one's personal memory. Some scholars have helpfully developed the directive idea further as "possible selves," that is, as the repertoire of life scenarios that guide our behavior.[101] In this view, the images of the land would serve to shape Israel's ideas of who it might become, for good or ill, and thus direct it to act accordingly. The main theme of the images, that of abundance and flourishing, shows Israel "the possibility of a special kind of life—good, undefiled, life in community, life in the worship of Yahweh."[102] But this is dependent upon Israel's ability to obey the Torah; its level of success there predicts its level of flourishing in the land (Deut 28:1–14).[103] Within the images of abundance, though, there is also the warning of an inherent danger of complacency. If not guarded against, the comfortable life in the land will cause forgetfulness and, consequently, disobedience (6:12; 8:11–18). Such a situation is no mere trifle, for its consequences would be catastrophic (28:15–68). Here in 28:15–68, we find the mnemonic aspect of the land that stands opposite of flourishing: famine, disease, destruction, and exile. It is what Assmann calls Deuteronomy's "death fugue."[104] Also dramatic and vivid, this text provides Israel with the negative side of its "possible self." Indeed, the land is the goal, the directive, of Israel's memory; but the other possibility is that it will not do its part. Together, therefore, the depictions of flourishing, its dangers, and the images of punishment formulate the life scenarios of the promised land that guide Israel's autobiographical memory.

The Exodus

We now turn to the three episodes that Assmann forwards. How well do they meet the above criteria and what does their composition reveal about their workings? In regard to the exodus, it is the most frequent reference of the "eyes" motif (seven times).[105] This indicates to begin with that the exodus is meant as a key episode of memory. It is interesting that the event itself never receives detailed visual rehearsal in Deuteronomy. Instead, it is typically accompanied by a "concatenation of terms for [Yahweh's] great acts in saving Israel from Egypt."[106] Deut 4:34 is a good example of this: Yahweh delivered Israel "by trials (מסת), by signs (אתת), and by wonders (מפתים),[107] and by war (מלחמה), and by a mighty hand (יד חזקה), and by an outstretched arm (זרוע נטויה), and by great terrors (מוראים גדלים)."[108] Such deliberate use of vivid words, repetition of the inseparable preposition ב ("by") to emphasize agency, the inordinate use of modifiers, and coupled with the fact that this appears in the recitation of firstfruits (26:8), indicates at the very least that the rhetoric is meant to be memorable. But other factors suggest that there is something more going on. Weinfeld argues that "mighty hand" and "outstretched arm" belong to "Egyptian royal typology,"[109] the latter of which Othmar Keel identifies as part of Egyptian iconography.[110] If this can be maintained, then these terms are not only depicting Yahweh as divine warrior,[111] but also evoking—and supplanting—Egyptian imagery.[112] Their use with the "eyes" motif would indicate that this idea is at least tenable, and at the very least, it shows an emphasis on visualization.

What is more, the exodus is mentioned frequently in Deuteronomy, in fact, no less than thirty-four times.[113] Many of these contain imagery overlapping with that of the "eyes" motif, and some use visual details beyond that. For instance, it is said that Yahweh brought Israel out of the "house of bondage" (בת עבדים) (5:6; 6:2; 7:8; 8:14; 13:5, 10), the "iron furnace" (מכו הברזל) (4:20), by "night" (לילה) and in "hurried flight" (חפזון) (16:3).[114] It is noteworthy that the previous visual terms concern Yahweh's action, whereas these concern the situation in Egypt and the departure from it. As such, they contain references to time ("night") and place ("house of bondage," "iron-furnace"). Beyond these instances, the exodus is often invoked in memory, too.[115] This memory is at the heart of Israel's community life. Moses establishes the exodus story as the foundation of the covenant by weaving it into the practices of the family and community realms. In family life, Moses places the story at the heart of the religious education of children (6:20–24; 11:2–4, 19–21). The retelling of the Exodus is what grafts them into covenantal life. In community life, the Exodus story is recounted, and embodied, yearly in the Feast of Passover and Unleavened

Bread (16:1–8); once in the land, the recitation in the offering of firstfruits recounts the *Heilsgeschichte*, of which the exodus is part (26:6–8). In this brief sketch, we have seen that the exodus is indeed a key episode that is accompanied by visual features. But it is not just Yahweh's activity as divine warrior that is visually laden; it is also Israel's situation in Egypt and its leaving from it. This suggests that Deuteronomy is indeed seeking to help Israel visualize the exodus, but broadly so—from the environment itself, to its leaving, to Yahweh's activity.

Autobiographically speaking, these things build a particular kind of memory. The use of imagery, though varied, in this case works toward one end: visualizing an episode in which Israel was suffering terribly but was delivered by Yahweh mightily. Yahweh's deliverance is obviously the theme of the imagery, but it depends on the depiction of Israel in dire circumstances. Together they portray an image that evokes from Israel not only awe of Yahweh's deeds, but more importantly gratitude for them. On its own, the motif of Yahweh as a mighty warrior is, in the biblical depiction, incomplete; it must be coupled with the fact that it was done on Israel's behalf and for its deliverance. This dynamic, we notice, is what in the last chapter we elucidated as a key piece of connective memory. The exodus is to evoke deep gratitude and obligation to Yahweh; thus, it forms the moral and ethical fabric of Israel's memory.

So, what does the imagery mean for the workings of autobiographical memory? At the ESK level, it seems that of the four particular kinds of episodes—origins event, turning point, anchoring event, or analogous event—the exodus functions as an origins event. The exodus is the origination of Israel as a defined people, the point at which it became Yahweh's redeemed community (Deut 31:6).[116] This becomes clearer when we look at the Mount Horeb episode. How, then, does the exodus function at the next level of general event? It seems apparent that the exodus serves as a redemptive event, setting the theme of Israel as a redeemed people.[117] More than just an example, though, the exodus stands in Israel's memory as the archetype of redemption.[118] It is *the* defining episode of Yahweh's deliverance of Israel. We should note further that as the initial event of Israel's formative period, the exodus generation,[119] the exodus then characterizes the whole generation as one of deliverance. The events of Mount Horeb and the wilderness are framed in memory as constituent parts of Yahweh's redemption of his people. This comes to light when considering the self-concepts and goal orientation that arises from the exodus episode. Self-conceptually, Israel sees itself as the redeemed of Yahweh and therefore, in terms of goal orientation, obligated to remain loyal to him. On its own, the target of the goal remains undefined; but it will become concrete through the revelation at Horeb.

Mount Horeb

In regard to the Horeb event, it is not the referent of the "eyes" motif as much as the exodus, but it does feature twice (4:9; 9:17). As already discussed, 4:9 leads into the locus classicus for aniconism in Deuteronomy. That passage especially shows that the "seeing" of Horeb must continue if Israel is to continue "hearing" the words from there. The "seeing" depicted especially emphasizes the nature of the theophany: "The mountain blazed with fire (בער באש) to the heart of the heavens—darkness (חשך), clouds (ענן), and thick cloud (ערפל)" (4:11).[120] Miller aptly calls this an intentional "heaping up" of terms to drive home the image.[121] From verse 11 onward, the motif of "fire" (אש) continues to elicit Horeb imagery in the chapter (vv. 11, 12, 15, 24, 33, 36 [two times]). Miller points out that such fire imagery is common in ANE depictions of divine beings and their warfare.[122] When it appears in relation to Yahweh, he argues, it typically combines divine warring with theophany.[123] While divine warring is not at the forefront of Deut 4, verse 24 does root the theophany in warring language: Yahweh is a "consuming fire (אש אכלה), a jealous God." This is significant because it pairs fire as a symbol of Yahweh's presence with fire as a symbol of Yahweh's judgment on idolaters (5:9).[124] As with the exodus, then, we see that Deuteronomy employs imagery common to the ANE for its own ends, but more importantly for our work here is the fact that Deuteronomy purposefully leverages the ANE's images.

Interestingly, 9:17 depicts not the theophany, but Moses's breaking of the tablets on the mountain. In verse 16, Moses "sees" Israel's sin of idolatry and in verse 17, he reacts: "I seized (תפש) the two tablets and cast (שלך) them out of my two hands, and I shattered (שבר, Piel) them before your eyes."[125] In comparison to the Exodus account (32:19), Deuteronomy's is more dramatic.[126] Exodus does have Moses getting angry and "casting" and "shattering" the tablets, but it does not draw visual emphasis with the repetition of "two tablets" from "my two hands" and "before your eyes." Taken together, Deut 4:9 and 9:17 show that, like the exodus, Horeb visualization is multifaceted. The rhetoric gives visual detail not only of the theophany at Horeb, but also of Moses's reaction to Israel's idolatry. It is not accidental, we suggest, that the two episodes intersect at the point of visual representations in worship.

There are other aspects, too, that betray the emphasis on Horeb. Indeed, the event is mentioned frequently in Deuteronomy: at least twenty-four times.[127] But what sets it apart from the exodus is its narrative rehearsals, namely, in chapters 4, 5, 9, and 10.[128] Typical of chapters 4 and 5 is the vivid language describing the mountain: "blazing with fire" (בער באש), shrouded in "cloud" (ענן) and "deep darkness" (חשך). The longest recounting however, 9:7–10:11, employs only the "fire" motif. It also differs from the other two in focusing not on the theophany but on the consequences of Israel's idolatry. As pointed out above, it seeks to emblazon Moses's reaction to the sin. In addition to the visual language used to describe his shattering of the tablets (9:17), this passage deploys a detailed narrative surrounding the idolatry. Israel's sin sends Moses up and down the mountain, fasting and remaining up there for intervals over forty days and nights, and interceding on behalf of the people. Finally, he prevails and is able to chisel out two new tablets and carry on with the covenant intact.[129] The express purpose of this rehearsing, 9:7 establishes, is so that Israel may "remember" its history of provoking Yahweh. In light of the visual imagery and extended recounting of both the Horeb theophany and Moses's reaction to Israel's sin, it seems clear that Horeb is a key episode of Israel's memory. This finding runs counter to von Rad's view, but neither am I comfortable giving it the supremacy that Lohfink does. Craigie, then, gives the best summary: "Horeb (Sinai) . . . was one of the cardinal points of the faith which was to be remembered."[130]

In regard to its autobiographical workings, then, the Horeb episode betrays unique function. The diversity of images again point to a multifaceted construal. In particular, the episode's ESK betrays two key strands. The foundational strand is of the theophany itself, focusing on its nature and substance. As already discussed, the visualization of the voice coming from a mountain shrouded and blazing means, first, that Israel saw no form, and second, that the voice is the basis of the covenant stipulations. Now captured in the Torah, that voice is to continue to direct community worship; the memory of the clouds and fire, and not a graven image, is what should continue to accompany the voice. Integrally connected to this is the second strand, which focuses on the consequences of not heeding the meaning of the theophany. The motif of fire connects the first strand with the second, issuing a warning: if the revelatory fire of Horeb is not heeded, then the consuming fire of Yahweh's jealousy will devour the idolaters. Consequences of idolatry are further highlighted in relation to the covenant in Moses's breaking of the tablets. Here the warning is not of destruction, but of covenant nullification (represented in the tablet breaking).

So what kind of event is Mount Horeb? I suggest that it, too, is primarily an origins event, though different from that of the exodus. Whereas the exodus stands as the point at which Israel became a redeemed people, Yahweh's possession, Mount Horeb is where they became a covenanted people. The theophany imagery emphasizes how things began at the mountain and how worship should continue in the land (and what happens if it does not). Interestingly, the imagery of Moses's breaking the tablets is of a different nature, though it does serve to support that of the Horeb origins. The tablets imagery, I suggest, serves as an analogous event. It portrays an event that models how idolatry affects the covenant relationship. The function is to perpetually warn Israel about the perils of "forgetting" the Horeb episode. What is the next level, the general event, of Mount Horeb? It seems that if the exodus stands as a redemptive event, then Horeb stands as a revelatory and covenanting event. Growing out of these are self-concepts and goal orientation. Self-conceptually, Israel is to see itself as in covenant with Yahweh, distinctly shaped by the revelation that is now the Torah. We notice that this dovetails into Deuteronomy's program of generational conflation. The goal that arises from it is for Israel to worship rightly, heeding the warnings, obeying the Torah and particularly abstaining from images. As such, we observe how the exodus goal of living as redeemed people becomes concrete in the revelation of Horeb.

The Wilderness

In regard to the wilderness, the "eyes" motif is referred to three times (1:30–31; 4:3; 11:7). In the first instance, the "eyes" motif occurs initially with the exodus (1:30), but then serves to link into what Israel "saw" (ראה) in the wilderness (1:31). What Israel saw was "how the Lord your God carried you, as a father carries his son." The imagery here is not descriptive, per se, but it is visual in its metaphorical depiction. This idea of sonship also comes up in Deut 8:5 and 14:1 (also 32:5–6), and the former context shares with 1:31 the theme of divine provision. In the other two examples, however, there is a very different focus. Deut 4:3 refers to the event at Baal Peor: "The Lord God destroyed from among you everyone who followed the Baal of Peor, but all of you who held fast to the Lord your God are still alive today." Deut 11:7 refers to "all the great work" (כל־מעשה הגדל) the Lord did. In context, this comes after a litany of Yahweh's deeds, beginning with the exodus and continuing through the wilderness to the present at Moab. McConville is probably right to see "all the great work" as a unifying phrase referring to the whole of Yahweh's activity.[131] And he also points out that there are two events found only here in Deuteronomy's rehearsal of salvation history: the Red Sea crossing and the destruction of Dathan and Abiram.

The latter is yet another vivid depiction of a cautionary event: "in the midst of all of Israel, the earth opened its mouth and swallowed them, their households, their tents, and every living thing at their feet." Against its full account in Numbers 16, several features in Deuteronomy are unique. To begin with, the passage singles out Dathan and Abiram without mentioning Korah. Whatever the reason for this,[132] it does not appear central to it as the referent of the "eyes" motif. Perhaps more pertinent is Deuteronomy's use of language. Deut 11:6 most closely resembles Num 16:32, but unlike the Numbers verse it mentions the people's "tents" (אהלים),[133] uses a different word for "opened up" (פצה),[134] and says that every "living thing" (יקום) "at their feet" (ברגליהם)

was consumed. Though we must be careful not to take this too far, it does seem that Deuteronomy shows a sharpening of imagery. It accomplishes this by employing the concrete nouns of "tents" and "feet," compared to the use in Numbers of either abstract or nondescript nouns. These make the traumatic event even more vivid in the mind's eye. Further, the phrase "in the midst of all Israel" emphasizes "that it happened in full sight of all the people."[135] The point of recounting this, therefore, is not to highlight Yahweh's salvation,[136] but rather to serve as a cautionary tale.[137] As we have been seeing, Israel's memory is a two-sided entity, at once illumining Yahweh's power to save and to judge and the significance of these for Israel's behavior.

This reality is developed further if we consider the wilderness event apart from the "eyes" motif. While not as frequent as the exodus or Horeb references, the "wilderness" (מדבר) occurs at least nineteen times.[138] What is more, it appears in fuller narratives and with vivid imagery.[139] Deut 1–3 is important in that, as already discussed, it sets out places of failure and places of success. The visual imagery further illumines this dynamic in that it juxtaposes what Israel saw with what it should have seen. At Kadesh Barnea, the people lost heart because of the spies' report. It is important that in Numbers 13:27–29, the report comes from the spies, but in Deuteronomy 1:28, it comes from the people's perspective:[140] "[The spies] say, 'The people are greater and taller than us; the cities are great and fortified into the heavens. We even saw the Anakites there.'" The use of "greater" (גדול), "taller" (רם), "cities fortified into the heavens" (ערים גלות וצורת שמים), and "seeing" (ראה) the "Anakites" who were deemed giants, I suggest, is intentionally visual. This, then, contrasts the descriptions seen in Deut 1–3 of other visual phenomena associated with the desert. Despite Israel "seeing" (ראה) that the desert was "great" (גדול) and "dreadful" (נורא) (1:19; 2:7), and "seeing" how the Lord provided throughout (1:30–31; 2:7)—"with fire (אש) by night" and "cloud (ענן) by day"—she could not trust and obey Yahweh.

Deut 8 picks up on and develops these aspects even more. There it says specifically that Israel is to "remember" the wilderness as a definitive example of Yahweh's leading and provision (v. 2). It juxtaposes the imagery of the promised land with that of the wilderness. Again, Deuteronomy employs visually laden language for the desert: it was "great" (גדול) and "dreadful" (נורא), "thirsty and waterless" (צמאון אין־מים), and with "fiery snakes" (נחש ושרף) and "scorpions" (עקרב) (v. 15). Despite these conditions, though, the Lord provided manna (vv. 2, 16) and water from the "rock of flint" (צור החלמש) (v. 15);[141] and Israel's "clothes did not wear out" nor did its "feet swell" (v. 4). Weinfeld points out that parts of this wilderness portrait arise elsewhere in the ANE.[142] Esarhaddon described the Arabian territory of Bazu as a waterless region with serpents and scorpions and spoke of Egypt as having venomous and fiery (or flying) serpents.[143] And Herodotus similarly describes the Sinai desert.[144] Further, Keel shows that images of such serpents were part of Egyptian iconography.[145] As with the exodus and Horeb events, then, Deuteronomy employs powerful images from the ANE world to portray the wilderness.

What, then, of the autobiographical workings of the wilderness event? In this case, there are again a couple of complementary strands of imagery. The first of these depicts the wilderness as a severe and unyielding place. The text connects this depiction to Israel's sonship, which contains the ideas both of Yahweh's provision (1:31) and discipline (8:5).[146] Thus the imagery serves to highlight Yahweh's ability to care for and correct his people even in such a place. The other strand portrays cases of rebellion, such as the spies event at Kadesh Barnea (1:28) and the judgment of Dathan and Abiram (11:7).[147] Especially in view are the consequences of the rebellions: the former causes the wilderness experience in the first place and the latter details the horrible judgment of rebels in a particular case. It is also noteworthy that Deut 9:7 commands the people to "remember" and never "forget" that Israel's rebellion is what characterized the entire wilderness experience (9:22–24).

At the specific events level, I suggest that these two strands are purposely juxtaposed as anchoring events. The rebellion imagery characterizes the wilderness period as one of rebellion and, as such, anchors the idea that by nature Israel is a stiff-necked people. The imagery depicts the severity of the wilderness, however, highlights Yahweh's provision for and discipline of his people. It therefore anchors the notion of Yahweh's fatherhood and Israel's sonship (8:2–5). While each imagery set evokes a distinct notion, it also seems that the text envisions them under the single rubric of Israel's time "in the wilderness" (במדבר).[148] Thus the wilderness experience supports a tandem: Israel as both petulant child and beloved son. For the general events level, the identification of these episodes are predictable: cases of rebellion and times of Yahweh's provision and correction. As already hinted at, the imagery frames Israel's identity within the self-concepts of an inherently rebellious child but also as Yahweh's son. The goals arising from these intersect, for the former warns Israel to be wary of its own belligerence while the latter calls it to a deep trust in Yahweh's fatherly guidance.

CONCLUSION

I have tried to show how Israel's collective memory comes to inhabit individual Israelites, and how this, in turn, shapes them into the kind of people desired by Deuteronomy: lovers of Yahweh and listeners of his voice (Deut 6:4–9). In light of memory theory's gap on the question of how group memory becomes individual memory, I leveraged two key areas, psychology of memory and autobiographical memory, to build my own scaffolding. And from this, we peered into the workings of memory as found in the book of Deuteronomy.

Fundamental here were the two long-term memory systems of the mind, semantic (informational) and episodic (scenic) memory, and how they combine to create a person's autobiography. In general, semantic memory provides the overarching story and episodic memory the scenes of that story. I followed the perspective that sees episodic memory as primary, which means that scenes, not semantic threads, are what form the spine of a person's autobiography. As such, the presence of visual, or scenic, features are vitally important, for they determine the fundamental nature of one's autobiography. Leveraging the notions of "Picture-Superiority Effect" and "Imagination Conflation," I argued further that visual features provide the all-important point of exchange between collective memory and autobiographical memory. They provide, in other words, a kind of "wrinkle in time"[149] through which individuals travel to ancient events and come to see those events as part of their own experiences. This, I noted, makes for an important point of connection with Deuteronomy's theology, which insists that visual memory is necessary for motivating covenantal obedience.

As for the shape of memory in Deuteronomy, I suggested five constituent elements: patriarchal promises, exodus, Mount Horeb, wilderness, and promised land. The patriarchal promises and the promised land, it was argued, serve a different role than the others, providing a semantic framing for memory. The patriarchal promises establish the semantic grounding for memory, with the key ideas of Yahweh's promise of land, seed, blessing, and divine presence serving as a connective web of covenantal memory. It was noted that this part of memory is purely semantic, never invoking the "eyes" motif or using the telltale visual language. The other part of the semantic frame, the promised land, serves somewhat differently. It does use visual imagery, but in a semantic way—to set the trajectory of memory. That is, rather than using visual imagery to create identification with past events, it uses the imagery to shape people's longings for the future. In mnemonic terms, this is meant to establish "possible selves," images of what might be if people behave in a certain way. Here Deuteronomy portrays two possibilities: a paradise-like life in the land (result of obedience) or a life of famine, disease, destruction, and exile from the land (result of disobedience).

The other three components are different again, in that they are the pillar episodes of Israel's memory, that is, the events that each Israelite is to identify with. Each is accompanied with the "eyes" motif and highly visual language. The exodus serves as Israel's origins event and therefore defines the people's DNA. It does so by balancing two sets of imagery: the misery of Egypt and the might of Yahweh's deliverance. As such, it characterizes Israel as a redeemed people and infuses in them awe of Yahweh's power and gratitude for his goodness. The second component, Mount Horeb, serves in tandem with the exodus as an origins account. But while the exodus characterizes Israel as a redeemed people, Mount Horeb portrays them as a covenanted people. The distinctive part of Mount Horeb, then, is that it depicts the essence of the covenant relationship: one where God speaks and his people listen. This is displayed in the episode's two sides of visual imagery: the terrifying nature of Yahweh's revelation, especially emphasizing fire from which God spoke, and Moses's shattering of the tablets of the covenant due to Israel's disobedience. The third component, the wilderness, serves as an anchoring memory, that is, a memory that grounds foundational ideas in past events. For Deuteronomy, the foundational ideas are Israel's sonship and Yahweh's fatherhood. Israel is characterized as a rebellious son through an emphasis on the spies' event at Kadesh Barnea and the judgment on Dathan and Abiram, and Yahweh is characterized as a good and faithful father through an emphasis on his provision and discipline of Israel in the wilderness wasteland.

These five components of memory are not novel in themselves, for they are all well-worn from scholarly discussions. What is novel, though, is the proposal for how they work together to shape Israel's autobiography, an autobiography meant to create the ideal Israelite. To my knowledge, this has not been attempted elsewhere. As such, it would represent a development on the classic notion of *Heilsgeschichte*, which views events as if they were purely positive and inherently simple.

NOTES

1. Jan Assmann is one of the few who attempts to address this, proposing a fourfold model of psyche, consciousness, society, and culture. Assmann's notion of psyche would appear closest to personal memory, though even here he calls it "communicative memory" and speaks of it in ways akin to social memory. See Assmann, "What is 'Cultural Memory?,'" in *Religion and Cultural Memory*, trans. R. Livingstone (Palo Alto, CA: Stanford University Press, 2006) 1–30, and "Collective Memory and Cultural Identity," trans. John Czaplicka, in *New German Critique* 65 (1995): 125–33.

2. Jeffrey Olick shows how, from Halbwachs till now, collective memory study has not accounted enough for the individual. See Olick, "Collective Memory: The Two Cultures," *Sociological Theory* 17, no. 3 (1999): 334–36. Olick describes the situation like this: while there are "mutual affirmations of psychologists who want more emphasis on the social and sociologists who want more emphasis on the cognitive . . . actual cross-disciplinary research . . . has been much rarer than affirmations about its necessity and desirability." See Jeffrey Olick, "Collective Memory: A Memoir and Prospect," *Memory Studies* 1, no. 1 (2008): 19–25; 23. And according to John Sutton, this has created a situation so impoverished that nearly all aspects are in need

of analysis: "neural, cognitive, habitual, interpersonal, organizational, archival, and so on." See John Sutton, "Between Individual and Collective Memory: Coordination, Interaction, Distribution," in *Social Research* 75, no. 1 (2008): 23–48, 39.

3. Mary Jean Carruthers, *The Book of Memory*, 2nd ed. (Cambridge, UK: Cambridge University Press, 2008), 18–55. Carruthers rightly notes that the wax tablet must be seen as the governing metaphor for memory. In these pages, she offers an excellent history of the concept. See also Anne Whitehead, *Memory* (Abingdon, UK: Taylor & Francis, 2009), 17–32.

4. I use Schacter not only because he is a leading voice but also because he provides a cohesive phenomenological view of memory—the focus of our study—that is rooted in three key areas: cognitive psychology, clinical observation, and neuroscience (Schacter, *Searching for Memory* [New York: Basic Books, 1996], 7). For another accessible introduction, see *The Seven Sins of Memory*, repr. (Boston, MA: Houghton Mifflin, 2002). For more specialized treatments that Schacter has edited and contributed to, see *Memory Systems 1994*, ed. Daniel Schacter and Endel Tulving (Cambridge, MA: Massachusetts Institute of Technology, 1994); *Memory Distortion*, ed. Daniel Schacter and Joseph Coyle (Cambridge, MA: Harvard University Press, 1997); *The Cognitive Neuropsychology of False Memories*, ed. Daniel Schacter (London: Psychology Press, 1999); *Memory, Brain, and Belief*, ed. Daniel Schacter and Elaine Scarry, 3rd ed. (Cambridge, MA: Harvard University Press, 2001); *Scientific American Reader to Accompany Schacter/Gilbert/Wegner*, ed. Daniel Schacter, Daniel Gilbert, and Daniel Wegner (Macmillan, 2008).

5. Schacter, *Searching for Memory*, 5. A brief overview of the physical workings of memory out of which this statement arises: What most people think of in the brain is the wrinkly structure called the cerebral cortex, which can be understood as having different regions (lobes). The occipital lobe (rear cortex) is involved in perception more than memory; the parietal lobe (central cortex) is involved in aspects of memory involving visual items or spatial manipulation; the temporal lobes (lower central cortex, in front of parietal lobe) are the parts of the cortex most associated with memory, as they probably store long-term memories (especially autobiographical and conceptual memories); and the frontal lobe (front cortex) is also important to memory in that it coordinates various types of information. Beneath this cortex, however, are smaller structures (subcortical structures) that are not so commonly known but that are crucial to memory. The diencephalon, serving as an information router to other areas of the brain, is involved in the conscious, factual elements of memory and possibly also the temporal sequence of events. The amygdala, a small almond-shaped structure, is responsible for processing emotional elements of memory. The basal ganglia, a collection of subcortical structures, and the cerebellum deal with aspects of unconscious memory such as knowledge necessary for habits and motor skills. The hippocampus is the subcortical structure most involved with memory, especially majoring in the processing of conscious, episodic memories (Schacter, *Searching*, 27–32).

6. Schacter, *Searching*, 42.

7. Schacter, *Searching*, 58. Schacter's division follows that of the nineteenth-century German biologist Richard Semon who, until Schacter's research, was virtually lost from the history of memory scholarship.

8. Schacter, *Searching*, 58. For a history of the idea of the engram, see Schacter, *Forgotten Ideas, Neglected Pioneers* (London: Psychology Press, 2001), 163–80. For a helpful discussion on current views of the engram, see Morris Moscovitch, "Memory: Why the Engram is Elusive," *Science of Memory*, ed. Henry Roediger III, Yadin Dudai, and Susan Fitzpatrick (Oxford: Oxford University Press, 2007), 17–22.

9. Moscovitch, "The Engram," 18.

10. Pribram, *Brain and Perception* (New Jersey: Lawrence Erlbaum Associates, 1991). Pribram's own work is much more far-reaching than this, arguing that the basic functioning of the human mind are analogous to that of a hologram. I simply employ his metaphor for memory.

11. Schacter, *Searching*, 42.

12. Schacter, *Searching*, 46.

13. Schacter, *Searching*, 43.

14. Schacter, *Searching*, 45.

15. This idea was first forwarded by Fergus I. M. Craik and Robert Lockhart in "Levels of Processing: A Framework for Memory Research," *Journal of Verbal Learning and Verbal Behaviour* 11 (1972): 671–84. For discussions on the state of the theory at present, see *Human Memory and Cognitive Aging*, ed. Moshe-Naveh Benjamin, Morris Moscovitch, and Henry Roedigger III (London: Psychology Press, 2001). It should be noted that I follow Craik and Lockhart only in their basic idea of how memories are engrained. The more technical distinction that they draw—that encoding does not actually exist in its own right but only as a by-product of perception-cognition—seems untenable. For a good critique, see Endel Tulving, "Does Memory Encoding Exist?," in *Human Memory*, 6–27. In this sense, the view adopted here would be in line with Tulving's "general abstract processing system."

16. It would seem that this contradicts the phenomenon that, since Roger Brown and James Kulick, has been called "flashbulb" memory ("Flashbulb Memories," *Cognition* 5 [1977]: 73–99). Brown and Kulick argued that the reason surprising events are suddenly and indelibly emblazoned on the mind is because of a special kind of encoding called the "Now Print" mechanism. The issue has been under ongoing scrutiny (e.g., D. B. Pillemar, "Flashbulb Memories of the Assassination Attempt on President Reagan," *Cognition* 16 [1984]: 63–80; Sven-Áke Christianson, "Flashbulb Memories: Special, But Not So Special," *Memory and Cognition*, 17: [1989]: 435–43; Martin A. Conway, Stephen J. Anderson, and Steen F. Larsen et al., "The Formation of Flashbulb Memories," *Memory and Cognition* 22 [1994]: 326–43). Schacter and others, however, argue that such memories are still the result of normal encoding but manifest differently (Schacter, *Searching*, 195–201). Further evidence for this view comes from research showing that so-called flashbulb memories are indeed vivid but are not any more reliable than normally encoded memory. See J. M. Talarico and D. C. Rubin, "Confidence, not Consistency, Characterizes Flashbulb Memories," *Psychological Science* 14, no. 5 [2003]: 455–61.

17. See Scott C. Brown and Fergus I. M. Craik, "Encoding and Retrieval of Information," *The Oxford Handbook of Memory*, ed. Endel Tulving and Fergus I. M. Craik (Oxford: Oxford University Press, 2000), 93–108.

18. Schacter, *Searching*, 82.

19. Schacter, *Searching*, 58.
20. Schacter, Searching, 66.
21. Schacter, Searching, 66.
22. For a good discussion on this, see Brown and Craik, "Encoding and Retrieval."
23. Endel Tulving and Donald M. Thomson, "Encoding Specificity and Retrieval Processes in Episodic Memory," *Psychological Review* 80 (1973): 352–73.
24. Such an idea has immediate echoes in Assmann's argument that Deuteronomy aims to construct a counter memory for Israel in the promised land.
25. Brown and Craik, "Encoding and Retrieval," 100–102.
26. This was first discussed by D. R. Godden and A. D. Baddeley, "Context-Dependant Memory in Two Natural Contexts: On Land and Under Water," *British Journal of Psychology* 66 (1975): 325–31. See also Schacter, *Seven Sins*, 202; J. R. Anderson and L. J. Schooler, "Reflections of the Environment in Memory," *Psychological Science* 2, no. 6 (1991): 396–408.
27. These systems were first articulated as such by Endel Tulving in "Episodic and Semantic Memory," in *Organization of Memory*, ed. Endel Tulving and Wayne Donaldson (Cambridge, MA: Academic Press, 1972), 381–402. He further developed his ideas in the landmark work, *Elements of Episodic Memory* (Oxford: Clarendon Press, 1983). Semantic and episodic memory are two of what is typically considered a triad of long-term memory; the third system is procedural memory, that which is embodied in particular skills such as bicycling or typing. These systems can be further grouped as explicit and implicit memory (see Larry Squire and Eric Kandel, *Memory* [New York: Henry Holt, 2003]). Explicit, or declarative, memory is the kind that a person is aware of and can articulate, and it includes the semantic and episodic kinds. Implicit memory, however, is that which is present, but which is either unknown or unable to be articulated; procedural is of this kind. While the division of memory into semantic and episodic systems is generally accepted, there are others who disagree. See Arthur M. Glenberg, "What Memory is For," *Behavioral and Brain Sciences* 20 (1997): 1–55; Mark Howe, *The Fate of Early Memories* (American Psychological Association, 2000).
28. Richard Thompson and Stephen Madigan, *Memory* (Princeton, NJ: Princeton University Press, 2007), 8.
29. Schacter, *Searching*, 151. Schacter advocates a network model. There is, however, still much discussion as to what model best represents the workings of semantic memory. For instance, see Thomas L. Griffiths, Mark Steyvers, and Alana Firl, "Google and the Mind: Predicting Fluency with Page Rank," *Psychological Science* 18, no. 12 (2007): 1069–76; Thomas K. Landauer and Susan T. Dumais, "A Solution to Plato's Problem: The Latent Semantic Analysis Theory of the Acquisition, Induction, and Representation of Knowledge," *Psychological Review* 104 (1997): 211–40; John Anderson, *The Adaptive Character of Thought* (New Jersey: Lawrence Erlbaum, 1990).
30. See Phyllis Koenig and Murray Grossman, "Process and Content in Semantic Memory," in *Neural Basis of Semantic Memory*, ed. John Hart and Michael Kraut (Cambridge, UK: Cambridge University Press, 2007), 247–64.

31. The seminal work on this is Tulving's aforementioned *Elements of Episodic Memory*. For a helpful discussion on developments of the idea since that work, see Tulving, "Episodic Memory: From Mind to Brain," *Annual Review of Psychology* 53 (2002): 1–25.

32. Tulving, "From Mind to Brain," 1, and "Origin of Autonoesis in Episodic Memory," in *The Nature of Remembering*, ed. Henry Roediger III et al. (American Psychological Association, 2001),1–25; Mark A. Wheeler, "Episodic Memory and Autonoetic Awareness," in *The Oxford Handbook of Memory*, 597–608.

33. Tulving, "From Mind to Brain," 2. The phrase "mental time travel" is usually attributed to Thomas Suddendorf and Michael Corballis, "Mental Time Travel and the Evolution of the Human Mind," *Genetic Social and General Psychology Monographs* 123 (1997):133–67. Suddendorf himself uses it earlier, though, in his thesis, *Discovery of the Fourth Dimension: Mental Time Travel and Human Evolution* (master's thesis: University of Waikato, 1994).

34. This distinguishes it from mental disorders whose sufferers perceive such mental events as real. It is also interesting to note that a growing body of research shows that this "mental time travel" is a feature of memory unique to humans (see Tulving, "From Mind to Brain," 2).

35. As already noted, Tulving originally saw the two systems as independent, which meant that episodic was the one handling AM. However, it is now widely held (including by Tulving himself) that semantic and episodic are inextricably bound in creating AM, which should become clear. For other works on AM, see David C. Rubin, ed., *Autobiographical Memory* (Cambridge, UK: Cambridge University Press, 1986); Martin A. Conway et al., *Theoretical Perspectives on Autobiographical Memory* (Dordrecht, The Netherlands: Kluwer Academic, 1992); David C. Rubin, ed., *Remembering Our Past* (Cambridge, UK: Cambridge University Press, 1995); Robyn Fivush and Catherine A. Haden, eds., *Autobiographical Memory and the Construction of the Narrative Self* (New Jersey: Lawrence Erlbaum Associates, 2003); Denise R. Beike, James M. Lampinen, and Douglas A. Behrend, eds., *The Self and Memory* (London: Psychology Press, 2004); Anita Kasabova, *On Autobiographical Memory* (Newcastle upon Tyne, UK: Cambridge Scholars, 2009); Hans J. Markowitsch and Harald Welzer, *The Development of Autobiographical Memory* (London: Psychology Press, 2010).

36. Helen Williams, Martin Conway, and Gillian Cohen, "Autobiographical Memory," in *Memory in the Real World*, ed. Gillian Cohen and Martin Conway (London: Psychology Press, 2008), 22.

37. Williams, Conway, and Cohen, "Autobiographical Memory," 22–23.

38. Williams, Conway, and Cohen, "Autobiographical Memory," 22.

39. See Denise R. Beike, James M. Lampinen, and Douglas A. Behrend, "Evolving Conceptions of the Self and Memory," in *The Self and Memory*, 3–10.

40. Beike, Lampinen, and Behrend, "Evolving Conceptions of the Self and Memory," 6.

41. E.g., Robyn Fivusch, "The Social Construction of Personal Narratives," *Merrill-Palmer Quarterly* 37 (1991): 59–82; Dan McAdams, *The Stories We Live By* (New York: Guilford Press, 1997); Donna Rose Addis and Lynette Tippett, "The

Contributions of Autobiographical Memory to the Content and Continuity of Identity," in *Self-Continuity*, ed. Fabio Sani (London: Psychology Press, 2008), 71–84.

42. Denise Beike, Erica Kleinknecht, and Erin T. Wirth-Beaumont, "How Emotional and Nonemotional Memories Define the Self," 141–60; and Constantine Sedikides, Jeffrey D. Green, and Brad Pinter, "Self-Protective Memory," in *The Self and Memory*, 161–80; David Pillemer, *Momentous Events, Vivid Memories* (Cambridge, MA: Harvard University Press, 1998) and "Momentous Events and the Life Story," *Review of General Psychology* 5 (2001): 123–34.

43. Martin A. Conway and Christopher W. Pleydell-Pearce, "The Construction of Autobiographical Memories in the Self-Memory System," *Psychological Review* 107 (2000): 262–88. Conway himself furthered the view in "Memory and the Self," *Journal of Memory and Language* 53 (2005): 594–628.

44. Conway and Pleydell-Pearce, "Self-Memory System," 262–64.

45. Conway and Pleydell-Pearce, "Self-Memory System," 262–63.

46. Conway and Pleydell-Pearce, "Self-Memory System," 263–64.

47. D. B. Pillemer, "Momentous Events and the Life Story," *Review of General Psychology* 5 (2001): 123–34.

48. Pillemer, "Momentous Events," 127.

49. Pillemer, "Momentous Events," 127–28.

50. C. S. Lewis, *Surprised by Joy* (Fort Washington, PA: Harvest Books, 1955), 228–29. Technically, this describes his conversion to theism in 1929, followed by one to Christianity proper in 1931.

51. Pillemer, "Momentous Events," 127–28.

52. Pillemer, "Momentous Events," 128.

53. Conway calls these "goal structures" and "self-conceptual knowledge" ("The Self," 597).

54. Conway, "The Self," 597.

55. Conway, "The Self," 597.

56. Conway and Pleydell-Pearce, "Construction," 266. For a discussion of how exactly this works, see Conway, "The Self," 597.

57. We should also note that these goals often exist implicitly; if asked, a person may or may not be able to articulate them.

58. Conway and Pleydell-Pearce, "Construction," 274. Of course, Conway and Pleydell-Pearce make clear that there can be many "subsidiary mappings to other lifetime periods and . . . many mappings to other associated general events."

59. As Jon Levenson says, "History is not only rendered contemporary; it is internalized. One's people's history becomes one's personal history." Jon Levenson, *Sinai and Zion: An Entry into Jewish Bible* (San Francisco: Harper-SanFrancisco, 1985), 39.

60. We should note that this differs from delusion and confabulation, which tends to refer to the same fictional memories but which stem from brain damage or disorder. Giuliana Mazzoni and Amina Memon, "Imagination Can Create False Autobiographical Memories," *Psychological Science* 14 (2003): 186–88.

61. For academic work on this, see Elizabeth Loftus, "The Reality of Repressed Memories," *American Psychologist* 48 (1993): 518–37; Elizabeth Loftus and Katherine Ketcham, *The Myth of Repressed Memory* (New York: St. Martin's Griffin, 1996).

For a devastating popular account of false memory, see Lawrence Wright, *Remembering Satan* (New York: Alfred A. Knopf, 1994).

62. Karen J. Mitchell and Marcia K. Johnson, "Source Monitoring: Attributing Mental Experiences," in *Oxford Handbook of Memory*, 187.

63. Mitchell and Johnson, "Source Monitoring." See also Marcia K. Johnson, Shahin Hashtroudi and D. Stephen Lindsay, "Source Monitoring," *Psychological Bulletin* 114 (1993): 3–28; Marcia K. Johnson, "Source Monitoring and Memory Distortion," *Philosophical Transactions of the Royal Society of London* 352 (1997): 1733–45; Karen J. Mitchell and Marcia K. Johnson, "Source Monitoring 15 Years Later: What Have We Learned from MRI About the Neural Mechanisms of Source Memory?," *Psychological Bulletin* 135 (2009): 638–77; Siegfried L. Sporer and Stefanie J. Sharman, "Should I Believe This? Reality Monitoring of Accounts of Self-Experienced and Invented Recent and Distant Autobiographical Events," *Applied Cognitive Psychology* 20 (2006): 837–54.

64. For helpful work on this, see Maryanne Garry et al., "Imagination Inflation: Imagining a Childhood Event Inflates Confidence That it Occurred," *Psychonomic Bulletin and Review* 3 (1996): 208–14; Maryanne Garry et al., "Imagination Inflation is a Fact, Not an Artifact: A Reply to Pezdek and Eddy," *Memory and Cognition* 29 (2001): 719–29; Mazzoni and Memon, "Imagination Can Create False Autobiographical Memories," 186–88; Stefanie J. Sharman and Amanda J. Barnier, "Imagining Nice and Nasty Events in Childhood or Adulthood: Recent Positive Events Show the Most Imagination Inflation," *Acta Psychologica*, 129 (2008): 228–33.

65. Lyn M. Goff and Henry L. Roediger, "Imagination Inflation for Action Events: Repeated Imagining Leads to Illusory Recollections," *Memory and Cognition* 26 (1998): 20–33.

66. Mara Mather, Linda A. Henkel, and Marcia K. Johnson, "Evaluating Characteristics of False Memories: Remember/Know Judgments and Memory Characteristics Questionnaire Compared," *Memory and Cognition* 6 (1997): 827.

67. Mitchell and Johnson, "Source Monitoring 15 Years Later"; Marcia K. Johnson, "Reality Monitoring: An Experimental Phenomenological Approach," *Journal of Experimental Psychology* 117 (1988): 390–94; Siegfried L. Sporer and Stefanie J. Sharman, "Should I Believe This? Reality Monitoring of Accounts of Self-Experienced and Invented Recent and Distant Autobiographical Events," *Applied Cognitive Psychology* 20 (2006): 837–54.

68. Helene Intraub and Susan Nicklos, "Levels of Processing and Picture Memory: The Physical Superiority Effect," Journal of Experimental Psychology. *Learning, Memory, and Cognition* 11 (1985): 284–98.

69. Andrew J. O. Whitehouse, Murray T. Maybery and Kevin Durkin, "The Development of the Picture-Superiority Effect," *British Journal of Developmental Psychology* 24 (2010): 767–73.

70. Ira E. Hyman, Jr. and Joel Pentland, "The Role of Mental Imagery in the Creation of False Childhood Memories," *Journal of Memory and Language* 35 (1996):101–17; Ayanna K. Thomas and Elizabeth F. Loftus, "Creating Bizarre False Memories Through Imagination," *Memory and Cognition* 30 (2002): 423–31; Ayanna K. Thomas, John B. Bulevich, and Elizabeth F. Loftus, "Exploring the Role

of Repetition and Sensory Elaboration in the Imagination Inflation Effect," *Memory and Cognition* 31 (2003): 631–32; Mazzoni and Memon, "Imagination Can Create False Autobiographical Memories."

71. Lyn M. Goff and Henry L. Roediger, "Imagination Inflation for Action Events: Repeated Imagining Leads to Illusory Recollections," *Memory and Cognition* 26 (1998): 20–33.

72. This shift, I suggest, is related to the two different perspectives of remembering: field and observer. To remember as an observer is to see oneself from a bird's-eye view, looking down on the event and seeing oneself as part of it. This is typical of older, distant memories. To remember from the field perspective, however, is to see the events as if through one's own eyes. This is typical of more recent and monumental memories. On this, see John A. Robinson and Karen L. Swanson, "Field and Observer Modes of Remembering," *Memory* 1 (1994): 169–84.

73. Because this theory addresses a lacuna in current scholarship, I have presented it to the preeminent scholar of autobiographical memory, David Pillemer. Dr. Pillemer agrees that this is indeed an important though overlooked issue, and says of my own theory: "I do like your idea that visually detailed collective episodes may be 'shared' with individuals and become a sort of 'synthetic personal memory'" (quoting my original correspondence) (personal correspondence, September 26, 2011).

74. This does not mean, of course, that the ancient writers had all this in mind. Rather, it means that the ancients would have understood that certain things were more potent and enduring in mnemonics, and they employed those accordingly. We note, too, that scholars in related areas have begun to investigate the role of visual features in collective memory. For example, see Maria Luiselli, "The Ancient Egyptian Scene of 'Pharaoh Smiting his Enemies': An Attempt to Visualize Cultural Memory?," in *Cultural Memory and Identity in Ancient Societies*, ed. Martin Bommas (Contiuum, 2011), 10–25.

75. Assmann, *Religion and Cultural Memory*, 17–18.

76. Von Rad, *Hexateuch*, 13–26, argues that Horeb's absence from the credo statements shows it was originally a tradition separate from that of the exodus. The absence is curious, and we engage this more in the next chapter.

77. Norbert Lohfink, *Die Väter Israels im Deuteronomium: Mit einer Stellungnahme von Thomas Römer* (Freiburg, Switzerland: Universitätsverlag, 1991), 104–5.

78. Nathan MacDonald, "Chewing the Cud: Food and Memory in Deuteronomy," in *Not Bread Alone* (Oxford: Oxford University Press, 2008), 76: "[the *Heilsgeschichte*'s] memorization is crucial to the Deuteronomic reform program. Fathers, exodus, wilderness, and conquest together articulate Israel's relationship to YHWH, his law, and his land."

79. J. D. W. Watts, "The Deuteronomic Theology," *Review and Expositor* 74 (1977): 326. See also Marvin E. Tate, "Deuteronomic Philosophy of History," *Review and Expositor* 61 (1964): 311–19.

80. Watts, "Deuteronomic Theology," 326.

81. For a host of examples: Deut 1:8, 35; 4:31; 6:10, 18, 23; 7:8, 12, 13; 8:1, 18; 9:5; 10:11; 11:9, 21; 13:7; 19:8; 26:3, 15; 28:11; 29:13; 30:20; 31:7, 20, 21, 23.

82. Deut 1:8, 35; 4:31; 6:10, 18, 23; 7:8, 12, 13; 8:1, 18; 9:5; 10:11; 11:9, 21; 13:7; 19:8; 26:3, 15; 28:11; 29:13; 30:20; 31:7, 20, 21, 23.

83. Pillemer, *Momentous Events, Vivid Memories*, 99.
84. David J. A. Clines, *The Theme of the Pentateuch*, 2nd ed. (Sheffield: Sheffield Academic Press, 1997).
85. Watts, "Deuteronomic Theology," 328. See Deut 6:31–33; 7:18; 26:1, 15. Also 5:16; 27:3b.
86. Von Rad, *Hexateuch*, 95.
87. Deut 6:3; 11:9; 26:9, 15; 27:3; 31:20. See also S. Douglas Waterhouse, "A Land Flowing with Milk and Honey," *Andrews University Seminary Studies* 1 (1961): 152–66; Patrick D. Miller, "The Gift of God: The Deuteronomic Theology of the Land," *Interpretation* 23 (1969): 454–65; 456–57.
88. The classic study of the promised land is Peter Diepold, *Israels Land* (Stuttgart: Kohlhammer, 1972). It is important to note, too, the traditional debate about the unconditional and conditional aspects of the land. Is it a gift or is it a reward issued by Yahweh for Torah obedience? Von Rad, for one, played the two aspects against each other, arguing that they represent strands of conflicting ideology (*Hexateuch*, 85). Others, however, have seen more purpose in the tension (e.g., Josef Plöger, *Literarkritische, formgeschichtliche und stilkritische Untersuchungen zum Deuteronomium* [Peter Hanstein, 1967], 121–29; Mayes, *Deuteronomy*, 78–79; Polzin, *The Deuteronomist*, 26). Perhaps the simplest and most powerful theological argument for the tension is by Christopher J. H. Wright, who argues that Deuteronomy's conception of Israel's sonship perfectly situates the conditional and unconditional elements (*God's People in God's Land* [Milton Keynes, UK: Paternoster, 1990], 15).
89. Mayes, *Deuteronomy*, 78–79.
90. J. Gary Millar, *Now Choose Life: Theology and Ethics in Deuteronomy* (Leicester, UK: Apollos, 1998), 60–62.
91. Michael Carasik also picks up on this difference (*Theologies of the Mind in Biblical Israel* [Bern, Switzerland: Peter Lang, 2006], 193). His argument, however, is based on the faulty idea that the audience at Moab is the same as that of the exodus. As such, he argues that the lack of visual images in the patriarchal promises, compared to vividness of the other pieces of memory, is due to the fact that it is the only aspect the people have not themselves experienced. Other than the confusion of the generations, his argument also fails to make sense of the functions of the various pieces of memory.
92. Deut 1:25, 35; 4:21; 6:18; 8:7, 10; 9:6; 11:17.
93. Deut 6:3; 11:9; 26:9, 15; 27:3; 31:20.
94. For a good, brief discussion, see Jeffrey Tigay, *Deuteronomy* (Philadelphia, PA: The Jewish Publication Society, 1996), 437–38.
95. Miller, "The Gift of God," 457.
96. Philip D. Stern, "The Origins and Significance of the 'Land Flowing with Milk and Honey,'" *Vetus Testamentum* XLII (1992): 554–57.
97. Stern, "Milk and Honey," 556.
98. McConville, following Gösta Ahlström, identifies Yahweh's provision of cities here with the same practice of Mesopotamian kings when incorporating new territories into their kingdom (*Deuteronomy*, 143). See also Ahlström, *Royal Administration and National Religion in Ancient Palestine* (Leiden: Brill, 1982), 27; Norbert Lohfink, "Kerygmata des Deuteronomistischen Geschichtwerks," in *Die Botschaft*

und die Boten, eds. Jorg Jeremias and Lothar Perlitt (Neukirchener Verlag, 1981), 87–100.

99. McConville, *Deuteronomy*, 170. Emphasis mine. He also notes that such ideal depictions are found in Egypt, namely, in the story of Sinuhe (p. 171, citing Miriam Lichtheim, *Ancient Egyptian Literature* 1 [Berkeley, CA: University of California Press, 1975], 226–27).

100. Williams, Conway, and Cohen, "Autobiographical Memory," 24.

101. See Hazel Markus and Paula Nurius, "Possible Selves," *American Psychologist* 41 (1986): 954–69. Though Conway and Pleydell-Pearce, "Construction," 266, do not use identical language, they discuss a similar phenomenon: "the self is separated into three major domains: the actual self (some approximately accurate representation of one's self, perhaps, even the system's mental model of itself), the ideal self (what the self aspires to), and the ought self (the self one should be as specified by one's parents, educators, other significant persons, and society generally)."

102. Miller, "The Gift of God," 458.

103. It should be noted that we are aware of the issue of how, ultimately, Israel will inherit the land. While Deuteronomy indicates that Israel can only be obedient through a divine work on her heart (30:6), the present call of the book is to obey. Therefore, this call to Torah obedience is what shapes the role of the promised land in Israel's autobiography. For a good work on how the optimistic and pessimistic strands work together in Deuteronomy, see Paul Barker, *The Triumph of Grace in Deuteronomy*, repr. (Eugene, OR: Wipf & Stock, 2007).

104. Assmann, *Religion and Cultural Memory*, 55. Though we note that Assmann does not identify it as part of Deuteronomy's memory for Israel. He argues it is a "traumatizing text" that gives rise to the Freudian dynamics necessary to create a repressed memory in Israel, something that we have already disagreed with.

105. Deut 1:30; 4:34; 6:22; 7:19; 10:21; 29:2, 3.

106. McConville, *Deuteronomy*, 112.

107. "Signs" and "wonders" are typically understood as referring to the plagues, though Deuteronomy is not explicit on this. See Ronald Hendel, "The Exodus in Biblical Memory," *Journal of Biblical Literature* 120 (2001): 608–615.

108. 6:22; 7:19; 10:21; 29:2, 3, which use permutations of the collection of these terms. Also, 11:2–4. For a more exhaustive list of the terms and their combinations, see Weinfeld, *The Deuteronomic School*, 326–30. The terms "mighty hand" and "outstretched arm" are particularly common in Deuteronomy. Weinfeld identifies this pairing as first appearing in Deuteronomy and then continuing in literature impacted by it (*Deuteronomy*, 212; *The Deuteronomic School*, 329).

109. Weinfeld, *Deuteronomy*, 212.

110. Othmar Keel, *Wirkmächtige Siegeszeichen im alten Testament* (Frieberg: Universitätsverlag Freiburg Schweiz, 1974), 158–60.

111. Richard Nelson, "Divine Warrior Theology in Deuteronomy", in *A God So Near*, 256–57.

112. For a good discussion on how the Old Testament takes up and adapts ANE images in order to transmit its own social energies, see Mark George, *Israel's Tabernacle as Sacred Space* (Atlanta: Society of Biblical Literature, 2009).

113. Deut 1:27, 30; 4:20, 34, 37; 5:6, 15; 6:12, 21, 22; 7:8, 18; 8:14; 9:7, 26, 29; 10:19–20; 11:3–4; 13:5, 10; 15:15; 16:1, 3, 6, 12; 20:1; 23:4; 24:9, 18, 22; 25:17; 26:8; 29:2, 25.

114. For the shifting nature of the exodus references, see George W. Coats, "Traditio-Historical of the Reed Sea Motif," *Vetus Testamentum* 17 (1967): 258–60, n. 6. Coats's point is that the exodus reference is not crystallized into one item but can in different contexts refer to different aspects of the experience.

115. "Remember" (זכר): Deut 5:15; 7:18; 15:15; 24:18. "Not forget" (לא שכח): Deut 6:12; 8:11–14.

See Deut 6:20–25 and 11:2–4.

116. Craigie supports this, saying in regard to Deut 31:6, "the phrase *he created you*, in its context, alludes to both the exodus and Sinai as the events connected with the 'creation' of the people of the Lord" (*Deuteronomy*, 379).

117. For an interesting discussion on the exodus as a narrative of asylum seeking that, in turn, shapes biblical law, see Johnathan P. Burnside, "Exodus and Asylum: Uncovering the Relationship between Biblical Law and Narrative," *Journal for the Study of the Old Testament* 34 (2010): 243–66.

118. For succinct discussions, see Michael Coogan, "The Exodus," in *The Oxford Companion to the Bible*, ed. Bruce M. Metzger and Michael David Coogan (Oxford: Oxford University Press, 1993), 209–12; *The Dictionary of Biblical Imagery*, ed. Leland Ryken, James C. Wilhoit, and Tremper Longman (Westmont, IL: InterVarsity Press, 1998), 253–55.

119. The exodus generation, I argue, is the most general level of autobiographical memory, the lifetime period, in which the exodus, Mount Horeb, and the wilderness are found. It seems such a view is made clear by our previous discussion on Deuteronomy's contemporizing, that is, on its collapsing of the present with the past. The very notion of treating each new generation as if it were the one from the exodus, after all, presupposes that the original is both discrete and unique. In Deuteronomy's construal, the generation is roughly forty years: beginning with Yahweh's mighty deeds against Egypt (6:21) and finishing with Israel crossing the Zered Valley after all the fighting men had died (2:13–15). As with all lifetime periods, the exodus generation establishes an important theme for Israel's self-memory. We suggest that it stands as Israel's formative years. This is not only logical from the text, but also follows the pattern of religious memory in general. The memory of formation contains the DNA of the community, and so to become part of it individuals must absorb that DNA. Exactly what this means for Israel we hope to elucidate here. I should also mention a corollary. Does the above notion of memory assume that Yahweh's activity will cease once Israel is in the land? The simple answer is no. If the above view of memory speaks to the issue at all, it is only in an ancillary way. The point is that Israel, like all communities, must be rooted in a defining formative memory. That memory serves as the fundamental identity for members of the community, but it does not necessarily speak to whether miracles will continue in a similar way. In the New Testament, for instance, Christ's life, death, resurrection, and ascension form a memory of Christianity's formative events; however, at the close of this formative period the miraculous activity does not decrease but actually increases into the next period of the apostles.

120. The Exodus depictions (19:18; 20:18) are similar in imagery, though they also mention lightning and the sound of trumpets (Weinfeld, *Deuteronomy*, 204).

121. Miller, *Deuteronomy*, 58.

122. On the fire motif, see Miller, *Deuteronomy*, 59; "*Fire in Mythology*."

123. "Fire in Mythology," 260. See Deut 9:3; 33:2; Isaiah 29; Psalm 50:3. Notice that the fire can come as judgment both against Israel's enemies and on her own iniquity.

124. McConville, *Deuteronomy*, 109; Tigay, *Deuteronomy*, 51; Miller, *Deuteronomy*, 59.

125. Though I do not have space to discuss it here, we should note the interplay between Moses's "seeing" in v. 16 and Israel's in v. 17. Verse 16 says that Moses "looks" (ראה), then it shifts the perspective from external to internal through "behold!" (הנה), so that the audience sees through his eyes: the people had made a molten calf. Then in v. 17 Moses reacts by breaking the tablets "before your eyes," which shifts the perspective back to external but while still emphasizing what Israel saw. The Exodus version (32:19) does not contain this perspective shift. For discussions of the use of הנה in shifting the point of view, see Adele Berlin, *Poetics and Interpretation of Biblical Narrative* (Stirling, Scotland: The Almond Press, 1983), 62–63; Gary Yamasaki, *Watching a Biblical Narrative* (London: T. & T. Clark, 2007), 11–151.

126. Weinfeld, *Deuteronomy*, 410. He rightly emphasizes that this event is vivid not only because of its visual nature, but because it depicts the dissolving of the covenant.

127. "Horeb": Deut 1:2, 6, 19; 4:10, 15; 5:2; 9:8; 10:1; 18:16; 29:1. "Mountain," referring to Horeb: Deut 4:11; 5:4, 5, 22, 23; 9:9, 10, 15, 21; 10:1, 3, 4, 5, 10.

128. Deut 4:9–20; 5:2–31; 9:7–21, 25–29; 10:1–11.

129. On the differences between this account and the one in Exodus, see McConville, *Deuteronomy*, 178–79.

130. Craigie, *Deuteronomy*, 133.

131. McConville, *Deuteronomy*, 202; con. Weinfeld, *Deuteronomy*, 432.

132. A typical way of explaining the absence of Korah is literary-critical, with the Numbers account being from the priestly material (Weinfeld, *Deuteronomy*, 444). However, McConville points out that it can also be understood in terms of "Deuteronomy's habit of passing over the priest-Levite distinction, thus picking out Dathan and Abiram as representing rebellion in general" (*Deuteronomy*, 203).

133. "Tents" are mentioned in the Numbers account, but earlier in 16:26–27 when Moses tells people to move back from their tents.

134. Though this, too, is used earlier in 16:30 in the Numbers version.

135. Tigay, *Deuteronomy*, 111.

136. Con. McConville: "The inclusion of this event in the list makes it primarily a saving act, that is, from an enemy within" (*Deuteronomy*, 203). However true this may be as a consequence, it does not seem the chief concern of the cautionary tale.

137. In line with Tigay, though he goes too far in saying "the rest of the context refers only to punitive acts" *Deuteronomy*, 111). Indeed, judgment is a theme running through the exodus, the Sea of Reeds, and the Dathan and Abiram events, but it plays a different role in each. In the exodus, it is the background to Israel's redemption;

in the Sea of Reeds, it is in the foreground but coupled with redemption; and in the Dathan and Abiram account, redemption is, at most, in the background and judgment is in the foreground.

138. 1:1, 19, 31, 40; 2:1, 7, 8, 26; 4:43; 8:2, 15, 16; 9:7, 28; 11:5, 24; 29:5; 32:10, 51.

139. The longest wilderness accounts are Deut 1–3 and 8. Of course, 9:7–10:11 is also an account of the wilderness, as signaled by its introduction in 9:7. But its focus quickly turns to the Horeb event.

140. McConville, *Deuteronomy*, 69.

141. It is noteworthy that here, too, Deuteronomy heightens the imagery by adding "flint," which the parallel accounts in Exod 17:6 and Num 10:8, 11 do not have. See Weinfeld, *Deuteronomy*, 395.

142. Weinfeld, *Deuteronomy*, 395.

143. Riekele Borger, *Die Inschriften Asarhaddons Königs von Assyrien* (New Jersey, US: Weidner, 1956), 56, 112.

144. Weinfeld, *Deuteronomy*, 395.

145. Keel, *Wirkmächtige Siegeszeichen*, 77.

146. On the meaning of יסר (Piel, "discipline"), see R. D. Branson, "יסר," in *The Theological Dictionary of the Old Testament*, vol. 6, eds. G. Johannes Botterweck and Helmer Ringgren, trans. D. E. Green (Grand Rapids, MI: Eerdmans, 1990), 130.

147. There are others, of course, such as the destruction of rebels at Baal Peor (Deut 4:3–4) and, as discussed already with Mount Horeb, the golden calf episode (9:7–10:11).

148. Representative examples of each are found in 8:2 and 9:7.

149. Echoing Madeleine L'Engle, *A Wrinkle in Time* (New York: Farrar, Straus and Giroux, 1962). Or in more technical language, "Both remembering the past . . . and imagining the future . . . are a matter of imaginatively projecting oneself into a mentally simulated event. In both cases, one has a subjective sense of mentally travelling in time." Kourken Michaelian, "Mental Time Travel: What Is Memory?," *The Brains Blog*, May 16, 2016, philosophyofbrains.com/2016/05/16/mental-time-trav el-what-is-memory.aspx. Michelian has developed his thoughts more extensively in *Mental Time Travel: Episodic Memory and Our Knowledge of the Personal Past* (Cambridge, MA: The MIT Press, 2016).

Chapter 4

Making Memories
Identifying Deuteronomy's Memory Vectors

There has been one goal at the center of this work: to study Deuteronomy as a memory-making agent, that is, as a shaper of Israel's collective memory. In the past two chapters, I have looked at the what and the why questions: why Deuteronomy focuses on memory in the first place and what kind of memory it cultivates to accomplish its purposes. Having examined these, I now turn to the how question. *How* does Deuteronomy cultivate this memory in Israel? I shall approach this in two stages. First, I look to elucidate mechanisms of memory building, the avenues by which memory is inculcated into communities in general. The point is to clarify the nature of such mechanisms and so be able to identify them in Deuteronomy. And second, following on from this, I seek to identify Deuteronomy's main memory mechanisms. Having done this, I shall then move, in the chapters that follow, to elucidate each mechanism's role in building Israel's autobiographical memory.

MEMORY VECTORS IN SOCIETY

How, then, do cultures establish collective memory, their shared cultural autobiography? What mechanisms do they employ and, critical to our own study of Deuteronomy, how can we identify these? Perhaps the most interesting thing about this last question is that, though fundamental,[1] it is not easily answered. This is due to the fact that in collective memory literature there is a marked paucity of discussion on the issue. Jeffrey Olick indicates that this is part of a larger lack of "conceptual and methodological" clarity endemic to the field, ultimately stemming from the founding work of Maurice Halbwachs.[2] When he refers to the resulting situation as "a rather unproductive hodgepodge,"[3] he aptly describes the treatment of memory mechanisms, too. The most puzzling aspect is that studies do focus on particular situations and discuss their mechanisms, though without a word about what actually constitutes such mechanisms, how to recognize them, and how to distinguish them from other cultural elements.[4]

Jo McCormack's work on the memory of the Algerian War in contemporary France is representative of the field.[5] Early in her work, she offers this broad definition for memory mechanisms: they are

> carriers or channels—that can, for example, be associative, official (commemorations), cultural, or scholarly—[that] transmit or carry memories and historical representations between individuals, groups, and the Nation.[6]

But while this definition is a good starting point, it needs quite a bit of tightening to prove conceptually helpful. After all, arguably any cultural element could in some way fit this definition. McCormack moves on without narrowing the idea to focus on three "key vectors" for her own study: the education system, the family, and the media.[7] The rest of the book then expounds the roles of the vectors in French representations of memory. The glaring problem, of course, is that having failed to establish what a vector is and how to identify one, her own emphases might be taken as arbitrary and her larger work seen as unfounded.[8] I do, however, find the term "memory vector" helpful for reasons that should become clear.

While McCormack emphasizes just a few vectors, another scholar, Pierre Nora, has offered an extensive list of them. Especially in view is the multivolume work he directed and contributed to, *Realms of Memory*,[9] which seeks to identify all "the 'memory places' [*lieux de mémoire*] of French national identity as they have been constructed since the middle ages [*sic*]."[10] By the work's own admission, it operates on a broad notion of memory vectors: including "geographical place or locus," "historical figures," "literary and artistic objects," "emblems, commemorations, and symbols," and also the "conflictual spaces and symbolic divisions" within France.[11] The majority of the list is predictable, being comprised of obvious sites of memory, but the latter two items are not. What Nora seems to mean by these are the ideological spaces at which conflicting viewpoints come together, such as the *Ancien Régime* and the French Revolution or the French people and foreigners. As such, they are not so much sites as conceptual realms.[12]

If Nora's construal of vectors is rather wide, it is predictable based on the trajectory of his work. To begin with, Nora aims to counteract the writings of Ernest Lavisse, which in the nineteenth century served to inculcate French loyalty through what, in Nora's opinion, was a rather synthetic view of history.[13] Nora's own work, then, seeks to portray the past in a more diverse and polyphonic way. Additionally, and arising from this point, Nora offers a refiguring of Halbwachs's social frameworks (*cadres sociaux*) of memory. Whereas Halbwachs focused on frameworks as unifiers of people, Nora examines "self-consciousness by dividing the 'unitary framework' of collective memory into smaller configurations or identities resulting in the politicization of memory."[14] So Nora aims to see how multitudes of fragmented identities can still exist within, and even give rise to, larger unified identities. With these aims in mind, it is understandable that Nora's handling of memory vectors would display a similar lack of unity and centeredness. This is not to say that he offers no center whatsoever, for he says, "*lieux de mémoire* [are] those [things] that reshape memory in some fundamental way."[15] Rather, the point is that, like McCormack, Nora does not sufficiently establish exactly what a memory vector is. While Nora does provide a spectrum of things that *can* be vectors, he never establishes *if* and *when* they are. Olick says it well that Nora's approach really "rais[es] the question of what is not a *lieu de mémoire*"![16]

In the midst of this widespread lack of precision, however, there is at least one study that seeks to address the issue. Nancy Wood engages it in the introduction to her work on memory in postwar Europe.[17] While her discussion spans only fourteen pages, it offers a helpful starting point for identifying memory vectors. Wood says this:

> [P]ublic memory—whatever its unconscious vicissitudes—testifies to a will or desire on the part of some social group . . . to select and organize representations of the past so that these will be embraced by individuals as their own. If particular representations of the past have permeated the public domain, it is because they embody an intentionality—social, political, institutional, and so on—that promotes or authorizes their entry.[18]

Here Wood is articulating her view of collective (or "public") memory generally, but this view directly shapes her understanding of vectors.

There are two key points to highlight. First, Wood distinguishes between intentional and unintentional memory production. That memory may arise from arbitrary items and avenues is not disputed; what is disputed is that these can be considered an integral part of memory *production*. For Wood, then, the distinctive mark of collective memory, and also its vectors, is "intentionality."[19] Thus, something qualifies as a vector only if it produces memory purposely.[20] Second, Wood emphasizes human agency.[21] Intention is something that can arise only from a mind, and so to speak of it is to ask the question of who enacts the commemoration. As her example illustrates, the enactor can take a variety of shapes: "social, political, institutional, and so on." And the nature of the enactor influences the nature of the vectors it

102   *Chapter 4*

employs. However, there is something else important here that Wood does not sufficiently address: the target of the vectoring. That is, the issue is not only who does the vectoring but also for whom.[22] At whom is a memory aimed—certain socioeconomic groups, families, people of particular ages? This is important because it shapes the nature and purpose of a memory vector.

Wood further elucidates the aspects of intention and agency by drawing them together under the canopy of performance. She explains:

> [My] book develops Halbwachs's insight further by treating "collective" memory . . . as essentially *performative*—i.e. as only coming into existence at a given time and place through specific kinds of memorial activity . . . I mobilize the concept of "vector" to designate the conduits of this performativity, whether these be commemorations, historical narratives, political debates or other cultural forms.[23]

Halbwachs's insight here is the idea, discussed in the last chapter, that collective memory is not a "repository of images," but the "selective reconstruction and appropriation of aspects of the past that respond to needs of the present."[24] Performativity, then, refers to the purposeful ways in which groups transmit this memory to the people. Now, Wood's notion of performativity seems relatively novel, but, interestingly, she attributes part of it to Pierre Nora.[25] The connection is not entirely clear, but perhaps she is referring to how Nora contrasts mute markers on a landscape with things that are part of a dynamic commemorative process. Whatever the connection, Wood's coupling of intention and performance is insightful for demarcating memory vectors. It shows that for something to be a vector, it must include intention and agency in a mnemonic act. Why this is important is made clear by the example of the commemorative coin. By most definitions, such a coin would be considered a conduit of memory: the coin was created with images and text whose purpose, when viewed, is to create memory. But while the coin meets the criteria of intentionality and agency, it fails in the performance category. Granted, a person's viewing and reading of it is a kind of performance, but it is unlikely anybody would consider it truly "performative."[26]

At this point, however, we encounter an issue with Wood, for exactly what she construes as "performative" is not clear. One may point to her discussion and deduce, simply, that she envisions a purposeful *act* of memory making. But even this does not solve but only shifts the problem of defining performance. One may then say that Wood has in mind ceremonies and rituals. However, this is too reductionist and does not fit with the vectors that Wood herself examines.[27] Ultimately, it seems that Wood leaves the issue somewhat open. I would like to suggest another characteristic that helps mark a vector as performative: programming. Consider the following quote:

> [Memory] was established in the ancient world through the concept of *ars memorativa,* by which mnemonic devices are based on repetition, rhythm, reference points, and spatial ordering.[28]

The authors are speaking of *ars memorativa,* which is a particular notion of memorization associated first with the ancient Greeks. And while this is somewhat different from our own topic,[29] I think it is still instructive. It shows that for something to be a memory vector, it needs to be part of a program—a purposeful, systematic, and sustained memory-making effort.[30] As indicated in the quote above, these features are even more poignant for the ancient world, where memory and enculturation depended on the structuring of social and religious media. Common folk did not have archives of information or personal media resources readily available to them as we do today.[31]

Some might argue that programming is too restrictive a criterion, for it excludes aspects of culture that are known to affect memory. We soon shall look at this very issue in regard to Deuteronomy's command to destroy Canaanite worship sites and paraphernalia and to erect commemorative stones across the Jordan and on Mount Ebal. The validity of programming as a criterion is found at the intersection of individual memory and its generational transmission. We recall from the last chapter that memory is inherently selective and constructive, ever refiguring itself according to incoming stimuli. In psychological terms, this means that self-memory arises from the ongoing encoding, cueing, and retrieval of key episodes and ideas. This has obvious implications for transmitting cultural memory. Because each new generation must come to see itself through the memories of the past, memories that are not its own, there must be sustained exposure. Such exposure comes only through regular intervals of mnemonic inculcation. Whatever the impact of one-time or erratic commemorations, therefore, they are not vectors for they are not integral to generational memory. They do not seek to keep memory "alive through regularly repeated commemorative processes."[32]

Having defined vectors as mnemonic devices that show intentionality, performativity, and programming, I now introduce another idea: distribution. Typically, when scholars use the term "distributed" they are referring to memory's location (for lack of a better term). A common position in the social sciences is represented by the following quotes:

> [M]emory appears to reside not in perceiving consciousness but *in the material*: in the practices or institutions of social or psychic life.[33]

> [C]ollective memories are material. They have texture, existing in the world rather than in a person's head.[34]

We notice here that material and mind are juxtaposed as locales of memory, with preference falling on material. Thus, in this view, collective memory is "distributed" across material objects that, when coming in contact with the mind, evoke unique forms of memory. But while material serves an important role in memory vectoring, I suggest that the opposition of material and mind is unhelpful. This much has been especially highlighted by memory studies of the philosophical bent.[35] These tend to see material and mind not as opposed but as "complementary."[36]

Complementary distribution, in brief, "stresses that biological resources and external resources" interface to produce the matrices of collective memory.[37] Clark describes it as "the computational power and expertise . . . spread across a heterogeneous assembly of brains, bodies, artifacts, and other external structures."[38] In this conceptualization, an individual's mind and agency work in concert with the minds of others[39] and with the various mnemonic objects to produce collective memory. Importantly, the "engrams and exograms," that is, the memory embedded in the individual mind and in the external objects, give rise to particular types of memory.[40] These types have significant implications for the substance and nature of the remembering. Moreover, their agency then determines the target audience: "families, professions, political generations, ethnic and regional groups, social classes, and nations" to name some.[41]

This notion of distribution, therefore, provides us a more nuanced conceptualization of memory vectoring. It depicts vectors as spread throughout a cultural landscape, with each having a particular form and function and with each requiring a certain kind of agency; each also has a target audience. This produces what might be called a vectoring triangle, composed of "memory maker, memory consumer, and the visual and discursive objects . . . of representations."[42] As such, each of the three parts must be present if vectoring is to occur. A commemorative stone, for example, cannot be considered a vector unless accompanied by a maker (agent) and a consumer. What is more, in light of our previous criteria the object must be used by the agent in an intentional and performative act of mnemonics.[43] When all of the parts are present for each vector and a variety of vectors are part of a program, the end result is a dynamic community memory. Zelizer captures the dynamic well: material "texture" provides the long-term structures that "offset the fluctuations" of human remembering.[44] These structures, put into the service of human agents and consumers, produce "axes of remembering" around which "collective memory 'vibrates'" and "bounces to and from between all of them on its way to gaining meaning."[45]

MEMORY VECTORS IN DEUTERONOMY

With the criteria established (intentional, performative, and programmatic agents), we turn to see what in Deuteronomy may be called a memory vector. Here again, Jan Assmann has been at the forefront of the discussion:

> The mnemotechnique that Moses devised in order to constantly remind the people of the covenant, its various obligations and the story that frames and explains it, is laid out not in the Book of Exodus, but in Deuteronomy, the testament of Moses. Deuteronomy prescribes *how* to remember, but Exodus narrates *what* to remember. This mnemotechnique exceeds by far anything comparable in the ancient world.[46]

Aside from pitting the *how* of Deuteronomy against the *what* of Exodus (for, as we have seen, Deuteronomy has a unique what as well), Assmann is right: Deuteronomy's prescribing of how to remember ("mnemotechnique") is exceptional.

For his part, Assmann proposes a list of seven memory vectors: (1) learning by heart; (2) education; (3) making visible; (4) storing and publishing; (5) festivals; (6) oral transmission; and (7) canonization.[47] But these run into difficulties almost immediately.[48] To begin with, at least five of the seven are so generic that they are almost impossible to pin down. Learning by heart, education, making visible, storing and publishing, and oral transmission all have the appearance of mechanisms but, in reality, can mean and include a host of things. Being so general they may, of course, encompass true vectors. Making visible, for example, seems to refer most directly to the practices in Deut 6:6–9 and 11:18–20 of inscribing the commands in visible places as signs. This in itself would indeed qualify as a memory vector. The problem with Assmann's conceptualization, however, is that in other places "making visible" seems to mean the larger transmuting of memory into "signs, symbols, images, texts, and rituals."[49] What is more, the mechanisms of learning by heart, education, and making visible overlap greatly; it is difficult to tell where one begins and the other ends. Now, it is true that identifying vectors is not always clear-cut, for the relationship between agent and object fluctuates. But it seems safe to say that the five general mechanisms above cannot be called memory vectors.

What about the other two mechanisms, festivals and canonization? Festivals is the one that meets all four criteria for memory vectors. I shall explore this more in a later chapter on ritual. Canonization, on the other hand, is a curious one, although it does make better sense in light of another of Assmann's essays.[50] There he employs Konrad Ehlich's concept of texts as "extended contexts," that is, as messages that endure beyond their original situations.⁵¹ In such cases, it becomes important to preserve and transmit the message in order to extend it. Canonization, then, is a particular kind of extension. It is unique in that it crystallizes not only the message but also the very words and structure of that message. Canonization takes texts and makes them "culturally institutionalized" as sacred authorities;⁵² they become "like verbal temples that enshrine divine presence."⁵³ For Assmann, this means that the memory such texts contain also becomes crystallized. Thus, the act of canonization is key in that it freezes particular memories and makes them sacred and binding for the community. But while it is true that canonization affects cultural memory, the act itself is not a vector. Most notably, this is because canonization is a one-time event; it is not something that serves repeatedly to inculcate memory.

Canonization serves as a good segue into two other things in Deuteronomy that, although at some level are related to memory, cannot be considered vectors. First is the command for Israel to destroy the Canaanite worship paraphernalia and apparatus (Deut 7:5, 25; 12:2–3).⁵⁴ Consider 12:2–3:

> You shall completely destroy all the places where the nations you are dispossessing served their gods—on the high mountains and on the hills and under every green tree. You shall break down their altars, shatter their sacred stones, and burn their Asherim with fire; and the graven images of their gods you shall hack down and abolish their name from that place.⁵⁵

The destruction of these items is part of the larger חרם, and it sits at the intersection of the חרם's dual ideas of destroying the nations and worshipping rightly.⁵⁶ The basic idea is that the demolishing of the Canaanite sacral items is the first step in devotion to Yahweh in the land.⁵⁷ The text indicates this in how it structures Deut 7, where the demolishing of false worship brackets Israel as a holy people (vv. 1–6, 17–26),⁵⁸ and how in Deut 12 it introduces true Yahwistic worship (vv. 5–32) by juxtaposing it to that of the Canaanites (v. 4), embodied in the accoutrements that Israel is to destroy (vv. 2–3).⁵⁹

Latent in the command to destroy items of worship, lest they become a "snare" (נקש) for Israel (12:30), is the notion that their presence is a *reminder* of other gods.⁶⁰ This is highlighted by the fact that said destruction will "abolish" (אבד, Piel) the "names" of the deities from those places (12:3), while Yahweh's "name" will come to dwell in the chosen place (12:5, 11, 21).⁶¹

> [T]he logic of this command is, then, that the only sure way to protect Israel from sliding into the worship of the gods of the land was to eradicate the physical remains of it, with their long and powerful *memories*.⁶²

This may be understood in terms of an aspect of collective memory that, though necessary, is often overlooked: forgetting.⁶³ Just as healthy individual memory is based on the interplay of remembering what is important and letting go what is not, so too is collective memory.[64] As Aleida Assmann succinctly puts it: "The continuous process of forgetting is part of social normality."[65] Assmann then points out that such forgetting exists in passive and active forms.[66] Passive forgetting is when the things of memory are infrequently accessed and so move to the periphery or fade away altogether. Active forgetting, however, is when things are intentionally omitted or censored in order to starve them from memory.[67]

The act of destroying the accoutrements of Canaanite worship, therefore, is a kind of active forgetting.[68] It is meant to clear the landscape of reminders of Canaanite gods so that there are no rivals when Israel fills the space with its own mnemonics. The act of destruction, as such, is an important step in establishing Israel's memory program. But it cannot be considered part of the program proper, much less a memory vector. That is to say, it does not have an ongoing role, for once the Canaanite paraphernalia is gone, the phase is finished. As we shall see, this stands in contrast to other conduits that are explicitly linked with Israel's transmission of memory and identity throughout the generations.

The second activity in Deuteronomy that is related to memory but which is not a vector, is the act of erecting stones on Mount Ebal (27:1–8).[69] This setting up of stones is part of the covenant ceremony commanded for when Israel crosses the Jordan into the land (27:9–26).[70] The ceremony is comprised of three parts: (1) on Mount Ebal, stelae are to be erected, an altar built, and sacrifices offered (vv. 1–8); (2) on Mount Gerizim half the tribes are to pronounce the covenantal blessings,[71] while the other half shall do the same with the curses from Mount Ebal (vv. 11–13);[72] and (3) representative Levites are to recite curses for crimes that may easily go undetected.[73] The point of the larger ceremony, then, is to "inaugurate Israel's life in the promised land with acts that drastically express the message that its life must be based on obedience to God's instruction."[74] More specifically, the act is an important gesture of time and place: the ceremony enacts Israel's subservience to Yahweh both geographically in the land and chronologically as a new era.

What role do the erected stones play in this? To begin with, the "great stones" (אבנים גדלות)—not "standing stones" (מצבת)[75]—are to be erected, plastered, and inscribed with "all the words of Torah" (v. 3). But when and where are they to be erected—immediately upon entry or at Mount Ebal?[76] While "on that day" seems to indicate a conflict in time, for Ebal is more than a day's journey from the Jordan, Deuteronomy's typical usage of ביום helps to explain this. The significance of the timing is not literal but typological: the ceremony at Mount Ebal is to happen "on that day," that is, on yet another key moment of decision in the chain that began at Horeb, in this case the first covenant ceremony in the land.[77] According to Richter, this journey motif may also help to untangle the issue of where the ceremony is meant to occur.[78] Instead of seeing locales as terminals, we should view them as part of a trajectory.[79] The only place named is Mount Ebal, but even this is just a link in the chain leading to the "chosen" place. It should not be surprising that other places, such as Gilgal, serve as points of commemoration and rededication along the way. So, while Deuteronomy envisions the full ceremony—replete with an altar and monuments—occurring at Mount Ebal, it does not exclude (and may even assume) other commemorative acts in route.[80]

The erecting of "great stones" reflects a common Canaanite practice of plastering and writing in ink on stelae.[81] Typically, Richter argues, this practice was employed for the royal construction of votive or triumph monuments.[82] She indicates that both of these fit Deuteronomy's monumentalizing on Mount Ebal.[83] On the one hand, such a practice indicates that the particular sovereign is staking ownership, or triumphing, over the previous powers of the land. This idea is strengthened by the nature of Mount Ebal: the highest local mountain overlooking the most influential town of the area (Shechem). On the other hand, the stones on Ebal are to be monuments witnessing to Israel's covenantal vow to Yahweh. This much is evident in the fact that the inscription will include "all the words of this Torah" (27:3), that is, the covenantal instruction. In ANE custom, such an inscription would include the heroic or benevolent acts of the sovereign, something that Richter implies is also true of the inscriptions on Ebal.[84] While Deuteronomy does not mention this overtly, it is plausible in light of the use of the global term "Torah" (תורה) instead of more specific ones such as "commands" (מצות) and "statutes" (חקים) (e.g., v. 10).[85] Thus, the inscription would feature Deuteronomy's Mosaic framework, which recounts Yahweh's deeds, and not just the particular laws in chapters 12–26.[86] All of this is, according to Richter, part of the larger ANE ceremony of "placing the name" (e.g., Deut 12:5).[87] While Ebal is not the final destination of Yahweh's name, it is the first "chosen" place in the land.

In regard to mnemonics, most scholars assume that the plastered stones serve a commemorative role.[88] However, very little is ever said as to what this role is. Even the detailed work of Richter is only marginally helpful, for it seems to presume that the notion of commemoration is immediately transparent. And while this is true at a general level, for the stones are certainly a kind of witness,[89] it is unlikely that the stones have an ongoing mnemonic role in Deuteronomy's program. The first evidence for this comes from the nature of the stones themselves. It has been noted that the plaster on which the words are written would, being outdoors, soon wash off.[90] Tigay says it indicates that the stones were part of a "one-time ceremony."[91] Noticing the temporary role of the stones but wanting to validate their ongoing significance, Craigie says that from then on they stood on Mount Ebal as "silent witnesses to the renewal of the covenant."[92] The problem, of course, is that there is no such thing as a silent witness; it must be given voice by some kind of continued exposition.[93] Not to mention, Deuteronomy itself never overtly ties the stones into memory nor portrays the accoutrements on Mount Ebal as anything but part of this unique, one-time event.[94] Arising from this is the second piece of evidence: to see Ebal's stones as having a continuing role is to run against the flow of Deuteronomy's theology of journey and of the chosen place. As I have already argued, Mount Ebal is "simply presented as the next place on the itinerary of the journey of Israel" into the land and toward the chosen place: here "the 'day of decision' of Moab becomes the 'day of response' in Canaan."[95] Critically, Ebal is not *the* chosen place, the place to which all Israel will pilgrimage and worship. Ultimately, the stones on Mount Ebal cannot be considered memory vectors, for they are not part of Deuteronomy's ongoing memory program.

CONCLUSION

If these do not qualify as memory vectors, then what do? I suggest that three major vectors can be discerned in Deuteronomy: song, story, and ritual. We now move to examine these vectors in Deuteronomy in two ways: (1) to show that they meet the criteria laid out previously (intentional, performative, and programmatic); and (2) to elucidate each vector's unique function, that is, the dynamics of its agency triad: object (vector), maker, and consumer.

NOTES

1. Ultimately, "All culture is a struggle with oblivion." Thomas Macho quoted by Jan Assmann, *Religion and Cultural Memory*, trans. Rodney Livingstone (Stanford: Stanford University Press, 2006), 81.

2. Jeffrey Olick, "Collective Memory: The Two Cultures," *Sociological Theory* 17 (1999): 336.

3. Olick, "Two Cultures," 338.

4. This reality is borne out even in the most recent works of biblical studies that leverage memory research. See the discussion in the introductory chapter by Althalya Brenner and Burke O. Long, *Performing Memory in Biblical Narrative and Beyond*, ed. Althalya Brenner and Frank. H. Polak (Sheffield, UK: Sheffield Phoenix Press, 2009), 4.

5. Jo McCormack, *Collective Memory: France and Algerian War (1954–1962)* (Lanham, MD: Lexington Books, 2007). Other examples that follow this pattern are Arthur G. Neal, *National Trauma and Collective Memory* (New York: M. E. Sharpe, 1998) and Bridget Fowler, *The Obituary as Collective Memory* (Abingdon, UK: Routledge, 2007).

6. McCormack, *Collective Memory*, 3. Here she is following the ideas of Henry Rousso.

7. McCormack, *Collective Memory*, 5.

8. This is not, of course, to say that McCormack fails to discuss her choice of the education system, the family, and the media. She does this in chapter one, "Critical Literature and Recent Developments," 11–56. The point is that, in the absence of an articulation of memory vectors, her discussion amounts to a treatment of general avenues of enculturation.

9. Pierre Nora, *Realms of Memory*, 3 vols., ed. Lawrence D. Kritzman, trans. Arthur Goldhammer (New York: Columbia University Press, 1996–1998). Wulf Kansteiner makes a similar statement: "Pierre Nora's work in the tradition of Halbwachs lacks . . . conceptual precision" ("Finding Meaning in Memory: A Methodological Critique of Collective Memory Studies," *History and Theory* 41 [2002]: 183).

10. Lawrence D. Kritzman, Foreword to *Realms of Memory*, vol. 1, ix–xiv; ix.

11. Kritzman, *Realms of Memory*, x.

12. For a good overview and discussion of the *Realms of Memory*, see Nancy Wood, "Memory's Remains: *Les Lieux de mémoire*," *History and Memory* 6 (1994): 123–51; it can also be found under the same name as the first chapter in her book, *Vectors of Memory* (Oxford: Berg, 1999), 15–38.

13. See Hue-Tam Ho Tai, "Remembered Realms: Pierre Nora and French National Memory," *The American Historical Review* 106 (2001): 38 pars., accessed October 12, 2011, http://www.historycooperative.org/journals/ahr/106.3/ah000906.html. Tai's article offers a good treatment on the weaknesses of Nora's approach, particularly highlighting areas—in addition to the one I discuss—of conceptual ambiguity.

14. Kritzmann, *Realms of Memory*, xi.

15. Nora, *Realms of Memory*, 17.

16. Olick, "Two Cultures," 336.

17. Nancy Wood, *Vectors of Memory: Legacies of Trauma in Postwar Europe* (Oxford: Berg, 1999), 1–14.

18. Wood, *Vectors of Memory*, 2.

19. Wood roots her notion of intentionality in power, a common theme in political studies of collective memory. Power, however, is often too emphasized as the impetus of collective memory. Therefore, a memory vector can be intentional without being inherently rooted in an exertion of power.

20. The idea of intentionality runs counter to much thinking, which prefers to see collective memory as a result of unintentional processes, too. See Richard Terdiman, *Present Past* (New York: Cornell University Press, 1993), 34, and Mieke Bal, "Introduction," in *Acts of Memory*, ed. Mieke Bal, Jonathan Crewe, and Leo Spitzer (New Hampshire: University Press of New England, 1999), vii. Terdiman explores the idea of "materials memory," that is, the notion that carriers of memory store aspects of it that manifest in an "unforeseeable *productivity* of its representations," 35, 60. Curiously, Bal forwards the idea of performavity, like Wood, but insists that often "such acts are not consciously and wilfully contrived" (vii).

21. The way in which Wood emphasizes agency and intentionality, Kansteiner argues, draws on "conventional methods of historical studies . . . without returning to simplistic notions" ("Finding Meaning," 188).

22. See Kansteiner, "Finding Meaning," 197.
23. Wood, *Vectors of Memory*, 2.
24. Wood, *Vectors of Memory*, 2.
25. Wood, *Vectors of Memory*, 17. Although he uses different terms, Edward Casey defines commemoration similarly to what we are here calling vectoring (*Remembering*, 2nd ed. [Bloomington, IN: Indiana University Press, 2000], 217–19).
26. Of course, there may be exceptions to this. Consider, for example, a case in which someone injures another as punishment, with the express purpose of leaving them with a physical reminder (this was brought to my attention by Pekka Pitkänen, personal communication). If the injury produces a lasting symptom that finds regular reminder, such as walking with a gimp, then the mnemonic continues even though the initial "performance" has finished. Such an example, I would suggest, is not a true exception, for it still meets the essential criteria though in a unique way. It rather is a question of the agency involved.
27. Wood's own discussion focuses on the vectors of historiography, war crimes trials, novels, and films which, in my opinion, seems to obscure rather than clarify her own conceptualization of vectors (*Vectors of Memory*).
28. Peter Meusburger, Michael Heffernan, and Edgar Wunder, "Cultural Memories: An Introduction," in *Cultural Memories*, ed. Peter Meusburger, Michael Heffernan, and Edgar Wunder (Berlin: Springer, 2011), 7–8.
29. The main difference is that *ars memorativa* focused on the raw memorization of facts, concepts, and ideas, and not necessarily on memory for enculturation and identity formation. The same basic principles of making things memorable, however, still hold true. For a classic discussion on *ars memorativa* in history, see Frances A. Yates, *The Art of Memory*, 2nd ed. (Chicago, IL: University of Chicago Press, 1966).
30. See the definition given by Rudy Koshar: "It is a continuity based on recurring forms and symbols of collective memory" (*From Monuments to Traces* [Berkeley: University of California Press, 2000], 286).
31. Terdiman similarly speaks of memory since the industrial revolution as an "archival consciousness" transmitted by "'extra-individual' mnemonic mechanisms" (*Present Past*, 37).
32. Meusburger, Heffernan, and Wunder, "Cultural Memories," 7.
33. Terdiman, *Present Past*, 34.
34. Barbie Zelizer, *Remembering to Forget* (Chicago, IL: University of Chicago Press, 1998), 4.
35. This view typically comes out of the philosophical notion of the "extended mind." For a good recent article that integrates philosophical views with those of the social sciences, see John Sutton et al., "The Psychology of Memory, Extended Cognition, and Socially Distributed Remembering," *Phenomenology and the Cognitive Sciences* 9 (2010): 521–60. See also Mark Rowlands, *The New Science of the Mind* (Cambridge, MA: MIT Press, 2010).
36. Sutton et al., "Psychology of Memory," 525; See Andy Clark, *Being There* (Cambridge, MA: MIT Press, 1997), 220.
37. Sutton et al., "Psychology of Memory," 525.
38. Clark, *Being There*, 77.

39. This idea, similar to what Assmann refers to as communicative memory, has been shown to play a key role in memory. So-called collaborative remembering between people is an essential way of calibrating and constructing group memory. See Sutton et al., "Psychology of Memory," 520–23; Amanda J. Barnier and John Sutton, "From Individual to Collective Memory: Theoretical and Empirical Perspectives," *Memory* 16 (2008): 177–82; Amanda J. Barnier et al., "A Conceptual and Empirical Framework for the Social Distribution of Cognition: The Case of Memory," *Cognitive Systems Research* 9 (2008): 33–51.

40. Sutton et al., "Psychology of Memory," 526.

41. Kansteiner, "Finding Meaning," 188–89.

42. Kansteiner, "Finding Meaning," 197, following Marius Kwint, *Material Memories*, ed. Marius Kwint, Christopher Breward, and Jeremy Aynsley (Oxford: Berg, 1999), 3. While these studies focus on the three aspects as a triangle of hermeneutics, their observation also represents well the general vectoring relationship of maker, consumer, and object. A similar triangle is forwarded by Casey in *Remembering*. Casey's aim, it should be noted, is slightly different: to identify the ways in which memory is represented outside of the individual mind. He concludes that it is in "body memory," "place memory," and "commemoration" (xi). (For in-depth discussions of each, see the chapters by the same names: respectively, pp. 146–180; 181–215; 216–257.)

43. Admittedly, there are some gray areas concerning agency. First, it would seem that in some instances, there need be only one person and an object to vector memory. For instance, a man might perform an act with the express intention that, in so doing, he himself will better remember something. He is then the agent and the consumer. Second, in cases where there is a separate agent and consumer, it is not clear whether the consumer need be aware of the intention of the vectoring. After all, one would assume that many a memory program is meant to mold people who are more or less unaware.

44. Zelizer, *Remembering to Forget*, 4.

45. Zelizer, *Remembering to Forget*, 4–5.

46. Jan Assmann, "Exodus and Memory," in *The Afterlife of Events: Perspectives on Mnemohistory*, ed. Marek Tamm (Basingstoke, UK: Palgrave Macmillan, 2015), 123.

47. Assmann, *Cultural Memory*, 18–19.

48. Karin Finsterbusch has also critiqued Assmann's mechanisms of memory (*Weisung für Israel* [Heidelberg: Mohr Siebeck, 2005], 2). She acknowledges that Assmann's work is important in that it shows how cultural memory helps preserve and transmit identity. In the end, though, Finsterbusch finds the approach wanting because it does not give proper attention to Deuteronomy's focus on teaching and learning. What is curious about her critique, however, is that it fails to take Assmann's model on its own terms, viewing it instead through the teaching/learning lens. What is more, she seems to assume that memory and learning are one and the same. As the voluminous research on this topic shows, the two are indeed related, but cannot be considered the same. As such, Finsterbusch's own work would seem to suffer from a lacuna similar to the kind she levels against Assmann's.

49. Finsterbusch, *Weisung für Israel*, 95.

50. Jan Assmann, "Form as a Mnemonic Device: Cultural Texts and Cultural Memory," in *Performing the Gospel*, ed. Richard A. Horsley, Jonathan A. Draper, and John M. Foley (Minneapolis, MN: Fortress Press, 2011), 67–82.

51. Assmann, "Form as a Mnemonic Device," 75.

52. Assmann, "Form as a Mnemonic Device," 76.

53. Assmann, "Form as a Mnemonic Device," 80.

54. See 16:21–22 for the mirroring of this in prohibitions of such paraphernalia in Israelite worship.

55. Moshe Weinfeld notes the differences between Deuteronomy's account and that found in Exodus 34:13 (*Deuteronomy 1–11* [New York, Doubleday, 1991], 366–67, 376). In particular, Deuteronomy adds to the elements of destruction "burning" (שרף) (graven images [7:5, 25] and Asherim [12:3]) and to the paraphernalia of worship "graven images" (פסילים); also, for cutting down the Asherim (7:5) and graven images (12:3) it uses "hack" (גדע) instead of Exodus' "cut" (כרת).

56. On the intrinsic connection of these two ideas, see Gordon McConville, *Deuteronomy* (Westmont, IL: InterVarsity Press, 2002), 149–50. See also Josh 4–6 and 1 Sam 4, both of which focus on the destruction of the nations but also feature the ark of the covenant. *Pace* A. D. H. Mayes, *Deuteronomy* (London: Oliphants, 1979), 181.

57. First, it represented the rejection of other gods generally (Peter Craigie, *Deuteronomy* [Grand Rapids, MI: Eerdmans, 1976], 216). (It should also be noted, though, that in other places standing stones were deemed legitimate [see Gen 28:22]. For more on the archaeology of מצבת, see Richard Hess, *Israelite Religions* [Ada, MI: Baker Academic, 2007], 198–99.) Second, some of the items would have been plated with precious metals (see 7:25). The act of destroying them, instead of taking them as booty or reusing them for worship accoutrements, was therefore a strong showing of devotion to Yahweh.

58. McConville forwards this structure (*Deuteronomy*, 151).

59. See also J. Gary Millar, *Now Choose Life* (Westmont, IL: InterVarsity Press, 1998), 109. He argues that in Deut 12, vv. 2–4 and 29–31 form an inclusion that frame the whole chapter with an anti-Canaanite theme.

60. Of course, this refers to the larger gamut of worship practices, not just the use of the paraphernalia (see 12:4). McConville aptly notes the juxtaposition of the plurality of "places" in Canaanite worship (12:2) and the singularity of the chosen "place" of Yahwistic worship (12:5) (*Deuteronomy*, 218). But while there is probably a negative view of the plurality versus the singularity generally, the main idea is the establishment of worship that is "qualitatively different from the nations" (p. 219).

61. There, of course, has been a lot of discussion on the so-called "name theology" of Deuteronomy. Traditionally, it has been seen as a way of expressing Yahweh's absolute transcendence (Gerhard von Rad, *Studies in Deuteronomy* [London, SCM Press, 1953], 39; Moshe Weinfeld, *Deuteronomy and the Deuteronomic School* [Oxford: Oxford University Press, 1972], 191–209), though there have been convincing counterarguments (J. G. Millar and J. G. McConville, *Time and Place in Deuteronomy* [Sheffield, UK: Sheffield Academic Press, 1994], 111–23; Ian Wilson, *Out of the Midst of the Fire* [Atlanta, GA: Scholars Press, 1995]; Sandra Richter, *The*

Deuteronomistic History and the Name Theology [Berlin: Walter de Gruyter, 2002]). For our present discussion, I follow McConville in arguing that the context focuses not on Yahweh's presence but on the place of worship as "one that is known to belong wholly and unequivocally to Yahweh" (*Deuteronomy*, 220).

62. McConville, *Deuteronomy*, 219, emphasis mine.

63. On this idea, see Edward Casey, *Remembering*, xii–xiii, and more fully "Remembering Forgotten: The Amnesia of Anamnesis," 1–18.

64. For a recent study, see Barry Schwarz, "Collective Remembering and the Symbolic Power of Oneness: The Strange Apotheosis of Rosa Parks," *Social Psychology Quarterly* 72 (2009): 123–42.

65. Jan Assmann, "Canon and Archive," in *The Collective Memory Reader*, ed. Jeffrey K. Olick, Vered Vinitzky-Seroussi, and Daniel Levy (Oxford: Oxford University Press, 2011), 334. Originally found in full in "Canon and Archive," in *Cultural Memory Studies*, ed. Astrid Erll and Ansgar Nünning (Berlin: Walter de Gruyter, 2008), 97–107.

66. Assmann, "Canon and Archive," 334.

67. It should be noted that though active forgetting is often viewed in the negative, as propaganda or social mind control (a tendency probably due in a large part to the fact that active forgetting was first discussed by Nietzsche, in the second of his *Untimely Meditations*, trans. Anthony Ludovici and Adrian Collins [Digireads, 2010], 96–133), this is not inherently so. Paul Ricoeur, for example, has shown that active forgetting needs to be understood as a spectrum ranging from manipulation on the one end to forgiveness on the other (*Meaning and Representation in History*, ed. Jörn Rüsen [New York: Berghahn Books, 2006], 9–19). Thus, it is not the act of forgetting itself but its *telos* that determines the bent. See also Miroslav Volf, *The End of Memory* (Grand Rapids, MI: Eerdmans, 2006).

68. A related idea has been forwarded by Mark Smith in *The Memoirs of God* (Minneapolis, MN: Augsburg Press, 2004), esp. chapter 4: "The Formation of Israel's Concepts of God: Collective Memory and Amnesia in the Bible," 124–58. The key difference, however, is that Smith analyzes active forgetting not so much as something the text is seeking to accomplish as a dynamic that, through the evolution of religion, led to the portrait of God now found in the text. It seems Smith sees active forgetting playing a role in differentiation, the second of his three stages of development (in order, the stages are convergence, differentiation, and reinterpretation).

69. We note that "Mt. Ebal" is the reading of the Masoretic Text in v. 4, but the Samaritan Pentateuch locates the altar and standing stones on "Mt. Gerizim." Opinions differ on which is correct: for instance, John Wevers (*Notes on the Greek Text of Deuteronomy* [Atlanta, GA: Scholars Press, 1995], 417) and Craigie (*Deuteronomy*, 328, n. 5) like the "Mt. Ebal" reading, while Georg Braulik (*Deuteronomium II* [Würzburg: Echter Verlag, 1992], 200) and Mayes (*Deuteronomy*, 341) favor "Mt. Gerizim," following the BHS suggestion. On archaeological evidence for Mt. Ebal, see Hess, *Israelite Religions*, 216–21. For counterarguments, see William Dever, *Who Were the Early Israelites and Where Did They Come From?* (Grand Rapids, MI: Eerdmans, 2003), 89–90. A recent article by Sandra Richter examines the literary, archaeological, epigraphic, and geographical evidence and convincingly shows that

Mt. Ebal is in fact the correct designation ("The Place of the Name in Deuteronomy," *Vetus Testamentum* 57 [2007]: 342–66).

70. See Josh 8:30–35. Some have seen Deut 27 as intrusive into the flow between Chs. 26 and 28. Others, however, have highlighted connections to Deut 11, thus making Chs. 11 and 27 a bracket for the laws found in 12–26. See McConville, *Deuteronomy*, 387; Craigie, *Deuteronomy*, 212; Norbert Lohfink, *Das Hauptgebot* (Rome: Pontifical Biblical Institute, 1963), 233–34.

71. Simeon, Levi, Judah, Issachar, Joseph, Benjamin.

72. Reuben, Gad, Asher, Zebulun, Dan, Naphtali.

73. On this threefold breakdown, see Jeffrey H. Tigay, *Deuteronomy* (Philadelphia: Jewish Publication Society, 1996), 246–47; on the third point, see also McConville, *Deuteronomy*, 392. That the curses recorded here are examples of crimes that might go undetected seems to be the best explanation of their unique nature (esp. their differing from the curses found in Ch. 28).

74. Tigay, *Deuteronomy*, 247.

75. Because Deuteronomy commands Israel to destroy the Canaanite מצבת, it seems likely the term "great stones" is used deliberately to avoid that connotation.

76. The difficulty arises between v. 2, which says, "And it shall be *on the day* when you cross over the Jordan," and v. 4, which has "when you cross the Jordan, erect . . . on Mt Ebal." The former indicates that the stones are to be erected the very day of the crossing, as Israel's first act in the land; the latter, however, dictates that this is to happen at Mt. Ebal near Shechem, which is more than a day away. This has raised questions since ancient times, witnessed to by a manuscript of Joshua from Qumran, and discussions in Josephus, Pseudo-Philo, and rabbinic commentators (see Tigay, *Deuteronomy*, 486; Richter, "Place of the Name," 352, n. 29).

77. See McConville, *Deuteronomy*, 388; Paul Barker, "The Theology of Deuteronomy 27," *Tyndale Bulletin* 49 (1998): 298.

78. Richter, "Place of the Name," 353–54. The discrepancy is often explained in traditio-historical terms (e.g., Mayes, *Deuteronomy*, 340–41; Tigay, *Deuteronomy*, 486–87). In this view, Deut 27:1–8 (and 11:29–32) reflects the conflation of two competing traditions. One is an altar tradition centered in Shechem (Mt. Ebal), commemorating Sinai (vv. 5–7; Josh 8:30–35; 24; see also Gen 33:18–20; 35:2–4), the other a stelae tradition based in Gilgal, commemorating the settlement (vv. 2–4; Josh 4–5). However, see Duane Christensen on the possibility that the repetitiveness of Deut 27:1–10 is due to the presence of a chiasm (*Deuteronomy 21:10–34:12* [Nashville, TN: Thomas Nelson, 2001], 652).

79. Richter does not make this point explicit, but it seems to be the logical conclusion ("Place of the Name," 353, n. 32). She proposes, further, that this is not just a figurative journey, but that it actually refers to an eastwest highway (i.e., Deuteronomy 11:30's "Sunset Road") running from two kilometers north of Jericho, through Ai, and onto Bethel (pp. 353–54. See David Dorsey, *The Roads and Highways of Ancient Israel* [Baltimore, MD: Johns Hopkins Press, 1991], 201–7). Significantly, at Bethel this road intersects the so-called "National Highway," which connects Shechem to Jerusalem.

80. Richter also notes that, contra the common assumption that altar and stelae were not complementary in Levantine religion, just the opposite is true ("Place of the

Name," 358). She mentions a variety of examples, most important of which are the Shechem and Bull sites. These were both functioning during Iron Age I and in the region of Manasseh, and both employed an altar and stelae.

81. *Pace* Craigie (*Deuteronomy*, 328) and McConville (*Deuteronomy*, 388), who see this as reflecting an Egyptian practice, Richter argues that it is reflective of Iron Age Canaan ("Place of the Name," 359–60; Richter seems surprised that commentators are largely unaware of this fact). She cites examples such as Deir Allah and Kuntilat 'Ajrud.

82. Richter, *The Name Theology*, 153. For her larger discussion on inscriptions in the ANE, see pp. 130–153; 184–203.

83. Though Richter seems to see the monuments as both votive and triumphant in nature ("Place of the Name," 344, 358, 361).

84. Richter, *The Name Theology*, 133; "Place of the Name," 345.

85. Commentators note this usage but disagree as to what it means. There are a range of views as to what the "Torah" entails: the Decalogue (Eugene Merrill, *Deuteronomy* [Nashville, TN: Broadman and Holman, 1994], 342); the laws of the covenant in Exodus 19–24 (Craigie, *Deuteronomy*, 328); the legal section of Deuteronomy (12–26) (Samuel Rolles Driver, *Deuteronomy* [New York: Charles Scriber's Sons, 1895], 296); the whole of Deuteronomy (Tigay, *Deuteronomy*, 248; Braulik, *Deuteronomium*, 202).

86. Arguments against this on the grounds that the writing would not fit onto mere commemorative stones are unfounded. The whole of Deuteronomy would fit onto just two stones the size of Hammurabi's (Tigay, *Deuteronomy*, 248; see also Barker, "Theology of Deuteronomy 27," 286).

87. Richter, *Name Theology*, 153–84; "Place of the Name," 351, 361.

88. E.g., Richter, *Name Theology*, 130; McConville, *Deuteronomy*, 388; Christensen, *Deuteronomy*, 655; Miller, *Deuteronomy*, 191; Mayes, *Deuteronomy*, 341.

89. See Gen 31:45–54; Exod 28:12; Josh 4:20–22; 1 Sam 7:12.

90. Tigay, *Deuteronomy*, 249; Moshe Anbar, "The Story About the Building of an Altar on Mount Ebal," in *Das Deuteronomium*, ed. Norbert Lohfink (Leuven, Belgium: Leuven University Press, 1985), 305, n. 8. Contra Miller, *Deuteronomy*, 191.

91. Tigay, *Deuteronomy*, 249. We should note that even if the writing on the plaster was meant to inscribe through it onto the stone, the notion of a one-time ceremony is clear from the context.

92. Craigie, *Deuteronomy*, 328.

93. To be fair, the stones do in some sense find ongoing exposition in the reading of the book of Deuteronomy. But this can hardly be considered intentional commemoration via the stones.

94. Although the account of the stones by the Jordan in Josh 4:20–22 would meet most of the criteria of memory vectors.

95. Millar, *Time and Place*, 71, 72.

Chapter 5

Emplotting Memory
Story as Memory Vector

This, the first of Deuteronomy's memory vectors, is perhaps the most enduring, for we find forms of it in Jewish practice still today. Best known are the practices of affixing little scrolls with Scripture to doorposts (*Mezuzot*) and wearing them in capsules on the arm and forehead (*Tefillin*), and the practice, during Passover, of having a child ask about the meaning of the rites. These are derived from various texts, especially Deuteronomy 6. But while they appear as independent practices today, in Deuteronomy they are presented, I shall argue, as a single unit. To be sure, the unit is comprised of two parts: religious *habitus* (Deut 6:6–9) and storytelling (Deut 6:20–25). But it is the latter part, the storytelling, that encompasses the whole.

HABITUS: DEUTERONOMY 6:6–9

The first part, the *habitus*, is found in Deut 6:6–9.[1] And by "*habitus*" I mean simply the religious habits that people practice in cultivating their faith. Since the role of Deut 6 is "extending the laws given at Horeb [from Deut 5] into the regular lives of the people,"[2] then Deut 6:6–9, the practical means of doing this, offers a prime example of *habitus*.[3]

The purpose of the *habitus* is to help children fulfill the call of the *Shema* (6:4–5): to love Yahweh singularly. And the crucial way in which the *habitus* do so is by inscribing "these words" (הדברים האלה) (v. 6) on their hearts. But here we come upon an interpretive problem, for the meaning of "these words" is debated. Before moving on to the *habitus* themselves, therefore, we must discern the nature of this phrase.

There are various views on the reference of "these words," ranging from the whole of Deuteronomy to just part of Deut 6:4, "Yahweh our God,

Yahweh is one."[4] For those who hold that "these words" refer to Chapters 5–26 or all of Deuteronomy, the argument is that this reflects a common usage of דברים.[5] The same can be said for the Decalogue, which at least eight times is the referent.[6] Nathan MacDonald, however, suggests that there are complicating issues with the above positions. First, there are cases in which דבר, as a singular or plural, appears in conjunction with "that I am commanding you today" and refers not to a body of items but an individual command;[7] and, what is more, in each of these the referent is the command immediately preceding it.[8] Second, the practical implementation of "these words" precludes a large text, for a person could not, for example, wear something the size of a book between their eyes.[9] The above factors, MacDonald argues, point to the *Shema* (Deut 6:4–5) as the referent of "these words": it is a text of manageable size that immediately precedes the command.[10] But he also says that this does not "absolutely exclude a reference to the rest of the book since . . . the command to love YHWH is the 'quintessence of the entire teaching of the book.'"[11] Perhaps it is best to see the primary reference as the *Shema*, with the implication being that it would naturally lead into the distillation of the Torah found in the Decalogue.

What about the *habitus* themselves—how do they inculcate "these words"? Again, MacDonald is helpful, suggesting six ways:[12]

1. They are to be upon your heart (v. 6)
2. Repeat them to your sons (v. 7)
3. Recite them when you rest at home, when you walk, when you lie down and when you rise (v. 7)
4. Bind them as a sign on your hand (v. 8)
5. They are to be as a frontlet between your eyes (v. 8)
6. Write them upon the doorposts of your house and on your gates (v. 9).

But here we come upon another interpretive issue: Are these to be taken literally or metaphorically? Scholarly views have been mixed on this, but even those who tend toward the literal usually see "upon your heart" as a figurative goal of the practices that follow. MacDonald, however, argues that this too should be taken literally.

The root of MacDonald's argument is that a figurative meaning of "upon your heart" cannot be assumed and that textual examples may point toward a literal understanding. For one, he suggests that a figurative conception presumes על־לבבך is equivalent to בלבב.[13] And while MacDonald acknowledges that the former can have the sense of "in the mind," he sees the closest parallel coming from Exod 28:30.[14] There it is said that the Urim and Thummim are to be put in the breastplate, in order to "be upon Aaron's heart" (והיו על־לב אהרן). The difficulty with this, though, is that it may not be as similar to Deut 6:6 as it seems. Indeed, Exod 28:30 employs the similar construction of על-לב with the verb היה. However, it also precedes this with an explicit material object, the "breastplate of judgment" (חשן המשפט), whereas Deut 6 only has "these words." So, while there are similarities, there is also a key difference that marks the former as obviously literal. What is more, apart from the two cases of Aaron's breastplate in Exod 28:29–30, the vast majority of occurrences of (על-לב(ב are figurative in nature.[15] So for me the linguistic evidence does not settle the issue.[16]

Stronger support comes from the way in which the linguistic intersects the material. Material findings from Egypt and Assyria have been the primary sources of evidence for those in favor of the literal interpretation.[17] They show that the practice of wearing a small plaque or amulet on a string around the neck and over the heart was well known.[18] One could also point to the Ketef Hinnom amulets from seventh-century BC Judah, discovered in burial caves south of Jerusalem, which contain inscriptions of Num 6:24–26 and Deut 7:9.[19] More recently, other items have come to light.[20] First, amulets of the same nature as those from Ketef Hinnom have been found from fifth- to sixth-century Tyre.[21] These testify to how common the practice was in Israel's immediate neighbors. Second, and perhaps more tellingly, we now know of a small oval pendant that is bilingual (Neo-Assyrian and Aramaic) that gives precise instructions for where it is to be worn: "between the arms and *the heart*."[22] This object is important for how it links key features: it is an (1) inscribed object (2) worn over the heart that is (3) self-aware of its location. While this does not prove that Deut 6:6 is literal, it provides a suggestive bridge between the language of the text and a particular ANE practice. As Lemaire says, it "show[s] that an inscription, specifically a religious inscription, could literally be placed 'on the heart,' especially if it was a short inscription such as [the *Shema*]."[23]

The second of MacDonald's six instructions is to "repeat them to your sons" (Deut 6:7).[24] Here the crux interpretive issue concerns the meaning of שנן in the Piel, which is a *hapax legomenon*. In the Qal, this word means "to sharpen" and is used both literally ("sword," Deut 32:41) and figuratively ("tongue," Ps 64:4).[25] This fact, alongside Deut 11:19's use of למד in its place, has led some to render שנן in the Piel as "to teach diligently or incisively."[26] However, MacDonald is probably right to argue instead for the notion of "to recite, repeat."[27] Cognate studies show that similar forms have this same meaning in both Akkadian and Ugaritic.[28] Further, philological evidence may point toward שנ (pi.) being a by-form of שנה, which means "to rehearse, teach, do once again" (1 Kgs 18:34).[29] It seems that the idea in view, therefore, is for parents to instruct their children by rehearsing the *Shema* with them.

The third instruction is to recite the words when sitting at home or out walking and when sleeping or waking (6:7). Traditionally, דברת בם has been understood to mean "talk about them," as in making the words the object of conversation between parent and child.³⁰ Since the article by Fischer and Lohfink, however, there has been a shift toward seeing the phrase as referring to recitation.³¹ MacDonald follows this line of thinking.³² A key point of this view is that דבר typically denotes "the physical act of speaking" and not "speech *about* speech" (emphasis added).³³ Eep Talstra has strengthened this position through his analysis of דבר + ב.³⁴ With this said, Finsterbusch has recently raised a strong counterargument. She argues, first, that understanding דבר as "recite" presents an unnecessary repetition of ideas, for the preceding שנן carries the same notion.³⁵ She suggests the larger teaching context, namely 6:20–25, indicates that there is more than recitation in view.³⁶ Second, developing the first notion, she avers that the parallel passage 11:18–21 provides the governing interpretive framework for 6:6–9. In particular, Finsterbusch notes how chapter 11 uses למד ("to teach") in place of שנן ("to rehearse") and the infinitive לדבר + ב instead of the perfect.³⁷ The resulting idea is that "teaching" is the main verb, which is modified by "reciting." Perhaps the greatest strength of the above analysis is that it shows the interconnections of the various pieces of Israel's educational program; indeed, the recitation of the words cannot be separated from the narrative exposition in 6:20–25. However, this does not in my opinion change the fact that in Deut 6:7 דבר + ב means "recite them" to your children.

Finsterbusch identifies a further issue arising from the passage if one understands דבר + ב as "recite them": "Wem gilt das 'Reden'?"³⁸ The question of who does the talking, she suggests, has been answered in two main ways. The first way is to see the recitation happening between adults.³⁹ She traces this to the work of Fischer and Lohfink, who intimate it could happen even through an individual humming the words to himself.⁴⁰ In this view, presumably the children would learn through hearing the adults speak the words. The second way is to see recitation more traditionally, through parents perpetually speaking the words to their children.⁴¹ She traces the idea to Talstra, who says, "to instruct the Torah to next generations is to be done by recitation, making the text of the Torah heard by means of *performance*" (emphasis added).⁴² Exactly what "performance" entails is unclear, but Finsterbusch seems to envisage a two-way act: parents reciting the words to their children and the children repeating them back to the parents.⁴³ While I have argued that דבר + ב itself refers to recitation, it is reasonable to assume with Finsterbusch that such activity provides the impetus for the questions and Torah exposition that arise in 6:20–25.⁴⁴

The remaining issue with the recitation performance in Deut 6:7 concerns where and when it is practiced. The verse gives two contrasting pairs: "when you sit in your home and when you walk along the way" (בשבתך בביתך ובלכתך בדרך) and "when you lie down and when you rise up"

(ובשכבך ובקומך). These are nearly universally understood as merisms representing totality. There is however a question about what the merisms might refer to. MacDonald suggests two possibilities.[45] One is that the merisms refer to the words themselves—everywhere and always being recited. Another is that they refer to the timing of the actions: as in Jewish custom, the recitation would occur in the morning and evening as a merism for the whole day. MacDonald does not make clear which he prefers, but the two options are not mutually exclusive. It is hard to imagine that there is anything in view here but the call to recite the words continually.[46] But this does not negate the possibility that set times of morning and evening recitation were part of the original idea, providing a concrete framework to propel and inculcate the ideal.

The fourth and fifth instructions from MacDonald's list are the binding of signs on hand and head. Once again, the chief question is whether these are to be understood figuratively or literally. The notion of a figurative interpretation might arise from passages in Exodus and Proverbs, where similar ideas are found with metaphorical meanings. In Exod 13:9, 16 the context concerns consecrating the firstborn and celebrating the Passover, two acts which it then says are to be "like a sign on your hand and a reminder between your eyes." It is hard to see this as anything but figurative.[47] In Proverbs, there are several instances in which the language of binding things to one's body is used in reference to instruction.[48] While there may have been cases in which this was supplemented or reinforced with literal binding, the metaphorical appears to be the chief intent and, in some cases (e.g., Prov 3:3), is the only possible interpretation.[49] In the immediate context of Deut 6:7–9, however, there are at least two aspects that give pause to a figurative interpretation.[50] First, the object in view is *particular words*. The idea that concrete words are to serve as a "sign" would suggest more than a metaphor. Second, crystallizing the first point, verse 9 envisions inscribing "these words" on architectural features. The writing of particular words on particular items "would be hard to take in a metaphorical sense."[51]

MacDonald argues that further evidence for a literal interpretation is found in archaeology and other biblical parallels.[52] As for archaeology, it has been shown that the practices in Deut 6:8—the אות on the arm and the טטפת between the eyes[53]—are consonant with those known from the ANE. The wearing of armbands appears in Egypt and that of headbands in representations of Syrian goddesses.[54] At times the goddesses' headbands sport a letter (ת) on them. MacDonald also points to the aforementioned Ketef Hinnom amulets as evidence of such practices in pre-exilic Israel. In particular, he notes that one of the inscribed texts, Num 6:24–26, may in its scriptural context corroborate the idea, for it appears to provide the impetus for a literal practice: "So will they set my name on the sons of Israel" (6:27).[55] MacDonald's discussion of biblical parallels offers more evidence. He notes that Isaiah 44:5 portrays the

Israelites as writing ליהוה on their hands and that Ezekiel 9:4–6 depicts a man marking the repentant of Jerusalem with a ת.[56] As already pointed out, there is also the inscription on Aaron's breastplate in Exodus 28 and, further, the plate on his headdress inscribed with קדש ליהוה ("holy unto Yahweh") (v. 36). While this does not prove the literal nature of the אות and טטפת, it shows that such a conception was at home in the ANE and in the biblical text and is therefore likely in Deut 6:8. We should note also that unlike the later practice of the *tefillin*, in which written words were inside of capsules, these words were probably written on the outside to be visible.[57]

The sixth and final instruction on MacDonald's list is for Israel to write "these words" on the doorposts of the house and on the city gates (6:9).[58] Here, too, he garners much of the same evidence to demonstrate that this should be taken literally. First, various texts witness to the importance of doorposts in connection to symbols.[59] In Exod 12:7 the blood of the Passover lamb is smeared on doorposts, and in Isa 57:8 the people are chastised for using them in ways akin to foreign worship. Second, ANE evidence shows that it was common for both doorposts and gates to be inscribed. Following Keel, MacDonald highlights the written instructions upon temple doorways in Egypt,[60] which he connects to practices known from the Old Testament.[61] Perhaps more illuminating for Deut 6:9, though, are the Northwest Semitic inscriptions recently pointed out by Lemaire.[62] He divides these into three groups, with the first two relating to doorways and the third to gates.

The first kind is exemplified at Kuntillet 'Ajrud and dates to the early eighth century BC. While the focus typically centers on the Hebrew and Phoenician wall writings that mention Yahweh, there is also at least one doorpost *in situ* that bears an inscription.[63] Due to partial publishing of the inscriptions, it is not clear what the doorpost says; but the location—leading from the benchroom into the courtyard—"corresponds exactly with the instructions in Deut 6:9a."[64] The second group is that of so-called "house amulets." Lemaire especially cites the entrance to the palace of the Aramean King Kilamuwa in Zencirli, dating to the eighth and ninth centuries BC, which bore Phoenician inscriptions on amulets. Too big for personal use, it is a thought that these hung on the frames of entrances. One of these is inscribed on the outside, invoking the blessing of a deity over the house, but the other seems to have been written on perishable material and held in a capsule.[65] Lemaire notes that the latter, if his construction is correct, may be the antecedent to the later Jewish *mezuzot*.[66] The third and final group is that of monumental inscriptions. Lemaire admits that direct parallels have not been found *in situ*, but shows that inscriptions on stelae from gates in Samaria (Hebrew, eighth century BC) and at Dan (Aramaic, ninth century) are at least suggestive.[67] Understood in this way, Deut 6:9b could refer to writing either on the gates themselves or on a separate stone set alongside them. These examples show that a literal interpretation of Deut 6:9 fits well with what the material evidence shows of Israel's closest neighbors and perhaps even of some of its own cities.

Another point arises from Lemaire's discussion that may further illumine the performative aspect of these practices. He notes that at Deir 'Alla the "inscriptions clearly were copied from a manuscript containing a literary tradition."[68] While this much is not as obvious at Kuntillet 'Ajrud, its similarities to Deir 'Alla leads to the assumption that its inscriptions also "contain fragments from literary texts."[69] Thus he avers that the inscriptions on doorposts and gates are frequently part of larger literary texts.[70] The same may be said of the aforementioned bodily practices, especially in light of the Ketef Hinnom amulets which are known to fit within the larger text of Numbers.[71] What this shows for Deuteronomy is that its instruction to inscribe part of the larger text on body and architecture is, in fact, consistent with other ANE practices. More important than the issue of the origin of the inscribed text, however, is its purpose. What is the goal of the inscription compared to that of the text corpus?

David Carr is helpful at this point.[72] Against the traditional view that memory/mind and writing/text were conflicting ways of storing information in the ancient world, Carr argues for a more complementary relationship:

[T]he *mind* stood at the center of the often discussed oral-written interface. The focus was on inscribing a culture's most precious traditions on the insides of people. Within this context . . . texts served as solidified reference points for the recitation and memorization of tradition.[73]

If this was the *telos* of texts generally, what was the role of inscriptions? Inscriptions such as those envisaged in Deut 6:6–9 would appear to fit within Carr's notion of "visual presentation."[74] This was when visible objects, sometimes as simple as symbols or individual letters, were used as cues into larger texts. As such, the inscriptions would have served in concert with parents' recitation to children, both as an accuracy check and as a mnemonic trigger. Following Braulik, Carr sees the domestic practices as triggering the whole of chapters 5–26.[75] But while the larger Torah is always in sight, the rehearsal of the *Shema* here would more naturally lead into the Decalogue. It makes sense practically, with the Decalogue being of manageable size, and also contextually, for Deut 6 provides the practical means of extending the ten words of chapter 5 into the community.

In summary, it seems best to interpret the instructions of Deut 6:6–9 as literal means by which the Israelites were to inscribe "these words" on their heart. "These words" probably refers to the *Shema* (6:4–5), but may well include, or at least imply entry into, the Decalogue. Conceptually, the practices themselves represent the intersection of key areas of life. On the one hand, they demarcate chronological, spatial, and social boundaries: morning and evening, coming and going, doorposts and gates.[76] This shows that the practices are to gain and keep the constant attention of the Israelites, much like the *Shema* demands all of them. On the other hand, they also show how domestic practices connect the individual to the community.[77] In this way, the external practices of the home serve as the fulcrum for internalizing the covenant of the community in the individual.

HABITUS IN DEUTERONOMY'S MEMORY-MAKING

What, then, is the role of these things in the formation of Israel's memory? In order to answer this question, I leverage the notion of *habitus* developed by Mary McClintock Fulkerson.[78] Her conceptualization is particularly helpful because of the way in which it integrates faith habits with memory. McClintock Fulkerson understands *habitus* as the bodily practices through which people become enculturated into traditions of faith.[79] An important underlying idea here is that the process occurs through not only the creeds and doctrines of the mind but also the practices of the body.[80] Building on this, McClintock Fulkerson takes up Paul Connerton's distinction between inscribed and incorporated memory.[81] Inscribed memory, in this view, is that which is stored on physical objects, whereas incorporated memory is "sedimented" in the body through practice.[82] While McClintock Fulkerson uses these categories, pairing the mind with inscribed memory and with the body incorporated, her own treatment reveals that she sees them as complementary. This is important for examining Deut 6:6–9, which "holds together inscribed and incorporated memories . . . as mutually supportive."[83]

A couple of McClintock Fulkerson's ideas about *habitus* are helpful here. First, she highlights how mind and body function symbiotically in memory inculcation. While it is true that embodied knowledge (incorporated memory) resides in particular skills—such as bike riding or swimming—and is not reducible to propositions, it is also true that such knowledge is inherently interwoven with that of the mind (inscribed memory).[84] In a religious sense, this is observable by the way in which the bodily memory of *habitus* ultimately finds meaning and purpose in the larger frameworks of tradition and texts of faith.[85] These frameworks both exposit the *habitus* and contain the impetus for practicing them. Deuteronomy, for instance, locates its *habitus* within the trajectory of Israel's covenantal relationship with Yahweh; the governing story and the resulting *Torah* situate the particular practices. Apart from the text, therefore, the practices would have neither a catalyst nor an explanation. But the interconnectivity is deeper yet, for in some cases, the *habitus* itself turns in on the textual tradition. That is, the very practice is bent toward mastering words of the text. This is what we find in Deut 6:6–9. The *habitus* of placing "these words" on the body and on doorposts and gates is part of the rehearsal and recitation of them between parents and children. Through McClintock Fulkerson's model, then, we view the body and mind in reciprocal mnemonic relationship here. The point is not simply to memorize words in the mind but also to have those words sedimented within the body.[86] She mentions it only briefly, but the grand *telos* of such practices is to create and condition "creaturely desire."[87] The intermingling of memory in body and mind is to shape the desires of the heart which, in the case of Deuteronomy 6:6–9, is the absolute love of Yahweh expressed in the *Shema*.

The second of McClintock Fulkerson's ideas is what she calls "situational competence."[88] This term refers to the notion that *habitus* are not ends in themselves, but rather extend their skills and principles to apply to other contexts. In regard to situation, *habitus* establish a foundational symbolic context, that is, their own *place* "fundamental in generating knowledge."[89] In the case of Deut 6:6–9, we may add to this the aspect of time: through morning and evening recitation, a particular time is demarcated. Together with the inscriptions on doorposts and gates, which set out the particular place, the *habitus* establish a temporal-placial context. We note that in Deut 6:6–9 this is anchored in the domestic sphere. The nodes of time and place, then, serve as points between which the *habitus* reverberate and ultimately inculcate an idea of the good.[90] Thus, the "context" that the *habitus* creates functions as springboard into other situations in which the good can be manifest. This idea would seem to fit well in Deut 6:4–9. We already noted that the object of the *habitus* here is at least the *Shema* (and maybe the Decalogue), but that it also serves as an entry point into the larger Torah. Of course, even the Torah has concrete instances of the law and so does not exhaust the situational possibilities for embodying the *Shema*.

When McClintock Fulkerson speaks of competence, she means not only the skills to perform a particular skill but also the "bodily wisdom" about how to extend it into other contexts.[91] She does not make clear exactly how this works, but suggests that people learn the ability through watching others and hearing concrete examples in stories.[92] If this is true, then again it fits Deuteronomy, which employs not only particular laws but also stories to flesh out how the love of Yahweh is to be manifest. Interestingly, McClintock Fulkerson avers that competence in extending bodily knowledge into other contexts is proportionate to mastery of the *habitus* itself: "To do a practice well is to enhance one's capacities and to realize goods internal to the practice."[93] This also rings true of Deuteronomy's logic, which construes the vigilant keeping of its *habitus* as a chief means of taking to heart the *Shema*. In this, therefore, we see the deep interconnectivity between memory of the body and mind found in Deuteronomy's domestic *habitus*.

It is good to summarize by tying these findings in with previous ones. How does the *habitus* in Deut 6:6–9 reflect the two aspects of memory making discussed in the last chapter—encoding and retrieving? The encoding aspect largely concerns the way in which *habitus* inculcate memory in both the mind and body. By practicing the *habitus*, Israelite parents accomplish two things. First, they engrain the *Shema* into the minds of their children. We note that the *Shema* itself is strictly semantic in nature, a unique feature of the *habitus* vectoring of memory. Second, parents sediment this memory through particular practices. So, while the object of memory here is semantic, the manner of inculcation means that its storage extends beyond the mind into the body of the practitioners. In regard to retrieval, the efforts of parents ensure that at particular intervals and in particular places children must recall from memory the words of the *Shema*. The constancy of this retrieval is pivotal in cementing the mental and bodily features of memory in the children. An important part of successful retrieval are the mnemonic triggers: the inscriptions on pendants, headwear, and armbands, and on doorposts and gates stood as constant reminders of the *Shema*. These create an environment rich in mnemonic triggers which, as already noted, serve to infuse the teachings of the nation into the domestic and individual spheres.

Before moving on, we should point out something else about the memory resulting from *habitus*. The nature of the agency triad is perhaps clear by now: the vector is the *habitus* that reverberates between inscriptions and the continued recitations; the agent is the Israelite parents; and the consumer is their children.[94] What may not be quite as clear, though, is the role of this particular memory in Israel's larger autobiography. We learned in the last chapter that in autobiographical memory, semantic knowledge serves to set the trajectory and *telos* of episodic memories. The same is true here, I suggest, in that the memorizing of the *Shema*, a purely semantic memory, establishes the governing *telos* of Israel's autobiographical memory: to love the Lord completely. Moreover, this reflects the complementary relationship between "hearing" and "seeing" that I identified in Deut 4. The memorizing of "these words" puts the words into the minds and bodies of the people, but they cannot be fully "heard" or taken to heart unless accompanied by the "seeing." This "seeing," I have argued, comes in the form of vivid episodic memories. Being that stories are a primary carrier of such vivid images, it is fitting that we now turn to Deut 6:20–25.

STORYTELLING: DEUTERONOMY 6:20–25

Deuteronomy 6:20–25 resumes the theme of verses 6–9 and so brackets the chapter with the notion of the education of children.[95] In general, the chapter shows a progression of instruction that moves from the recitation of the *Shema* ("these words") (v. 6), into the "commands," "testimonies," and "statutes" (v. 17), and concludes with the exposition of these through the story of the exodus (vv. 21–23).[96] The key questions here, then, concern the nature and purpose of the exodus story in Israel's education.

Though not as many as in Deut 6:6–9, there are a few key issues in the interpretation of verses 20–25. The first concerns the object of the exposition: the "testimonies" (עדות), "statutes" (החקים), and "ordinances" (המשפטים). While the latter two terms are common, even functioning as an important *Struktursignal* in the book, the term "testimonies" is not.[97] What, then, is the reason for עדות here? One view sees the term as referring to the body of laws generally,[98] serving as a collective idea of witness: not only "denoting the act of witnessing" but also the "thing which is witnessed, viz. the laws themselves."[99] But while this may be true, it fails to make sense of why this unique term is employed here. After all, if the point is to refer to the body of laws, surely "statutes" (החקים) and "ordinances" (המשפטים) adequately accomplish this on their own.[100] Some may want to nuance it further, saying that עדות, which is a cognate of technical terms in ANE treaties,[101] adds to the basic idea of "laws" overtones of covenantal obligation.

Against this, however, another view has been forwarded. Bernard Couroyer argues that the best understanding of עדות in Deuteronomy is "doctrines." Braulik and Lohfink have followed this.[102] For them the idea is not so much one of covenantal "testimonies" to be preserved as "doctrines" to be taught. In the present context, this view makes the most sense. In addition to deciphering עדות, we must also account for the presence of the three terms as a whole, which differ from the Exodus account. In Exod 13:14 the same kind of questioning occurs, except within the Passover festival and in regard to the rite of the firstborn (Josh 4:6–7). But in Deuteronomy the question is part of domestic education and exposits not one particular command but the whole of the law body—the "doctrines" (עדות), "statutes" (החקים), and "ordinances" (המשפטים). As is frequently noted, this is yet another example of what we observed in Deut 6:6–9: the extension of the sacred into everyday life.[103] Here it is the entire body of laws, not just one particular rite, that is supported by recounting Israel's redemption.

Arising from this is a second issue of whether there stands behind the text an actual practice. As with Deut 6:6–9, the issue is highlighted by the traditional Jewish celebration of the Passover seder. In this tradition, the meal is punctuated by "The Four Questions," asked at intervals by the youngest child at the table, which inquires about the meaning of the rite.[104] These are more akin to Exodus than Deuteronomy, but they raise the question of whether something similar was in view in the ancient context. Some have answered this in the negative, seeing the questioning described in Deut 6:20 as merely rhetorical[105] or as derived from the cultic context but without background in an actual domestic practice.[106] In support of such views, one may point out that Deuteronomy does not, like Exodus, embed the questioning within other concrete practices. By this, what is typically meant is that Deut 6:20–25 is not cultic in nature. But whether one can assume that being noncultic in nature excludes the possibility of concrete practices is questionable. We need look no further than Deut 6:6–9 to see that.

Other scholars, however, have answered in the positive. Mayes, for one, argues that Deut 6:20–25 should be read together with verses 6–9, that is, as part of the aforementioned domestic ritual.[107] For him the idea is strengthened by viewing verses 10–19 as a late insertion, which means that verses 6–9 and 20–25 were once seamlessly linked. However, one does not need to do this to link the two sections. To begin with, scholars have frequently noted that there is a natural connection between Deut 6:7 and verses 20–25:[108] namely, both concern parents' teaching of children in the home. As pointed out already, this results in a structural bookending of the chapter with the theme of education. Braulik goes so far as to say that, in its present form, verses 6–9 and 20–25 are complementary, with the latter supporting the former.[109] Finsterbusch picks up on this idea and seeks to elucidate its supporting role further. What she concludes is that the role of the instruction in verses 20–25 is to provide for verses 6–9 a *Deutehorizont*, that is, an interpretive horizon.[110] For her this is not a supplementary role, however; it is *essential*. Without an interpretive horizon, Finsterbusch says, the recitation of the *Shema* and the laws would be an incomplete pedagogical program.[111] While she does not expand on this, Finsterbusch seems to have in mind a fundamental principle of education: that abstract knowledge must be shown to have saliency and that demanding practices must be motivated by purpose.[112] While her idea may not carry the argument on its own, combined with the aforementioned thematic and structural relationships it adds credence to the view that verses 6–9 and 20–25 are one entity. And if one entity, then it follows that the practice envisaged in the latter is, like those in the former, concrete in nature. We must be clear that the text does not articulate a set pattern for the question asking. But it is reasonable to assume that the practice fits within the patterns in view in verses 6–9.

A third issue regards whether verses 21–25, the answer given by the parents, betrays an Israelite creed. The idea was first forwarded by Gerhard von Rad, who argued that in Deuteronomy two passages in particular show the marks of a "short historical creed": 6:20–24 and 26:5–9.[113] For him these derived from a creedal formula employed in the cultic context. Such derivations are what he called "free modifications," that is, flexible recapitulations used in other situations.[114] Since the time it first appeared, the merits of von Rad's view have been much discussed. But while many of these discussions have concerned the genetic relationship between creed and text, our own concern is elsewhere. Our concern primarily lies in the question of the substance of Deut 6:21–25 and the appropriateness of calling it a creed.

Contemporary scholars tend to follow the idea that the passage has creedal qualities, though rarely go so far as calling it a creed.[115] A typical understanding is that Deut 6:21–25 is a "condensation of the principle elements of the faith of the Israelites."[116] But while this description is generally helpful, Aelred Cody has offered an important critique.[117] At the heart of his critique is the idea that "creed" is an inherently problematic category for verses 21–25.[118] He defines creed as "a statement of . . . article[s] of religion whose acceptance is required of anyone who wishes to be part of the religious group."[119] Key here is the idea that creeds are *statements of belief*, typically about the attributes of God. The issue then with passages such as Deut 6:21–25, Cody argues, is that they do not fit the creedal description. Instead of statements of belief, we find recollections of key events from Israel's past. Therefore, Cody prefers to call these *anamnesis*, that is, rehearsed or liturgical commemorations.[120]

While I would not make such a sharp distinction between creed and anamnesis, Cody's view does provide some illuminating points. First, he argues that in anamnesis what is called to mind is "not a static attribute but an event."[121] This is not in itself enough to demarcate anamnesis, for even the Apostles' Creed recounts items of belief by way of events: "[Jesus Christ] suffered under Pontius Pilate, was crucified, dead, and buried." The difference is in the function of these events. In anamnesis, and this is our second point, the events serve to affect a response: past events are to produce present dispositions.[122] Cody particularly identifies that the exodus is to elicit the effect of gratitude. In the present context, this effect is meant to motivate obedience to the law. As we discussed in the last chapter, though, while the exodus is central to Israel's memory, it is not alone. Third and most importantly, Cody avers that the aim of such anamnesis is for the participant to "own" the events and "identif[y] himself with those who actually experienced" them.[123] That is, the person is in some sense to see oneself as part of said memory. The strength of Cody's view for the present study, then, is that it shows the practice of storytelling in Israel's educational program has an inherently mnemonic function. Thus, the parents' retelling of the stories is more akin to anamnesis than creedal recitation.

The only issue left in this section is one that we have already addressed in the last chapter: the substance of Israel's storytelling. I review the key points here and tie them into the present text. I argued for five main aspects of memory: patriarchal promises, promised land, exodus, Horeb, and the wilderness. Each plays a particular role in demarcating Israel's identity and motivating obedience to Yahweh; and they all interlock to form a sophisticated mnemonic matrix. What we observe in Deut 6:20–25, then, is the distillation of that matrix. Consider the following: verse 22 evokes the exodus, the foundational event which serves to motivate obedience out of gratitude and obligation; verse 23 evokes ideas of both the patriarchal promises and the promised land, the integrating bookends to Israel's memory, tying together its constituent pieces; verse 24 then weaves the law into the above elements, implicitly evoking Mount Horeb;[124] and verse 24 further links the laws of Horeb with Israel's taking and keeping the land, thus interweaving another type of motivation for obedience. As such, it appears that even in its distilled form, the integrity of Israel's memory remains intact. We should note something implicit in the present text: the distillation is representative, not exhaustive. In line with the creedal view, the substance of the parents' storytelling in verses 20–25 is part of larger and relatively fixed constellation of key memories. So when they are told to recall this for their children, the telling can range from the sparse version in Deut 6:20–25 up to larger versions of the stories contained in Deuteronomy proper.[125] Whatever the version, it would appear that the visual aspect of the recollection is important, for verse 22 invokes the "eyes" motif discussed previously. Thus, the storytelling in verses 20–25 serves "als Grundmodell religiöses Sozialisation," that is, as the foundation of Israel's family catechism.[126]

STORYTELLING IN DEUTERONOMY'S MEMORY-MAKING

What, then, is the particular role of story as a memory vector? While the strength of the *habitus* of Deut 6:6–9 is that it vectors memory in a unique embodied way, story is different. Eviatar Zerubavel expresses well the key role of story when he says that social storytelling "transform[s] essentially unstructured series of events into seemingly coherent *historical narratives*."[127] He aptly labels this as the process of "emplotment,"[128] through which key images, ideas, and concepts are woven together into a particular "sociomental topography," that is, a mnemonic mindscape.[129] What this means is that storytelling is the central organizing force that allows the coherent whole of Israel's memory, as articulated last chapter, to pass from one generation to the next. While other vectors engrain things more narrowly, such as an abstract idea (*habitus* and the *Shema*) or particular moments (Passover and Israel's leaving from Egypt), story engrains things as an integrated and fully functioning identity.[130]

Having discussed the contours of Israel's memory at length in the last chapter, here we review the key contours as they relate to the aforementioned roles of storytelling: as a *Deutehorizont* and as a medium of identification.

As a medium of identification, story engrains in the Israelites the complex and calibrated matrix of semantic and episodic memory necessary for self-understanding. Semantically, it causes Israel to see itself as rooted in the patriarchal promises and aiming toward life in the promised land.[131] Episodically, it causes the people to see themselves in some sense as participants in the events of the exodus, Mount Horeb, and the wilderness.[132] It is important to pause here to note the central role of story in inculcating visual memory. While other vectors play a part in this, it is primarily through story that the visual features of the episodes, which I highlighted last chapter, pass into the minds of individuals. As such, storytelling also stands at the center of the key dynamic of "imagination conflation," that is, the portal between collective and individual memory. In addition to these aspects, story also serves to engrain the necessary "dialectic negation." We recall that this is the tension undergirding the episodes: by envisaging itself as part of the events, Israel is to identify with the redemption, revelation, and provision of the exodus generation, while seeing itself as called to learn from—and eschew—its failures. Thus, storytelling is a main way in which the people come to see themselves, to use Millar's language, as perpetually at a moment of decision.

Growing out of this generational identification is storytelling's second mnemonic role as *Deutehorizont*, or interpretive framework. If the previous role serves to engrain the various aspects of the narrative, this one engrains their meaning and significance. By meaning and significance we are referring to how storytelling inculcates in Israel both "why?" and "so what?" information: it exposits why certain events are central and what they mean for covenantal life. While variegated in form and content, the three key episodes typically serve to motivate some kind of obedience to Yahweh. The exodus, as Finsterbusch points out, shows that the call to absolute devotion to Yahweh, concretized in the Torah, is born not out of abstraction but out of the reality of Israel's redemption. Through story, then, Israel also absorbs the affective aspects, perceiving itself as obliged to Yahweh due to his benevolence. Mount Horeb then explains the reason for the unique, aniconic nature of Israel's worship, which reflects the nature of the original revelation. It motivates not only through explanation but also through the warning of the consequences of disobedience: judgment and dissolution of the covenant. Serving somewhat differently, the wilderness represents not so much a defining moment as a defining time, typifying the character of Yahweh as long-suffering father and of Israel as the petulant, rebellious child. What it serves to explain, then, is the nature of the covenant relationship, assuring Israel of Yahweh's enduring love but also warning of the consequences of disobedience. Finally, story roots the significance of these episodes in Israel's future in the promised land. If it heeds these, then it will flourish; if it does not, it will suffer punishment and, ultimately, expulsion from the land.

How, then, should we envisage storytelling functioning in Israel? In light of our discussion of Deut 6:20–25, it seems the primary retrieval mechanism for Israel's story is the domestic *habitus*. The text portrays that children, by practicing the *habitus*, will naturally come to ask about the significance of the covenant commands. Whether this means that the questioning is a formalized part of the practice is not clear. But, per Finsterbusch, the close connection between storytelling and *habitus* indicates that these were seen as complementary pieces of the same process. As such, the vectoring of memory through story reflects the same makers and consumers as *habitus*: parents and children, respectively. The natural reading of this is that children would ask their parents the question and the parents would respond with Israel's story. But it is not impossible that the children would, in turn, be asked to repeat the story themselves, perhaps like the firstfruits in Deut 26.

We should note something else about the nature of story's encoding. While there are distilled and expanded versions of Israel's defining story, and even some variety in its contours, the pattern is generally stable. This is why scholars have often thought of it as a creed. The importance of such a set pattern should not be overlooked, for it plays an important role in what we previously called "deep" encoding. For one thing, it makes the story more memorable. The pattern not only allows children to absorb the details quickly but also to access and retrieve them more readily. For another thing, the fact that story serves in an explanatory role means that it causes deeper encoding for both itself and for the things that it exposits (Torah obedience). The same is true for the way in which storytelling serves as a carrier for visual images and affective elements. As a memory vector, therefore, story's power resides in its ability to transmit not isolated abstractions or events, but complete plotlines interwoven with ideas and images. Through story, children come to see themselves as part of the ancient plotline and begin to share in its privileges and obligations: "Stories are the secret reservoir of values: change the stories individuals or nations live by and tell themselves, and you change the individuals and nation."[133]

NOTES

1. Deuteronomy 6:6–9 is very similar to 11:18–21. We shall discuss the important differences below. According to some, the exhortation beginning in 6:4–9 then closes with the parallel passage in 11:18–21 (Moshe Weinfeld, *Deuteronomy 1–11: A New Translation with Introduction and Commentary* (New York: Doubleday, 1991), 448; Georg Braulik, "Deuteronomy and the Commemorative Culture," in *The Theology of Deuteronomy*, trans. Ulrika Lindblad [North Richland Hills, TX: BiBAL Press, 1994], 190–91.

2. J. G. McConville, *Deuteronomy* (Westmont, IL: InterVarsity Press, 2002), 138. See Norbert Lohfink, *Das Hauptgebot* (Rome: Pontifical Biblical Institute, 1963), 290–91. Moshe Weinfeld has highlighted Deuteronomy's tendency to extend the sacral beyond the priesthood and into the nation, calling it "secularization" (*Deuteronomy and the Deuteronomic School* [Oxford: Clarendon Press, 1972], 227–28). However, Nathan MacDonald is right to say that "secularization" actually obscures said dynamic (*Deuteronomy and the Meaning of "Monotheism"* [Tübingen: Mohr Siebeck, 2003], 133).

3. It should be noted, though, that some see these domestic practices, with their assumption of literacy, as evidence of a utopian bent. The most recent argument is by Kåre Berge, "Literacy, Utopia, and Memory: Is There a Public Teaching in Deuteronomy?," *Journal of Hebrew Scriptures* 12 (2012): 1–19.

4. MacDonald, *Monotheism*, 125. MacDonald also points out that the question cannot be answered from history. Since the Talmud, Jews have put into *tefillin* (also called phylacteries: capsules worn on the forehead and left arm during prayer) Exod 13:1–10, 11–16, Deut 6:4–9, and 11:13–21 and into *mezuzot* (capsules put on doorposts) Deut 6:4–9 and 11:13–21. The logic is that these passages contain the instructions for *tefillin* and *mezuzot*. At Qumran, however, the *tefillin* contained different texts, such as the Decalogue, and the Samaritans placed in *mezuzot* the Decalogue or even just Deut 6:4.

5. Deuteronomy 1:1; 4:2; 13:1. See esp. Georg Braulik, "Die Ausdrücke für 'Gesetz' in Buch Deuteronomium," *Biblica* 51 (1970): 39–66, who is followed by Georg Fischer and Norbert Lohfink, "'Diese Worte sollst du summen': Dtn 6, 7 w^{e}dibbarta bam—ein verlorener Schlüssel zur meditativen Kultur in Israel," *Theologie und Philosophie* 62 (1987): 59–72. See Jean-Pierre Sonnet, *The Book Within the Book* (Leiden: Brill, 1997), 51–58; Duane Christensen, *Deuteronomy 1–11* (Nashville, TN: Thomas Nelson, 2001), 144; Jeffrey H. Tigay, *Deuteronomy* (Philadelphia: Jewish Publication Society), 68.

6. 4:10, 13, 36; 5:5, 22; 9:10; 10:2, 4.

7. Deut 12:28; 15:15; 24:18, 22.

8. MacDonald, *Monotheism*, 127. We note, too, that MacDonald (p. 126) points out a flaw in Braulik's argument on למד (Braulik, "Deuteronomy and the Commemorative Culture in Israel," 183–98. According to Braulik (p. 187) למד, which appears in the parallel passage of 11:18, only occurs in reference to the entire Mosaic law. MacDonald shows, however, that למד occurs in Deut 31:19, 22, referring only to the Song of Moses.

9. MacDonald, *Monotheism*, 125.

10. MacDonald, *Monotheism*. As MacDonald himself notes, others have also forwarded the *Shema* as the object of "these words," albeit without very much justification. For example, see Samuel Rolles Driver, *A Critical and Exegetical Commentary on Deuteronomy*, 2nd ed. (Edinburgh: T. & T. Clark, 1896), 92, and Weinfeld, *Deuteronomy*, 340.

11. MacDonald, *Monotheism*, 128, quoting Driver, *Deuteronomy*, 92.

12. MacDonald, *Monotheism*, 124–25. Formatting has been modified.

13. MacDonald, *Monotheism*, 128–29.

14. See also Johannes de Moor, "Poetic Fragments in Deuteronomy and the Deuteronomic History," in *Studies in Deuteronomy in Honour of C. J. Labuschagne on the Occasion of His 65th Birthday*, ed. F. García Martínez et al. (Leiden: Brill, 1994), 190–91.

15. על־לבב: Deut 6:6; 11:18; Jer 51:50; Ezek 38:10; Nah 2:7; 2 Chr 32:6. על־לב: Gen 34:3; 50:21; Judg 19:3; 1 Sam 1:13; 2 Sam 19:7; 2 Kings 12:4; Isa 40:2; 42:25; 46:8; 47:7; 57:1; 57:11; 65:17; Jer 3:16; 7:31; 12:11; 19:5; 31:33; 32:35; 44:21; Ezek 14:3; Hosea 2:14; Mal 2:2; Prov 6:21; 25:20; Ruth 2:13; Dan 1:8; 2 Chr 7:11; 30:32.

16. See Yehudah Cohn, *Tangled Up in Text* (Providence, RI: Brown University, 2008), 46.

17. For Egyptian: Othmar Keel, "Zeichen der Verbundenheit: Zur Vorgeschichte und Bedeutung der Forderungen von Dt 6,8f und par," in *Mélanges Dominique Barthèlémy*, ed. Pierre Casetti, Othmar Keel, and Adrian Schenker (Göttingen: Vandenhoeck and Ruprecht, 1981), 213–14; B. Couroyer, "La Tablette du Coeur," *Revue Biblique* 90 (1983): 416–34; Nili Shupak, "Learning Methods in Ancient Israel," *Vetus Testamentum* 53 (2003): 416–26. For Assyrian: Weinfeld, *Deuteronomy*, 340.

18. MacDonald suggests that this may be indicated by the way in which Deut 11:18 speaks of placing them on the "heart" and "throat" (נפש) (*Monotheism*, 129).

19. For discussion of the amulets in relation to Deut 6:6–9 and 11:18–21, see Cohn, *Tangled Up*, 49–50.

20. See André Lemaire, "Deuteronomy 6:6, 9 in the Light of Northwest Semitic Inscriptions," in *Birkat Shalom*, vol. 1, ed. Chaim Cohen et al. (University Park, PA: Eisenbrauns, 2008), 525–30.

21. Lemaire, "Semitic Inscriptions," 526–27. An important difference is that at least one of these contains an image on the opposite side of the writing, while those from *Ketef Hinnom* do not.

22. Lemaire, "Semitic Inscriptions," 526 (emphasis mine). This was originally brought to light by A. R. Millard ("Some Aramaic Epigraphs," *Iraq* 34 [1972]: 131–37) but has since been retranslated by Frederick Fales, *Aramaic Epigraphs on Clay Tablets of the Neo-Assyrian Period* (Rome: La Sapienza, 1986), 222–24, n. 45.

23. Lemaire, "Semitic Inscriptions," 527.

24. MacDonald, *Monotheism*, 129.

25. Ludwig Koehler and Walter Baumgartner, "שנן I," *The Hebrew and Aramaic Lexicon of the Old Testament*, vol. 2, study ed., trans. and ed. M. E. J. Richardson (Leiden: Brill, 2001), 1606.

26. Christensen, *Deuteronomy*, 144.

27. MacDonald, *Monotheism*, 129.

28. Tigay, *Deuteronomy*, 358–59, n. 25; Peter Craigie, *The Book of Deuteronomy* (Grand Rapids, MI: Eerdmans, 1976), 170, n. 17. Also, see Koehler and Baumgartner, "שנן II," 1606–7, *Hebrew Lexicon*, vol. 2; Godfrey Rolles Driver, *Canaanite Myths and Legends*, repr. (Edinburgh: T. & T. Clark, 1956), 151.

29. Koehler and Baumgartner, "שנן II," *Hebrew Lexicon*, vol. 2, 1606–7; "שנה II," 1598–99. This is also witnessed to by *Targum Onkelos* and the Peshitta.

30. McConville, *Deuteronomy*, 142; Tigay, *Deuteronomy*, 78; Christensen, *Deuteronomy*, 144; Craigie, *Deuteronomy*, 170. Interestingly, writing for the JPS

commentary series Tigay inherits the translation "recite," which he attempts to explain away.

31. Fischer and Lohfink, "Diese Worte."
32. MacDonald, *Monotheism*, 129–30; Also, Weinfeld, *Deuteronomy*, 341.
33. MacDonald, *Monotheism*, 130.
34. Eep Talstra, "Texts for Recitation: Deuteronomy 6:7; 11:19," in *Unless Someone Guide Me* . . ., ed. J. W. Dyk (Maastricht: Shaker Publishing, 2001) 67–76. What he finds is that in cases in which ב serves as the complement of דבר, such as in Deut 6:7, there are a few possible functions, two of which are pertinent here: "person" and "means of communication". When the complement is a person, the speech can in fact be *about* (or against) the individual (e.g., Ezek 33:30); but when the complement is a means of communication—for example, words, text, vision, dream—its function is instrumental: "to speak by means of." Deut 6:7 would fit into this latter category.
35. Karin Finsterbusch, *Weisung für Israel: Studien zu religiösem Lehren und Lernen im Deuteronomium und in seinem Umfeld* (Tubingen: Mohr Siebeck, 2005), 246.
36. Finsterbusch, *Weisung*, 247.
37. Finsterbusch, *Weisung*, 246.
38. Finsterbusch, *Weisung*, 245.
39. Finsterbusch, *Weisung*, 245.
40. Fischer and Lohfink, "Diese Worte." This view, she says, stems largely from Fischer and Lohfink's dividing between the two instructions in Deut 6:7a.
41. Finsterbusch, *Weisung*, 245–46.
42. Talstra, "Texts," 75.
43. Finsterbusch, *Weisung*, 247.
44. Finsterbusch, *Weisung*, 247.
45. MacDonald, *Monotheism*, 130.
46. See Weinfeld, *Deuteronomy*, 333; *The Deuteronomic School*, 299–300; Christensen, *Deuteronomy*, 144; Mayes, *Deuteronomy*, 177.
47. Although, some do see it as literal. See Brevard Childs, *Exodus* (London: Westminster Press, 1974), 203; Umberto Cassuto, *Exodus*, trans. Israel Abrahams (Jerusalem: Magnes Press, 1967), 152–53; and Terence Fretheim, *Exodus* (Louisville, KY: John Knox Press, 1991), 147–48. One wonders if this has more to do with the tradition of phylacteries than the context of this passage.
48. Prov 1:8–9; 3:3, 21–22; 6:20–23; 7:1–3.
49. MacDonald rightly notes that "where abstract qualities are to be bound to the body, a metaphorical interpretation must be envisaged" (*Monotheism*, 131).
50. For these two, see Driver, *Deuteronomy*, 92–93, and McConville, *Deuteronomy*, 142, who follows Driver on this.
51. McConville, *Deuteronomy*, 142.
52. MacDonald, *Monotheism*, 131–32.
53. Of course, the exact meaning of טטפת, the object between the eyes, is unclear (see also Exod 13:16; Deut 11:18; Exod 13:9 uses זכרון in place of טטפת). In his article, Jeffrey H. Tigay outlines just how long and varied the understanding of the word's etymology and meaning has been ("On the Meaning of *T(W)TPT*," *Journal of Biblical*

Literature 101 [1982]: 321–23). Contemporary translations, he notes, highlight the various opinions: "frontlets" (RSV), "phylactery" (NEB), "circlet" (JB), "pendant" (NAB), and "symbol" (NJV). The versions betray a similar lack of clarity and resultant diversity of opinion. For his part, Tigay argues the word should be understood as a singular segholate (contra MT pointing) related to a root meaning "to encircle, encompass." Building on this, he argues the notion of an encircling item fits well with Egyptian/Assyrian depictions of the headbands worn by Syrian goddesses. The view that טטפת depicts some kind of an encircling object worn on the head is perhaps most common (Cohn, *Tangled Up*, 38), though it is widely acknowledged that there is still much ambiguity surrounding the word (see Cohn's translation of Weinfeld's Hebrew quote, p. 38, n. 37).

54. Keel, "Zeichen," 212–15; 193–211.
55. MacDonald, *Monotheism*, 132.
56. The use of ל in Isaiah is a common way of showing ownership, but the function may be in view for the ת in Ezekiel. See Daniel Block, *The Book of Ezekiel*, vol. 1 (Grand Rapids: Eerdmans, 1997), 307.
57. MacDonald, *Monotheism*, 132; Lemaire, "Semitic Inscriptions"; David Carr, *Writing on the Tablet of the Heart* (Oxford: Oxford University Press, 2005), 5.
58. MacDonald, *Monotheism*, 132–33.
59. Of course, we also have the *mezuzot*, which in Judaism are small cases attached to doorways that contain parchment with the words of Deut 6:4–9 and 11:13–21 (though in the Samaritan tradition the *mezuzot* were tablets on which the words were inscribed). The reason we do not include this as evidence is because, while reaching back to Qumran, it is difficult to forward this as evidence for biblical Israel.
60. MacDonald, *Monotheism*, 132–33; Keel, "Zeichen," 183–92. MacDonald suggests that the movement from writing on temple doorways and on Aaron's garments, which represent the priestly sphere, to that of the houses/gates and common Israelites, representing the domestic sphere, may reflect Deuteronomy's extension of the sacral to the larger nation.
61. 1 Sam 1:9; 2 Chr 23:19; Pss 15 and 24.
62. Lemaire, "Semitic Inscriptions," 528–29.
63. For more on this, see Ze'ev Meshel, "Kuntillet 'Ajrud," in the *Anchor Bible Dictionary*, vol. 4, ed. David Noel Freedman (New York: Doubleday, 1992), 103–9.
64. Lemaire, "Semitic Inscriptions," 528.
65. Lemaire, "Semitic Inscriptions," 528–29.
66. Lemaire strengthens this idea by comparing it to silver amulets inscribed with Phoenician from the sixth century, which also dedicate a house and show similar characteristics. The question remains, though, whether something such as silver, which is surely not intended for frequent unrolling, can be considered part of an education program such as Deuteronomy's. It would instead appear more closely related to internal types of building inscriptions, which are symbolic or protective but not inherently educational. Thus, it is still preferable to see the inscriptions in view in Deuteronomy as visible.
67. Lemaire, "Semitic Inscriptions," 529. For more on the Samaria inscription: Solomon A. Birnbaum, "The Fragment of a Stele," in *The Objects from Samaria*, ed. J. W. Crowfoot et al. (London: Palestine Exploration Fund, 1957), 33–34; Nahman

Avigad, "Samaria (City)," in *New Encyclopedia of the Archaeological Excavations of the Holy Land*, vol. 4, ed. Ephraim Stern (University Park, PA: Eisenbrauns, 1993), 1300–10. For the Tel Dan inscription: Avraham Biran and Joseph Naveh, "An Aramaic Stele Frament from Tel Dan," *Israel Exploration Journal* 43 (1993): 81–88; see also their discussion on the fragments found after the writing of the first article: Avraham Biran and Joseph Naveh, "The Tel Dan Inscription: A New Fragment," *Israel Exploration Journal* 45 (1995): 1–18; Aaron Dembsky, "On Reading Ancient Inscriptions: The Monumental Aramaic Stele Fragment from Tel Dan," *Journal of the Ancient Near Eastern Society* 23 (1995): 29–35; William M. Schniedewind, "Tel Dan Stela: New Light on Aramaic and Jehu's Revolt," *Bulletin of the American Schools of Oriental Research* 302 (1996): 75–90.

68. Lemaire, "Semitic Inscriptions," 528.
69. Lemaire, "Semitic Inscriptions," 528.
70. Lemaire, "Semitic Inscriptions," 528–29.
71. The amulets appear to be copied from a larger, stable text. See Erik Waaler, "A Revised Date for Pentateuchal Texts? Evidence from Ketef Hinnom," *Tyndale Bulletin* 53 (2002): 29–55.
72. Carr, *Writing on the Tablet of the Heart*.
73. Carr, *Writing on the Tablet of the Heart*, 6.
74. Carr, *Writing on the Tablet of the* Heart, 5.
75. Carr, *Writing on the Tablet of the* Heart, 136.
76. MacDonald, *Monotheism*, 132.
77. Craigie, *Deuteronomy*, 171; See also Miller, *Deuteronomy*, 105.
78. Mary McClintock Fulkerson, *Places of Redemption* (Oxford: Oxford University Press, 2007), esp. 42–48.
79. Here she extends Pierre Bourdieux's cultural notion of *habitus* (originally set out in *Outline of a Theory of Practice*, trans. Richard Nice [Cambridge, UK: Cambridge University Press, 1977]) to faith practices.
80. Bourdieux, *Outline of a Theory of Practice*, 42–43.
81. Paul Connerton, *How Societies Remember* (Cambridge, UK: Cambridge University Press, 1989).
82. Connerton, *How Societies Remember*, 72. We shall discuss the idea of memory sedimentation further in our discussion of ritual.
83. Nathan MacDonald, *Not Bread Alone* (Oxford: Oxford University Press, 2008), 96.
84. "*Habitus* signals a range of understanding from the tacit to the explicit" (McClintock Fulkerson, *Places*, 43).
85. McClintock Fulkerson, *Places*, 47.
86. Bourdieux has aptly called this "the internalization of externality and the externalization of internality" (*Theory of Practice*, 72).
87. McClintock Fulkerson, *Places*, 237. For a good discussion of this, see James Smith, *Desiring the Kingdom* (Ada, MI: Baker Academic, 2009).
88. McClintock Fulkerson, *Places*, 46.
89. McClintock Fulkerson, *Places*, 25.
90. McClintock Fulkerson, Places, 39. Here she follows in part the ideas of Alasdair MacIntyre, *After Virtue* (Notre Dame, IN: Notre Dame University Press, 1984).

91. McClintock Fulkerson, *Places*, 43.
92. McClintock Fulkerson, *Places*, 45–47.
93. McClintock Fulkerson, *Places*, 39.
94. Of course, as in any pedagogical task, the parents would have gained from the process too, with the object of their teaching—the *Shema*—becoming more and more engrained in them along the way.
95. Some scholars see the chapter as a chiasm. Tigay's basic structure, which follows the division of the MT, is helpful (*Deuteronomy*, 76):
   A) Educating children: the *Shema* (vv. 4–9)
   B) Warning about forgetting (vv. 10–15)
   B') Exhortation to keep the commands (vv. 16–19)
   A') Educating children: the exodus story (vv. 20–25)
96. See Finsterbusch, *Weisung*, 175–78.
97. It occurs in similar usage only in Deut 4:45 and 6:17.
98. We should note, too, the singular form, עדות, is employed in Exodus to refer to the Decalogue specifically (Exod 31:18; 32:15; 34:29). See Mayes, *Deuteronomy*, 160.
99. Mayes, *Deuteronomy*, 160. See also Barnabas Lindars, "Torah in Deuteronomy," in *Words and Meanings*, ed. P. R. Ackroyd and B. Lindars, repr. (Cambridge, UK: Cambridge University Press, 2009), 127–28. Weinfeld argues that in v. 20 עדות refers to the body of laws and not to the "basic command to keep loyalty" (*Deuteronomy*, 347–48).
100. Braulik, "Die Ausdrücke."
101. See Delbert Hillers, *Covenant* (Baltimore, MD: Johns Hopkins Press, 1969), 160.
102. Braulik, "Commemorative Culture," 185; Norbert Lohfink, "*'D(w)t* im Deuteronomium und in den Königsbüchern," *Biblische Zeitschrift* 35 (1991): 86–93.
103. Tigay, *Deuteronomy*, 82.
104. These questions date back to the Mishnaic times, though different versions existed in the Jerusalem and Babylonian Talmud. Also, Sephardic practice is somewhat different, with the questions being asked by the assembled company and at times including aspects of physical reenactment.
105. Lohfink, *Hauptgebot*, 113.
106. Weinfeld, *Deuteronomic School*, 34.
107. Mayes, *Deuteronomy*, 179. See also J. Alberto Soggin, "Kultätiologische Sagen und Katechese im Hexateuch," *Vetus Testamentum* 10 (1960): 341.
108. E.g., Gottfried Seitz, *Redaktionsgeschichtliche Studien zum Deuteronomium* (Stuttgart: Kohlhammer, 1971), 70; Weinfeld, *Deuteronomy*, 356; Tigay, *Deuteronomy*, 82; Finsterbusch, *Weisung*, 255.
109. Braulik, "Commemorative Culture," 188. It should be noted that Braulik sees vv. 20–25 as originally coming from a later hand than vv. 6–9.
110. Finsterbusch, *Weisung*, 255.
111. Finsterbusch, *Weisung*, 255.
112. One might ask whether this theory runs aground in Deut 11, which does not contain the question-and-answer format found in Deut 6. This problem is only

illusory, however, because ch. 11:2–7 expresses a similar idea although through the language of memory. As has been pointed out, memory and education are interwoven in Deuteronomy.

113. Von Rad, *The Problem of the Hexateuch and Other Essays*, trans E. W. Trueman Dicken (Oliver & Boyd, 1965), 3.

114. In fact, von Rad saw creed as the ancient kernel from which the so-called Hexateuch grew.

115. For example, Craigie, *Deuteronomy*, 174–75; Mayes, *Deuteronomy*, 180; Christensen, *Deuteronomy*, 151; McConville, *Deuteronomy*, 144; Nelson, *Deuteronomy*, 94. Others, however, such as Braulik ("Commemorative Culture," 266, n. 41) and Walter Brueggemann (*Deuteronomy* [Abingdon Press, 2001], 88), appear comfortable with the traditional designation.

116. Craigie, *Deuteronomy*, 175.

117. Aelred Cody, "'Little Historical Creed' or 'Little Historical Anamnesis'?," *Catholic Biblical Quarterly* 68 (2006): 1–10. While Cody's article focuses on Deut 26, much of his argument applies also to Deut 6:21–25.

118. For other important critiques of von Rad's notion of a historical credo, see: James Barr, *Old and New in Interpretation* (New York: Harper & Row, 1966), 65–102 and Hans-Joachim Kraus, *Die biblische Theologie* (Neukirchen-Vluyn: Neukirchener Verlag, 1970), 355–60.

119. Kraus, *Die biblische* Theologie, 5. He develops this idea on pp. 4–6.

120. Kraus, *Die biblische Theologie*, 6–9. It is interesting to note that Cody makes the observation that we made in the last chapter: that too often anamnesis is limited to mnemonic actualization. Says he, "the idea of reactualization is not necessarily included in the concept of anamnesis itself" (p. 4).

121. Cody, "Anamnesis," 6.

122. Cody, "Anamnesis," 6–7.

123. Cody, "Anamnesis," 9.

124. Contra von Rad's classic view. See also Theodore Christiaan Vriezen and Adam Simon van der Woude, *Ancient Israelite and Early Jewish Literature* (Leiden: Brill, 2005), 160.

125. On the idea that in Deuteronomy Moses is portrayed as the storytelling teacher of Israel *par excellence* and therefore the model to be imitated, see esp. Johannes Taschner, *Die Mosereden im Deuteronomium* (Heidelberg: Mohr Siebeck, 2008). Though from a different angle, Taschner forwards an idea similar to Cody's: that storytelling is a primary conduit through which remembrance should shape the community (338–39). While this idea is generally accepted, it should be noted that Taschner's work as a whole has come under strong critique. See reviews by Dominik Markl, *Review of Biblical Literature* 4 (2009) and Eckart Otto, *Zeitschrift für Altorientalische und Biblische Rechtsgeschichte* 14 (2008): 463–74.

126. Hans Jürgen Fraas, "Gemeinschaft-Geschichte-Persönlichkeit: Dtn 6, 20 als Grundmodell religiöses Sozialisation," in *Von Wittenberg nach Memphis*, ed. Walter Homolka and Otto Ziegelmeier (Vandenhoeck & Ruprecht, 1989), 21–37.

127. Zerubavel, *Time Maps* (Chicago, IL: University of Chicago Press, 2003), 13. See also his earlier work, *Social Mindscapes* (Cambridge, MA: Harvard University

Press, 1997), which deals more with the interface of cognitive and social structures. *Time Maps*, 13.

128. Another excellent study on this is David Pillemer, *Momentous Events, Vivid Memories* (Cambridge, MA: Harvard University Press, 1998).

129. Zerubavel, *Time Maps*, 7, 13.

130. As we shall see later, the Song of Moses overlaps somewhat with story in this sense, for it has a narratival structure.

131. This demarcating of time is what Zerubavel discusses as "staccato" and "legato" time (*Time Maps*, 34). Staccato time establishes differentiation in eras. It is what causes the promises and the land to be seen as generations distinct from that of the exodus. Legato time, then, establishes continuity. Because of it, the different events of the exodus, Mt. Horeb, and the wilderness are depicted as part of one era, that of the exodus generation.

132. Zerubavel calls this "mental bridging" (*Time Maps*, 40).

133. Ben Okri, *Birds of Heaven* (London: Phoenix, 1996), 21.

Chapter 6

Sedimenting Memory

Ritual as Memory Vector

The second memory vector, ritual, occupies a unique place in Deuteronomy's memory-making program. I shall especially focus on Deut 16:1–17, which contains Israel's annual festival calendar[1] outlining the celebration of the three pilgrimage feasts: Passover-Unleavened Bread (vv. 1–8), Weeks (vv. 9–12), and Booths (vv. 13–15). While other books of the Pentateuch contain these feasts as well, Deuteronomy is unique in one key way: it weaves these rites into a single commemorative fabric, making Israel's calendar into a yearlong commemoration of the exodus pilgrimage. As such, the text provides an important resource for understanding Deuteronomy's use of ritual in memory making.[2] We shall take the festivals in turn, first analyzing them exegetically and then considering them as memory vectors.

RITUAL: DEUTERONOMY 16:1–17

The discussion on Deut 16:1–17 has chiefly revolved around its relationship to the other Pentateuchal accounts of the festivals.[3] Those found in Exodus have served as a primary backdrop in this comparison,[4] with the Covenant Code (CC) in Exod 20–23 (23:14–19) being what many scholars see as the central *Vorlage* for Deuteronomy's festival calendar.[5] Arising from this, then, is the question not only of how Deut 16:1–17 differs from its source(s) but also why this is so. One common way of answering the why question has been to root the differences in the growth of the text.[6] In this view, "the text achieves its form as the result of prior cultic or tradition history."[7] However, the problem with such an approach, as Bernard Levinson points out, is that it understands the distinctives of Deuteronomy as a result of "merely playing catch-up, bringing law into conformity with existing practice."[8] Levinson himself has forwarded an alternative, and now widely accepted,[9] approach. It holds that the reason for the shape of Deuteronomy's festive calendar is to be found in its purpose: to innovate the CC to fit the theology and needs of Deuteronomy, namely the centralization of worship.

While Levinson's approach is quite helpful, a couple of its tenets give pause. First, Karl Weyde has shown that it is not necessary to restrict Deuteronomy's source to the CC (and Exod 13:3–10).[10] Rather, he argues it is tenable to see Exod 34:18–26 (and even Exod 12) as an important piece of Deut 16's *Vorlagen*. And second, it is perhaps best not to understand Deuteronomy's legal innovation as revolutionary, as a *replacement* of the CC.[11] Neither is it necessary to go to the other pole and cast it merely as legal supplementation.[12] A more middling road seems preferable, such as is expressed by Peter Altmann:[13]

> The DC [Deuteronomic Code] reformulates the CC not only to reaffirm it, but it also attempts to redefine what it means to act as or to be "Israel," and the DC incorporates rhetoric about ritual in order to envision this change.[14]

Altmann goes on to articulate the role of Deut 16's festive calendar in this redefining. Deut 16:1–17, he argues, is a "textual complex"[15] narrativized in such a way so as to create in Israel a spatial and temporal sense of the "exodus pilgrimage."[16] The festivals move participants from their homes to the chosen place and back on a calendrical rhythm, paralleled by the remembrance of Israel's movement from Egypt to the promised land. In so doing, the festivals perpetuate in Israel a distinctively Deuteronomic identity.

The Feast of Passover-Unleavened Bread

When it comes to Deuteronomy's presentation of this feast, the main interpretive issue revolves around the book's blending of Passover (פסח) and Unleavened Bread (מצות). The fact that these are not found clearly united elsewhere in (assumed) older Pentateuchal material has led to the conclusion that they were originally separate; and that, as such, what we find here in Deut 16 is the unification of those historically distinct entities.[17] Whether this is the necessary conclusion from the text "is not wholly clear,"[18] but what is clear is that Deuteronomy presents a distinctive portrait of their relationship. Levinson offers perhaps the most widely accepted view on this, so I use him as my main discussion partner and bring in other scholars as necessary.

Levinson calls the blending a "double transformation of Passover and Unleavened Bread."[19] By this he means that Deuteronomy carefully transforms each festival to fit the prescriptions of Deut 12, namely, the centralization of worship at the chosen place. In so doing, Deuteronomy essentially reverses key elements of each observance. Unleavened Bread, previously called a pilgrimage festival (חג) and assumed to have been performed at local sanctuaries, is reduced to a non-cultic ("secular") practice observed only in the home. Passover, conversely, is transformed from a domestic apotropaic rite to a sacrifice practiced only at the chosen place.[20]

An important aspect of Levinson's argument is the idea that Deuteronomy accomplishes the transformation by carefully redeploying lemmas.[21] In this view lemmas, or key words, originally associated with one feast are applied to the other. The aim is to shift the conceptual freight between the feasts, so as to present a thoroughly intertwined and revised version as subtly as possible. Deut 16:1–2 begins this with its use of the lemmas "observe" (שמר) and "month of Abib." Consider it alongside Exod 23:15 (emphasis added):

The Festival of *Unleavened Bread* you shall *observe* in the *month of Abib.* (Exod 23:15)

Observe the *month of Abib* and offer the *Passover* unto Yahweh your God; for in the *month of Abib* Jehovah thy God brought thee forth out of Egypt by night. You shall sacrifice the *Passover.* . . . (Deut 16:1–2)

The most obvious difference is that Exod 23:15 uses the terms for Unleavened Bread, while Deut 16:1–2 does so for Passover. But Levinson argues that, upon closer inspection, Deuteronomy betrays something further: the aim to evoke the idea of Unleavened Bread in order to invest it in Passover.[22] For him this is evidenced especially in the structuring of these verses. Twice the so-called "Unleavened Bread" framing is followed directly by a reference to Passover.[23] Further, Deuteronomy tweaks the terms, so to put them in places of emphasis and draw attention to the idea of Unleavened Bread.[24] The significance of this, according to Levinson, is that by beginning its festive calendar with language that evokes the idea of Unleavened Bread—a חג—but only mentioning Passover, Deuteronomy accomplishes two things. First, it conceptually blends Unleavened Bread and Passover. And second, without ever mentioning the term, it frames Passover as if it were a חג.[25] Levinson therefore argues that the resulting portrait, which we shall discuss more, casts Unleavened Bread as a local (non-pilgrimage) festival and Passover as a חג to the central sanctuary. But while Levinson's use of lemmas is helpful, his conclusion on Unleavened Bread seems problematic. He deduces from Deut 16:1–8 that Unleavened Bread is "to be celebrated locally, with the original pilgrimage element entirely voided."[26] A pale image of its former self (Exod 23:17), the practice is thus relegated to a "weeklong local observance distinguished only by its unleavened diet and by its final assembly and work stoppage."[27] For him this transformation is so extreme that, in Deuteronomy, "Unleavened

Bread becomes nearly an antipilgrimage festival."²⁸ Weyde, however, forwards some convincing objections against this.²⁹ For one thing, he points out that if Unleavened Bread is not to be conceived of as a pilgrimage festival, then it is odd that in Deut 16:16 we find חג המצות. Indeed, "it is strange that the assumed legislator retained the old name if he intended to substitute passover [sic] for the *massot* festival as a pilgrimage festival."³⁰ McConville says much the same, suggesting that the kind of innovator envisaged by Levinson likely would have renamed the feast something more appropriate like "the feast of the Passover."³¹ So while Weyde agrees that the designation חג המצות in verse 16 includes the Passover, he argues that it must also denote the most obvious reference of its name: Unleavened Bread.

Another aspect that Weyde draws attention to is the curious mention of "tents" (אהל) in Deut 16:7b. After the command to sacrifice, boil, and consume the Passover at the chosen place at sunset, it says, "then in the morning return to your tents." This is a well-known interpretive issue, with two traditional options. One interpretive option, which Levinson follows, is that the "tents" refer to the people's homes.³² In this view, the pilgrims travel to the chosen place to sacrifice the Passover and then return to their homes to celebrate Unleavened Bread and the final "solemn assembly." The problem, however, is that elsewhere in Deuteronomy אהל refers to temporary dwellings,³³ not permanent ones, for which "house" (בית) is used.³⁴ The other traditional option, which Weyde follows, is that "tents" refers to the camps erected around the chosen place. In this view, the command envisages the people's return to their temporary dwellings for the duration of Unleavened Bread, appearing back at the sanctuary for the solemn assembly. Weyde concludes thus: Unleavened Bread "had pilgrimage status . . . but the participants were not under the obligation to remain at the sanctuary throughout the seven days it lasted; only on the seventh day such presence was required."³⁵

Although Weyde's construal makes sense of Unleavened Bread as a pilgrimage feast, there are still unresolved issues. For one thing, the reason for the people's leaving the sanctuary after the first day is not transparent. And further, the concluding "solemn assembly" (עצרת) (Deut 16:8), rather than a "feast unto the Lord" (חג ליהוה) (Exod 13:6), "suggests that Deuteronomy envisages the people in their own local settings and not at the sanctuary."³⁶ Two scholars in particular have offered explanations here. McConville suggests that the command intentionally echoes Deut 5:30, which recounts the Israelites' witnessing of the Horeb revelation and the Lord's subsequent command for them to "return to your tents."³⁷ In his understanding, Deut 5:30 juxtaposes Horeb and the people's tents in order to represent the relationship between Yahweh's presence/revelation and everyday life. Because Deut 16:7 echoes this, it evokes a "structural parallel": like Horeb, the chosen place represents gathering before Yahweh; and like the wilderness setting, the festive return to tents represents the "extension of the worship life of Israel into the land."[38] In this view, then, the referent of "tents" is purposely ambiguous, for the real point is what it symbolizes. Although McConville's is a viable possibility,[39] it does not in my opinion offer the most satisfying resolution of the issues.[40]

Another possibility has been forwarded by MacDonald. Like McConville, MacDonald sees "tents" as an intentional echo of previous images and ideas. But while McConville roots it in the juxtaposition of Horeb and regular life, MacDonald ties it into the wilderness motif.[41] Thus conceived, the command to "return to your tents" is meant to establish a practice that parallels Israel's wilderness experience. "In common with their ancestors the celebrating Israelites leave the Passover and move immediately into an existence of living in tents."[42] Though he does not expound it, MacDonald seems to envisage the "solemn assembly" occurring then in the camps around the city and not at the sanctuary (thus the use of תרצע instead of חג).

If this is true, the view offers a helpful nuancing of Weyde's position. Indeed, both Passover and Unleavened Bread are to be understood as pilgrimage festivals; but while Passover occurs at the sanctuary, Unleavened Bread—including its "solemn assembly"—takes place in the tent camps around the city. There are other advantages to MacDonald's view as well. First, this understanding of "tents" resonates with Deuteronomy's larger usage of the term, which typically portrays tent living as part of the wilderness experience. And second, it aligns well with the "central role" that Deuteronomy assigns feasts "in Israel's recollecting of the past."[43] It shows, in particular, that the historical symbolism of Passover–Unleavened Bread extends beyond the eating of certain foods. Interestingly, Koch suggests that "tent" at times serves as a formal solemn expression.[44] One such case, he says, is when worshippers depart from the cult for their tents, à la Deut 16:7.[45] If this can be maintained, it illumines how the term "tents" fits within and supports the emotive theme of Passover-Unleavened Bread: by adding solemnity. We shall discuss shortly just how important this theme is mnemonically.

Having nuanced Levinson's view of the Feast of Unleavened Bread, we return to his discussion of lemmas. In particular, we focus on another issue pertinent to this study: the recasting of the exodus commemoration. Levinson explains that while "[t]he original cultic commemoration of the Exodus is not the Passover but the Festival of Unleavened Bread," Deut 16:1–8 seems to locate the commemoration squarely in the Passover.[46] Again Levinson focuses on particular lemmas to illustrate his point. First, he notes the usage of "by night" (לילה) in reference to the exodus (v. 1): "in the month of Abib he brought you out of Egypt by night."[47] While he recognizes that other texts also place the exodus at night,[48] Levinson argues that the biblical tendency is to portray the exodus in daylight[49] and the Passover at night.[50] This fact, coupled with the text's use of "observe" and "the month of Abib," to Levinson indicates that the night motif is used purposely to complete the merging of the two feasts. So merged, it is the Passover rite, not Unleavened Bread, that commemorates the exodus from Egypt. Levinson goes on to say that this shift is necessary to preserve a place for the Passover which, viewed through his paradigm, would be almost entirely divested of its original features.[51] Though the logic makes sense in his view, I wonder whether it is possible to see another reason for commemorating the exodus with Passover.

And second, Levinson flags up Deuteronomy's use of "appointed time" (מועד). Deut 16:6b says the following: "There you shall sacrifice the Passover in the evening, at the setting of the sun, at the appointed time when you came out from Egypt." Levinson suggests that מועד typically refers to "significant dates within the lunar or solar calendar," a fact borne out, he says, in the biblical accounts that refer to the seven-day period of eating unleavened bread in Abib.[52] What he says is not common is the way in which Deuteronomy uses the term for a specific time of day. Thus, in Deuteronomy we observe that "[w]hat was originally an adverbial phrase to specify the *date* of the Festival of Unleavened Bread becomes recontextualized rather to specify the *hour* of the performance of the Passover slaughter!"[53] Although Levinson may make too much of the contrast between the usages of מועד,[54] his larger point remains valid. Deut 16:6 employs the lemma מועד to root the commemoration of the exodus in the celebration of Passover. Once again, the motivation that Levinson posits, though consistent with his view, is somewhat unsatisfying. He intimates that the use of מועד in verse 6 is merely a byproduct of the night motif from verse 1.[55] It would be surprising for such a deft and subtle reworking to become straightjacketed at this point.

So while Levinson is right that these two lemmas are important in Deuteronomy's recasting of the exodus memory, his view of their significance and function is not completely satisfying. Gesundheit forwards a construal that might provide a better framework for the lemmas. He argues that the governing dynamic in Deut 16:1–8 is the desire to bring both feasts under the unifying theme of the Passover.[56] The aim, then, is not only to integrate Passover and Unleavened Bread uniquely, but also to imbue the substance of the *Vorlagen* (esp. Exod 23:15 and 34:18), which focus on Unleavened Bread, with a distinctively Passover flavor. This contrasts Levinson's views in a couple of important ways. First, it sees the process as one of enrichment, with Passover enriching Unleavened Bread. Levinson's view, we remember, portrays the act as one that occurs at the cost of the rites, with each leaching the other's distinctives in order to become unified. Second, and central to the mnemonic aspect, it sees the lemmas as employed in the service of supporting the Passover theme. At one level, Levinson has a similar understanding, but he focuses on how the lemmas are forced to link the rites in ways that are glaringly tenuous.

How, then, is Gesundheit's view helpful for understanding the exodus commemoration? Beyond offering a better conceptualization for the relationship between Passover and Unleavened Bread in general, it may also illumine the underlying mnemonic intention. Deuteronomy aims to evoke the memory of the exodus, which, I have argued, is a central event undergirding the moral/ ethical fabric of Israel's collective memory. But as we shall see, Deuteronomy also seeks to create through the festive calendar a symbolic annual journey that moves the people from Egypt to the wilderness to the promised land.[57] An important way in which it accomplishes this mnemonic journey is through characterizing the movement not only geographically but also emotively: from sorrow to joy. Thus, the people move from the sorrow of slavery to the joy of the abundant land. If, however, the construction of such a movement is in fact an aim of Deuteronomy,[58] a problem would accompany it: how to cast the mood of the exodus, a benevolent event, as something solemn and even sorrowful. This problem, I suggest, may help explain why Deuteronomy emphasizes Passover in its commemoration of the exodus.

If one views Passover–Unleavened Bread through the need to cast the exodus as solemn, then it helps explain other features, too. Levinson's lemmas, "by night" (לילה) and "appointed time" (מועד), could be seen not only as key words from Exod 23 but also as contributors to mood. It is noteworthy that the imagery in Deut 16:1–8 is nocturnal: the text uses nighttime to characterize the exodus event[59] and, as such, the event is dramatized by ritual at the "appointed time," "in the evening, at the setting of the sun" (v. 6). While rooting the commemoration in the paschal slaughter, and all the notions that accompany it, itself casts a solemn mood, and the emphasis on nighttime seems to contribute further. It may be that the darkness is meant to enact a symbolic topography, a situation in which the dark environment of the rite represents the solemn mood and so evokes a corresponding mood in the participants.[60] Another aspect that may contribute to mood is the term "tents" (v. 7), which we noted often carries solemn overtones. In addition to symbolizing the wilderness, then, it may also serve a subtle role in projecting solemnity. Finally, I highlight the characterization of *mazzot* as "bread of affliction" (לחם עני) eaten in "haste" (חפזון) (16:3).[61] It seems that these modifiers, which drive home the harsh reality of Israel's oppression in Egypt,[62] serve an important role in creating a sense of sorrow.[63] Combined with Passover–Unleavened Bread's express aim to create memory (v. 3),[64] the above features suggest that the feast's shape significantly reflects its aim to establish a dark mood.

The Feast of Weeks

The Feasts of Weeks (16:9–12) and Booths (vv. 13–15) have not attracted near the attention of Passover–Unleavened Bread. This is probably owing to the fact that these two, as they appear in Deut 16, are rather generic in nature.⁶⁵ Such a nature, though, fits well within Deuteronomy's larger distinctives. First, Deuteronomy tends to show a lack of concern for ritual detail and is bent toward the common, "nonspecialist" person.⁶⁶ Not to mention, Deut 16 seems to presuppose a certain amount of knowledge of the festivals. And second, it fits with the book's emphasis on "its theology of grateful response to Yahweh's blessing."⁶⁷ That is to say:

> in the case of the Feasts of Weeks and Booths, the essential aspects of the festivals have been outlined as a framework for the habitual deuteronomic themes of blessing (vv 10, 15, 17), rejoicing (vv 11, 15), kindness to the poor (vv 11, 14), and the contrast of life in the land with Egypt (v 12).⁶⁸

The general nature of the feasts, then, is probably tailored to the larger theological purposes of the festive calendar. We now look at their inclusions and omissions with this in mind.

As for the Feast of Weeks (חג שבעות) (vv. 9–12), it is again instructive to set Deuteronomy's version against those of the other festive calendars, especially Exodus 23.⁶⁹ At the outset we notice that Exod 23:16 calls it the Feast of Harvest (חג הקציר) and does not mention a seven-week period at all.⁷⁰ The difference here may be explained in general by Deuteronomy's focus on centralization. Due to the different regions of the land, which would mean varying dates for harvesting, the centralized feast would need to allow for the readiness of all regions.⁷¹ Seven weeks would accomplish this.⁷² The differences between Exod 23:16 and Deut 16:9 may also be explained rhetorically. We notice, for example, that Deuteronomy carefully structures its expression of the feast's name and timing:⁷³

    Seven weeks (שבעה שבעת)
      Count (ספר)
        Begin (חלל)
        Begin (חלל)
      Count (ספר)
    Seven weeks (שבעה שבעת)

As such, Deut 16:9's language may not be so much (or not exclusively) a rendering of time for centralization as a theological shifting. Weinfeld's views are helpful here: Deuteronomy's rhetoric seeks to preserve the "sacral calendrical reckoning," through using the significant number seven as a framework, while it omits the "sacral exigencies for [that] reckoning."⁷⁴ Weinfeld identifies two "exigencies" in particular: the sheaf-waving ceremony (Firstfruits), marking the beginning of the counting, and the new cereal offering, marking its end.

Of these two omissions, that of Firstfruits is the most conspicuous. Firstfruits is, in all other cases, explicitly connected to the Feast of Weeks.[75] The question, then, is why Deuteronomy treats the Feast of Weeks as independent of Firstfruits, which it expounds later in chapter 26. One way of answering this is again to view it as addressing a practical issue caused by Deuteronomy's centralization. Gesundheit, for instance, argues that the centralizing of worship creates a problem for the farmer who, at a critical time in the harvest season, cannot afford to take a pilgrimage all the way to the chosen place (instead of a local sanctuary).[76] In this view, the rite of Deut 26:1–11 allows for a window of time in which the farmer can come to give his offering. Support for this might be found in the Mishnah Bikhurim, which appears to read it in this way, saying that "the firstfruits could be offered during the whole summer, that is, from the feast of weeks onward."[77] This idea runs aground, however, if one takes Deuteronomy's depiction of Firstfruits as a foundations ceremony, a one-time event upon entering the land, and not as an annual rite.[78]

Another way of explaining the absence of Firstfruits is to view it as a theological move. A good example is that forwarded by McConville.[79] McConville argues that a couple of structural features associated with Firstfruits betray the conceptual importance of its placement. For one thing, Deut 26:1–11 itself is framed in such a way as to highlight a central Deuteronomic idea: "As Yahweh gives the land to Israel, so Israel gives back to him in response."[80] The same framework is found in both Deut 1–11 and 12–26 and, significantly, seems to link the two sections. As such, and this is McConville's second point, the placement of Firstfruits in Deut 26, the conclusion of the legal material, is suggestive. "Chapter 26 seems to have the function of returning to this theme, dwelling on it, and bringing the legal corpus to a climax in doing so."[81] Thus, Firstfruits is pruned from the Feast of Weeks and transplanted into Deut 26 in order to structurally highlight a central theological theme: Israel's response to Yahweh's benevolence is to give back to him.[82] This move does not, however, subtract from the theme's presence in Deuteronomy's Feast of Weeks. As we shall look at now, the feast's unique portrait employs distinctive features to place the theme at center.

Apart from the naming of the feast and its relation to Firstfruits, Deuteronomy's depiction of Weeks differs from Exod 23:16 in four other significant ways: its emphases of the freewill offering, caring for the needy, rejoicing, and remembering. These are all integrally connected to each other and contribute to the aforementioned theme. The "appropriate freewill offering" prescribed by Deut 16:10, in line with its treatment of Firstfruits, differs from that found elsewhere. In the first place, "appropriate" (מסת) is a *hapax legomenon* whose origin is obscure.[83] It seems best, though, to retain the above idea rather than "tribute" or the harmonized "gifts" (מתנה).[84] But the larger idea is unique, too, for Exod 23:16 requires "the firstfruits of your deeds" and Lev 23 the first sheaf of reaping and a male sheep (at the beginning of the season) and two loaves of bread and two male sheep (at the end of the seven weeks). Thus the requirement to offer an "appropriate freewill offering . . . according to Yahweh your God's blessing of you" reflects Deuteronomy's theology of Israel's obedience as its response to Yahweh's benevolence.

Similarly, Deuteronomy includes in the Feast of Weeks the command to share it with those within one's midst, which may be understood in two groups: daughters, maidservants, and manservants; and Levites, aliens, orphans, and widows (16:11). In both cases, Deuteronomy is unique in its depiction. In regard to the first group, the only mention of worshippers in Exod 23 specifies the attendees as men (v. 17).[85] And while it cannot be assumed that women were wholly out of view (1 Sam 1), it serves as a foil to show Deuteronomy's aim even more clearly: to "extend [the feast's] application to all members of the Israelite household, male and female alike."[86] Water Houston notes that this reflects the book's egalitarian view of the feasts, which has the purpose of establishing *communitas* in Israel.[87] In regard to the second group, the *personae miserabiles*,[88] Deuteronomy is again unique. Exodus includes legislation for the poor, but it is not interwoven into the feast; it has the basic command to leave the land lie unused every seven years, "so that the poor among you may get food from it" (23:10). Leviticus likewise stipulates land usage for the good of the needy apart from the feast, requiring farmers to leave the field edges and straggling fruit for the poor to glean (19:9). We observe, as such, that Deuteronomy is distinctive not only in its manner of charity, coming via the feast itself, but also in the substance of its charity.[89] In Exodus and Leviticus, the substance is found in the leftovers of crops and vineyards; in Deuteronomy (in Weeks and Booths, at least), it is presumably in the repasts of the festivals. Thus, Deuteronomy envisages the charity coming not so much through the Israelite's giving as his *sharing*; he and his family were to include the needy in their own feasting. So strong is this humanitarian bent that Weinfeld says this: "one gains the impression that the primary purpose of the festal repasts at the 'chosen place' is to provide nutriment for *personae miserabiles*."[90] In light of Deuteronomy's other provisions for the poor, however, it is probably better to see the humanitarianism here as part of what, in Houston's language, is the goal of establishing *communitas*.[91]

Tied into this is perhaps the most distinctive feature of Deuteronomy's Feast of Weeks: the command to "rejoice" (שׂמח). While joy is associated with the Feast of Booths in other texts (Lev 23:40), it is only here that it appears with Weeks.[92] What, then, is the reason for its presence? A common feature in discussions on this question is what Lohfink articulates thus: the emphasis on joy "indicates that the people had to be talked out of feeling that they had lost something."[93] Implicit here is the idea that the joy command is responding to a historical situation. MacDonald has suggested that perhaps the Assyrian tribute demands deprived the land, and so its feasts, of the precious element of meat.[94] While Houston acknowledges this historical situation, he disagrees with its effects on the feasts.[95] He prefers instead to see the impetus for the joy command coming from the shift in worshipping at local sanctuaries to doing so at the singular chosen place. In his view, then, the command addresses the perceived loss of "local solidarity."[96] Deuteronomy's command to rejoice is in essence a pledge that what was lost in the local gatherings will be replaced with a more global cohesion of *communitas*. Houston's highlighting of *communitas* is insightful, but whether it derives from the proposed situation is uncertain. Braulik also forwards an underlying historical background, though somewhat differently from the others.[97] For him, the use of joy is meant to juxtapose the biblical practice with that found in Canaanite feasts. The latter, he suggests, was rooted in an "orgiastic exultation" characterized by an excess of pagan practices (sex, drunkenness, etc.).[98] Deuteronomy seeks to contrast this, then, by portraying a properly motivated and modulated notion of joy, a fact made apparent by the text's lack of references to eating and drinking. Houston has rightly critiqued Braulik's view, however, arguing that it is based on outdated ideas of Canaanite practices and makes too much out of the text's silence on eating and drinking.[99]

Although historical background cannot be disregarded, the above views evidence the difficulty in identifying a particular situation as the impetus of the joy command. More satisfying is an explanation derived from the text's rhetoric. It is typically understood, rhetorically, that the exhortation to rejoice is tied to Yahweh's provision for Israel. "[T]he joy of the feast arises from gratitude to YHWH for his bounty."[100] Beyond just the bounty of the land, though, the gratitude is rooted in Yahweh's larger work to bring Israel into the land. "Hence the joy demanded by Deuteronomy is gratitude for the success which God granted, for the material prosperity and for the *fulfillment of the meaning of religious existence*."[101] Braulik goes on to say that the bounty of the Feast of Weeks, as such, is meant to inculcate in the Israelites their "special obligation" to Yahweh.[102] We recall that this is an important aspect of Deuteronomy's memory program. MacDonald's aforementioned view, that the calendar symbolizes Israel's move from Egypt to the land, ties the above points together nicely.[103] The emotion of rejoicing fits well with a harvest feast, which would naturally be a joyous affair; but the command to do so, coupled with the festive calendar's symbolic movement, imbues the gifts of the land with the so-called "special obligation." By enjoying the gifts, the Israelites experience the goodness and faithfulness of the giver which, in turn, is meant to renew their affection for him.[104] It is important to remember that in Deuteronomy's festive calendar gratitude does not arise from good gifts alone; it also depends on those gifts being backlit by Israel's life of slavery. That is one of the main functions of the "narrativized" festival calendar:[105] it forever keeps the blessing of the land juxtaposed to life in Egypt, joy juxtaposed to sorrow.

The joy command, then, serves as a fitting transition into the final unique aspect of the Feast of Weeks: memory. Deut 16:12 says, "You shall remember that you were a slave in Egypt and keep and do these statutes." The command is noteworthy for a variety of reasons, not least because "only here is the feast [of Weeks] expressly made a memorial of the deliverance from Egypt."[106] The appearance of the command is, at a superficial level, typical: the vocabulary and syntax reflect Deuteronomy's usual formula.[107] But on closer inspection there are some subtle differences. The formula typically occurs like this: specific command, exhortation to remember, reference to Israel's deliverance, and a return to the initial specific command.[108] Deut 16:12 differs, first, in the specific commands that frame the memory exhortation. Whereas the passage begins with the command to "keep the Feast of Weeks" (v. 10), it concludes with the command to keep and do "these statutes" (האלה החקים) (v. 12). The usage of "these statutes" is odd in its own right, for it usually refers to the totality of the particular laws from Yahweh.[109] This does not appear to be the case in Deut 16:12, however, where the reference is to the covenant obligations more generally.[110] Christensen intimates that the usage may stem from the fact that Weeks and Booths are, in his opinion, structured around one chiasm, whose center pivots on "these statutes."[111] If the outer frame is the joy of Weeks and Booths (vv. 10–11, 15), then it reinforces the idea that covenant loyalty arises from gratitude.

Apart from the usage of "these statutes," attention has been given to the relationship between memory and the treatment of the needy in verses 11–12. The usual view is that here, as elsewhere in Deuteronomy, Israel's memory of Egypt is meant to motivate its good treatment of the less fortunate.[112] However, Childs has argued against this interpretation. He suggests that the dynamic is just the opposite:

> Memory does not serve to arouse a psychological reaction of sympathy for slaves. Rather, quite the reverse is true. Israel observes the [feasts] *in order to* remember her slavery and deliverance. . . . The festival arouses and incites the memory.[113]

He suggests, in fact, that this memory-making emphasis is precisely how Deuteronomy's conception of remembrance differs from that found in Exodus.[114] But while Childs is right to emphasize Deuteronomy's ambition to create memory, he goes too far in juxtaposing it to the treatment of the poor. Indeed, I have argued the creation of memory and the embodiment of its obligations go hand in hand; Deuteronomy portrays them as being in symbiotic relationship. And that is what we observe in Deut 16:11–12: memory undergirds both joy and ethical behavior, even while joy helps engrain memory (more on that later).

There is a second way in which Deut 16:12 differs from the usual formula: it does not mention Yahweh's deliverance of Israel. In other examples, the call to remember is followed by some description of Israel's rescue from Egypt.[115] Deut 5:15, for instance, says, "and the Lord your God brought you out from there with a mighty hand and an outstretched arm." Explicit mention of the deliverance is not necessary to motivate obedience, of course, for it is implicit in the memory command itself.[116] But when it is absent, the question must be asked whether the abbreviated version serves a purpose. This may well be true in the case of Deut 16:12. We recall that the symbolic movement between verses 1–8 and 9–12 is one from the sorrow of Egypt to the joy of the land. If it is true, as Altmann argues, that the author seeks to "narrativize" the festival calendar, then this author has a difficult task in bridging Passover-Unleavened Bread and Weeks adequately. In particular, the author must use his references to Egypt in the Feast of Weeks carefully. If he emphasizes Egypt too much, the movement from Egypt (in Passover) to the land (in Weeks) is obscured. But if he emphasizes it too little, the land is not cast in sharp relief to Egypt and so the characterization of joy is diminished. Perhaps it is to achieve this calibration, therefore, that Weeks has the people remember their slavery without mentioning their deliverance.

The Feast of Booths

As already mentioned, the Feast of Booths in Deut 16:13–15 shares much in common with Weeks, particularly the themes of blessing (vv. 15), rejoicing (vv. 15), and concern for the poor (vv. 14). Further, in viewing the festival calendar as a symbolic movement from Egypt to the land, it is assumed that Weeks and Booths together represent the land.[117] But while this is true, Booths still displays distinctives that, when compared to the other festive calendars, prove instructive. What I seek to do here, then, is highlight important features of Booths that were not covered in our discussion of Weeks.

The first distinctive we notice is that Deut 16:13 uses the name the "Feast of Booths" (חג הסכות), while in Exodus 23:16 it is the "Feast of Ingathering" (חג האסיף).[118] There are also differences between the language surrounding the feast, with Deuteronomy again omitting the timing aspect ("at the end of the year") and drawing attention to the agricultural situation ("after you have gathered from your threshing floor and from your winepress"). While the differences in language are understandable in light of Deuteronomy's tendencies,[119] the matter of the name requires further explanation. One view is that Deuteronomy's use of "booths" reflects a vestigial term from the custom of farmers staying in temporary dwellings in their vineyards, either during the harvest or to celebrate the vintage.[120] Implicit in this is that the Feast of Booths, which celebrates the vintage, had a separate origin from Ingathering, which celebrates the storage of grain.[121] The problem with applying this to Deuteronomy, though, is that the book clearly sees Booths as celebrating both.[122]

Another view is that Deut 16:13 uses "booths" assuming knowledge of Lev 23, which provides a more detailed account.[123] Accordingly, the meaning of "booths" is articulated in Lev 23:42–43: "You shall live in booths for seven days . . . so your descendants will know that I had the Israelites live in booths when I brought them out of Egypt." The usual understanding here is that the Feast of Booths then commemorates the wilderness wandering, during which time the Israelites lived in temporary shelters.[124] As such, it is not only the clearest identification of what "booths" means, but also the most explicit historicizing of the feast in the Pentateuch. If this information can be read into Deuteronomy, then here again the Feast of Booths would commemorate Israel's wilderness experience. The problem with such a view, however, is that it clashes with various points of emphasis that we have already highlighted. Most notably, it would disrupt the very symbolic movement that makes Deuteronomy's festive calendar so unique: the movement from the sorrow of Egypt to the joy of the land. The wilderness would then be commemorated not only in "tents" of 16:7, but also again in 16:13, placing it squarely in a section that is meant to symbolize the land.

What, then, is the significance of the title "Booths"? It is difficult to discern what exactly Deuteronomy knows of an extant feast, but apart from the name there is little to indicate that the text is leaning on such information.[125] This is perhaps most obvious in regard to commemoration. While Leviticus establishes a direct link between the name and the nature of commemoration, Deuteronomy is rather opaque. Booths joins Weeks, it is true, in commemorating the land; but, strictly speaking, the only mention of memory occurs in the description of Weeks. The text still invites us to see Booths as a memory conduit, through its connection to Weeks and, as we shall see shortly, its reading of the Torah in 31:9–13. But in the festal calendar itself, the connection between the term "booths" and remembrance is unclear. It would appear, as such, that we are left with a couple of options. Either the text has no knowledge of a feast akin to that in Leviticus, and so acts out of ignorance, or it has knowledge and purposely avoids making the connection. In either case, one must construct a notion of "booths" according to the information Deuteronomy itself provides.

There is another subtle difference between Booths and Weeks that helps us to do this. The difference can be found in Israel's treatment of the poor.

In Weeks, we recall, the command to include the less privileged is motivated by remembrance of Egypt (v. 12). In Booths, however, the command is followed by something else: "for the Lord your God will bless you in all your harvest and in all the work of your hands" (v. 15). It therefore appears that Booths motivates the command with the blessings of the land and its bounty. Also, Booths ends with "and you shall be joyful indeed," that shows the commensurate response to the totality of blessing. And as we have already said, this should not be viewed as separate from Weeks; together the two celebrate the land. "The Israelite landowner *remembers Egypt from the vantage point of the land* which has yielded the produce with which he can be generous."[126]

The final aspect of Booths meriting mention is the reading of the Torah in Deut 31:9–13. There Moses gives the book of the law to the Levitical priest[127] and elders and commands that it be read before the people every seven years at the Feast of Booths. The purpose of doing so, it seems, is to establish the reading as one of three successors to Moses (the others being Joshua and the Song of Moses).[128] A short while later in verse 26 the song is said to function as a "witness" (עד) to the generations of Israel. For this reason, it is often discussed alongside the song in Deut 32:1–43. But while this is an important part of Deut 31–32's trajectory, I suggest that the notion of witness highlights a different aspect of Torah from 31:9–13. We shall talk more about that in the section on the song. Another comparison drawn is between the writing of the law here to that found in the ceremony at Mounts Ebal and Gerizim (27:1–8).[129] Because I previously argued that this ceremony does not constitute a memory vector, it is worth discussing how the reading of the law differs from it. A couple of features are especially pertinent.

The first feature of note is that Deut 31:9–13 roots the reading of the Torah[130] in the Festival of Booths. Unlike the ceremony in Deut 27, then, this reading is made part of the rhythm of worship, once every seven years (15:1), and thus is established as a central conduit of enculturation in Israel.[131] Deut 31:9–13 also shows thematic affinities with the portrayal of Booths in the festival calendar. Once again there is the language of "appearing before Yahweh" at the "place he will choose" (v. 11). There also seems to be a similar audience: "the men, women, little ones, and your alien who is within your gates" (v. 12). An issue arises here, however, for if this list is taken in the same way, it would run against the ontological distinctions drawn between Israelite and "alien" (גר). Indeed, Deuteronomy goes to great lengths to afford the alien ethical treatment and even enjoyment of the land,[132] which is the sense in the festive calendar. But the book also drives home that there is a categorical difference between Israelite and alien (14:21).[133] Simply said, the difference is that the former is in covenant with Yahweh, the latter is not. So how can the reading of the Torah, the covenant document, prescribe the presence of people outside of the covenant?[134]

Van Houten has proposed a helpful solution. She sees "alien" in Deut 31:12 as akin, though perhaps not identical, to that found in 29:11, which she identifies as the Gibeonites.[135] As such, the alien

> referred to here is not the vulnerable individual or family who came without connections into a strange place, and needed the protection of an Israelite household. Instead, the aliens referred to here are a group of people . . . who have entered into a legal relationship with Israel and hence with Israel's God. They are second-class citizens, being mentioned with the wives and children, and yet they are involved in a legally binding relationship . . . They are obliged to observe the law of Moses because it is the law of the land in which they are residing.[136]

The usage of "alien" in Deut 31:12 is therefore different from that in the festival calendar. The latter ensures that the Israelite farmer, by remembering Egypt, is moved to care for the underprivileged; the former ensures that the Israelites know the history and stipulations of their covenant with Yahweh. Of course, the two of them are not unconnected, for by teaching "all Israel" (v. 11) to "fear" Yahweh (v. 12)[137] the reading of the Torah in that way ensures an ethical treatment of the needy.

The second important feature in this passage is its didactic nature. Some understand the Torah reading here further as part of a covenant renewal ceremony.[138] While the reasons for this are not always explicit, it seems a few may be assumed. To begin with, two key instances of the public reading of the law in Scripture are accompanied by covenant renewals (2 Kgs 23; Neh 8:1—9:37). Each instance, though, is also attended by other circumstances that would make renewal an expected reaction to the reading: the discovery of the book of the covenant and the return from exile, respectively.[139] The reaction in such cases is natural, but it does not make it inherent to the process itself.[140] Other reasons for positing a renewal setting are the resemblance to Hittite vassal treaties and the use of certain concepts and words. The reading of Israel's law, it has been frequently noted, closely resembles the periodic reading of stipulations prescribed in Hittite treaties.[141] In these, the purpose was to remind the vassal of the benevolence of the overlord and his due obligation to the stipulations within the treaty. The command to read Israel's law also includes concepts and words akin to passages about covenant ceremonies: it includes "'assemble the people,' 'hear,' 'learn/teach,' 'fear,' 'words' . . . and imitates the pattern of writing and handing over laws that Yahweh practiced [at Horeb]" (see also Deut 4:10).[142]

But while the above points are valid, they do not require that a renewal ceremony be in view. In fact, they just as easily lend themselves to the idea that Deut 31:9–13 envisages a didactic enterprise.[143] Like a vassal treaty, the book of Torah "is to be read periodically in the presence of the leader and his subjects *so that they may know and observe it.*"[144] And in regard to the affinities with the Horeb revelation in Deut 4, we should highlight that, as already discussed, Deuteronomy portrays Horeb coming through Moses's sermon at Moab, which is crystallized into the Torah. Indeed, the reading of the Torah is meant to cause an existential encounter—a perpetual moment of decision—but it also seeks to imbue identity (via memory) and educate the generations.[145] That education is in view is evident from the fact that the aforementioned words connect this passage to other key pedagogical ones: Deut 4:9–14, 32–40; 6:6–9, 20–25; 11:2–9.[146] What is noteworthy about this public reading, then, is how it fits into the larger educational program. With Moses soon to die, it ensures that Yahweh's words will continue through the reading of the Torah, which will now be mediated through the Levitical priests and elders. In light of the audience, "all Israel," the aim is clear: to educate those "who do not know" (v. 13) about Yahweh and to use this public education to feed into the domestic practices. In this way, "the purpose of the reading is no different from the general aim of the preaching in Deuteronomy, and the regular teaching that it advocates (6:6–9)."[147]

If this is true pedagogically, then much of the same can be said of the role of public reading in Deuteronomy's memory program.[148] Perhaps that is why Craigie shies away from the idea of the ceremony as a covenant renewal in favor of highlighting its commemorative function.[149] It is not incidental, I suggest, that the above passages on pedagogy are rich in references to memory, as we have previously seen. As such, the question is how the public Torah reading contributes to the larger program. A few brief points should suffice.

First, the reading perpetuates the mnemonic system. Through it the system and its substance are at once authorized and made normative: the *habitus* in 6:6–9; the story exposition in 6:20–25; the ritual in 16:1–17; and the song in 32:1–43 (and even the reading itself!). All of these are, in some sense, branches whose sustenance depends on the public reading. Second, arising from the first point, Moses's style in Deuteronomy serves as a model for the Israelite's storytelling in their own domiciles. I noted that visual features play an especially important role in memory in Deuteronomy, something that would most naturally be transmitted through storytelling. Being that Moses is portrayed as the teacher *par excellence*, it is no surprise that his own recounting in Deuteronomy is wrought with the visual. Thus, the audience is invited to recount things at home in a similar manner. Third and lastly, the reading would expose families that otherwise neglect the domestic practices to Israel's memory.[150] If an Israelite neither witnesses the *habitus* nor hears the stories or the song, the public reading exposes him to the meaning of covenantal life.[151] What is more, as he listens to the reading, he is existentially fused to the past, bringing him again to a moment of decision.

Summary

Deut 16:1–17 presents a unique portrait of the festival calendar. Especially helpful for our own study is the way in which the festive calendar leads participants through key movements. Symbolically, MacDonald has shown that the Israelites move from Egypt and the wilderness, commemorated in Passover–Unleavened Bread, into the promised land, represented in Weeks and Booths. While this is not a true historicizing of the feasts, it is clear that the annual progression is one that dramatizes Israel's movement from Egypt to the land. Attending this dramatic movement is an emotional movement. Woven into the fabric of Passover–Unleavened Bread is the feeling of sorrow, but into that of Weeks and Booths is joy. It seems the idea is that, through emotive elements, the people are more fully invested in Israel's defining journey. And spatially, Altmann has noted a pattern that is common to all of the feasts: each one moves from dispersed locales, to the chosen place, and then back to the locales. The significance here is that each feast embodies the covenantal solidarity of the twelve tribes and the rippling of worship at the chosen place outward to the borders of the land. Surely, then, Altmann is right to say that the festive calendar "is a literary *topos* for the construction and maintenance of the common Israelite story and shared identity in Deuteronomy."[152]

RITUAL IN DEUTERONOMY'S MEMORY-MAKING

So how exactly do these three feasts contribute to the construction of Israel's memory? One study is especially helpful here: Paul Connerton's *How Societies Remember*.[153] In Connerton's understanding, ritual is a unique memory vector because it gives memory a "ceremonially embodied form."[154] So while other vectors convey memory through "words and images," ritual does so through "bodily behavior."[155] This, in turn, affects where memory is stored: not so much in the ideas of the mind as in the habits of the body.[156] At this point one may ask how ritual differs from *habitus* in memory making. While there is certainly overlap, the crux is in how each relates to knowledge. *Habitus*, we recall, uses rehearsed practices to sediment ideas and words (i.e., the *Shema*) into one's body. As such, their main function concerns the mastery of abstract knowledge (albeit with the hope of taking it to heart and producing related competencies). Ritual, however, tends toward the sedimenting of events. It seeks through action to dramatize important moments from the past. The performance of ritual, then, compresses the usual process of recollection-action: instead of having to recall an idea/image and then implement it in behavior, embodied memory is at once recollection and action. Having learned to swim, for example, we no longer need to recall instruction each stroke of each lap; we simply swim. Thus, according to Connerton's view, the strength of Israel's feasts as memory vectors lies in the fact that through them "the past is, as it were, sedimented in the body."[157]

But how, in Connerton's understanding, would Israel's feasts specifically serve to sediment memory in the people? He suggests that it occurs through three kinds of commemorative acts: calendrical, verbal, and gestural repetition.[158] Calendrical repetition commemorates by having the ritual occur at the same time as the original event. This could be general, such as a season, or specific, such as the precise time, day, and month of the year. Verbal repetition commemorates by replicating important words (spoken or written) used during the initial event. Connerton notes that often these words have an archaic form, in order to maintain the sense of the original language.[159] Deuteronomy 16's festive calendar does not make use of verbal repetition,[160] but as we shall see, the Song of Moses does. The final of Connerton's types of repetition, gestural, commemorates by mimicking physical actions or postures from the initial event. To these I should like to add another, emotive repetition, which as we have already seen plays an important part in the festival calendar.

What, then, do we find if we apply these types of repetition to Deuteronomy's feasts? In regard to Passover–Unleavened Bread, the most obvious is calendrical repetition. The text prescribes that the people "observe the month of Abib . . . for in the month of Abib he brought you out of Egypt by night" (v. 1). Thus, it aligns the ritual with the time in which Israel left Egypt. It goes even further, though: "you must sacrifice the Passover in the evening, at the setting of the sun, the appointed time of your coming out from Egypt" (v. 6). The syntax here makes it clear that Deuteronomy seeks to commemorate the exodus not only in a certain month or day, but in an exact moment. At the setting of the sun on that day in Abib, the people will reenact a piece of their history and so be brought into the memory of the exodus. It is not unimportant, I suggest, that at least three times the text draws attention to the fact that the "appointed time" is at night.[161] This has a couple of key functions. Firstly, as pointed out before, synchronizing a commemorative act to a time marked with visual features, in this case darkness, is mnemonically powerful. It makes the event especially memorable and allows participants to see themselves as part of the original moment. And secondly, the presence of darkness serves to establish a symbolic typography. Observing this rite under darkness helps create a solemn mood. Before leaving calendrical repetition, we should note the connection between Passover–Unleavened Bread and the following feasts of Weeks and Booths. While the former is patterned according to calendrical repetition, the latter are based instead on agricultural rhythms. This should not, however, be taken to mean that these "constitute two basic forms of liturgy";[162] as already argued, Deuteronomy seeks to portray them as a single "remembered narrative" continuum.[163]

In addition to calendrical repetition, Passover–Unleavened Bread also employs the gestural. This is evidenced generally in that the rite includes things that originally attended Israel's deliverance: the animal slaughter at sunset, which must be devoured before dawn, the ban on leaven, and the eating of *mazzot*. Of course, the text does not highlight the animal sacrifice mnemonically, for due to theological emphases it no longer mirrors the original act.[164] What the text does emphasize is the eating of *mazzot*. *Mazzot* is meant to commemorate Israel's affliction and anxious state of waiting: "for seven days eat unleavened bread, the bread of affliction, because you left Egypt in haste, so that you may remember the time of your departure from Egypt" (v. 3). As with the nighttime aspect, the *mazzot* serves a powerful role in the commemoration. In ancient times, the whole process of making and consuming the bread—with its distinctive preparations, aromas, flavors, and textures—would evoke and engrain the images and memories that accompanied Israel's waiting in darkness. These memories, in turn, would be laden not with the joy characterizing Weeks and Booths but with the sorrow of Egypt's "affliction" (v. 3). Also gestural is the use of tents to commemorate the wilderness experience (v. 7). Combined with the eating of unleavened bread, the remaining days in the tents around the chosen place would function doubly to recall the movement out of Egypt into the desert and to imbue that movement with the solemn tone.

Intertwined with calendrical and gestural repetition is the emotional. I have pointed out that Passover–Unleavened Bread purposely uses the elements of nighttime, *mazzot*, and even tent living to characterize the rite as a time of solemnity. Such a dynamic betrays what in memory research is called "mood congruency." Mood congruency refers to the fact that people retrieve memories well when their current mood matches the mood of content of their memory (or the mood in which the memory was created).[165] This is true across the spectrum of emotions, from happy to sad. While mood congruence was first noticed in natural contexts, recent research has shown that it can be, and often is, induced.[166] Interestingly, such mood "facilitation"[167] can be accomplished through a range of means, from a simple command to feel an emotion to the use of a particular piece of music.[168] Mood facilitation may thus be understood as a subset of context-dependent memory retrieval: by employing the right features, a community creates an emotional "context" mirroring that of the remembered event. The effect is that the participants not only recall the memory more vividly, but also feel grafted into that historical moment. In the case of Passover–Unleavened Bread, the aforementioned elements facilitate the feelings of that night in Egypt: sorrow, anxiety, and solemnity. This is important not only in its own right, but also to establish a stark contrast against which the joy of Weeks and Booths can be celebrated.

In regard to participants, or the intended memory consumers, of Passover–Unleavened Bread, the text is clear: the rite is only for Israelites. While Weeks and Booths make provision for including the needy and even the non-Israelite, the same cannot be said here. In light of the text's own silence, the only sure thing is that the ritual included Israelite men (v. 16). It is not necessary, however, to conclude that women and children were excluded. The role of *mazzot* in the festival—occurring all seven days, presumably in the surrounding family encampments—would seem to indicate that, though altered from its domestic context, Passover–Unleavened Bread was still a family affair. Mnemonically speaking, it is significant that the feast is restricted to Israelites,[169] for it commemorates their defining event, the exodus. This may seem paradoxical, considering Deuteronomy's concern to extend covenantal values beyond the Israelite, but it is in fact essential. For Israel to treat others ethically and justly, it must first understand itself rightly. This it does by remembering the exodus and seeing itself as both redeemed by and obliged to Yahweh. Having entered itself within the moral fabric of the exodus memory, Israel is then in a position to live out the vision of life found in Weeks and Booths.

While Passover–Unleavened Bread's use of mnemonics is fairly straightforward, that of Weeks and Booths is not as obvious. This largely derives from their nature which, as we discussed, is tuned not so much to a point on the calendar as to the rhythms of the agricultural seasons. Even that, though, does not alone explain the difference in mnemonics. Exactly why this is so is best exemplified by considering the later historicizing of the calendar. At some point, the calendar came to commemorate the three key events in Israel's exodus generation: the exodus (Passover–Unleavened Bread), the revelation at Horeb (Weeks), and the wilderness experience (Booths). Even in the Pentateuch we find two of these explicitly tied to feasts, the exodus (Deut 16:1–8), and the wilderness (Lev 23:42–43), and the other possibly suggested by its timing.[170] To apply this to Deuteronomy's version, however, is to obscure its purposes. As I have said, it instead seeks to signify the movement from Egypt to the land, which means that Weeks and Booths commemorate the promised land. But how do these commemorate something that, from Deuteronomy's perspective, is yet to be gained? Not only this, but do not these feasts, as a tandem, also speak of remembering the exodus?

These questions bring us to the heart of the commemoration in Weeks and Booths. In the first place, it is important to note that the frame of reference of the festive calendar is not that of Moab, looking into the land, but that of settled life in the land looking back. It envisages the people enjoying the blessing of Yahweh. This does not contradict my previous argument that, in Deuteronomy's memory, the land serves as the *telos* and trajectory; rather, it adds depth to it. The land, we know, serves in the Mosaic covenant as an enduring *telos*—for the Israelites in exile and even for some Jews still today.

Therefore, the use of the land's bounty to evoke gratitude and thanksgiving drives home the obligational fabric undergirding Israel's memory. Yahweh has been faithful to his promises, and if Israel wants to continue enjoying his favor then it needs to continue *remembering* the exodus, Horeb, and the wilderness.

That it is true, and this is my second point, is evidenced by the call for Israel to remember its own servitude in Egypt (v. 12). Here one finds again that the elements of memory are inextricably bound to one another; the joy of the land arises properly only in juxtaposition to Israel's slavery in Egypt. Implicit, of course, is the fact that Yahweh delivered Israel from its bondage. It is in the juxtaposition that the mnemonics of Weeks and Booths come out fully. The grain and the vintage stand in stark contrast to the *mazzot*, and when the people eat of them they serve to bring their minds to a different place. Of course, the very bounty of the land poses its own dangers (Deut 8) and so must be enjoyed while keeping one eye cast back toward Egypt. In this way, the inclusion of the needy in the feasts may not be only a charitable action, but also a mnemonic one. The presence of "the poor and impoverished leads to reflection on the relations of past and present for the community."[171] And lastly, the joy prescribed for Weeks and Booths (vv. 11, 14, 15) also helps juxtapose Egypt and the land. Whereas Passover–Unleavened Bread employs nighttime ritual, *mazzot*, and tent dwelling to imbue the feeling of sorrow and anxiety, Weeks and Booths leverage simple commands and feasting on the land's bounty to evoke joy. Though the command to feel a certain way seems unfruitful, we have already noted that research shows it in fact does produce positive results. Such results are not, of course, as good as those arising from feasting on the land's bounty; but together they form a reliable force in mood shaping. Put into rotation with Passover–Unleavened Bread, then, Weeks and Booth complete the cycle of bringing Israel from the sorrow of Egypt to the joy of the land.

As far as mnemonic consumer, these two feasts are again less clear than Passover–Unleavened Bread. The festal participants are certainly more diverse, explicitly including children and servants, Levites, aliens, orphans, and widows. And while this may mean that all of the above are meant as consumers of memory, there are reasons to see it otherwise. In the first place, we previously discussed how the Torah reading in 31:9–13 possibly includes only those who are, in some sense, under the covenant. In this case, it would mean that the alien is not meant as a memory consumer. Second, arising from the first point, it would make little sense for Passover–Unleavened Bread to exclude non-Israelites in commemorating the exodus only to include them in remembering it here. One must be careful not to split hairs, but it seems reasonable that the commemoration in view in Weeks and Booths envisages different strands. For the Israelites, they are to remember Egypt and so rejoice in the bounty and show gratitude to Yahweh. Part of this remembering is manifest in their charity toward the needy. Though non-Israelites are included in the celebration, as such, their participation is not so much as commemorators themselves as recipients of the fruit of Israel's commemoration.

We should note something further here in order to tie the festive calendar into our larger argument. It was forwarded that the common view of memory as actualization, as experiential dramatization, does not adequately represent Deuteronomy's notion. In my opinion, the notion is better understood as the aim to create autobiographical memory, through which ongoing identification with the past can occur. This being said, I argued that dramatization does play a part. Its role, however, is not as an end itself but as a component within the larger process of encoding Israel's autobiography. That this is true is indicated, I suggest, when the above analysis of ritual is set against our broader discussion of memory vectors. Of all four vectors, only one aspect of one vector can be seen as actualization:[172] Passover–Unleavened Bread, with its explicit use of reenactment to commemorate. Neither of the other feasts, Weeks and Booths, emphasize dramatization, nor do the other memory vectors. It is true that the festive calendar's journey motif and aspects of the Song of Moses do employ some sort of dramatization. But these could not be considered actualization in the traditional sense. In light of Deuteronomy's aim to relate the sacral to the everyday lives of the people, this subsuming of actualization within autobiographical memory is not surprising.

NOTES

1. I recognize the issues associated with calling Deut 16:1–17 a festival "calendar." See D. J. A. Clines, "The Evidence for an Autumnal New Year in Pre-exilic Israel Reconsidered," *Journal of Biblical Literature* 93 (1974): 37; Donn F. Morgan, *The So-Called* Cultic *Calendars* in the Pentateuch (PhD thesis: Claremont Graduate School, 1974), 30, 93, 159; Bernard R. Goldstein and Alan Cooper, "The Festivals of Israel and Judah and the Literary History of the Pentateuch," *Journal of the American Oriental Society* 110 (1990): 23; Rolf Rendtorff, "Die Entwicklung des altisraclitischen Festkalenders," in *Das Fest und das Heilige*, ed. Jan Assmann and Theo Sundermeier (Gütersloh: Gütersloher Verlagshaus G. Mohn, 1991), 196. With this said, I refer to Deut 16:1–17 as a calendar in line with Bernard Levinson's view: "I employ the term 'festival calendar,' to stress (1) the focus of these units upon the three major pilgrimage festivals and (2) that the units intentionally span the calendar year" (*Deuteronomy and the Hermeneutics of Legal Innovation* [Oxford: Oxford University Press, 1997], 67, n. 45).

2. While ritual is seen as less important in many Protestant circles, we are reminded that "Rituals reveal values at their deepest level . . . men express in ritual what moves them most." Monica Wilson as quoted in Victor Turner, *The Ritual Process: Structure and Anti-Structure* (London: AldineTransaction, 2008 [1969]), 6.

3. Exod 23:14–18; 34:18–26; Lev 23; Num 28–29. See also Exod 12–13, which focuses on the Feast of Unleavened Bread.

4. There are a couple of notable exceptions to this. John Van Seters, "Cultic Laws in the Covenant Code and Their Relationship to Deuteronomy and the Holiness Code," in *Studies in the Book of Exodus*, ed. Marc Vervenne (Leuven: Peeters, 1996), 319–34, and Christoph Levin, "Das Deuteronomium und der Jahwist," in *Liebe und Gebot*, ed. Reinhard G. Kratz and Hermann Spieckermann (Göttingen: Vandenhoeck & Ruprecht, 2000), 121–36, both argue that Deuteronomy's laws come before the CC.

5. For example, Levinson, *Legal Innovation*; Timo Veijola, "The History of Passover in Light of Deuteronomy 16, 1–8," *Zeitschrift für Altorientalische und Biblische Rechtsgeschichte* 2 (1996): 53–75. In contrast to this view, Moshe Weinfeld (*The Deuteronomistc School*; *Deuteronomy*; *The Place of the Law in the Religion of Ancient Israel* [Leiden: Brill, 2004]) and Jacob Milgrom (*Leviticus*, 3 vols. [New York: Doubleday, 1991–2001]) have offered a rather different approach, which forwards an early priestly corpus as part of Deuteronomy's *Vorlagen*.

6. Jan Gertz, "Die Passa-Massot-Ordnung im deuteronomischen Festkalender," in *Das Deuteronomium und seine Querbeziehungen* (Göttingen: Vandenhoeck & Ruprecht, 1996), 56–80; Veijola, "The History of Passover"; Corinna Körting, *Der Schall des Schofar* (Berlin: Walter De Gruyter, 1999).

7. Levinson, *Legal Innovation*, 55.

8. Levinson, *Legal Innovation*, 55.

9. Though for critiques, see Peter Vogt, *Deuteronomic Theology and the Significance of Torah* (University Park, PA: Eisenbrauns, 2006), 68; Eckhart Otto, "The Pre-exilic Deuteronomy as a Revision of the Covenant Code," in *Kontinuum und Proprium* (Wiesbaden: Harrassowitz, 1996), 115; J. Gordon McConville, "Deuteronomy's Unification of Passover and Massot—A Response to B. M. Levinson," *Journal of Biblical Literature* 119 (2000): 47–58.

10. Karl Weyde, *The Appointed Festivals of Yahweh* (Heidelberg: Mohr Siebeck, 2004), 43–52. Shimon Gesundheit has also recently articulated a similar notion: "Intertextualität und literarhistorische Analyse der Festkalender in Exodus und im Deuteronomium," in *Festtraditionen in Israel und im Alten Orient*, ed. Erhard Blum and Rüdiger Lux, VWGT 28 (Gütersloh: Gütersloher Verlagshaus, 2006), 198, 205; and "Der deuteronomische Festkalender," in *Das Deuteronomium*, ed. Georg Braulik (Bern: Peter Lang, 2003), 57–67. For other scholars who include Exod 34, see Norbert Lohfink, "Zur deuteronomischen Zentralisationsformel," in *Studien zum Deuteronomium und zur deuteronomistischen Literatur II* (Stuttgart: Katholisches Bibelwerk, 1991), 172–77; Georg Braulik, *Die deuteronomischen Gesetze und der Dekalog* (Stuttgart: Katholisches Bibelwerk, 1991), 116; Eckart Otto, *Das Deuteronomium* (Berlin: Walter de Gruyter, 1999), 325–35.

11. For critiques of this idea, see Jürg Hutzli, *Die Erzählung von Hanna und Samuel* (Zurich: Theologischer Verlag Zürich, 2007), 251–52; Joachim Schaper, "Schriftauslegung und Schriftwerdung im alten Israel: Eine vergleichende Exegese von Ex 20, 24–26 und Dtn 12, 13–19," *Zeitschrift für Altorientalische und Biblische Rechtsgeschichte* 5 (1999): 125–26.

12. See Hindy Najman, *Seconding Sinai* (Leiden: Brill, 2003), 1–40. For a summary of the replacement vs. supplementation conversation, see Jeffrey Stackart, *Rewriting the Torah* (Heidelberg: Mohr Siebeck, 2007), 211–14.

13. Peter Altmann, *Festive Meals in Ancient Israel* (Berlin: De Gruyter, 2011).

14. Altmann, *Festive Meals*, 22.

15. By this Altmann means a couple of things (*Festive Meals*, 198, n. 259). First, he interprets Deut 16:1–17 as an integrated whole, rather than separating vv. 1–8 from 9–17 as some scholars do. And second, he reminds us that the passage is a text about ritual action but is not a ritual in itself.

16. Altmann, *Festive Meals*, 198–99.

17. For summaries of this discussion, see Alfred Cholewinksi, *Das Heiligkeitsgesetz und Deuteronomium* (Rome: Biblical Institute Press, 1976), 179–81; A. D. H. Mayes, *Deuteronomy* (London: Oliphants, 1979), 254–57.

18. McConville, "Unification of Passover and Massot," 50; also, Weyde, *Appointed Festivals*, 39–41.

19. Levinson, *Legal Innovation*, 72.

20. Indeed, the "most striking addition" to Passover is the "application of Deuteronomy's technical language for sacrifice" (Levinson, *Legal Innovation*, 78). Exod 12 offers a picture of the previously sanctioned practice: the animal is to be one of the small cattle (either sheep or goat) (v. 5), "slaughtered" (שחט) (v. 6), "fire-roasted" (צלי־אש) (v. 8)—not "boiled" (בשל) (v. 9)—and consumed at home. Deut 16, however, says this: the animal is to be from the flocks or *herds* of larger cattle (בקר) (v. 2), "sacrificed" (זבח) (vv. 2, 4–6), "boiled" (בשל) (v. 7), and consumed not domestically but rather at the chosen place (v. 5–8). As Levinson notes, these changes reflect Passover becoming centralized and "assimilated to the standard sacrificial protocol" (p. 72).

21. Levinson, *Legal Innovation*, 75–81.

22. Levinson, *Legal Innovation*, 75–76. Gesundheit ("Intertextualität und literarhistorische," 198–200; "Der deuteronomische Festkalender," 60–62) comes to similar conclusions here. Interestingly, although Gesundheit shows an awareness of Levinson's work in this very section ("Intertextualität und literarhistorische," 200, n. 29), he does not reference or interact with it in regard to these features (his reference is limited to Levinson's view of Deut 16's *Vorlagen*).

23. Levinson, *Legal Innovation*, 75–76.

24. Instead of beginning with the verbal object, the Feast of Unleavened Bread, Deut 16:1 starts with the verb itself, although it is in the form of an infinitive absolute and not the imperfect.

25. In this sense, it is not accidental that the explicit mention of חג in connection to this feast is never stated, only implied, until the closing of the festive calendar in Deut 16:16.

26. Levinson, *Legal Innovation*, 69.

27. Levinson, *Legal Innovation*, 72.

28. Levinson, *Legal Innovation*, 93.

29. Weyde, *Appointed Festivals*, 54–56. We focus on two of his arguments. His other arguments deal in detail with Levinson's assumptions of when certain passages should be dated and which ones served as sources for the others. In particular,

Weyde focuses on the relationship between Exod 23 and 34, which he regards as pre-Deuteronomic, and concludes that these show signs of already portraying Passover and Unleavened Bread as united and as pilgrimage festivals (*Appointed Festivals*, 53). In his opinion, then, the true innovation of Deuteronomy's festive calendar lies elsewhere, namely, in the centralization of the feasts.

30. Weyde, *Appointed Festivals*, 54.
31. McConville, "Unification," 51.
32. Levinson, *Legal Innovation*, 89.
33. Deut 1:27; 5:30; 11:6; 33:18. There are other occurrences of אהל, namely, for the tent of meeting; but we are speaking here of domestic dwellings.
34. Deut 6:7; 19:1; 20:5; 21:12–13; 22:8; 28:30.
35. Weyde, *Appointed Festivals*, 56.
36. Nathan MacDonald, *Not Bread Alone* (Oxford: Oxford University Press, 2008), 81.
37. McConville, "Unification," 54–55.
38. McConville, "Unification," 56.
39. *Pace* Levinson, who argues that McConville's is not a "coherent alternative" ("The Hermeneutics of Tradition in Deuteronomy: A Reply to J. G. McConville," *Journal of Biblical Literature* 119 [2000]: 276).
40. It is also noteworthy that the Hebrew verb for "return" differs from 5:30 to 16:7. In 5:30 we find שוב, while in 16:7 it is פנה. If Deut 16:7 were intentionally echoing 5:30, one would expect not only the repetition of "tents" but also that of the same verb for "return."
41. MacDonald, *Not Bread Alone*, 81.
42. MacDonald, *Not Bread Alone*, 81.
43. MacDonald, *Not Bread Alone*, 80.
44. Klaus Koch, "אהל," in *Theological Dictionary of the Old Testament* (*TDOT*), vol. 1, ed. G. Johannes Botterweck and Helmer Ringgren, trans. John T. Willis (Grand Rapid, MI: Eerdmans, 1974), 120–21.
45. Josh 22:4–8; 1 Kgs 8:66; 2 Chr 7:10.
46. Levinson, *Legal Innovation*, 78.
47. Levinson, *Legal Innovation*, 77–78.
48. We should note that Levinson recognizes that elsewhere in the text there seems to be variant notions of the time of the exodus. Following Samuel Loewenstamm, *The Evolution of the Exodus Tradition* (Jerusalem: Magnes Press, 1992), Levinson roots this in the idea that two independent strands originally existed: a daytime exodus (Exod 12:22) and a nighttime exodus (Exod 12:30–31) (Levinson, *Legal Innovation*, 77, n. 78).
49. Num 33:3.
50. Exod 12:6 and 12:22.
51. Levinson, *Legal Innovation*, 78. He says it thus: "The Deuteronomic assertion that Passover commemorates the Exodus is therefore nearly an admission of despair," for it does so "however tendentiously" in order to keep the rite from disappearing altogether in the merger.
52. Levinson, *Legal Innovation*, 78. Exod 23:15; 34:18.
53. Levinson, *Legal Innovation*, 78.

54. Overall there is a wide variety of uses, ranging from specific to general. See Klaus Koch, "מועד," in *TDOT*, vol. VIII, 167–73. But as Levinson suggests, the usage in Deuteronomy is rather unique for the festive calendars. Although, see Exod 13:10.

55. Levinson, *Legal Innovation*, 78.

56. Gesundheit, "Intertextualität und literarhistorische," 198; "Der deuteronomische Festkalender," 61.

57. MacDonald, *Not Bread Alone*, 82–83. *Pace* J. Gordon McConville, who sees this broader movement occurring in Passover–Unleavened Bread by itself (*Law and Theology* [Sheffield: JSOT Press, 1984], 115).

58. Besides MacDonald and McConville, other scholars have also argued for the importance of commemoration in the shaping of the feast. Most notable is Georg Braulik, who seems to see the exodus commemoration as *the* governing principle of composition ("Commemoration of Passion and Feast of Joy: Popular Liturgy According to the Festival Calendar of the Book of Deuteronomy [Deut 16:1–17]," in *The Theology of Deuteronomy*, 67–85). Says Braulik, "the central position of the exodus motif in the composition of [Deut 16:]1–7 corresponds perfectly with the function of this topic as the common denominator which made the cultic interweaving of the Passover and the Feast of Unleavened Bread possible" (p. 74).

59. "By night" initiates things in v. 1, but other references to nighttime are found in vv. 4 and 6 (cf. v. 7, which does not mention night but juxtaposes the time of the feast to "morning").

60. The term "symbolic typography" is common in literary circles, typically referring to when an author uses the features of the story environment to represent the mood of the scene. Biblically, we find a similar textual phenomenon in the Gospel of John, which in chapter 3 uses "night" to symbolize spiritual darkness (Craig R. Koester, *Symbolism in the Fourth Gospel*, 2nd ed. [Minneapolis, MI: Augsburg Fortress, 2003], 9). That lighting is used in ritual to symbolize or create mood is a truism. What differs from ritual to ritual is the way in which lighting is employed. For instance, while darkness frequently represents things such as evil or sorrow, it can also stand, as in ancient Mesopotamia, for something such as a mother's womb before birth (William S. Sax, Johannes Quack, and Jan Weinhold, *The Problem of Ritual Efficacy* [Oxford: Oxford University Press, 2010], 34).

61. Sax, Quack, and Weinhold, *The Problem of Ritual Efficacy*, 74. Braulik points out that the phrase "bread of affliction" (לחם עני) is found only here in all of the Old Testament, and "haste" (חפזון) occurs only in two other places: Exod 12:11 and Isa 52:12.

62. *Pace* Braulik, who wants to make a sharp division between the rite commemorating Israel's departure but not its oppression ("Commemoration of Passion," 75). As noted in our discussion in chapter 4 on the variegated nature of mnemonic imagery, Deuteronomy frequently holds together such seeming dichotomies on purpose.

63. This fact is significant, for unleavened bread plays a central role in Deuteronomy's conceptualization of the feast (Braulik, "Commemoration of Passion," 73) and its use to symbolize negative feelings is unique (MacDonald, *Not Bread Alone*, 81).

64. "Do not eat unleavened bread ... so that [למען] you may remember all the days of your life the day that you came out from the land of Egypt" (v. 3). On the

uniqueness of this intent, see Brevard Childs, *Memory and Tradition in Israel* (London: SCM Press, 1962), 53.

65. See Weinfeld's discussion on this (*Deuteronomic School*, 220–21).

66. Richard D. Nelson, *Deuteronomy* (Louisville, KY: Westminster John Knox, 2002), 209.

67. McConville, *Deuteronomy*, 275.

68. McConville, *Law and Theology*, 111.

69. For a detailed discussion of the Feast of Weeks throughout the various festive calendars (and even that found in the Temple Scroll), see Nathan MacDonald, "Ritual Innovation: The Feast of Weeks from the Covenant Code to the Temple Scroll," unpublished paper presented at the Society of Biblical Literature annual meeting (San Francisco, 2011).

70. Other calendars do use the name Feast of Weeks (Exod 34:22; Num 28:26) and Lev 23:15–16 articulates the timing of the seven weeks further.

71. E.g., MacDonald, "Ritual Innovation," 8; Mayes, *Deuteronomy*, 259. See Nelson, however, who understands the seven-week period in the traditional sense of the countdown to harvest, maintaining that the impracticality of such a schedule for a centralized festival betrays its idealistic or "utopian" bent, that is, its aim to portray an ideal and not something historically viable (*Deuteronomy*, 209).

72. For a discussion of how this would work, see Jan Wagenaar, *Origin and Transformation of the Ancient Israelite Festival Calendar* (Leipzig: Harrassowitz Verlag, 2005), 33–34.

73. Nelson, *Deuteronomy*, 209.

74. Weinfeld, *The Deuteronomic School*, 220. Weinfeld, we recall, considers this part of Deuteronomy's secularizing program (see also Gesundheit, "Intertextualität und literarhistorische," 195–96). Though I follow his general idea, I prefer to see it not as secularization but as the extending of the sacred into everyday life.

75. Exod 23:16; 34:22; Num 28:26; Lev 23:9–21.

76. Gesundheit, "Intertextualität und literarhistorische," 195–96. This presumes, of course, that Firstfruits is an annual feast, not just one upon entry to the land, and that it requires pilgrimage to the chosen place.

77. Weinfeld, *The Deuteronomic School*, 221.

78. See MacDonald, "Ritual Innovation," 10; Nelson, *Deuteronomy*, 307.

79. McConville, *Law and Theology*, 119–21.

80. McConville, *Law and Theology*, 120. McConville roots this especially on the chiastic patterning of the verb בוא: bring (hiphil), go (qal), go (qal), bring (hiphil) (see pp. 33–35).

81. McConville, *Law and Theology*, 120.

82. This view may be supported by Calum Carmichael, who detects in Deut 26:1–11 echoes of the spies' narrative from Num 13 (*The Laws of Deuteronomy*, repr. [Eugene, OR: Wipf & Stock, 2008], 247). The effect would be not only to portray right response to the land and its blessings, but also to warn of the consequences of not doing so.

83. There have been a handful of translations offered on this: e.g., Peter Craigie, "sufficient" (*The Book of Deuteronomy* [Grand Rapids, MI: Eerdmans, 1976], 245);

Altmann, "fullness" (*Festive Meals*, 197); William Morrow, "appropriate" (*Scribing the Center* [Atlanta, GA: Scholars Press, 1995], 152).

84. This conclusion derives from several points: the closest related root is an Aramaic word with this meaning; the word is well attested with this meaning in Mishnaic Hebrew; and the end of the verse clarifies this phrase with "according to Yahweh your God's blessing of you" (see Mayes, *Deuteronomy*, 260; Craigie, *Deuteronomy*, 245, n. 11; Duane Christensen, *Deuteronomy 1:1—21:9*, revised 2nd ed. [Nashville, TN: Thomas Nelson, 2001], 342). "Tribute," used by some translations, is based on the spurious connection to מס ("forced labor"). The BHS suggests the gloss כמתנת, which occurs in v. 17, without offering warrant for doing so.

85. While Deuteronomy takes up and uses this verse in its closing framework (16:16), the language must be understood in light of Deuteronomy's other emphases. Perhaps the reference to men, as such, refers to them as representatives of the family units.

86. Weinfeld, *The Deuteronomic School*, 292. Weinfeld suggests that the omission of wives from this list does not exclude them but, rather, implies that they are assumed as addressees of the law already.

87. Walter J. Houston, "Rejoicing Before the Lord: The Function of the Festal Gathering in Deuteronomy," in *Feasts and Festivals*, ed. Christopher M. Tuckett (Leuven: Peeters, 2009), 10–11.

88. Weinfeld, *The Deuteronomic School*, 212.

89. Weinfeld, *The Deuteronomic School*, 220–21. Here we are, of course, talking about the festal arrangements; Deuteronomy also makes provision for the needy in its other legislation (14:28–29).

90. Weinfeld, *The Deuteronomic School*, 290.

91. Houston, "Rejoicing," 10–11.

92. For other instances in Deuteronomy, see 12:12, 18; 14:26; 26:11; 27:7.

93. Norbert Lohfink, "The Cult Reform of Josiah of Judah: 2 Kings 22–23 as a Source for the History of Israelite Religion," in *Ancient Israelite Religion*, ed. P. D. Miller (Minneapolis, MN: Fortress Press, 1987), 469. See also Rainer Albertz, *A History of Israelite Religion in the Old Testament Period* (London: SCM Press, 1994), i. 211.

94. A personal communication cited in Houston, "Rejoicing," 8, n. 31. See also Nathan MacDonald, *What Did the Ancient Israelites Eat?* (Grand Rapids MI: Eerdmans, 2008), 69.

95. Houston, "Rejoicing," 8–9.

96. Houston, "Rejoicing," 9.

97. Georg Braulik, "The Joy of the Feast: The Conception of the Cult in Deuteronomy: The Oldest Biblical Festival Theory," in *The Theology of Deuteronomy*, 27–65.

98. Braulik, "Joy of the Feast," 34.

99. Houston, "Rejoicing," 3. For a fuller and more recent critique, see Altmann, *Festive Meals*, 205–7.

100. Houston, "Rejoicing," 3.

101. Braulik, "Joy of the Feast," 43 (emphasis mine).

102. Braulik, "Joy of the Feast," 43–44, quoting Raphael Schulte, "Zum christlichen Verständnis von Religion und Kult," *Theologisch-praktische Quartalschrift* 115 (1967): 34–44; 42.

103. MacDonald, *Not Bread Alone*, 82. See also Altmann, *Festive Meals*, 98.

104. Houston seeks to illumine the role of the giver by viewing the feast through the lens of social patronage ("Rejoicing," pp. 11–13). While I do not agree with all of Houston's conclusions, his basic understanding of Yahweh as chief patron and the feast's function in establishing *communitas*, is helpful. Also, see Altmann's discussion and development of Houston's view (*Festive Meals*, 209–10).

105. Altmann, *Festive Meals*, 199.

106. McConville, *Deuteronomy*, 275.

107. On the language, see Weinfeld, *The Deuteronomic School*, 327; on the syntax, see Childs, *Memory and Tradition*, 46, 52.

108. For example, Deut 5:12–15; 15:12–15; 24:17–18.

109. Braulik, "Die Ausdrücke."

110. On this, see Christensen (*Deuteronomy*, 342–43), who likens it to the usage in 17:19, which parallels "these statutes" to "all the words of this Torah."

111. See Christensen, *Deuteronomy*, 340–41.

112. For example, Craigie, *Deuteronomy*, 245; Mayes, *Deuteronomy*, 260; Christensen, *Deuteronomy*, 342–43; MacDonald, *Not Bread Alone*, 82.

113. Childs, *Memory and Tradition*, 53.

114. Childs, *Memory and Tradition*, 55.

115. Deut 5:15; 15:15; 24:18. Each of these is slightly different from the others, though they all share the aspect of mentioning the deliverance.

116. Deut 24:22.

117. See MacDonald, *Not Bread Alone*, 82; Altmann, *Festive Meals*, 204.

118. Lev 23:34 also calls it "booths." See also Zech 14:16, 18; Ezra 3:4; 2 Chr 8:13.

119. Altmann sees this as part of another movement within the festal calendar (*Festive Meals*, 202). While he agrees that the larger movement is one from Egypt to the land, he argues that within each feast there is also movement from dispersed individual residences to the chosen place, and then, in v. 16, back to the wider land. In this view, the language of v. 13 represents the individual residences.

120. Mayes, *Deuteronomy*, 261; Nelson, *Deuteronomy*, 209.

121. Traditionally this view was rooted in the idea that the Israelites took over the feasts from Canaanite culture. See George W. MacRae, "The Meaning and Evolution of the Feast of Tabernacles," *Catholic Biblical Quarterly* 22 (1960): 251–76.

122. MacDonald, *Not Bread Alone*, 82.

123. Craigie, *Deuteronomy*, 246; Christensen, *Deuteronomy*, 350.

124. Some sensibly point out that the reference to "booths" does not align well with the wilderness account, which portrays the people as living in tents and not booths. Tigay, for instance, devotes an excursus to discussing this issue and concludes that "booths" should be understood as a "screen" or "covering" (*Deuteronomy*, 469–70). In this view, סכות symbolizes not the nature of Israel's dwellings in the wilderness, but Yahweh's protective covering (Ps 105:39). Other than linguistic considerations,

Tigay further bases his view on the idea that "commemorative symbols prescribed by Torah normally commemorate miracles, and there is nothing miraculous about living in booths or tents" (p. 469). The problem with this statement, though, is that it is patently untrue. As we have already seen in a previous chapter, the nature of commemoration is variegated and subtle, and it cannot be reduced to a one-to-one correspondence between symbol and miracle.

125. With this said, it may be that Deuteronomy does have knowledge of the portrayal found in Leviticus, and that for this very reason it employs the name with none of the details, so that it might forge its own version.

126. MacDonald, *Not Bread Alone*, 82 (emphasis mine).

127. For Deuteronomy's usage of "priests" and "Levites," see McConville, *Law and Theology*, 137–38.

128. This theme of succession will be discussed in the section on the song.

129. For example, Nelson, *Deuteronomy*, 359. However, for a succinct discussion on the differences, see Arie van der Kooij, "The Public Reading of Scriptures at Feasts," in *Feasts and Festivals*, 32.

130. There is some discussion as to what "this Torah" (v. 11) refers to. As discussed previously, it seems best to take it as Moses's sermons now crystallized as the book of Deuteronomy (Christensen, *Deuteronomy*, 765; Mann, *Deuteronomy*, 165). In regard to how long it would take to read, Tigay suggests three to four hours (*Deuteronomy*, 292).

131. On the relationship between Yahweh's revelation at Horeb, Moses's sermon at Moab, and this perpetual reading of the Torah, see Jean-Pierre Sonnet, *The Book Within the Book: Writing in Deuteronomy* (Leiden: Brill, 1997), 137–38.

132. Regarding justice, see Deut 1:16; 24:14, 17, 19, 21; 27:19. Regarding enjoyment of the land, see Deut 14:29; 16:11, 14; 26:11, 12, 13.

133. For a thorough discussion of the alien in Deuteronomy, see Christiana van Houten, *The Alien in Israelite Law* (Sheffield: Sheffield Academic Press, 1991), 68–108.

134. This is even clearer in Deut 29:10–11, the covenant renewal ceremony prescriptions that include in the audience the "alien." See also Josh 8:30–35.

135. See also A. D. H. Mayes, "Deuteronomy 29, Joshua 9, and the Place of the Gibeonites in Israel," in *Das Deuteronomiums*, ed. Norbert Lohfink (Leuven: Leuven University Press, 1985), 321–25.

136. Christiana Van Houten, *Alien in Israelite Law* (Sheffield: Sheffield Academic Press), 105–6.

137. On the notion of fear here, see Weinfeld, *The Deuteronomic School*, 274–75.

138. John Arthur Thompson, *Deuteronomy* (Downers Grove, IL: InterVarsity Press, 1974), 291; Houten, *Alien in Israelite Law*, 102; Merrill, *Deuteronomy*, 399.

139. Not to mention, 2 Kgs 23 can hardly be taken as an exemplary manifestation of the reading of the Torah as envisaged in Deut 31:9–13.

140. It is important to note that in Deut 31:9–13 there is no obvious connection to a renewal ceremony.

141. Weinfeld, *The Deuteronomic School*, 64–65. Also, Viktor Korošec, *Hethitische Staatsverträge* (Leipzig: Leipziger rechtswissenschaftlicher Studien, 1931) and

George E. Mendenhall, *Law and Covenant in Israel and the Ancient Near East* (Pittsburgh: Biblical Colloquium, 1955). We recall, though, that Willy Schottroff affirms the similarities without positing a formal renewal ceremony (*Gedenken im Alten Orient und im Alten Testament* [Neukirchen-Vluyn: Neukirchener Verlag, 1967], 122).

142. Nelson, *Deuteronomy*, 358.

143. Nelson, *Deuteronomy*, 358–59.

144. Weinfeld, *The Deuteronomic School*, 275 (emphasis mine).

145. Not to mention, it is notable that the existential encounter now comes not through a cultic ceremony *per se*, but through listening to the reading.

146. See Weinfeld, *The Deuteronomic School*, 164; Tigay, *Deuteronomy*, 498–502; Miller, *Deuteronomy*, 222; Nelson, *Deuteronomy*, 358–59.

147. McConville, *Deuteronomy*, 439.

148. See Millar, *Choose Life*, 95. Van der Kooij makes the interesting point that the fact that the reading occurs at the year of release may implicitly evoke ideas of Israel's own deliverance from Egypt ("Public Reading," 32). For a recent discussion on the reading within Israel's pedagogy program, see Karin Finsterbusch, *Weisung für Israel: Studien zu religiösem Lehren und Lernen im Deuteronomium und in seinem Umfeld* (Tubingen: Mohr Siebeck, 2005), 281–94.

149. Craigie, *Deuteronomy*, 371.

150. This assumes that such families would attend the festivals, whatever their motivation for doing so.

151. McConville points out that the "institution of the seven-year reading would provide at least two memorable occasions in the formative years of every Israelite" (*Deuteronomy*, 439).

152. Altmann, *Festive Meals*, 2.

153. Paul Connerton, *How Societies Remember* (Cambridge, UK: Cambridge University Press, 1989).

154. Altmann, *Festive Meals*, 43. It is interesting to note that commemorative ritual is, for Connerton, not only a memory vector, but actually the chief one in culture.

155. See especially "Chapter 3: Bodily Practices," pp. 72–104.

156. Here Connerton differentiates between "inscribed" and "incorporated" memory (pp. 72–73). Inscribed memory is that which is stored by being emblazoned upon an object, such as is the case with a book. Inscribed items can display its message without physical performance, that is, without the performer being present. Incorporated memory, however, is that which is stored through bodily absorption, such as eating at commemorative feasts. This, in turn, means that incorporated memory can display its message only through performance, and thus only when the performer is present. However helpful this division may be heuristically, we recall that Deuteronomy holds the two together as complementary (MacDonald, *Not Bread Alone*, 96–98).

157. Connerton, *Remember*, 72.

158. Connerton, *Remember*, 65.

159. He also points out that the words can, in themselves, have a performative function. In the Lord's Supper, for example, "Do this in remembrance of me" (1 Cor

11:24–25) functions both as the substance of the verbal repetition and as the command to perpetuate the rite.

160. The offering of Firstfruits does, of course, though it appears later in Deut 26. It might be asked if the reading of the Torah at Booths qualifies. But it does not, for the reading is primarily didactic and not an attempt to reenact an event.

161. 16:1, 4, 6. These variously juxtapose "evening," "night," and "setting of the sun" against "morning."

162. *Pace* Braulik, "Passion and Feast of Joy," 84.

163. Altmann, *Festive Meals*, 204.

164. The original act, we recall, was an apotropaic "slaughter," while Deuteronomy's is that of a "sacrifice" at the chosen place.

165. John D. Mayer, Laura J. McCormick, and Sara E. Strong, "Mood-Congruent Memory and Natural Mood: New Evidence," *Personality and Social Psychology Bulletin* 21 (1995): 736–46; Penny A. Lewis and Hugo Critchley, "Mood-Dependent Memory," *Trends in Cognitive Sciences* 7 (2003), 431–33.

166. Penny A. Lewis et al., "Brain Mechanisms for Mood Congruent Memory Facilitation," *NeuroImage* 25 (2005): 1214–23.

167. Lewis et al., "Memory Facilitation," 1214.

168. Phuong T. Nguyen and Lauren Scharff, "A New Test of Music Mood Induction and Mood Congruency Memory," *Abstracts of the Psychonomic Society* 8 (2003): 114.

169. While the text of Deuteronomy does not make it clear, it is possible that, like in Exod 12:48–49, foreigners who have been circumcised can participate in more covenantal activities.

170. That is, if one takes the seven weeks as the time between Passover and Weeks, then it could understood as corresponding to the time between the Exodus and Mt. Horeb in the narrative (Exod 19:1). It would mean, then, that Weeks commemorates the revelation at Horeb.

171. MacDonald, *Not Bread Alone*, 82.

172. We shall see shortly that the Song of Moses betrays similar features but is not the same as Passover–Unleavened Bread.

Chapter 7

Emoting Memory

Song as Memory Vector

The third and final memory vector, song, is perhaps the most underappreciated of the three. This is the case even though the Song of Moses (Deut 32) has left an indelible mark on the biblical literature and beyond. In the Old Testament, "echoes of the Decalogue, the basic covenantal document, are rare" but "echoes of the Song . . . are ubiquitous."[1] We see this influence especially in the books of Psalms, Isaiah, Jeremiah, and Ezekiel. The song featured prominently in the Second Temple period as well, appearing in the literature of 2 Maccabees and Josephus's *Antiquities of the Jews*, and in a papyrus scroll (4Q44) at Qumran.[2] And the song's influence continued into the writings of the New Testament. There its echoes reverberate through the Gospels and Paul's Epistles,[3] and, apparently, will continue to reverberate even in the eschaton, where the faithful will sing "the song of God's servant Moses and of the Lamb" (Rev 15:3).[4] The Song of Moses, then, is a memory vector that deserves attention. As with the previous vectors, we will discuss it exegetically and then mnemonically.

SONG: DEUTERONOMY 32:1–43[5]

It has long been noted that the Song of Moses sits precariously in Deuteronomy. On the one hand, it is generally accepted that the song had a previous existence before being included in the present text.[6] Pointing to this is both its apparent lack of key themes from the larger book—namely the centralization of worship, the monarchy, the exodus, the exile, and Horeb and Moab covenants[7]—and its unique language and style.[8] But on the other hand, it is also recognized that the song is now grafted into the larger book, especially through its immediate context (31:19–13). As James Watts notes, this is not insignificant, for it means that it is "the only psalm in a narrative context of the Hebrew Bible for which this is the case."[9] The result, Watts goes on to say, is that the song is "decisively affected by the description . . . provided by the narrative itself": it thus characterizes the song both "as a witness" and "as a popularly accessible summary of Deuteronomy's theology and thus a counterpart to the law-book itself."[10] R. A. Carlson goes a step further, calling the song "a compendium of Deuteronomic ideology" that, for the common Israelite, would be more easily learned and recalled than the full Torah.[11] We now turn to flesh out this idea, especially in light of the aforementioned differences between the song and the larger book.

If the "narrative context" of Deut 31 is what establishes the role of the song, then we must begin there. The difficulty, though, is that the logic of Deut 31 is not immediately transparent. The first half of the chapter proceeds in an expected manner: Moses's impending death[12] leads to his encouraging of the people in general (vv. 1–6) and of Joshua in particular (vv. 7–8), and his writing down of the Torah, which he entrusts to the Levitical priests and elders for reading (vv. 9–13). Following that, the Lord calls Moses and Joshua to the Tent of Meeting for the express purpose of commissioning Joshua (v. 14). It is at this point, however, that the song seems to interrupt the commissioning (vv. 16–22). The tone turns grave, with Yahweh predicting Israel's apostasy and requiring that Moses write down the song and teach it to the people in order to guard against these events. Though the text does return to the commissioning of Joshua (v. 23), the event now seems obscured by the new trajectory set by the song's introduction. So much is this the case that the role of the written Torah, reintroduced in verse 24, is recast in the image of the song as a "witness" (v. 26).

A variety of textual proposals have been forwarded in attempt to address these issues.[13] What most of them have in common is the aim to alleviate the discontinuities presented by the text.[14] One scholar in particular, however, argues that it is precisely in the discontinuities that Deut 31 communicates its message.[15] Talstra puts it thus:

> The frequent change of actors in the narrative frame can be taken as a signal that the most effective way of entering the text is to analyze it *in terms of the various roles and actors presented*, rather than in terms of its chronological order or its theological concepts . . . I think it possible to analyze the narrative sections of the text in terms of the actors presented, the themes of their dialogues and the earlier texts in the book of Deuteronomy which these sections continue or comment upon.[16]

In this view, the entrance of the song (vv. 16–22) is supposed to be conspicuous in that it signals the redefining of participants' roles:

Torah (the instruction becomes a witness), Joshua (the finish becomes a start), the Levites (the teachers need to add the document of the witness to the text of their Torah) and the elders (readers of the instructions and leaders of the people are now in the same role as the people: listening to the witness).[17]

Coming at the end of the Pentateuch, at the death of Moses, and as the people prepare to cross the Jordan, the song then serves as a kind of transformer: it readies the agents and agencies for their new roles in Israel's future.

At this point, we come across the question of what the text means when it calls the song a "witness"(עד). Exactly what role does it envisage? The traditional view is that the notion is one of a trial witness: the song stands to testify against Israel's repeated infidelity against Yahweh.[18] Those who favor this view often point to the use of covenant lawsuit language in Deut 32. Such an idea of "witness," they say, is consonant with the song's legal ethos. The problem, however, is that it is now accepted that the song employs lawsuit language in a limited and unique capacity.[19] More central to the song's nature is its didactics.[20] Thompson sums up the resulting situation well: "it is not strictly a covenant lawsuit document, but a didactic poem based on covenant lawsuit pictures."[21] Another weakness in the trial witness view is that it makes poor sense of the song's actual use as portrayed in Deuteronomy. The dark premonitions are what will take place in the future; they have not yet come to pass.[22] What is more, their function appears to be not so much as a pronouncement of judgment as a cautionary for Israel. For these reasons, it has been suggested that the song is not a witness but a warning.[23] Allen articulates it so: "The song . . . must therefore be understood not so much as a trial witness, incriminating or indicting Israel, but rather as a cautionary exhortation that warns Israel of the importance of faithfulness in the land and the dire consequences of disobedience to YHWH."[24] Thus, the song is to have an important role in the ongoing life of Israel in the land and beyond, a point evidenced by the concluding frame in 32:45–47.[25]

What, then, is the substance of this warning? While space prohibits full-scale exegesis of the song, I would like to focus on its pertinent features. To begin with, the broad structure might be construed thus:[26]

1–6 God and Israel juxtaposed
7–18 Yahweh's care for Israel, Israel's apostasy
19–35 Yahweh's judgment on Israel
36–43 Yahweh's judgment on the nations, Israel's vindication

From this, we discern that the song reflects the basic trajectory of Israel's relationship with Yahweh: moving from Yahweh's taking of Israel for himself, through Israel's rebellion, to ultimate restoration. According to MacDonald, this "journey from past to future" is a key way in which the song serves as a mnemonic agent.[27]

Within this structure, we discern several central motifs by which the song progresses. As poetry typically does, the song begins (vv. 1–6) with the idea that it seeks to develop.[28] What this section establishes is that the theme of the poem is the contrast between faithful Yahweh and unfaithful Israel.[29] Key motifs for developing the theme are also introduced here, namely, Yahweh as rock and father and Israel as rebellious child.[30] The "rock" (צור) motif occurs throughout the song (vv. 4, 15, 18, 30, 31, 37), with the purpose of establishing Yahweh's faithfulness as the baseline of the relationship.[31] This much is made clear when the motif is introduced in verse 4: "The Rock—perfect is his work, for all his ways are justice; a God of faithfulness, without iniquity, righteous and upright is he." It is significant that here, at the outset, not only the character of the Rock but also his work is portrayed as good and reliable; these will be developed in the ensuing sections of the song.[32] Since the song is a summation of Israel's relationship with Yahweh, it is not unimportant that the rock motif occurs in all the major sections. This signifies that in all stages of Israel's life, in both blessing and curse, Yahweh remains the same and his ways are righteous.

Integrally connected to the rock motif is the image of Yahweh as father. The metaphor is paired with "rock" conceptually in the introduction (v. 6); and the two are structurally paralleled in verses 15b and 18. Each of these verses teases out what the song means by Yahweh as father: "who created you," "made you and sustained you" (v. 6); "the God who made them," "his savior" (v. 15b);[33] "the Rock who bore you," "the God who birthed you" (v. 18). Thus, verse 6 highlights the idea of Israel's creation,[34] whereas verse 18 emphasizes that of Israel's birth.[35] As Tigay notes, the language of verse 18 is quite powerful, for it frames the idea of Yahweh as the Rock in images typically used of mothers.[36] And while it is true that these terms collectively drive home the idea of Israel's election,[37] there is clearly a deeper affective purpose in view. In particular, the multifaceted image of Yahweh as father enlivens that of the Rock. Although it is important to establish the Rock as faithful and good, these qualities cannot be held as mere abstractions. The point is that this Rock is the same God who has established and cared for Israel. In deploying these images, therefore, the song seeks to kindle in Israel the appropriate affection for and obligation to Yahweh, the Rock.[38]

Juxtaposed to the image of Yahweh as father and rock is that of Israel as petulant child. Having articulated the character of the Rock in verse 4, the poem quickly turns in verse 5 to speak of Israel as "dealing corruptly" with Yahweh, a "blemished" people, a "perverse and crooked" generation. So far from Yahweh is Israel, in fact, that the text says that they are "not his children" (לא בניו). The petulant child motif occurs in other sections of the song as well. In verse 19, Yahweh is said to reject his "sons and daughters" because they have provoked him. And in verse 20 they are again called a "perverse generation" and then "children with no faithfulness in them" (בנים לא־אמן בם). This latter description, of course, stands in stark contrast to that of the Rock who is depicted as a "God of faithfulness" (אל אמונה) (v. 4). According to Carlson, within the description contained in verse 19 we find yet another key *leitmotif*: provocation.[39] At least four times in the song, Yahweh is said to be "provoked" (כעס) (vv. 16, 19, 21, 27). The significance of this particular motif, though, is greater than it might appear. Provocation is a key concept that connects the Yahweh/Israel juxtaposition introduced at the beginning (vv. 1–6) to the flow of the larger song. On the one hand, Israel's apostasy and idolatry are what provoke Yahweh to judge his people (vv. 16, 19, 21). His judgment (vv. 19–26) may be seen as echoing the covenant curses in Deut 28.[40] But on the other hand, the thought of Israel's complete destruction bringing on its enemy's provocation is what ultimately stems Yahweh's punishment and turns it back upon the enemy (v. 27). Thus, the motifs of Yahweh as rock/father, Israel as petulant child, and Yahweh's response to provocation serve as the backbone of the message of the song.

Another important part of the song's message is conveyed through the theme of memory. The song's treatment of memory is nicely demarcated by the use of "remember" (זכר) in verse 7 and "forget" (שכח) in verse 18. Within the section, we find elements that are at once similar to and different from those connected to memory elsewhere in Deuteronomy. First, the call to remember in verse 7 envisages something akin to other occurrences. The remembrance of Yahweh's benefactions on Israel's behalf is meant to motivate loyalty in her. Some assume, following the pattern of the larger book, that the reference here is to the events of the exodus generation.[41] Of these, Thompson offers the most reasonable explanation, arguing that the exodus is implied by the fact that the wilderness and land follow in verses 10–14. But while it is true that the latter two are present, the immediate context would suggest that something else is in view for the former. The object of זכר, "days of old," is often used biblically to denote the most ancient of time (Amos 9:11; Mic 7:14; 1 Sam 27:8; also Deut 4:32), and in ANE thought typically means mythic time.[42] Also, the events found in verses 8–9 would seem to confirm this view. For these reasons, scholars tend now to identify the reference with primeval events of the Bible, such as the parceling of land in Gen 10–11, and not the exodus.[43]

And the second aspect here that echoes the larger book is the wilderness portrait (vv. 10–12). While the language is not identical to that found in Deut 8, the example of wilderness memory *par excellence*, there are several striking similarities. For one thing, the father/son image that predominates the song is also central in Deut 8 (v. 5). Related to this, the song juxtaposes Yahweh's tender care for Israel with the harsh elements of the wilderness

(v. 10; also 8:15–17). As is the case in Deut 8 (vv. 6–14), the song connects the wilderness to the land (vv. 12–14). They follow similar logic, too, in that both portray the land as a place of plenty (vv. 12–14; 8:7–9), but whose primary danger to the people is satiety (v. 15; 8:12–14),[44] which in turn leads to apostasy and idolatry—the "forgetting" of Yahweh (vv. 16–18; 8:19). The song also employs the desert motif in a couple of distinctive ways. In describing the people's satiety, the song draws attention to the people's nature by calling Israel by the name "Jeshurun" (יְשֻׁרוּן) (v. 15). Deriving from the root יָשָׁר ("upright"), which is used to describe Yahweh in verse 4, "Jeshurun" is a scathing moniker that highlights the disparity in the character of the two parties. Harold Fisch says that "the great central image of this poem of Moses is the image of the burning heat of the desert."[45] While this is perhaps an overstatement, Fisch is right that the image of the desert heat serves a pivotal role in linking Israel's fickle character (vv. 10–18) to the punishment that it will bring (vv. 22–24).

In sum, the song is meant to serve as a mnemonic in Israel that will perpetually warn the people of the dangers of disloyalty. It accomplishes this through a variety of features, including word play, meter, and recurring motifs, all of which combine to create a kind of narrative summary of Israel's relationship with Yahweh. We especially noted the use of the rock and the father/son motifs in drawing a stark contrast between Yahweh and Israel: the former is forever faithful and good, the latter ever fickle and faithless. Mnemonically speaking, the song betrays a unique contour. It roots Israel's relationship with Yahweh not in the exodus but in the primeval past, at an indeterminate time. What it focuses on is the wilderness and the land: the wilderness typifies the relationship between Yahweh and Israel and in the land this will be writ large. Ultimately, though, the character of the Rock/father will manifest in the renewal of the land and the people (v. 43).

SONG IN DEUTERONOMY'S MEMORY MAKING

For understanding the song as a vector of memory, the recent work by Terry Giles and William Doan, *Twice Used Songs*, is helpful.[46] In their work, Giles and Doan seek to illumine so-called recycled songs—songs that have been inserted in the biblical narrative—through the lens of performance criticism.[47] What is more, they do so in conversation with collective memory research in hopes of elucidating the role of song in the creation of Israel's memory. The work thus draws together several strands important to my own study.

Giles and Doan begin by highlighting the importance of so-called "recycled songs" for memory in the Old Testament:

recycling song material represents a rich history of cultural memory, of internalizing the words and rhythms of life . . . constructed identity and the binding of a social unit with a belief or memory is a primary function of the twice-used songs of the Hebrew Bible.[48]

This, taken with the authors' later discussion of the Song of Moses, confirms my view that the song is an important memory vector in Deuteronomy. But it also raises a couple of further questions. First, how do Giles and Doan envisage song's agency in memory construction in general? In this regard, the authors follow a main line of memory scholarship, which emphasizes the transportive quality of song.[49] That is to say, Giles and Doan highlight the way in which song sweeps people into powerful and moving states of being.

A problem with this, perhaps deriving from the scholarship they draw upon,[50] is that Giles and Doan never articulate how they see the transportive quality of song functioning mnemonically. We pause, therefore, to consider a couple of key dynamics that are commensurate with their notion but never made explicit. We find from research, for one thing, that song encodes memory through inducing emotive experiences.[51] More than other agents, music moves us; it takes us places existentially with surprising quickness and intensity. In so doing, a song engrains its substance—particular images, ideas, affections—in memory with what we have called "deep encoding."[52] It should be noted at this point that while it is common to emphasize the positive, or euphoric, side of song's emotive state,[53] negative emotion can play just as important a role.[54] Some songs seek to induce in their audience a negative emotive state,[55] a point with significance for the Song of Moses. Another way in which song functions mnemonically is through creating in people a vision of what life could be.[56] We recall from a previous chapter that this is the teleological function of memory, that is, the projection of "possible selves." By envisaging a particular portrait of life, a person is motivated to act in a certain way, either to bring about the portrait or to avoid it. That song is emotively potent means that it is therefore powerful in its motivation of possible selves.

Having considered how song works within mnemonics in general, we now move to the second question of how Giles and Doan see the Song of Moses functioning in Israel's memory in particular. Their view of the song arises from their broader understanding of the Bible's twice-used songs:

Recycling allows us to place something from the past into a present moment, to perform what *was* in the *here* and *now*. If we sing along in the recycled version . . . we participate in the creation of a new reality, a time and space that we share through the performance of the song . . . The songs allow us to bind the past to some special moment of the present.[57]

On its own, this quote repeats for song something that we have already discussed for Deuteronomy: that it seeks to bridge the present with a particular moment from Israel's past. But what makes Giles and Doan's construal unique is how it applies this notion to the Song of Moses.

As with their view on the mnemonics of song in general, the details of Giles and Doan's notion of the Song of Moses are not entirely clear.[58] What they seem to be saying, though, is that the song seeks to bridge each new generation with the original giving of the Song at Moab (Deut 31:19–30). If this is true, it differs from the other vectors' generational bridging in a couple of important ways. On the one hand, it would mean that the song bridges not the moments of the exodus generation—the exodus, Mount Horeb, and the wilderness—but the final moment of decision at Moab. And on the other hand, it would mean that the song seeks generational identification not so much through its own substance, as story and ritual do, as through the song's original setting. In other words, in singing the song the Israelites primarily revisit the moment at Moab, not the various moments within the song itself.[59]

But what evidence is there that supports this idea? Giles and Doan identify two key supporting features: (1) the identification of the song's composer and (2) the assigning of the precise words of the song to that composer.[60] That Yahweh composed and commissioned the song (v. 19) and that Moses taught it to the people (v. 22) is significant, they argue. "Composition and commissioning are processes whereby the presence of the composer and commissioner is extended to audiences of the future."[61] By identifying these explicitly, then, the text signals something about the moment of the song's giving. When in each generation the song is sung, it will recall the moment in which it was originally issued. That moment, of course, is one of Moses's last acts, on the plains of Moab when he gives the people the song as an enduring covenantal warning.[62]

Bolstering this idea is Giles and Doan's second point, that the very words of the song are attributed to Yahweh and their transmission to Moses's teaching at Moab. The authors do not flesh this out mnemonically, but we recall Connerton's point that verbal repetition is often used in the dramatization of cultural memory. If such a dynamic can be found here, it seems that Deuteronomy casts each new singing of the song as a duplication of the original. Israel continues to enter the Moab situation, in some sense, through repeating the words that characterize it. With this said, there appears to be here a dynamic different from that found in Passover–Unleavened Bread. Most notable is that the feast creates an elaborate ritual environment in which the exodus is dramatized. With the song, however, there is no such environment.[63] So while the text envisages some kind of dramatization, it is perhaps not the full-scale type found in Passover–Unleavened Bread. To Giles and Doan's arguments for why the song bridges Israel back to Moab, not to the events sung about, we might add one more point: the nature of the song itself. We remember from our analysis above that the song employs ambiguous language as an intentional device, portraying Israel's relationship with Yahweh in a generalized, timeless fashion.[64] As such, the song also lacks the kind of visual imagery characteristic of the rest of the book. If this imagery is, as I have argued, central to generational conflation, then its absence here is instructive. It would thus add credence to the idea that the song's setting, not its substance, is meant for generational identification.

Let us now draw together these ideas to clarify how the song serves as a memory vector. The song is meant to cause Israel to identify with the moment of Moab, when the song was first given as an enduring warning. Storytelling and the reading of the Torah create the sense of a journey through moments of decision, but the song at Moab stands as the quintessential call to covenantal loyalty.[65] The substance of the song contributes to this call, then, by inducing an emotive state and projecting Israel's possible selves. Taking the people on a whirlwind tour of its relationship with Yahweh, which emphasizes him as the Rock/father and it as petulant child, the song evokes a deep dismay. Israel beholds its own infidelity against the backdrop of Yahweh's faithfulness. Connected to the emotion are Israel's possible selves. Although in the end Yahweh will renew his people, the near outlook looks bleak—punishment and expulsion from the land. The portrait is purposely negative, in the hope that it might motivate Israel to avoid such a reality. The song therefore stands in Israel's memory, in some sense, as a counterpart to the *habitus*: while the *habitus* encodes what *should* be (the *Shema*), the song encodes the warning of what *could* be.

How, then, does Deuteronomy envisage the mnemonic agency of the song? As for target audience, the text emphasizes that Moses teaches it directly to the Israelites (31:19, 22). It also assumes that the people will perpetuate the song generationally amongst themselves (v. 21). This suggests, therefore, that while Moses is the original giver of the song, the ongoing transmission occurs through the Israelites. Resembling the *habitus* and storytelling in this sense, the song appears to be transmitted from parents to children.[66]

As for the practical implementing, there are a couple of possibilities. Traditionally, it has been common to see the song as part of a periodic covenant renewal ceremony.[67] This notion is largely tied to the view that the song itself is a covenant lawsuit. If one does not assume a lawsuit view, however, there is little contextual reason for seeing the song as part of a formal ceremony. Another possibility is that the song is to be "displayed and taught in ways similar to the *Shema*."[68] A couple of factors make this the more likely view. For one thing, and as already noted, the transmission of the song seems to resemble that of the domestic practices: the *habitus* and storytelling. We see this most clearly in the song's conclusion in Deut 32:44–47:

Moses came with Joshua son of Nun and spoke all the words of this song in the hearing of the people. When Moses finished reciting all these words to all Israel, he said to them, "Take to heart all the words I have solemnly declared to you this day, so that you may command your children to obey carefully all the words of this law. They are not just idle words for you—they are your life. By them you will live long in the land you are crossing the Jordan to possess. (NIV)

Archeological finds from Qumran support this interpretation as well, for they reveal *tefillin* containing the song.[69] This further links the song to the domestic practices in Deut 6, adding a material connection to the rhetorical and theological ones.

It is noteworthy, therefore, that two of the three memory vectors in Deuteronomy—*habitus*/story and song—operate in the domestic sphere, and so reflect the same memory makers and consumers: parents and children, respectively. This strengthens the idea that memory in Deuteronomy is grounded more in daily life than cultic actualization. And the song plays a unique role in this. It infuses Israel's image of "possible selves" with a solemn warning of what might become of them if they continue to disobey. So at each singing in the home, the song evokes its original setting of Moab, where the people face the great moment of decision and hear the call to choose life. It is no wonder that the Song of Moses left such an indelible mark on the community, for, as the Scottish politician Andrew Fletcher once said, "Let me write the songs of a nation, and I care not who writes its laws."[70]

NOTES

1. Daniel Block, *Deuteronomy* (Grand Rapids, MI: Zondervan, 2012), 770.

2. See Armin Lange, "The Dead Sea Scrolls and the Date of the Final Stage of the Pentateuch," 287–304, in *On Stone and Scroll: Essays in Honour of Graham Ivor Davies*, ed. James Aitken, Katharine Dell, and Brian Mastin (Berlin: De Gruyter, 2011), 299.

3. On the many echoes and uses of the song in the New Testament, see: G. K. Beale and D. A. Carson, eds., *Commentary on the New Testament Use of the Old Testament* (Grand Rapids, MI: Baker Academic, 2007); Richard Hays, *Echoes of Scripture in the Letters of Paul* (New Haven: Yale University Press, 1989); Richard Hays, *Echoes of Scripture in the Gospels* (Waco, TX: Baylor University Press, 2016).

4. There is debate about the meaning of "the song of God's servant Moses," for it echoes various Old Testament texts including two songs associated with Moses: the Song of the Sea (Exod 15) and the Song of Moses (Deut 32). See G. K. Beale and Sean McDonough, "Revelation," in *Commentary on the New Testament Use of the Old Testament*, 1133–34.

5. I do not see Moses's blessing of the tribes (Deut 33) as a vector, for unlike the song the text does not mark it as an intentional agent of memory.

6. There have been a host of attempts to explain this existence, arguing for different dates on grounds ranging from historic situation, language, form, theology, and intertextual links (Nathan MacDonald, *Deuteronomy and the Meaning of "Monotheism"* [Tübingen: Mohr Siebeck, 2003], 140–42; see p. 140, n. 86 for scholarship on "no people," a focus of those seeking to identify the song's historical situation). For a summary of scholarship, see Paul Sanders, *The Provenance of Deuteronomy 32* (Leiden: Brill, 1996), 1–98. A sampling of the spectrum: Umberto Cassuto, proposes a twelfth-century date during the time of the Judges ("The Prophet Hosea and the Books of the Pentateuch," in *Biblical and Oriental Studies*, vol. 1 [Jerusalem: Magnes Press, 1975]) 1081–161; William Albright dates the song to the eleventh century, roughly the time of Samuel ("Some Remarks on the Song of Moses in Deuteronomy XXXII," *Vetus Testamentum* 9 [1959]: 339–346); David Robertson suggests the Davidic-Solomonic period (*Linguistic Evidence in Dating Early Hebrew Poetry* [Missoula, MT: Society of Biblical Literature, 1972], 155); Mark Leuchter argues for a date prior to the eighth century ("Why is the Song of Moses in the Book of Deuteronomy," *Vetus Testamentum* 57 [2007]: 295–317); Solomon A. Nigosian proposes more generally from the tenth to the eighth century ("Linguistic Patterns of Deuteronomy 32," *Biblica* 78 [1997]: 223–24); Jack R. Lundbom identifies the song as the very document discovered during Josiah's reign c. 622 ("The Lawbook of the Josianic Reform," *Catholic Biblical Quarterly* 38 [1976]: 293–302); Sanders himself forwards a general preexilic date (*Deuteronomy 32*, 432); Carl Steuernagel argues for an exilic date (*Das Deuteronomium* [Göttingen: Vandenhoek & Ruprecht, 1898], 168–169); and R. Meyer sees the song's composition reflecting the Persian period, sometime after 400 BC ("Die Bedeutung von Deuteronomium 32, 8f. 43 (4Q) für die Auslegung des Mosesliedes," in *Verbannung und Heimkehr*, ed. A. Kusche [J. C. B. Mohr, 1961]), 197–209.

7. See J. G. McConville, *Deuteronomy* (Westmont, IL: InterVarsity Press, 2002), 461.

8. Samuel Rolles Driver, *A Critical and Exegetical Commentary on Deuteronomy*, 2nd ed. (Edinburgh: T. & T. Clark, 1896), 337–38, especially notes this in regard to 32:14–23. He also points out the many *hapax legomena* and unusual words occurring in the song as a whole (p. 348).

9. James W. Watts, *Psalm and Story* (Sheffield: Sheffield Academic Press, 1992), 65. See pp. 67–74 for ways in which the song links to chs. 31–34 and the book as a whole.

10. Watts, *Psalm and Story*, 67.

11. R. A. Carlson, *David, the Chosen King* (Stockholm: Almqvist & Wiksell, 1964), 235, 237. The quote seems to play off the classic view that Deuteronomy is "a compendium of prophetical theology" (Carl Cornill, *Einleitung in das Alte Testament* [Frieburg: Mohr, 1891], 13.5, cited by Driver, *Deuteronomy*, 346). For a collection of those who espouse similar views, see David Allen's discussion (*Deuteronomy and Exhortation in Hebrews* [Tübingen: Mohr Siebeck, 2008], 20–22).

12. For a discussion of the song as an example of ANE last-words, see Steven Weitzman, *Song and Story in Biblical Narrative* (Bloomington, IN: Indiana University Press, 1997), 37–58; esp. 44–53.

13. S. Carrillo Alday, "Contexto redaccional del *Cántico de Moisés* (Dt 31, 1–32, 47)," *Estudios Bíblicos* 26 (1967): 283–93; Watts, *Psalm and Story*, 64–67; Norbert

Lohfink, "Zur Fabel in Dtn 31–32," in *Konsequente Traditionsgeschichte*, ed. Rudiger Bartelmus, Thomas Krüger, and Helmut Utzschneider (Göttingen: Vandenhoeck & Ruprecht, 1993), 255–79; Casper J. Labuschagne, "The Setting of the Song of Moses in Deuteronomy," in *Deuteronomy and Deuteronomic Literature*, ed. Marc Vervenne and Johan Lust (Leuven: Leuven University Press, 1997), 111–29; Jean-Pierre Sonnet, *The Book Within the Book* (Leiden: Brill, 1997), 147–48; Brian Britt, "Deuteronomy 31–32 as a Textual Memorial," *Biblical Interpretation* 8 (2000): 358–74.

14. Perhaps the one exception is Britt, "Textual Memorial," who does focus on the difficulties as an interpretive entry point, though in my opinion not entirely satisfactorily.

15. Eep Talstra, "Deuteronomy 31: Confusion or Conclusion? The Story of Moses' Threefold Succession," in *Deuteronomy and Deuteronomic Literature*, ed. Marc Vervenne and Johan Lust (Leuven: Leuven University Press, 1997).

16. Talstra, "Confusion," 96 (emphasis mine).

17. Talstra, "Confusion," 101.

18. See George Ernest Wright, "The Lawsuit of God: A Form-Critical Study of Deuteronomy 32," in *Israel's Prophetic Heritage*, ed. Bernhard W. Anderson and Walter J. Harrelson (New York: Harper, 1962), 26–67; A. D. H. Mayes, *Deuteronomy* (Edinburgh: Oliphants, 1979), 378; Jeffrey Tigay, *Deuteronomy* (Philadelphia: The Jewish Publication Society, 1996), 295; Helmer Ringgren, "עוד," *TDOT*, vol. 10, 504.

19. See Allen, *Deuteronomy and Exhortation*, 29–30.

20. See Weitzman, *Song and Story*, 44–46; Nigosian, "Song of Moses," 8. These offer balanced views of the legal language with the didactic. (It should be noted, though, that Weitzman still follows the traditional idea of the song as "witness against.")

21. John A. Thompson, *Deuteronomy* (London: InterVarsity, 1974), 297.

22. Pietro Bovati compares the song in this sense to the altar in Josh 22:27, 28, 34 and the stones in Gen 31:48. "These have an indisputable juridical function as the sign of a pledge or a contract between two partners, but they do not enter into the area of trial witness" (*Re-Establishing Justice*, trans. M. J. Smith [Sheffield: Sheffield Academic Press, 1994], 264).

23. See MacDonald, *Monotheism*, 144; Allen, *Deuteronomy and Exhortation*, 30–31.

24. Allen, *Deuteronomy and Exhortation*, 31.

25. See MacDonald, *Monotheism*, 144.

26. The verse divisions are adopted from J. P. Fokkelman, *Major Poems of the Hebrew Bible* (Assen: Van Gorcum, 1998), 62. Fokkelman's structure is based on careful analysis of the text's metrics. As important for me is that this division represents important thematic units, which should become clearer. I recognize that there are a host of views on structure at both the macro and micro levels of the song. For examples at the macro level, see Patrick Miller, *Deuteronomy* (Louisville, KY: Westminster John Knox, 1990), 226–32; Tigay, *Deuteronomy*, 299; Duane Christensen, *Deuteronomy 21:10—34:12* (Nashville, TN: Thomas Nelson, 1997), 786; McConville, *Deuteronomy*, 451; MacDonald, *Monotheism*, 148. For two thorough yet differing studies at the micro level, see Fokkelman, *Major Poems*, 54–149 and Sanders, *Deuteronomy 32*, 12–258.

27. MacDonald, *Monotheism*, 148. In addition to the movement from past to future, he identifies the movement from "heaven to earth to Sheol and back again." MacDonald forwards a total of five rhetorical features that the song employs to aid memorization (pp. 147–49). Other than that of Israel's journey, he points out the use of different speakers and "actors," word plays, measured rhythm, and recurring motifs (for a similar though slightly different list, see Carlson, *Chosen King*, 237).

28. For the basic ways in which biblical poetry accomplishes such development, see Robert Alter, *The Art of Biblical Poetry* (New York: Basic Books, 1985), 62–84.

29. See Driver (*Deuteronomy*, 344); Miller (*Deuteronomy*, 227); MacDonald (*Monotheism*, 148); Allen (*Deuteronomy and Exhortation*, 32).

30. For discussions on these motifs, see Alter (*Poetry*, 144); Miller (*Deuteronomy*, 227).

31. It seems that Braulik understands v. 3 as introducing some kind of new name for Yahweh, which v. 4 presents as "the Rock" (Georg Braulik, *Deuteronomium II: 16, 18—34, 12* [Würzburg: Echter Verlag, 1992], 228). This does not, however, make much sense of the rock motif.

32. See McConville, *Deuteronomy*, 453.

33. In light of the context, the term "savior" (ישועה) is probably best taken as another term for election generally rather than referring to the exodus deliverance in particular.

34. For the roots קנה and כון, see Tigay (*Deuteronomy*, 402, nn. 37 and 38); on these as creation language, see McConville (*Deuteronomy*, 453).

35. "Bore" (ילד) and "birthed" (חלל).

36. Tigay, *Deuteronomy*, 307. He suggests that this is similar to instances in ancient Syrian inscriptions in which kings are portrayed as both father and mother to their people.

37. Allen, *Deuteronomy and Exhortation*, 57.

38. The song also employs the image of an eagle caring for its young in a similar capacity (v. 11).

39. Carlson, *Chosen King*, 237. See also Richard D. Nelson, *Deuteronomy* (Louisville, KY: Westminster John Knox, 2002), 373.

40. Though see MacDonald, who argues that the song's curses are closer to those found in Leviticus (*Monotheism*, 146).

41. Mayes, *Deuteronomy*, 384; Thompson, *Deuteronomy*, 299; Christensen, *Deuteronomy*, 796.

42. See Nelson, *Deuteronomy*, 371.

43. See Tigay, *Deuteronomy*, 32; Nelson, *Deuteronomy*, 371; McConville, *Deuteronomy*, 453–54.

44. See Moshe Weinfeld, *Deuteronomy and the Deuteronomic School* (Oxford: Oxford University Press, 1972), 280; MacDonald, *Monotheism*, 146.

45. Max H. Fisch, "The Song of Moses: Pastoral in Reverse," 55–79, in *Poetry with a Purpose* (Bloomington, IN: Indiana University Press, 1988), 56. In this essay, Fisch offers one of the better literary readings of the song, sensitive to the interplay of images, motifs, and intertextual links. Having said this, his reading does suffer in that it sees the song as a witness in the lawsuit sense rather than as a warning.

46. Terry Giles and Bill Doan, *Twice Used Songs: Performance Criticism of the Songs of Ancient Israel* (Peabody, MA: Hendrickson Publishers, 2009).

47. For the role of music in the world of ancient Israel, see Joachim Braun, *Music in Ancient Israel/Palestine* (Grand Rapids, MI: Eerdmans, 2002) and Theodore Burgh, *Listening to the Artifacts* (New York: Continuum, 2006).

48. Giles and Doan, *Twice Used Songs*, 5.

49. Giles and Doan, *Twice Used Songs*, 6–7.

50. In this regard, Giles and Doan especially use the idea of Jill Dolan (*Utopia in Performance: Finding Hope at the Theatre* [Ann Arbor, MI: University of Michigan Press, 2005], 5–6) called "utopian performatives." The authors summarize this idea for song, saying it is the way in which singing has the ability to "lift [one] above the present" (Giles and Doan, *Twice Used Songs*, 6).

51. See Robert Jourdain, *Music, the Brain, and Ecstasy* (New York: Harper Perennial, 1998); Bob Snyder, *Music and Memory* (Cambridge, MA: MIT Press, 2000); Daniel Reisberg and Friderike Heuer, "Memory and Emotional Events," in *Memory and Emotion*, ed. Daniel Reisberg and Paula Hertel (Oxford: Oxford University Press, 2003), 3–41; James L. McGaugh, *Memory and Emotion* (New York: Columbia University Press, 2006), x; Daniel J. Levitin, *This is Your Brain on Music*, repr. (New York: Plume/Penguin, 2007).

52. There is an ongoing discussion on the relationship of a song's music and lyrics in eliciting emotion. For differing views, see Valerie N. Stratton and Annette H. Zalanowski, "Affective Impact of Music vs. Lyrics," *Empirical Studies of the Arts* 12 (1994): 173–84; Mireille Besson et al., "Singing in the Brain: Independence of Lyrics and Tunes," *Psychological Science* 9 (1998): 494–98; Felicity Baker and Tony Wigram, "Rehabilitating the Uninflected Voice: Finding Climax and Cadence," *Music Therapy Perspectives* 22 (2004): 4–10; Aniruddh Patel, *Music, Language, and the Brain* (Oxford: Oxford University Press, 2008).

53. Dolan seems to do this (*Utopia*, 5) and Giles and Doan follow her here (*Twice Used Songs*, 6).

54. Probably the most influential work on music and the evoking of negative emotion has been done by Jerrold Levinson, "Music and Negative Emotion," in *Music and Meaning*, ed. Jenefer Robinson (New York: Cornell University Press, 1997), 215–41; *Music, Art, and Metaphysics* (Oxford: Oxford University Press, 2011), esp. 306–35.

55. This point has been especially stressed in research on music therapy. It is common practice, for instance, for therapists to carefully control the music they employ to facilitate client progress. Positive music may be used liberally, but the negative kind is to be used with extreme caution, for fear of undermining a patient's development. See Jeanette Tamplin, "Singing for Respiratory Muscle Training: Using Therapeutic Singing and Vocal Interventions to Improve Respiratory Function and Voice Projection for People with a Spinal Cord Injury," in *Voicework in Music Therapy*, ed. F. Baker and Sylka Uhlig (London: Jessica Kingsley Publishers, 2011), 155. We also find this borne out in everyday life. Just the other day a couple told me of how they had come across an advertisement for a collection of songs from their younger years. At first, they were excited at the idea of reminiscing, but soon they realized that the songs brought up feelings and memories of things they did not wish to experience

again. In the end, they chose not to buy the collection because the negative emotions were too haunting.

56. Says Dolan, song creates "a hopeful feeling of what the world might be like if every moment of our lives were as emotionally voluminous, generous, aesthetically striking, and intersubjectively intense" (Dolan, *Utopia*, 5). Giles and Doan quote this in building their own point (*Twice Used Songs*, 6).

57. Giles and Doan, *Twice Used Songs*, 5.

58. See Giles and Doan, *Twice Used Songs*, 105–11.

59. In other words, "Poetry cannot report the event; it must *be* the event." Balachandra Rajan, *The Overwhelming Question: A Study of the Poetry of T. S. Eliot* (Toronto: University of Toronto Press, 1976).

60. Giles and Doan, *Twice Used Songs*, 105. They note that the other biblical song with similar features is the Song of David in 2 Sam 22.

61. Giles and Doan, *Twice Used Songs*, 108–109.

62. Giles and Doan argue that the Song of Moses, along with the Song of David (2 Sam 22), is spoken and taught, but never sung (*Twice Used Songs*, 105). However, this seems to me too rigid a reading of the text. Indeed, Moses is said to have "taught" (למד) (Deut 31:19, 22) and "spoken" (31:30) (דבר) the song to the people. But these descriptions follow suit with Deuteronomy's emphases, and they may reflect this more than a literal description of the mechanisms of the process. Even if one does take the terms rigidly, the "teaching" of the song would probably include more than just the recitation of its words, for after Moses's teaching the people will be able to sing the song (31:19).

63. It would seem, in light of Deut 32:44–47, that the song's environment is, like the *habitus* and storytelling, in the domestic sphere.

64. See Peter Craigie, *Deuteronomy* (Grand Rapids, MI: Eerdmans, 1976), 383; Mayes, *Deuteronomy*, 388; Jan Ridderbos, *Deuteronomy*, trans. E. M van der Maas (Grand Rapids, MI: Zondervan, 1984), 281; Fokkelman, *Major Poems*, 142–43; MacDonald, *Monotheism*, 140.

65. If this function of the song can be maintained, it is curious that Millar, who pioneered the notion of moments of decision, says very little about the song's role in it. See J. Gary Millar and J. Gordon McConville, *Time and Place in Deuteronomy* (Sheffield: Sheffield Academic Press, 1994), 86.

66. That the song is also written down (31:19) may imply the involvement of the priests and elders in a more formal dispersing of the song among the people.

67. Wright, "Lawsuit," 44; Craigie, *Deuteronomy*, 373; Watts, *Psalm and Story*, 66, n. 1. Yet see also Block, *Deuteronomy*, who portrays the song more generally as an "anthem" sung in "liturgical events" (p. 748).

68. MacDonald, *Monotheism*, 147.

69. See Roland de Vaux and J. T. Milik, eds., *Qumran Grotte 4*, vol. 2 (Oxford: Oxford University Press, 1977), 72–74.

70. Quoted in Gordon Wenham, *The Psalter Reclaimed* (Wheaton, IL: Crossway, 2013), 13.

Conclusion

A Wrinkle in Time: Memory as Portal into the Divine Presence

The goal of this study has been to explore an overgrown path in biblical scholarship: how Deuteronomy acts as a memory producer. While scholars were once interested in this path, times changed and it became overgrown, and when scholarship eventually did return to the study of memory, it came with a new focus: texts as *products* of memory, rather than as *producers* of memory. Whatever the value of this new focus, however, it represents only one side of the coin, and to focus on it nearly exclusively, as scholarship has done, is to leave out half of the picture. This is especially true for a book like Deuteronomy, which sees memory production as its chief priority. For Deuteronomy, memory is the "fulcrum" of covenant faithfulness, the very thing that determines whether Israel will remain loyal to Yahweh.

At the outset, I suggested that the situation with memory is representative of the larger field of biblical studies. For much of the past century, the focus has been on the world *behind* the text, especially the question of how the forces of that world influenced the biblical texts. In reaction to this, some began to focus more on the world *of* the text: its rhetoric, literary qualities, etc. Memory studies reflect this trend as well, as I highlighted in the chapter reviewing the history of scholarship. Where scholarship still needs to do more, in my opinion, is in studying the world *in front of* the text.[1] By this, I mean the world that Scripture projects, the world that it builds and bids us, as its readers, to enter and experience. This is my understanding of Luke Timothy Johnson's quote, with which I began the study:

> If Scripture is ever again to be a living source for theology, those who practice theology must become less preoccupied with the world that produced Scripture and learn again how to live in the world Scripture produces.[2]

What I would like to do in closing, therefore, is consider how my own study contributes to this goal of helping us to "live in the world Scripture produces."

TEXTS AND WORLD PROJECTION

Paul Ricoeur has been central in developing the idea that texts "project" worlds and that we enter these worlds through reading.³ To understand Ricoeur's perspective on texts, though, we must understand his larger work. Kevin Vanhoozer summarizes it like this:⁴

> Ricoeur's philosophy seeks to understand human being (What is man?) and thereby to achieve self-understanding (Who am I?). But the meaning of human being is gained only through interpretation of texts (including meaningful action) which attest to human existence . . . I attain self-understanding when I grasp the range of my possibilities. This self-understanding may be transformed when in reading I confront the "world of the text" and apply to myself the existential possibility, the way of living and being in the world.⁵

Human beings, in other words, are meaning-seeking creatures,⁶ and texts provide access to meaning in that they act as storehouses of portraits on what it means to be human: who humanity is, might be, and ought to be.

For Ricoeur, the key idea here is human *possibility*.⁷ Against the view that people are bound to turn out in a certain way, he argues that to be human is to be full of potential. People can become almost anything, he suggests, so long as they can first imagine it. And as such, imagination is vital, for "By changing his imagination, man alters his existence."⁸ On this point, Ricoeur diverges from some classic thinking in which imagination is seen as a second-rate imitation of the real thing.⁹ Quite to the contrary, imagination helps to project possibility: it does not merely reflect what is, but projects what could be.

To Ricoeur, the most powerful shapers of imagination are metaphor and narrative,¹⁰ with narrative occupying an especially central role in his thinking. The reason narrative is so important is because of how it produces "fiction." By "fiction" Ricoeur does not mean untrue stories, but rather that all stories, being selective in nature, tell certain events in a certain way to accomplish a certain effect. Stories, in other words, build a world by *emplotting* events, by weaving together disparate elements into one fabric. In this way, Ricoeur sees narrative as truer than history, for history can only disclose what happened once while narrative can reveal what might happen yet. Narrative thus plays a unique role in connecting the two realms of the real and the imaginary.

For Ricoeur, it is precisely because of this that narrative is so important to imagination: "fiction [narrative] changes reality, in the sense that it both 'invents' and 'discovers' it."[11] Here we come to the nub of Ricoeur's view on how texts transform readers. While he does not entirely discount the historical circumstances of a text's writing (the world behind the text),[12] Ricoeur finds little value there.[13] He argues that when real-time communication is captured in written form, it is severed from the original context and becomes a stand-alone message with "semantic autonomy":[14] what remains is the message of the text itself (the world of the text).[15] And when someone comes to read this, it is the things internal to the text itself—the plot, characters, images, etc.—that form the basis of the reading experience. These things, and not the historical factors of the text's writing, are what the text "projects" to the reader as the world in front of the text.

The emphasis in Ricoeur, therefore, is on "*how* a certain literary genre 'projects a world'" and how this world "redescribes reality and opens for us a new way of seeing and being."[16] In general, Ricoeur sees the biblical material as working in ways similar to all literature: they project possible worlds, invite us to enter them and consider new perspectives, and in so doing have our self-understandings transformed.[17] He develops his notion further in regard to narrative, though it seems he means it in some sense for all genres. What he says is that in the experience of reading we are in fact *reconstituted*. In having our horizons opened, we are first challenged by and then reconstituted according to the contours of the text. We become new people because of our encounter with the text's projected worlds.[18]

Now, one of the concerns with Ricoeur's work is that it is too vague, that it leaves open the question of how particular texts transform people in particular ways. This is seen to stem from two things. First, Ricoeur's work is ultimately one of philosophical hermeneutics. While he himself engages in biblical interpretation and while others have used his work to do so as well, the heart of his project is philosophical. As such, it looks at texts from the perspective of philosophical questions ("what is human being?") and treats their content largely as ideal symbols and archetypes, rather than real events. By itself, therefore, Ricoeur's hermeneutic leaves us closer to a "philosophy of existence" than a "theology of salvation history."[19]

Second, Ricoeur's work revolves around the notion of "distanciation." He places great emphasis on what he sees as the yawning distance ("distanciation") between the world behind the text and the text itself, on the one hand, and the text and the world it projects, on the other.[20] These distances create an estrangement between the text and the reader, which must be overcome: "To 'make one's own' what was previously 'foreign' remains the ultimate aim of hermeneutics."[21] Yet unlike Gadamer, Ricoeur does not see distanciation as wholly negative; it also preserves a healthy distance. Instead of the interpreter trying to overcome distanciation by fusing the two horizons (à la Gadamer),[22] therefore, Ricoeur suggests readers come to "a kind of sympathy-in-distance."[23] We do this by balancing "explanation" with "understanding" and thereby "appropriate" the text's meaning. With this said, it is not clear how Ricoeur imagines this working: "There seems to be some almost quasi-mystical dimension to 'appropriation' in Ricoeur's thinking. Exactly how the 'worlds' interact seems to be less than fully clear."[24] And since it is in the act of appropriation that people are transformed, this is no small matter.

It is at this point that memory studies may prove helpful. Not only do they have the power to describe how particular "worlds" are projected, but also how these transform people in particular ways. As my work has shown, memory studies articulate how the human mind absorbs, structures, and recalls events through the two systems of long-term memory: semantic (word-based) and episodic (image-based). This holds not only for lived events, but also events experienced through other mediums (such as texts, song, story, ritual, etc.). We might say, then, that memory provides a perfect bridge between Ricoeur's notion of the reading "event" and its role in transforming readers.

In regard to Deuteronomy, I showed that Israel's memory is built from five elements: patriarchal promises, exodus, Mount Horeb, wilderness, and promised land. The patriarchal promises and promised land serve different roles from the others, in that they provide the semantic framing for memory. The first one, the patriarchal promises, establishes the grounding and trajectory of memory; everything grows out of Yahweh's ancient promise of land, seed, blessing, and divine presence. Thus, covenant becomes the governing idea. Yet as I highlighted, it is noteworthy that the patriarchal promises are purely semantic, or conceptual, in nature, never invoking the "eyes" motif or employing the telltale visual language. This is important in what it reveals about function: the patriarchal promises are vital at a conceptual but not experiential level. To use Ricoeur's language, this introduces a healthy distanciation: the events of the patriarchal generation are foundational in that they generate the controlling concept for Israel's memory. But those events are not, in themselves, what Israel should identify with; that is reserved for the exodus and Moab events.

The other part of the memory frame, the promised land, is somewhat different. It does employ visual language, but not as a bridge backwards. Instead, it uses visual language to create visions for what might become of Israel in the future. Mnemonically, these visions are called "possible selves." They project the kind of worlds that certain behaviors will produce. The goal, of course, is to steer people toward right behavior and away from wrong behavior. Deuteronomy projects two sets of "possible selves." The first depicts the results of obedience: Israel living life in paradisal land, where food, water, health, progeny, and God's presence are abundant. The second, however, depicts the results of disobedience: Israel suffering famine, disease, destruction, and exile from the land and God's presence.

Within these two frames dwell the other elements of memory—the three pillar episodes at the heart of identification. In contrast to the semantic framework, these are the province of episodic memory, shown by their association with the "eyes" motif and the trademark visual language. The exodus acts as the founding or origins event and, as such, establishes Israel's DNA as a people. Two sets of imagery are prominent in this: the misery of Egypt and the might of Yahweh's deliverance. Together these cultivate in Israel an identity as a redeemed people and a sense of love and gratitude toward their deliverer Yahweh.

Mount Horeb, in turn, builds on the exodus event. Through its imagery the people are portrayed as a covenant people and Yahweh as a revealing God. Further, this portrays the relationship between Yahweh and Israel as: the God who speaks and the people who listen. Two sets of imagery paint this portrait: the fiery and thunderous revelation of Yahweh and Moses's breaking of the covenant tablets when the people fail to "listen" to Yahweh. The third and final episode, the wilderness, further develops the previous episodes by acting as an anchoring memory. As an anchoring memory, it grounds the covenant relationship in two foundational aspects: Yahweh's fatherhood and Israel's sonship. Yet the fatherhood and sonship are imbued further with defining characteristics: Yahweh is a good and faithful father, while Israel is a stubborn and rebellious son. Deuteronomy accomplishes this through its use of imagery in depicting the spies' episode at Kadesh Barnea and the judgment on Dathan and Abiram (Israel as rebellious son), and in depicting Yahweh's provision for and discipline of Israel in the wilderness wasteland (Yahweh as faithful father).

This then takes us beyond even Vanhoozer's salvation history concern. Memory studies do allow us to show how Ricoeur's reading "event" takes shape as salvation history. But as I suggested in a previous chapter, the notion of salvation history is not the be-all and end-all. For starters, the notion is concerned chiefly with the world of the text; it does not pursue questions of the world in front of the text. How salvation history projects a world that draws in and transforms readers is not its concern. Furthermore, discussions of salvation history typically treat the events as if they were simple in composition and positive in nature. But, as we have seen, that is not true. The events are finely calibrated with semantic and episodic features to highlight elements that are both positive and negative; and this, in turn, forms in each new generation a particular kind of autobiography—one that motivates people to love Yahweh and listen to his voice.

TEXTS AND REAL PRESENCE

To develop this further, it is helpful to introduce another perspective on how Scripture reading constitutes an "event": the theological interpretation of Scripture.[25] Recognizing the term "theological interpretation" can mean many things, I draw from a particular strand. Its starting point is simply "to read the texts as they wish to be read, and as they should be read in order to do them justice."[26] This stands in contrast to the practice of reading the Bible with suspicion, trying to get behind the surface message to discern what is "really" going on. And since "the principal interest of the Bible's authors, of the text itself, and of the original community of readers was theological," the "biblical texts are ultimately concerned with the reality of God."[27]

Speech act theory has proven especially helpful in illuminating the theological purposes of Scripture.[28] In moving beyond the traditional image of language—as stating facts and representing realities—to one where language *does things with words*, speech act theory casts light not just on what biblical texts mean but on what they seek *to do*.[29] And what then does Scripture seek to do? Vanhoozer has taken up this question in regard to the canon as a whole and developed the notions of "scripture acts" and "canonic illocution."[30] In this view Scripture, despite its internal diversity, is understood as having one governing intention—"*covenanting*"—"What God does with Scripture is covenant with humanity . . . bringing about the reader's mutual indwelling with Christ."[31] Elsewhere Vanhoozer describes this as causing readers "to know the triune God by participating in the triune life."[32] What Scripture does, in other words, is draw people into an encounter with God in order to draw them into relationship with him.

But how does Scripture accomplish this? Richard Briggs is helpful here. He argues that Scripture represents a *summoning*: the "summoning presence" of God calls out for readers to come and appear before him.[33] To read faithfully, therefore, is not to observe Scripture like a spectator. Rather, it is like going to the theater and suddenly finding yourself addressed by the main actor and invited up on stage. Here you would have only two choices: either accept or decline. You could not merely remain passive; you must choose to participate or not. And this is how Briggs sees Scripture working. It requires readers to either decline the summons and remain an observer or accept it and become a participant. He calls this a "hermeneutic of self-involvement."[34]

A common way of understanding this involvement is as an auditory experience: Scripture is God's address to us and our role, in turn, is to *listen*. One of the finest discussions of this is found in Craig Bartholomew's volume on hermeneutics.[35] There he develops what might be called a theology of listening, a theology that places listening at the very center of what it means to be human: "*Theologically* listening is an extension of our being creaturely."[36]

Bartholomew argues, as such, that listening is the entry point for all human understanding: "Listening should be epistemologically central; indeed, it functions like a midwife, opening the way to thought."[37] The reason for this is that language is for humans the "house of being" (à la Heidegger), the place where they are born and grow up, but this house can only be opened to the outside through listening.

Bartholomew develops his view further by building on George Steiner's notion of "real presences."[38] In contrast to the perspective of the modern age, where the loss of transcendent values has meant a "real absence" of meaning in texts, Steiner argues that texts do have meaning since they are endowed with a "real presence." Texts have meaning, he says, because creation is "underwritten" with God's spoken word, and life lived within creation, therefore, is made meaningful with words. And this "grammar of creation makes all the difference in the world to reading,"[39] for it means that texts are meaning*ful*, that in texts we encounter the "real presence" of the one who imbues language with meaning.

If this is true of texts in general, then it is all the more true of biblical texts, whose very purpose is to mediate the presence of God: "Scripture is *the* means by which God gives himself to us and draws us into his very life."[40] Bartholomew especially points to the Shema in Deut 6:4–5: "Hear, O Israel: the Lord our God, the Lord is one. You shall love the Lord your God will all your heart, with all your soul, and with all your might." For ancient Israel, this was the central confession of faith, and it began with the command to "hear" (שׁמע). As Bartholomew points out, the word "hear" can also be translated as "listen." Listening, then, was critical to knowing God rightly, and Deuteronomy sought to instill this through domestic and communal practices.

One of the most notable features in Bartholomew's work is his focus on the aural—on Scripture as God's *voice* and our reading of Scripture as *listening*. Indeed, one of his chief concerns is that "Biblical hermeneutics needs to recover the primacy of creative receptivity, of listening."[41] I wholeheartedly agree with this, yet I also wonder what role the visual might play? Bartholomew is clear that he does not wish to prioritize the auditory metaphor over the visual in Scripture, and that his own concern is with the misuse of the visual in modern analyses of texts.[42] Yet this leaves open the question of how the aural and the visual work together to create an encounter with God's "real presence."

This, I think, is where my own study contributes to the conversation. Despite opinion to the contrary, Deuteronomy does not subordinate the visual to the aural in Israel's worship. Rather, it pairs them in complementary relationship. If Israel is to continue "hearing" Yahweh's voice, it must continue "seeing" his deeds. This seeing, I have argued, occurs through acts of memory. That is why we find in Deuteronomy what would otherwise appear as perfect strangers: a fiercely aniconic theology supported by highly visual language. It explains, too, the curious command for Israel to remember what they saw with their own "eyes," even though they had not "seen" anything.

Critical in this was the discovery, from memory studies, that visual features are what open the secret passage between communal memory and personal autobiography. They are the "wrinkle in time"[43] that allows people to identify with events they did not experience and come to see them as part of their own identity. Here Bartholomew's discussion of "real presences" in Scripture provides an interesting point of contact. His view, it seems, is that we experience the presence of God in Scripture by hearing his voice. But from Deuteronomy's perspective, this is not the whole story. It portrays people as deaf to the divine voice until after they have "seen" God's deeds. It is in seeing his benevolence and majesty that people's ears are opened to his voice. What this suggests, therefore, is that before communities can learn to listen they must learn to remember, for in remembering they are drawn into God's presence and "see" themselves standing before him.

NOTES

1. A notable exception, we will recall, is Jerry Hwang's *The Rhetoric of Remembrance: An Investigation of the "Fathers" in Deuteronomy* (Winona Lake, IN: Eisenbrauns, 2012). But while Hwang does apply speech-act theory to the book of Deuteronomy, he does so without bringing it to bear specifically on the phenomena of memory (which he subsumes under "imaginative speech-acts").

2. Luke Timothy Johnson, "Imagining the World Scripture Imagines," in *Theology and Scriptural Imagination*, ed. L. Gregory Jones and James J. Buckley (Oxford: Blackwell, 1998), 3.

3. In my opinion, the most helpful entry points into Ricoeur's work are: Paul Ricoeur, *Interpretation Theory: Discourse and the Surplus of Meaning* (Fort Worth, TX: Texas Christian University, 1976) and *Hermeneutics and the Human Sciences*, ed. and trans. John Thompson (Cambridge, UK: Cambridge University Press, 1981).

4. Kevin Vanhoozer, *Biblical Narrative in the Philosophy of Paul Ricoeur* (Cambridge, UK: Cambridge University Press, 1990).

5. Vanhoozer, *Biblical Narrative*, 17.

6. Vanhoozer, citing T. M. van Leeuwen, calls this a "central intuition" of Ricoeur's work (*Biblical Narrative*, 6).

7. Indeed, Ricoeur's work might be summarized as "a passion for the possible," with texts serving to create "narrative hope" (Vanhoozer, *Biblical Narrative*, 8).

8. Ricoeur, cited in Vanhoozer, *Biblical Narrative*, 24.

9. Vanhoozer, *Biblical Narrative*, 9. See his discussion, following Ricoeur, on the false-dichotomy of "real" versus "imaginary" and its grounding in the platonic

view of being vs. non-being. Vanhoozer uses Plato and Jean-Paul Sarte as examples of this view, contrasting them with Aristotle who sees mimesis having a more productive role.

10. On this, see Ricoeur's two works that "form a pair": *The Rule of Metaphor: The Creation of Meaning in Language*, trans. Robert Czerny, Kathleen McLaughlin, and John Costello (London: Routledge, 1978) and *Time and Narrative*, vols. 1–3, trans. Kathleen McLaughlin and David Pellauer (Chicago: University of Chicago Press, 1984–1988). Ricoeur calls them a pair in the preface to *Time and Narrative*, vol. 1, ix.

11. Paul Ricoeur, quoted in Vanhoozer, *Biblical Narrative*, 10.

12. For "a text remains a discourse told by somebody, said by someone to someone else about something" (Paul Ricoeur, *Interpretation Theory*, 30).

13. He especially singles out the three classic elements of "authorial intention," "initial situation" (Sitz-im-Leben), and "primitive audience." See Paul Ricoeur, *Figuring the Sacred: Religion, Narrative, and Imagination*, ed. Mark Wallace, trans. David Pellauer (Minneapolis, MN: Fortress, 1995), 38.

14. Paul Ricoeur, *Interpretation Theory*, 30.

15. "This notion of the 'world of the text' is perhaps Ricoeur's most important contribution to interpretation theory. Indeed, Ricoeur recasts the whole hermeneutic enterprise in light of this notion." Vanhoozer, *Biblical Narrative*, 88.

16. Lewis Mudge, "Paul Ricoeur on Biblical Interpretation," in Paul Ricoeur, *Essays on Biblical Interpretation*, ed. Lewis Mudge (Philadelphia: Fortress Press, 1980), 26.

17. "The text speaks of a possible world and of a possible way of orientating oneself within it . . . here showing is at the same time creating a new mode of being" (Paul Ricoeur, *Interpretation Theory*, 88).

18. We may also summarize Ricoeur's hermeneutic arc as: "an initial moment of 'understanding' (a first, naïve encounter with the text), a critical moment of 'explanation,' and then a refigured moment of 'application' (a 'second naïveté')." Daniel Treier, *Introducing Theological Interpretation of Scripture: Recovering a Christian Practice* (Grand Rapids, MI: Baker, 2008), 133.

19. Vanhoozer, *Biblical Narrative*, 12. Vanhoozer's concluding chapter is especially helpful in outlining the strengths and weaknesses of Ricoeur's work in this regard (pp. 275–89).

20. Ricoeur's notion of distanciation is difficult to pin down, as it appears to have multiple meanings. For example, see Pierre Bühler, "Ricoeur's Concept of Distanciation as a Challenge for Theological Hermeneutics," in *Paul Ricoeur: Poetics and Religion*, ed. Jozef Verheyden, Theo Hettema, and Pieter Vandecasteele (Leuven: Peeters, 2011), 151–65. As indicated above, the sense I find most helpful is distanciation as "twofold distance." See Aaron Pidel, "Ricoeur and Ratzinger on Biblical History and Hermeneutics," *Journal of Theological Interpretation* 8, no. 2 (2014): 193–212.

21. Ricoeur, *Interpretation Theory*, 91.

22. "Therefore, I wouldn't speak of a fusion of horizons in Ricoeur's hermeneutics . . . If appropriation happens through distanciation, the distance between the different

horizons must be preserved and not surpassed." Bühler, "Ricoeur's Concept of Distanciation," 162.

23. Pidel, "Ricoeur and Ratzinger," 193.

24. Robin Parry, *Old Testament Story and Christian Ethics: The Rape of Dinah as a Case Study* (Milton Keynes, UK: Paternoster, 2004), 17.

25. For a good discussion on how this fits within the broader quest of hermeneutics, see Daniel Treier, *Introducing Theological Interpretation of Scripture: Recovering a Christian Practice* (Grand Rapids, MI: Baker, 2008), 103–56.

26. Kevin Vanhoozer, "Introduction," in *Dictionary for Theological Interpretation of the Bible*, gen. ed. Kevin Vanhoozer (Grand Rapids, MI: Baker, 2005), 22.

27. Vanhoozer, "Introduction."

28. For a good summary in regard to its use in theological hermeneutics, see Richard Briggs, "Speech-Act Theory," in *Dictionary for Theological Interpretation of the Bible*, gen ed. Kevin Vanhoozer (Grand Rapids, MI: Baker, 2005), 763–66.

29. Echoing the seminal work by J. L. Austin, *How to Do Things with Words* (Oxford: Oxford University Press, 1962).

30. Kevin Vanhoozer, *First Theology* (Downers Grove, IL: InterVarsity Press, 2002). He especially discusses this in "From Speech Acts to Scripture Acts," 159–203.

31. Vanhoozer, *First Theology*, 194, 203.

32. Vanhoozer, "Introduction," *Dictionary for Theological Interpretation*, 24.

33. See especially, Richard Briggs, "Summoned: The Virtue of Receptivity," in *The Virtuous Reader: Old Testament Narrative and Interpretive Virtue* (Grand Rapids, MI: Baker Academic, 2010), 167.

34. He develops this more fully in Richard Briggs, *Words in Action: Speech Act Theory and Biblical* Interpretation (New York: T. & T. Clark, 2001). For a short discussion of his view, see Richard Briggs, "Getting Involved: Speech Acts and Biblical Interpretation," *ANVIL* 20, no. 1 (2003): 25–34.

35. Craig Bartholomew, *Introducing Biblical Hermeneutics: A Comprehensive Framework for Hearing God in Scripture* (Grand Rapids, MI: Baker Academic, 2015), especially the chapter "Listening and Biblical Interpretation," pp. 17–47.

36. Bartholomew, *Hermeneutics*, 22.

37. Bartholomew, *Hermeneutics*, 20.

38. Bartholomew, *Hermeneutics*, 25–33. See also George Steiner, *Real Presences: Is There Anything in What We Say?* (London: Faber & Faber, 1989).

39. Bartholomew, *Hermeneutics*, 28.

40. Bartholomew, *Hermeneutics*, 35.

41. Bartholomew, *Hermeneutics*, 24.

42. Bartholomew, *Hermeneutics*, 24–25, especially n. 50.

43. À la Madeleine L'Engle, *A Wrinkle in Time* (New York: Farrar, Straus & Giroux, 1962).

Bibliography

Addis, Donna Rose, and Lynette Tippett. "The Contributions of Autobiographical Memory to the Content and Continuity of Identity." In *Self-Continuity*, edited by Fabio Sani, 71–84. London: Psychology Press, 2008.
Ahlström, Gösta Werner. *Royal Administration and National Religion in Ancient Palestine*. Leiden: Brill, 1982.
Albertz, Rainer. *A History of Israelite Religion in the Old Testament Period*. London: SCM Press, 1994.
Albright, William. "Deuteronomy XXXII." *Vetus Testamentum* 9 (1959): 339–46.
Allen, David. *Deuteronomy and Exhortation in Hebrews*. Tübingen: Mohr Siebeck, 2008.
Alter, Robert. *The Art of Biblical Narrative*. Rev. ed. New York: Basic Books, 2011.
Altmann, Peter. *Festive Meals in Ancient Israel*. Berlin: De Gruyter, 2011.
Anbar, Moshe. "The Story About the Building of an Altar on Mount Ebal." In *Das Deuteronomium*, edited by Norbert Lohfink, 304–9. Leuven, Belgium: Leuven University Press, 1985.
Anderson, John. *The Adaptive Character of Thought*. New Jersey: Lawrence Erlbaum, 1990.
Anderson, John R., and Lael J. Schooler. "Reflections of the Environment in Memory." *Psychological Science* 2, no. 6 (1991): 396–408.
Asmal, Kader, Louise Asmal, and Ronald Roberts. *Reconciliation Through Truth*. Cape Town: David Philip, 1996.
Assmann, Aleida. "Canon and Archive." In *The Collective Memory Reader*, edited by Jeffrey K. Olick, Vered Vinitzky-Seroussi, and Daniel Levy, 334–37. Oxford: Oxford University Press, 2011.
———. "Canon and Archive." In *Cultural Memory Studies*, edited by Astrid Erll and Ansgar Nünning, 97–107. Berlin: Walter de Gruyter, 2008.
Assmann, Jan. "Collective Memory and Cultural Identity." In *New German Critique* 65 (1995): 125–33. Translated by John Czaplicka.

———. "Exodus and Memory." In *The Afterlife of Events: Perspectives on Mnemohistory*, edited by Marek Tamm, 115–133. Basingstoke, UK: Palgrave Macmillan, 2015.

———. "Form as a Mnemonic Device: Cultural Texts and Cultural Memory." In *Performing the Gospel*, edited by Richard A. Horsley, Jonathan A. Draper, and John M. Foley, 67–82. Minneapolis, MN: Fortress Press, 2011.

———. *Moses the Egyptian: The Memory of Egypt in Western Monotheism*. Cambridge, MA: Harvard University Press, 1997.

———. *Religion and Cultural Memory*. Translated by Rodney Livingstone. Stanford, CA: Stanford University Press, 2006.

———. "What is 'Cultural Memory?'" In *Religion and Cultural Memory*, 1–6. Translated by R. Livingstone. Stanford, CA: Stanford University Press, 2006.

Austin, J. L. *How to Do Things with Words*. Oxford: Oxford University Press, 1962.

Avigad, Nahman. "Samaria (City)." In *New Encyclopedia of the Archaeological Excavations of the Holy Land*, vol. 4, edited by Ephraim Stern, 1300–10. University Park, PA: Eisenbrauns, 1993.

Baker, Felicity, and Tony Wigram. "Rehabilitating the Uninflected Voice: Finding Climax and Cadence." *Music Therapy Perspectives* 22 (2004): 4–10.

Bal, Mieke. "Introduction." In *Acts of Memory*, edited by Mieke Bal, Jonathan Crewe, and Leo Spitzer. New Hampshire: University Press of New England, 1999.

Baltzer, Klaus. *The Covenant Formulary in Old Testament, Jewish and Early Christian Writings*. Oxford: Blackwell, 1971.

Barker, Paul. "The Theology of Deuteronomy 27." *Tyndale Bulletin* 49, no. 2 (1998): 277–303.

———. *The Triumph of Grace in Deuteronomy*. Reprint, Eugene, OR: Wipf & Stock, 2007.

Barnier, Amanda J., and John Sutton. "From Individual to Collective Memory: Theoretical and Empirical Perspectives." *Memory* 16 (2008): 177–82.

Barnier, Amanda J., John Sutton, Celia B. Harris, and Robert A. Wilson. "A Conceptual and Empirical Framework for the Social Distribution of Cognition: The Case of Memory." *Cognitive Systems Research* 9 (2008): 33–51.

Barr, James. *Old and New in Interpretation*. New York: Harper & Row, 1966.

Bartholomew, Craig. *Introducing Biblical Hermeneutics: A Comprehensive Framework for Hearing God in Scripture*. Grand Rapids, MI: Baker Academic, 2015.

Beale, G. K., and D. A. Carson, eds. *Commentary on the New Testament Use of the Old Testament*. Grand Rapids, MI: Baker Academic, 2007.

Beale, G. K., and Sean McDonough. "Revelation." In *Commentary on the New Testament Use of the Old Testament*, 1133–34. Grand Rapids, MI: Baker Academic, 2007.

Beike, Denise R., Erica Kleinknecht, and Erin T. Wirth-Beaumont. "How Emotional and Nonemotional Memories Define the Self." In *The Self and* Memory, edited by Denise Beike, James M. Lampinen, and Douglas A. Behrend, 141–60. New York: Psychology Press.

Beike, Denise R., James M. Lampinen, and Douglas A. Behrend. "Evolving Conceptions of the Self and Memory." In *The Self and* Memory, edited by Denise Beike, James M. Lampinen, and Douglas A. Behrend, 3–10. New York: Psychology Press.

———. *The Self and Memory*. New York: Psychology Press, 2004.

Ben Zvi, Ehud. "Remembering the Prophets through the Reading and Rereading of a Collection of Prophetic Books in Yehud: Methodological Considerations and Explorations." In *Remembering and Forgetting in Early Second Temple Judah*, edited by Ehud Ben Zvi and Christoph Levin, 17–44. FAT 85. Tübingen: Mohr Siebeck, 2012.

Benjamin, Moshe-Naveh, Morris Moscovitch, and Henry L. Roediger III, eds. *Perspectives on Human Memory and Cognitive Aging: Essays in Honor of Fergus Craik*. London: Psychology Press, 2002.

Berge, Kåre. "The Anti-Hero as a Figure of Memory and Didacticism in Exodus: The Case of Pharaoh and Moses." In *Remembering and Forgetting in Early Second Temple Judah*, edited by Ehud Ben Zvi and Christoph Levin, 145–60. FAT 85. Tübingen: Mohr Siebeck, 2012.

———. "Literacy, Utopia, and Memory: Is There a Public Teaching in Deuteronomy?" *Journal of Hebrew Scriptures* 12 (2012): 1–19.

Berlin, Adele. *Poetics and Interpretation of Biblical Narrative*. Stirling, Scotland: The Almond Press, 1983.

Besson, Mireille, Frederique Faita, Isabelle Peretz, Anne-Marie Bonnel, and Jean Requin. "Singing in the Brain: Independence of Lyrics and Tunes." *Psychological Science* 9 (1998): 494–98.

BiCuM: The Centre for Bible and Cultural Memory. Accessed January 13, 2014. http://www.teol.ku.dk/english/dept/bicum/hoejrebokse/bicum/.

Biran, Avraham, and Joseph Naveh. "An Aramaic Stele Frament from Tel Dan." *Israel Exploration Journal* 43 (1993): 81–88.

Birnbaum, Solomon A. "The Fragment of a Stele." In *The Objects from Samaria*, edited by John Winter Crowfoot, Grace Mary Crowfoot, and Kathleen M. Kenyon, 33–34. London: Palestine Exploration Fund, 1957.

Block, Daniel. *The Book of Ezekiel*. Vol. 1. Grand Rapids, MI: Eerdmans, 1997.

———. *Deuteronomy*. Grand Rapids, MI: Zondervan, 2012.

Borger, Riekele. *Die Inschriften Asarhaddons Königs von Assyrien*. New Jersey: Weidner, 1956.

Bourdieux, Pierre. *Outline of a Theory of Practice*. Translated by Richard Nice. Cambridge: Cambridge University Press, 1977.

Bovati, Pietro. *Re-Establishing Justice*, trans. M. J. Smith. Sheffield: Sheffield Academic Press, 1994.

Branson, R. D. "יסר." In *The Theological Dictionary of the Old Testament*, vol. 6, edited by G. Johannes Botterweck and Helmer Ringgren, 130. Translated by D. E. Green. Grand Rapids, MI: Eerdmans, 1990.

Braulik, Georg. "Commemoration of Passion and Feast of Joy: Popular Liturgy According to the Festival Calendar of the Book of Deuteronomy (Deut 16:1–17)." In *The Theology of Deuteronomy*: Collected Essays of Georg Braulik, 67–85. N. Richmond, TX: BIBAL Press, 1994.

———. *Deuteronomium II: 16, 18–34, 12*. Würzburg: Echter Verlag, 1992.

———. "Deuteronomy and the Commemorative Culture." In *The Theology of Deuteronomy*, 190–91. Translated by Ulrika Lindblad. North Richland Hills, TX: BiBAL Press, 1994.

———. "Die Ausdrücke für 'Gesetz' im Buch Deuteronomium." *Biblica* 51 (1970): 39–66.
———. *Die deuteronomischen Gesetze und der Dekalog*. Stuttgart: Katholisches Bibelwerk, 1991.
———. "Die Mittel deuteronomischer Rhetorik." *Theology and Philosophy* 56, no. 2 (1981): 260.
———. "The Joy of the Feast: The Conception of the Cult in Deuteronomy: The Oldest Biblical Festival Theory." In *The Theology of Deuteronomy*, 27–65. N. Richmond, TX: BIBAL Press, 1994.
———. "Literarkritische und archaeologische Stratigraphie: Zu S Mittmanns Analyse von Deuteronomium 4: 1–40." *Biblica* 59, no. 3 (1978): 351–83.
Braun, Joachim. *Music in Ancient Israel/Palestine*. Grand Rapids, MI: Eerdmans, 2002.
Brenner, Althalya, and Burke O. Long. "Introduction: Memory Telling and the Art of (Self-) Definition." In *Performing Memory in Biblical Narrative and Beyond*, edited by Althalya Brenner and Frank. H. Polak. Sheffield, UK: Sheffield Phoenix Press, 2009.
Briggs, Richard. "Getting Involved: Speech Acts and Biblical Interpretation." *ANVIL* 20, no. 1 (2003): 25–34.
———. "Speech-Act Theory." In *Dictionary for Theological Interpretation of the Bible*, edited by Kevin Vanhoozer, 763–66. Grand Rapids, MI: Baker, 2005.
———. "Summoned: The Virtue of Receptivity." In *The Virtuous Reader: Old Testament Narrative and Interpretive Virtue*, 167. Grand Rapids, MI: Baker Academic, 2010.
———. *Words in Action: Speech Act Theory and Biblical* Interpretation. New York: T. & T. Clark, 2001.
Britt, Brian. "Deuteronomy 31–32 as a Textual Memorial." *Biblical Interpretation* 8 (2000): 358–74.
Brown, Roger, and James Kulick. "Flashbulb Memories." *Cognition* 5 (1977): 73–99.
Brown, Scott C., and Craik, Fergus I. M. "Encoding and Retrieval of Information." In *The Oxford Handbook of Memory*, edited by Endel Tulving and Fergus I. M. Craik, 93–108. Oxford: Oxford University Press, 2000.
Brueggemann, Walter. "Imagination as a Mode of Fidelity." In *Understanding the Word*, edited by James T. Butler, Edgar W. Conrad, and Ben C. Ollenburger, 13–36. Sheffield: JSOT Press, 1985.
Bühler, Pierre. "Ricoeur's Concept of Distanciation as a Challenge for Theological Hermeneutics." In *Paul Ricoeur: Poetics and Religion*, edited by Jozef Verheyden, Theo Hettema, Pieter Vandecasteel, 151–65. Leuven: Peeters, 2011.
Burnside, Johnathan P. "Exodus and Asylum: Uncovering the Relationship between Biblical Law and Narrative." *Journal for the Study of the Old Testament* 34 (2010): 243–66.
Carasik, Michael. *Die Mittel deuteronomischer Rhetorik erhoben aus Deuteronomium 4.1–40*. Rome: Pontifical Biblical Institute, 1978.
———. *Theologies of the Mind in Biblical Israel*. Bern, Switzerland: Peter Lang, 2006.
———. "To See a Sound: A Deuteronomic Rereading of Exodus 20:15." *Prooftexts* 19, no. 3 (1999): 257–76.

Carlson, R. A. *David, the Chosen King*. Uppsala: Almqvist & Wiksell, 1964.
Carmichael, Calum. *The Laws of Deuteronomy*. Reprint, Eugene, OR: Wipf & Stock, 2008.
Carr, David. *The Formation of the Hebrew Bible*. Oxford: Oxford University Press, 2011.
———. *Writing on the Tablet of the Heart: Origins of Scripture and Literature*. Oxford: Oxford University Press, 2005.
Carrillo Alday, Salvador. "Contexto redaccional del *Cántico de Moisés* (Dt 31, 1–32, 47)." *Estudios Bíblicos* 26 (1967): 283–93
Carruthers, Mary Jean. *The Book of Memory*, 2nd ed. Cambridge, UK: Cambridge University Press, 2008.
Casey, Edward. *Remembering*, 2nd ed. Bloomington, IN: Indiana University Press, 2000.
Cassuto, Umberto. *Exodus*. Translated by Israel Abrahams. Jerusalem: Magnes Press, 1967.
———. "The Prophet Hosea and the Books of the Pentateuch." In *Biblical and Oriental Studies*, vol. 1, 1081–161. Jerusalem: Magnes Press, 1975.
Childs, Brevard. *Exodus*. London: Westminster Press, 1974, 203.
———. *Introduction to the Old Testament as Scripture*. Minneapolis, MN: Fortress Press, 1979.
———. *Memory and Tradition in Israel*. London: SCM Press, 1962.
———. *Theologies of the Mind*. New York: Peter Lang, 2006.
Cholewinksi, Alfred. *Das Heiligkeitsgesetz und Deuteronomium*. Rome: Biblical Institute Press, 1976.
Christensen, Duane. *Deuteronomy 1–11*. Nashville, TN: Thomas Nelson, 2001.
———. *Deuteronomy 1:1—21:9*. Rev. 2nd ed. Nashville, TN: Thomas Nelson, 2001.
———. *Deuteronomy 21:10—34:12*. Nashville, TN: Thomas Nelson, 1997.
———. "The Numeruswechsel in Deuteronomy 12." In *A Song of Power and the Power of Song*, edited by Duane Christensen, 394–402. University Park, PA: Eisenbrauns, 1993.
Christianson, Sven-Åke. "Flashbulb Memories: Special, But Not So Special." *Memory and Cognition*, 17: (1989): 435–43.
Clark, Andy. *Being There*. Cambridge, MA: MIT Press, 1997.
Clines, David J. A. "The Evidence for an Autumnal New Year in Pre-exilic Israel Reconsidered." *Journal of Biblical Literature* 93 (1974): 22–40.
———. *The Theme of the Pentateuch*. 2nd ed. Sheffield: Sheffield Academic Press, 1997.
Coats, George W. "Traditio-Historical of the Reed Sea Motif." *Vetus Testamentum* 17 (1967): 253–65.
Cody, Aelred. "'Little Historical Creed' or 'Little Historical Anamnesis'?" *Catholic Biblical Quarterly* 68 (2006): 1–10.
Cohn, Yehudah. *Tangled Up in Text*. Providence, RI: Brown University, 2008.
Connerton, Paul. *How Societies Remember*. Cambridge, UK: Cambridge University Press, 1989.
Conway, Martin A. "Memory and the Self." *Journal of Memory and Language* 53, no. 4 (2005): 594–628.

Conway, Martin A., and Christopher W. Pleydell-Pearce. "The Construction of Autobiographical Memories in the Self-Memory System." *Psychological Review* 107 (2000): 262–88.
Conway, Martin A., David C. Rubin, Hans Spinnler, and Willem A. Wagenaar. *Theoretical Perspectives on Autobiographical Memory*. Dordrecht, The Netherlands: Kluwer Academic, 1992.
Conway, Martin A., Stephen J. Anderson, Steen F. Larsen, C. M. Donnelly, Mark A. McDaniel, A. G. R. McClelland, Richard Rawles, and R. H. Logie. "The Formation of Flashbulb Memories." *Memory and Cognition* 22, no. 3 [1994]: 326–43.
Coogan, Michael. *The Dictionary of Biblical Imagery*. Edited by Leland Ryken, James C. Wilhoit, and Tremper Longman. Westmont, IL: InterVarsity Press, 1998.
———. "The Exodus." In *The Oxford Companion to the Bible*, edited by Bruce M. Metzger and Michael David Coogan, 209–12. Oxford: Oxford University Press, 1993.
Cornill, Carl. *Einleitung in das Alte Testament*. Freiburg: Mohr, 1891.
Couroyer, B. "La Tablette du Coeur." *Revue Biblique* 90 (1983): 416–34.
Craigie, Peter. *The Book of Deuteronomy*. NICOT. Grand Rapids, MI: Eerdmans, 1976.
Craik, Fergus I. M. and Robert Lockhart. "Levels of Processing: A Framework for Memory Research." *Journal of Verbal Learning and Verbal Behaviour* 11 (1972): 671–84.
Culp, A.J. "Review of Ellman, Barat, *Memory and Covenant: The Role of Israel's and God's Memory in Sustaining the Deuteronomic and Priestly Covenants* (Emerging Scholars Series; Minneapolis, MN: Fortress, 2013)." *Journal of Hebrew Scriptures* 14 (2014). http://www.jhsonline.org/reviews/reviews_new/review723.htm.
———. "Review of Leveen, Adriane, *Memory and Tradition in the Book of Numbers* (Cambridge, UK: Cambridge University Press, 2008)." *Anvil: Journal of Theology and Mission* 26 (2009): 293–94.
De Boer, Pieter Arie Hendrick. *Gedenken und Gedachtnis in der Welt des Alten Testament*. Stuttgart: W. Kohlhammer, 1962.
Dembsky, Aaron. "On Reading Ancient Inscriptions: The Monumental Aramaic Stele Fragment from Tel Dan." *Journal of the Ancient Near Eastern Society* 23 (1995): 29–35.
De Moor, Johannes. "Poetic Fragments in Deuteronomy and the Deuteronomic History." In *Studies in Deuteronomy in Honour of C. J. Labuschagne on the Occasion of his 65th Birthday*, edited by Florentino García Martínez, Anthony Hilhorst, J. T. A. G. M. van Ruiten, and A. S. van der Woude, 190–91. Leiden: Brill, 1994.
De Tillesse, G. Minette. "Sections 'Tu' et Sections 'Vous' dans le *Deutéronome*." *Vetus Testamentum* 12 (1962): 29–87.
Deurloo, Karel. "The One God and All Israel in Its Generations." In *Studies in Deuteronomy*, edited by Florentino García Martínez, Anthony Hilhorst, J. T. A. G. M. van Ruiten, and A. S. van der Woude, 31–46. Leiden: Brill, 1994.
De Vaux, Roland, and J. T. Milik, eds. *Qumran Grotte 4*. Vol. 2. Oxford: Oxford University Press, 1977.

Dever, William. *Who Were the Early Israelites and Where Did They Come From?* Grand Rapids, MI: Eerdmans, 2003.

DeVries, Simon. *Yesterday, Today and Tomorrow*. Grand Rapids, MI: Eerdmans, 1975.

Dickens, Charles. *A Christmas Carol*. London: Chapman and Hall, 1843.

Diepold, Peter. *Israels Land*. Stuttgart: Kohlhammer, 1972.

Dolan, Jill. *Utopia in Performance: Finding Hope at the Theatre*. Ann Arbor, MI: University of Michigan Press, 2005.

Dorsey, David. *The Roads and Highways of Ancient Israel*. Baltimore, MD: Johns Hopkins Press, 1991.

Driver, Godfrey Rolles. *Canaanite Myths and Legends*. Reprint, Edinburgh: T. & T. Clark, 1956.

Driver, Samuel Rolles. *A Critical and Exegetical Commentary on Deuteronomy*. 2nd ed. Edinburgh: T. & T. Clark, 1896.

———. *Deuteronomy*. Edinburgh: T. & T. Clark, 1902.

———. *Deuteronomy*. New York: Charles Scriber's Sons, 1895.

Edelman, Diana. "Exodus and Pesach-Massot as Evolving Social Memory." In *Remembering (and Forgetting) in Judah's Early Second Temple Period*, edited by Christoph Levin and Ehud Ben Zvi, 161–93. Forschungenzum Alten Testaments, 85. Tübingen: Mohr Siebeck, 2012.

Ehring, Christina. "YHWH's Return in Isaiah 40:1–11* and 52:7–10: Pre-exilic Cultic Traditions of Jerusalem and Babylonian Influence." In *Remembering (and Forgetting) in Judah's Early Second Temple Period*, edited by Christoph Levin and Ehud Ben Zvi, 91–104. Forschungenzum Alten Testaments, 85. Tübingen: Mohr Siebeck, 2012.

Eliot, T. S. "Little Gidding." In *Four Quartets*. New York: Houghton Mifflin Harcourt, 1943.

Ellman, Barat. *Memory and Covenant: The Role of Israel's and God's Memory in Sustaining the Deuteronomic and Priestly Covenants*. Minneapolis, MN: Fortress, 2013.

Evans, Carl. "Cult Images, Royal Policies and the Origins of Aniconism." In *The Pitcher Is Broken*, edited by Steven Holloway and Lowell Handy, 192–212. Sheffield: Sheffield Academic Press, 1995.

Fales, Frederick. *Aramaic Epigraphs on Clay Tablets of the Neo-Assyrian Period*. Rome: La Sapienza, 1986.

Fentress James, and Chris Wickham. *Social Memory*. Oxford: Blackwell, 1992.

Finsterbusch, Karin. *Weisung für Israel: Studien zu religiösem Lehren und Lernen im Deuteronomium und in seinem Umfeld*. Tübingen: Mohr Siebeck, 2005.

Fisch, Max H. "The Song of Moses: Pastoral in Reverse." In *Poetry with a Purpose*, 55–79. Bloomington, IN: Indiana University Press, 1988.

Fischer, Georg, and Norbert Lohfink. "'Diese Worte sollst du summen': Dtn 6, 7 w^{e}dibbarta bam—ein verlorener Schlüssel zur meditativen Kultur in Israel." *Theologie und Philosophie* 62 (1987): 59–72.

Fivusch, Robyn. "The Social Construction of Personal Narratives." *Merrill-Palmer Quarterly* 37 (1991): 59–82.

Fivush, Robyn, and Catherine A. Haden, eds. *Autobiographical Memory and the Construction of the Narrative Self*. New Jersey: Lawrence Erlbaum Associates, 2003.

Fokkelman, J. P. *Major Poems of the Hebrew Bible*. Assen: Van Gorcum, 1998.

Foucault, Michael. *Language, Counter-Memory, Practice*. Edited by D. F. Bouchard. Ithaca, NY: Cornell University Press, 1977.

Fowler, Bridget. *The Obituary as Collective Memory*. Abingdon, UK: Routledge, 2007.

Fraas, Hans Jürgen. "Gemeinschaft-Geschichte-Persönlichkeit: Dtn 6, 20 als Grundmodell religiöses Sozialisation." In *Von Wittenberg nach Memphis*, edited by Walter Homolka and Otto Ziegelmeier, 21–37. Vandenhoeck & Ruprecht, 1989.

Fretheim, Terence. *Exodus*. Louisville, KY: John Knox Press, 1991.

Garry, Maryanne, Charles G. Manning, Elizabeth F. Loftus, and Steven J. Sherman. "Imagination Inflation: Imagining a Childhood Event Inflates Confidence That It Occurred." *Psychonomic Bulletin and Review* 3 (1996): 208–14.

Garry, Maryanne, Stefanie J. Sharman, Kimberley A. Wade, Maree J. Hunt, and Peter J. Smith. "Imagination Inflation Is a Fact, Not an Artifact: A Reply to Pezdek and Eddy." *Memory and Cognition* 29 (2001): 719–29.

Gedi, Noa, and Yigal Elam. "Collective Memory—What Is It?" *History and Memory* 8, no. 1 (1996): 30–50.

Geller, Stephen A. "Fiery Wisdom: Logos and Lexis in Deuteronomy 4." *Prooftexts* 14 (1994): 103–39.

———. *Sacred Enigmas*. London: Routledge, 1996.

George, Mark. *Israel's Tabernacle as Sacred Space*. Atlanta: Society of Biblical Literature, 2009.

Gertz, Jan. "Die Passa-Massot-Ordnung im deuteronomischen Festkalender." In *Das Deuteronomium und seine Querbeziehungen*, 56–80. Göttingen: Vandenhoeck & Ruprecht, 1996.

Gesundheit, Shimon. "Der deuteronomische Festkalender." In *Das Deuteronomium*, edited by Georg Braulik, 57–67. Bern: Peter Lang, 2003.

———. "Intertextualität und literarhistorische Analyse der Festkalender in Exodus und im Deuteronomium." In *Festtraditionen in Israel und im Alten Orient*, edited by Erhard Blum and Rüdiger Lux, VWGT 28. Gütersloh: Gütersloher Verlagshaus, 2006.

Giles, Terry, and Bill Doan. *Twice Used Songs: Performance Criticism of the Songs of Ancient Israel*. Peabody, MA: Hendrickson Publishers, 2009.

Glenberg, Arthur M. "What Memory is For." *Behavioral and Brain Sciences* 20 (1997): 1–55.

Godden, D. R., and A. D. Baddeley. "Context-Dependant Memory in Two Natural Contexts: On Land and Under Water." *British Journal of Psychology* 66 (1975): 325–31.

Goff, Lyn M., and Henry L. Roediger. "Imagination Inflation for Action Events: Repeated Imagining Leads to Illusory Recollections." *Memory and Cognition* 26 (1998): 20–33.

Goldstein, Bernard R., and Alan Cooper. "The Festivals of Israel and Judah and the Literary History of the Pentateuch." *Journal of the American Oriental Society* 110 (1990): 19–31.

Griffiths, Thomas L., Mark Steyvers, and Alana Firl. "Google and the Mind: Predicting Fluency with Page Rank." *Psychological Science* 18, no. 12 (2007): 1069–76.

Groves, Thomas L. *Actualization and Interpretation in the Old Testament*. Scholars Press, 1987.

Halbwachs, Maurice. *The Collective Memory*. New York: Harper & Row, 1980.

———. *La topographie légendaire des Évangiles en Terre Sainte* in 1941. Paris: Presses Universitaires de France.

———. *Les cadres sociaux de la mémoire*. Paris: Librairie Félix Alcan.

———. *On Collective Memory*. Edited, translated and introduction by Lewis Coser. Chicago, IL: University of Chicago Press, 1992.

Hartenstein, Friedhelm. "YHWH's Ways and New Creation in Deutero-Isaiah." In *Remembering (and Forgetting) in Judah's Early Second Temple Period*, edited by Christoph Levin and Ehud Ben Zvi, 73–89. Forschungenzum Alten Testaments, 85. Tübingen: Mohr Siebeck, 2012.

Hays, Richard. *Echoes of Scripture in the Gospels*. Waco, TX: Baylor University Press, 2016.

———. *Echoes of Scripture in the Letters of Paul*. New Haven: Yale University Press, 1989.

Hendel, Ronald. "The Exodus in Biblical Memory." *Journal of Biblical Literature* 120 (2001): 608–15.

———. *Reading Genesis*. Edited by Ronald Hendel. Cambridge: Cambridge University Press, 2010.

———. *Remembering Abraham*. Oxford: Oxford University Press, 2005.

———. "Social Origins of the Aniconic Tradition." *Catholic Biblical Quarterly* 50 (1988): 365–82.

Hervieu-Léger, Danièle. *Religion as a Chain of Memory*. Translated by Simon Lee. New Brunswick, NJ: Rutgers University Press, 2000.

Hess, Richard. *Israelite Religions*. Ada, MI: Baker Academic, 2007.

Hillers, Delbert. *Covenant*. Baltimore, MD: Johns Hopkins Press, 1969.

Hobsbawm, Eric, and Terence Ranger, eds. *The Invention of Tradition*. Cambridge: Cambridge University Press, 1992.

Hodgkin, Katharine, and Susannah Radstone, eds. *Memory, History, Nation*. Brunswick, NJ: Transaction Publisher, 2006.

Holter, Knut. *Deuteronomy 4 and the Second Commandment*. New York: Peter Lang, 2003.

Houston, Walter J. "Rejoicing Before the Lord: The Function of the Festal Gathering in Deuteronomy." In *Feasts and Festivals*, edited by Christopher M. Tuckett, 10–11. Leuven: Peeters, 2009.

Howe, Mark. *The Fate of Early Memories*. American Psychological Association, 2000.

Hutzli, Jürg. *Die Erzählung von Hanna und Samuel*. Zurich: Theologischer Verlag Zürich, 2007.

Hwang, Jerry. *The Rhetoric of Remembrance: An Investigation of the "Fathers" in Deuteronomy*. Winona Lake, IN: Eisenbrauns, 2012.

Hyman, Ira E. Jr., and Joel Pentland, "The Role of Mental Imagery in the Creation of False Childhood Memories." *Journal of Memory and Language* 35 (1996):101–17.

Intraub, Helene, and Susan Nicklos. "Levels of Processing and Picture Memory: The Physical Superiority Effect." *Journal of Experimental Psychology. Learning, Memory, and Cognition* 11 (1985): 284–98.

Johnson, Luke Timothy. "Imagining the World Scripture Imagines." In *Theology and Scriptural Imagination*, edited by L. Gregory Jones and James J. Buckley, 3. Oxford: Blackwell, 1998.

Johnson, Marcia K. "Reality Monitoring: An Experimental Phenomenological Approach." *Journal of Experimental Psychology* 117 (1988): 390–94.

———. "Source Monitoring and Memory Distortion." *Philosophical Transactions of the Royal Society of London* 352 (1997): 1733–45.

Johnson, Marcia K., Shahin Hashtroudi, and D. Stephen Lindsay. "Source Monitoring." *Psychological Bulletin* 114 (1993): 3–28.

Jourdain, Robert. *Music, the Brain, and Ecstasy*. New York: Harper Perennial, 1998.

Kansteiner, Wulf. "Finding Meaning in Memory: A Methodological Critique of Collective Memory Studies." *History and Theory* 41 (2002): 179–97.

Kasabova, Anita. *On Autobiographical Memory*. Newcastle upon Tyne, UK: Cambridge Scholars, 2009.

Keel, Othmar. *Wirkmächtige Siegeszeichen im alten Testament*. Freiberg: Universitätsverlag Freiburg Schweiz, 1974.

———. "Zeichen der Verbundenheit: Zur Vorgeschichte und Bedeutung der Forderungen von Dt 6,8f und par." In *Mélanges Dominique Barthèlémy*, edited by Pierre Casetti, Othmar Keel, and Adrian Schenker, 213–14. Göttingen: Vandenhoeck and Ruprecht, 1981.

Kleinert, H. W. P. *Untersuchungen zur alttestamentlichen Rechts—und Literaturgeschichte*. Vol. 1. Bielefeld: Verlhagen & Klasing, 1872.

Knapp, Dietrich. *Deuteronomium 4*. Göttingen: Vandenhoeck & Ruprecht, 1987.

Koch, Klaus. "אהל." In *Theological Dictionary of the Old Testament [TDOT]*, vol. 1, edited by G. Johannes Botterweck, Helmer Ringgren, 120–21. Translated by John T. Willis. Grand Rapid, MI: Eerdmans, 1974.

Koehler, Ludwig, and Walter Baumgartner. "שׁכן I." In *The Hebrew and Aramaic Lexicon of the Old Testament*. Vol. 2. Study ed., 1606. Translated and edited by M. E. J. Richardson. Leiden: Brill, 2001.

Koenig, Phyllis, and Murray Grossman. "Process and Content in Semantic Memory." In *Neural Basis of Semantic Memory*, edited by John Hart and Michael Kraut, 247–64. Cambridge: Cambridge University Press, 2007.

Korošec, Viktor. *Hethitische Staatsverträge*. Leipzig: Leipziger rechtswissenschaftlicher Studien, 1931.

Körting, Corinna. *Der Schall des Schofar*. Berlin: Walter De Gruyter, 1999.

Koshar, Rudy. *From Monuments to Traces*. Berkeley, CA: University of California Press, 2000.

Kostamo, Sonya. "Remembering Interactions Between Ahaz and Isaiah." In *Remembering (and Forgetting) in Judah's Early Second Temple Period*, edited by Christoph Levin and Ehud Ben Zvi, 55–72. Forschungenzum Alten Testaments, 85. Tübingen: Mohr Siebeck, 2012.

Kraus, Hans-Joachim. *Die biblische Theologie*. Neukirchen-Vluyn: Neukirchener Verlag, 1970.

Kwint, Marius, Christopher Breward, and Jeremy Aynsley, eds. *Material Memories.* Oxford: Berg, 1999.

Labuschagne, C. J. *Deuteronomium.* Vol. 1. Callenbach, 1987.

———. "The Setting of the Song of Moses in Deuteronomy." In *Deuteronomy and Deuteronomic Literature*, edited by Marc Vervenne and Johan Lust, 111–29. Leuven: Leuven University Press, 1997.

Landauer, Thomas K., and Susan T. Dumais. "A Solution to Plato's Problem: The Latent Semantic Analysis Theory of the Acquisition, Induction, and Representation of Knowledge." *Psychological Review* 104 (1997): 211–40.

Landy, Francis. "Notes Towards a Poetics of Memory in Ancient Israel." In *Remembering (and Forgetting) in Judah's Early Second Temple Period*, edited by Christoph Levin and Ehud Ben Zvi, 331–45. Forschungenzum Alten Testaments, 85. Tübingen: Mohr Siebeck, 2012.

Lange, Armin. "The Dead Sea Scrolls and the Date of the Final Stage of the Pentateuch." In *On Stone and Scroll: Essays in Honour of Graham Ivor Davies*, edited by James Aitken, Katharine Dell, and Brian Mastin, 287–304. Berlin: De Gruyter, 2011.

Lemaire, André. "Deuteronomy 6:6, 9 in the Light of Northwest Semitic Inscriptions." In *Birkat Shalom*. Vol. 1, edited by Chaim Cohen, Victor Avigdor Hurowitz, Avi M. Hurvitz, Yochanan Muffs, Baruch J. Schwartz, and Jeffrey H. Tigay, 525–30. University Park, PA: Eisenbrauns, 2008.

L'Engle, Madeleine. *A Wrinkle in Time.* New York: Farrar, Straus and Giroux, 1962.

Leuchter, Mark. "Why is the Song of Moses in the Book of Deuteronomy?" *Vetus Testamentum* 57 (2007): 295–317.

Leveen, Adriane. *Memory and Tradition in the Book of Numbers.* Cambridge: Cambridge University Press, 2008.

Levenson, Jon. *Sinai and Zion: An Entry into the Jewish Bible.* San Francisco: Harper-SanFrancisco, 1985.

Levin, Christoph. "Das Deuteronomium und der Jahwist." In *Liebe und Gebot*, edited by Reinhard G. Kratz and Hermann Spieckermann, 121–136. Göttingen: Vandenhoeck & Ruprecht, 2000.

———. "Days are Coming, When It Shall No Longer Be Said." In *Remembering and Forgetting in the Book of Jeremiah*," 105–24.

Levinson, Bernard, M. *Deuteronomy and the Hermeneutics of Legal Innovation.* Oxford: Oxford University Press, 1997.

———. "The Hermeneutics of Tradition in Deuteronomy: A Reply to J. G. McConville." *Journal of Biblical Literature* 119 (2000): 276.

Levinson, Jerrold. "Music and Negative Emotion." In *Music and Meaning*, edited by Jenefer Robinson, 215–41. New York: Cornell University Press, 1997.

———. *Music, Art, and Metaphysics.* Oxford: Oxford University Press, 2011.

Levitin, Daniel J. *This is Your Brain on Music.* Reprint, New York: Plume/Penguin, 2007.

Lewis, C. S. *The Silver Chair.* New York: HarperTrophy, 1953.

———. *Surprised by Joy.* Fort Washington, PA: Harvest Books, 1955.

Lewis, Penny A., and Hugo Critchley. "Mood-Dependent Memory." *Trends in Cognitive Sciences* 7 (2003): 431–33.

Lewis, Penny A., Hugo Critchley, Adam Paul Smith-Collins, and Raymond J. Dolan. "Brain Mechanisms for Mood Congruent Memory Facilitation." *NeuroImage* 25 (2005): 1214–23.

Lichtheim, Miriam. *Ancient Egyptian Literature* 1. Berkeley, CA: University of California Press, 1975.

Lindars, Barnabas. "Torah in Deuteronomy." In *Words and Meanings*, edited by P. R. Ackroyd and B. Lindars. Reprint, Cambridge, UK: Cambridge University Press, 2009.

Loewenstamm, Samuel. *The Evolution of the Exodus Tradition*. Jerusalem: Magnes Press, 1992.

Loftus, Elizabeth. "The Reality of Repressed Memories." *American Psychologist* 48 (1993): 518–37.

Loftus, Elizabeth, and Katherine Ketcham. *The Myth of Repressed Memory*. New York: St. Martin's Griffin, 1996.

Lohfink, Norbert. "The Cult Reform of Josiah of Judah: 2 Kings 22–23 as a Source for the History of Israelite Religion." In *Ancient Israelite Religion*, edited by P. D. Miller, 459–75. Minneapolis, MN: Fortress Press, 1987.

———. *Das Hauptgebot*. Pontifical Biblical Institute, 1963.

———. "Die '*huqqim umispatim*' im Buch Deuteronoium und ihre Neubegrenzung durch Dtn. 12.1." *Biblica* 70 (1989): 1–27.

———. *Die Väter Israels im Deuteronomium: Mit einer Stellungnahme von Thomas Römer*. Freiburg, Switzerland: Universitätsverlag, 1991.

———. "Dtn 28,69—*Überschrift* oder Kolophon?" *Biblische Notizen* 64 (1992): 44.

———. "'*D(w)t* im Deuteronomium und in den Königsbüchern." *Biblische Zeitschrift* 35 (1991): 86–93.

———. "Kerygmata des Deuteronomistischen Geschichtwerks." In *Die Botschaft und die Boten*, edited by Jorg Jeremias and Lothar Perlitt, 87–100. Neukirchen-Vluyn: Neukirchener Verlag, 1981.

———. "Moab oder Sichem—Wo Wurde Dtn 28 nach der Fabel das Deuteronomiums Proklamiert?" In *Studies in Deuteronomy in Honour of C. J. Labuschagne on the Occasion of His 65th Birthday*, edited by Florentino García Martínez, Casper Jeremiah Labuschagne, A. Hilhorst, Adam Woude, Masahiro Miyoshi, and J. T. A. G. M. Van Ruiten, 139–53. Leiden: Brill, 1994.

———. "Verkündigung des Hauptgebots in der jüngsten Schicht des Deuteronomiums (Deut. 4, 1–40)." In *Höre Israel!* Düsseldorf, 1965.

———. "Zur deuteronomischen Zentralisationsformel." In *Studien zum Deuteronomium und zur deuteronomistischen Literature II*. Stuttgart: Katholisches Bibelwerk, 1991.

———. "Zur Fabel in Dtn 31–32." In *Konsequente Traditionsgeschichte*, edited by Rudiger Bartelmus, Thomas Krüger, and Helmut Utzschneider, 255–79. Göttingen: Vandenhoeck & Ruprecht, 1993.

Luiselli, Maria. "The Ancient Egyptian Scene of 'Pharaoh Smiting his Enemies': An Attempt to Visualize Cultural Memory?" In *Cultural Memory and Identity in Ancient Societies*, edited by Martin Bommas, 10–25. Contiuum, 2011.

Lundbom, Jack R. "The Inclusio and Other Framing Devices in Deuteronomy." *Vetus Testamentum* 46 (1996): 296–315.

———. "The Lawbook of the Josianic Reform." *Catholic Biblical Quarterly* 38 (1976): 293–302.
MacDonald, Nathan. "Aniconism in the Old Testament." In *The God of Israel*, edited by Robert Gordon. Cambridge: University of Cambridge Press, 2007.
———. "Chewing the Cud: Food and Memory in Deuteronomy." In *Not Bread Alone*, 70–99. Oxford University Press, 2009.
———. *Deuteronomy and the Meaning of "Monotheism."* Tübingen: Mohr Siebeck, 2003.
———. "The Literary Criticism and Rhetorical Logic of Deuteronomy i–iv." *Vetus Testamentum* 56 (2006): 203–24.
———. *Not Bread Alone*. Oxford: Oxford University Press, 2008.
———. "Recite Them: Remembering 'Monotheism.'" In *Deuteronomy and the Meaning of "Monotheism,"* 124–50. Tübingen: Mohr Siebeck, 2003.
———. "Ritual Innovation: The Feast of Weeks from the Covenant Code to the Temple Scroll." Unpublished paper presented at the Society of Biblical Literature annual meeting. San Francisco, 2011.
———. *What Did the Ancient Israelites Eat?* Grand Rapids MI: Eerdmans, 2008.
MacIntyre, Alasdair. *After Virtue*. Notre Dame, IN: Notre Dame University Press, 1984.
MacRae, George W. "The Meaning and Evolution of the Feast of Tabernacles." *Catholic Biblical Quarterly* 22 (1960): 251–76.
Mann, Thomas W. *The Book of the Torah*. Louisville, KY: Westminster John Knox, 1988.
———. *Deuteronomy*. Louisville, KY: Westminster John Knox, 1995.
Markl, Dominik. "Review of Taschner, Johannes *Die Mosereden im Deuteronomium: Eine kanonorientierte Untersuchung* (Tübingen: Mohr Siebeck, 2008)." *Review of Biblical Literature* 4 (2009). https://www.bookreviews.org/pdf/6937_7517.pdf.
Markowitsch Hans J., and Harald Welzer. *The Development of Autobiographical Memory*. London: Psychology Press, 2010.
Markus, Hazel, and Paula Nurius. "Possible Selves." *American Psychologist* 41 (1986): 954–69.
Mather, Mara, Linda A. Henkel, and Marcia K. Johnson. "Evaluating Characteristics of False Memories: Remember/Know Judgments and Memory Characteristics Questionnaire Compared." *Memory and Cognition* 6 (1997): 827.
Mazzoni, Guiliana, and Amina Memon. "Imagination Can Create False Autobiographical Memories." *Psychological Science* 14 (2003): 186–88.
Mayer, John D., Laura J. McCormick, and Sara E. Strong. "Mood-Congruent Memory and Natural Mood: New Evidence." *Personality and Social Psychology Bulletin* 21 (1995): 736–46.
Mayes, A. D. H. *Deuteronomy*. London: Oliphants, 1979.
———. Deut 1–3 and 4 ("Deuteronomy 4 and the Literary Criticism of Deuteronomy"). *Journal of Biblical Literature* 100, no. 1 (1981): 23–51.
———. "Deuteronomy 29, Joshua 9, and the Place of the Gibeonites in Israel." In *Das Deuteronomiums*, edited by Norbert Lohfink, 321–25. Leuven: Leuven University Press, 1985).
McAdams, Dan. *The Stories We Live By*. New York: Guilford Press, 1997.

McClintock Fulkerson, Mary. *Places of Redemption*. Oxford: Oxford University Press, 2007.
McConville, J. Gordon. *Deuteronomy*. Westmont, IL: InterVarsity Press, 2002.
———. "Deuteronomy's Unification of Passover and Massot—A Response to B. M. Levinson." *Journal of Biblical Literature* 119 (2000): 47–58.
———. *Grace in the End*. Grand Rapids, MI: Zondervan, 1993.
———. *Law and Theology*. Sheffield: JSOT Press, 1984.
McCormack, Jo. *Collective Memory: France and Algerian War (1954–1962)*. Lanham, MD: Lexington Books, 2007.
McGaugh, James L. *Memory and Emotion*. New York: Columbia University Press, 2006.
Mendenhall, George E. *Law and Covenant in Israel and the Ancient Near East*. Pittsburgh: Biblical Colloquium, 1955.
Merrill, Eugene. *Deuteronomy*. Nashville, TN: Broadman and Holman, 1994.
Meshel, Ze'ev. "Kuntillet 'Ajrud." In the *Anchor Bible Dictionary*, vol. 4, edited by David Noel Freedman, 103–9. New York: Doubleday, 1992.
Meusburger, Peter, Michael Heffernan, and Edgar Wunder. "Cultural Memories: An Introduction." In *Cultural Memories*, edited by Peter Meusburger, Michael Heffernan, and Edgar Wunder, 7–8. Berlin: Springer, 2011.
Meyer, R. "Die Bedeutung von Deuteronomium 32, 8f. 43 (4Q) für die Auslegung des Moseliedes." In *Verbannung und Heimkehr*, edited by A. Kusche, 197–209. Heidelberg: J. C. B. Mohr, 1961.
Michaelian, Kourken. *Mental Time Travel: Episodic Memory and Our Knowledge of the Personal Past*. Cambridge, MA: The MIT Press, 2016.
———. "Mental Time Travel: What Is Memory?" *The Brains Blog*, May 16, 2016. philosophyofbrains.com/2016/05/16/mental-time-travel-what-is-memory.aspx.
Milgrom, Jacob. *Leviticus*. 3 vols. New York: Doubleday, 1991–2001.
Millar, J. Gary. "Ethics and Journey." In *Now Choose Life*, 67–98. Leicester: Apollos, 1998.
———. "Living at the Place of Decision." In *Time and Place in Deuteronomy*, edited by J. Gary Millar and J. Gordon McConville. Sheffield: Sheffield Academic Press, 1994.
———. *Now Choose Life: Theology and Ethics in Deuteronomy*. Leicester: Apollos, 1998.
Millar, J. Gary, and J. Gordon McConville. *Time and Place in Deuteronomy*. Sheffield: Sheffield Academic Press, 1994.
Millard, A. R. "Some Aramaic Epigraphs." *Iraq* 34 (1972): 131–37.
Miller, Patrick D. *Deuteronomy*. Louisville, KY: Westminster John Knox, 1990.
———. "Fire in the Mythology of Canaan and Israel." *Catholic Biblical Quarterly* 27 (1965): 256–61.
———. "The Gift of God: The Deuteronomic Theology of the Land." *Interpretation* 23 (1969): 454–65.
Mitchell, Karen J., and Marcia K. Johnson. "Source Monitoring: Attributing Mental Experiences." In *Oxford Handbook of Memory*, edited by Endel Tulving and Fergus I. M. Craik, 187. Oxford: Oxford University Press.

———. "Source Monitoring 15 Years Later: What Have We Learned from MRI About the Neural Mechanisms of Source Memory?" *Psychological Bulletin* 135 (2009): 638–77.

Mittmann, S. *Deuteronomium 1, 1–6, 3: Literarkritsch und traditionsgeschichtlich Untersucht*. Berlin: Alfred Töpelman, 1975.

Morgan, Donn F. *The So-Called Cultic Calendars in the Pentateuch*. PhD thesis: Claremont Graduate School, 1974.

Morrow, William. "Memory and Socialization in Malachi 2:17–3:5 and 3:13–21." In *Remembering (and Forgetting) in Judah's Early Second Temple Period*, edited by Christoph Levin and Ehud Ben Zvi, 125–42. Forschungenzum Alten Testaments, 85. Tübingen: Mohr Siebeck, 2012.

———. *Scribing the Center*. Atlanta, GA: Scholars Press, 1995.

Moscovitch, Morris. "Memory: Why the Engram is Elusive." *Science of Memory*, edited by Henry Roediger III, Yadin Dudai, and Susan Fitzpatrick. Oxford: Oxford University Press, 2007.

Mowinckel, Sigmund. *Psalmenstudien*. Amsterdam: P. Schippers, 1921–24. Reprinted 1961.

Mudge, Lewis. "Paul Ricoeur on Biblical Interpretation." In *Essays on Biblical Interpretation*, edited by Lewis Mudge, 1–40. Philadelphia: Fortress Press, 1980.

Muraoka, Takamitsu. *Emphatic Words and Structures in Biblical Hebrew*. Leiden: Brill, 1985.

Najman, Hindy. *Seconding Sinai*. Leiden: Brill, 2003.

Neal, Arthur G. *National Trauma and Collective Memory*. New York: M. E. Sharpe, 1998.

Nelson, Richard D. *Deuteronomy*. Louisville, KY: Westminster John Knox, 2002.

———. "Divine Warrior Theology in Deuteronomy." In *A God So Near: Essays on Old Testament Theology in Honor of Patrick D. Miller*, edited by Brent Strawn and Nancy Bowen, 256–57. Winona Lake: Eisenbrauns.

Nguyen, Phuong T., and Lauren Scharff. "A New Test of Music Mood Induction and Mood Congruency Memory." *Abstracts of the Psychonomic Society* 8 (2003): 114.

Nietzsche, Friedrich. *Untimely Meditations*. Translated by Anthony Ludovici and Adrian Collins. Digireads, 2010.

Nigosian, Solomon A. "Linguistic Patterns of Deuteronomy 32." *Biblica* 78 (1997): 223–24.

Nora, Pierre, and Lawrence D. Kritzman, eds. *Realms of Memory*. 3 vols. Translated by Arthur Goldhammer. New York: Columbiä University Press, 1996.

Noth, Martin. *The Deuteronomistic History*. 2nd ed. Sheffield: JSOT Press, 1991.

———. *Überlieferungsgeschichtliche Studien*. Vol. 1. Halle an der Saale: Niemayer Verlag, 1943.

O'Dowd, Ryan. "Memory on the Boundary: Epistemology in Deuteronomy." In *The Bible and Epistemology: Biblical Soundings on the Knowledge of God*, edited by Mary Healy and Robin Parry. Milton Keynes: Paternoster, 2007.

———. *The Wisdom of Torah: Epistemology in Deuteronomy and the Wisdom Literature*. Göttingen: Vandenhoeck & Ruprecht, 2009.

Okri, Ben. *Birds of Heaven*. London: Phoenix, 1996.

Olick, Jeffrey. Collective Memory: A Memoir and Prospect." *Memory Studies* 1, no. 1 (2008): 19–25.

———. "Collective Memory: The Two Cultures." *Sociological Theory* 17, no. 3 (1999): 333–48.

Olick, Jeffrey, Vered Vinitzky-Seroussi, and Daniel Levy, eds. *The Collective Memory Reader*. Oxford: Oxford University, 2011.

Olson, Dennis. "How Does Deuteronomy Do Theology? Literary Juxtaposition and Paradox in the New Moab Covenant in Deuteronomy 29–32." In *A God So Near: Essays on Old Testament Theology in Honor of Patrick D. Miller*, edited by Brent Strawn and Nancy Bowen, 201–13. Winona Lake: Eisenbrauns, 2003.

Osumi, Yuichi. *Die Kompositionsgeschichte des Bundesbuch Exod 20, 22b–23, 23*. Göttingen: Vandenhoek & Ruprecht, 1991.

Otto, Eckart. *Das Deuteronomium*. Berlin: Walter de Gruyter, 1999.

———. "The Pre-exilic Deuteronomy as a Revision of the Covenant Code." In *Kontinuum und Proprium*. Wiesbaden: Harrassowitz, 1996.

———. *Zeitschrift für Altorientalische und Biblische Rechtsgeschichte* 14 (2008): 463–74.

Pannell, Randall. *Those Alive Here Today*. Longwood, FL: Xulon Press, 2004.

Parry, Robin. *Old Testament Story and Christian Ethics: The Rape of Dinah as a Case Study*. Milton Keynes, UK: Paternoster, 2004.

Patel, Aniruddh. *Music, Language, and the Brain*. Oxford: Oxford University Press, 2008.

Patrick, Dale. "The Rhetoric of Collective Responsibility in Deuteronomic Law." In *Pomegranates and Golden Bells*, edited by David Wright, David Noel Freedman, and Avi Hurvits, 421–36. University Park, PA: Eisenbrauns, 1995.

Pidel, Aaron. "Ricoeur and Ratzinger on Biblical History and Hermeneutics." *Journal of Theological Interpretation* 8, no. 2 (2014): 193–212.

Pillemar, David B. "Flashbulb Memories of the Assassination Attempt on President Reagan." *Cognition* 16 (1984): 63–80.

———. "Momentous Events and the Life Story." *In Review of General Psychology* 5 (2001): 123–34.

———. *Momentous Events, Vivid Memories*. Cambridge, MA: Harvard University Press, 1998.

Plöger, Josef. *Literarkritische, formgeschichtliche und stilkritische Untersuchungen zum Deuteronomium*. Verlag: Peter Hanstein, 1967.

Polzin, Robert. *Moses and the Deuteronomist*. New York: Seabury Press, 1980.

Preuss, H. D. *Deuteronomium*. Darmstadt: Wissenschaftliche Buchgesellschaft, 1982.

Pribram, Karl H. *Brain and Perception*. New Jersey: Lawrence Erlbaum Associates, 1991.

Rad, Gerhard von. *Das Gottesvolk im Deuteronomium*. Stuttgart: Kohlhammer, 1929.

———. *Deuteronomium-Studien*. Göttingen: Vandenhoeck & Ruprecht, 1948.

———. *Old Testament Theology*. Vol. 1. Translated by D. M. G. Stalker. Manhattan: Harper & Row, 1962.

———. *The Problem of the Hexateuch and Other Essays*. Translated by E. W. Trueman Dicken. Edinburgh: Oliver & Boyd, 1965.

———. *The Problem of the Hexateuch and Other Essays*. New York: McGraw Hill, 1966.

———. *Studies in Deuteronomy*. Translated by David Stalker. London: SCM Press, 1953.

Rajan, Balachandra. *The Overwhelming Question: A Study of the Poetry of T. S. Eliot*. Toronto: University of Toronto Press, 1976.

Reisberg, Daniel, and Friderike Heuer. "Memory and Emotional Events." In *Memory and Emotion*, edited by Daniel Reisberg and Paula Hertel, 3–41. Oxford: Oxford University Press, 2003.

Rendtorff, Rolf. "Die Entwicklung des altisraclitischen Festkalenders." In *Das Fest und das Heilige*, edited by Jan Assmann and Theo Sundermeier. Gütersloh: Gütersloher Verlagshaus G. Mohn, 1991.

Richter, Sandra. *The Deuteronomistic History and the Name Theology*. Berlin: De Gruyter, 2002.

———. "The Place of the Name in Deuteronomy." *Vetus Testamentum* 57 (2007): 342–66.

Ricoeur, Paul. *Figuring the Sacred: Religion, Narrative, and Imagination*. Edited by Mark Wallace. Translated by David Pellauer. Minneapolis, MN: Fortress, 1995.

———. *Hermeneutics and the Human Sciences*. Edited and translated by John Thompson. Cambridge, UK: Cambridge University Press, 1981.

———. *Interpretation Theory: Discourse and the Surplus of Meaning*. Fort Worth, TX: Texas Christian University, 1976.

———. *Meaning and Representation in History*. Edited by Jörn Rüsen. New York: Berghahn Books, 2006.

———. *Memory, History, Forgetting*. Translated by Kathleen Blamey and David Pellauer. Chicago: IL: University of Chicago Press, 2004.

———. *The Rule of Metaphor: The Creation of Meaning in Language*. Translated by Robert Czerny, Kathleen McLaughlin, and John Costello. London: Routledge, 1978.

———. *Time and Narrative*. Vols. 1–3. Translated by Kathleen McLaughlin and David Pellauer. Chicago, IL: University of Chicago Press, 1984–1988.

Ridderbos, Jan. *Deuteronomy*. Translated by E. M van der Maas. Grand Rapids, MI: Zondervan, 1984.

Ringgren, Helmer. "עוד." In *TDOT*, vol. 10, 504.

Robertson, David. *Linguistic Evidence in Dating Early Hebrew Poetry*. Missoula, MT: Society of Biblical Literature, 1972.

Robinson, John A., and Karen L. Swanson. "Field and Observer Modes of Remembering." *Memory* 1 (1994): 169–84.

Robson, James. *Honey from the Rock: Deuteronomy for the People of God*. Nottingham: Apollos, 2013.

Rogerson, John. "History and Cultural Memory." In *A Theology of the Old Testament*, 13–40. Minneapolis, MN: Fortress Press, 2010.

Römer, Thomas. "Deuteronomy in Search of Origins." In *Reconsidering Israel and Judah*, edited by Gary Knoppers and J. Gordon McConville, 112–38. University Park, PA: Eisenbrauns, 2000.

———. *Israels Väter*. Göttingen: Vandenhoeck & Ruprecht, 1990.
Rowlands, Mark. *The New Science of the Mind*. Cambridge, MA: MIT Press, 2010.
Rubin, David C. ed. *Autobiographical Memory*. Cambridge, UK: Cambridge University Press, 1986.
———. *Remembering Our Past*. Cambridge, UK: Cambridge University Press, 1995.
Russell, Nicolas. "Collective Memory Before and After Halbwachs." *The French Review* 79, no. 4 (2006): 792–804.
Sanders, Paul. *The Provenance of Deuteronomy 32*. Leiden: Brill, 1996.
Schacter, Daniel L., ed. *The Cognitive Neuropsychology of False Memories*. London: Psychology Press, 1999.
———. *Forgotten Ideas, Neglected Pioneers*. London: Psychology Press, 2001.
———. *Memory, Brain, and Belief*. 3rd ed. Edited by Daniel Schacter and Elaine Scarry. Cambridge, MA: Harvard University Press, 2001.
———. *Memory Distortion*. Edited by Daniel Schacter and Joseph Coyle. Cambridge, MA: Harvard University Press, 1997.
———. *Memory Systems 1994*. Edited by Daniel Schacter and Endel Tulving. Cambridge, MA: Massachusetts Institute of Technology, 1994.
———. *Searching for Memory*. New York: Basic Books, 1996.
———. *The Seven Sins of Memory*. Reprint, Boston, MA: Houghton Mifflin, 2002.
Sax, William S., Johannes Quack, and Jan Weinhold. *The Problem of Ritual Efficacy*. Oxford: Oxford University Press, 2010.
Schaper, Joachim. "Schriftauslegung und Schriftwerdung im alten Israel: Eine vergleichende Exegese von Ex 20, 24–26 und Dtn 12, 13–19." *Zeitschrift für Altorientalische und Biblische Rechtsgeschichte* 5 (1999): 111–32.
Schmid, Konrad. *Erzväter und Exodus*. Neukirchen-Vluyn: Neukirchener Verlag, 1999.
Schniedewind, William M. "Tel Dan Stela: New Light on Aramaic and Jehu's Revolt." *Bulletin of the American Schools of Oriental Research* 302 (1996): 75–90.
Schottroff, Willy. *Gedenken im Alten Orient und im Alten Testament*. Neukirchen-Vluyn: Neukirchener Verlag, 1967.
Schroer, Silvia. *In Israel gab es Bilder*. Freiburg: Vandenhoeck & Ruprecht, 1987.
Schulte, Raphael. "Zum christlichen Verständnis von Religion und Kult." *Theologisch-praktische Quartalschrift* 115 (1967): 34–44.
Schwartz, Joan M., and Terry Cook. "Archives, Records, and Power: The Making of Modern Memory." *Archival Science* 2 (2002): 1–19.
Schwarz, Barry. "Collective Remembering and the Symbolic Power of Oneness: The Strange Apotheosis of Rosa Parks." *Social Psychology Quarterly* 72 (2009): 123–42.
Sedikides, Constantine, Jeffrey D. Green, and Brad Pinter. "Self-Protective Memory." In *The Self and Memory*, edited by Denise Beike, James M. Lampinen, and Douglas A. Behrend, 161–80. New York: Psychology Press.
Seitz, Gottfried. *Redaktionsgeschichtliche Studien zum Deuteronomium*. Stuttgart: Kohlhammer, 1971.
Sentilles, Sarah. *Draw Your Weapons*. London: The Text Publishing Company, 2017.
Seters, John Van. "Cultic Laws in the Covenant Code and Their Relationship to Deuteronomy and the Holiness Code." In *Studies in the Book of Exodus*, edited by Marc Vervenne, 319–34. Leuven: Peeters, 1996.

Sharman, Stefanie J., and Amanda J. Barnier. "Imagining Nice and Nasty Events in Childhood or Adulthood: Recent Positive Events Show the Most Imagination Inflation." *Acta Psychologica* 129 (2008): 228–33.

Shupak, Nili. "Learning Methods in Ancient Israel." *Vetus Testamentum* 53 (2003): 416–26.

Smith, James. *Desiring the Kingdom*. Ada, MI: Baker Academic, 2009.

Smith, Mark S. *The Early History of God*. 2nd ed. Grand Rapids, MI: Eerdmans, 2002.

———. *The Memoirs of God*. Minneapolis, MN: Augsburg Press, 2004.

———. *The Memoirs of God: History, Memory, and the Experience of the Divine in Ancient Israel*. Minneapolis, MN: Fortress, 2004.

———. *The Origins of Biblical Monotheism*. Oxford: Oxford University Press, 2001.

Snyder, Bob. *Music and Memory*. Cambridge, MA: MIT Press, 2000.

Soggin, J. Alberto. "Kultätiologische Sagen und Katechese im Hexateuch." *Vetus Testamentum* 10 (1960): 341.

Sonnet, Jean-Pierre. *The Book Within the Book: Writing in Deuteronomy*. Leiden: Brill, 1997.

Sporer, Siegfried L., and Stefanie J. Sharman. "Should I Believe This? Reality Monitoring of Accounts of Self-Experienced and Invented Recent and Distant Autobiographical Events." *Applied Cognitive Psychology* 20 (2006): 837–54.

Squire, Larry, and Eric Kandel. *Memory*. New York: Henry Holt, 2003.

Stackert, Jeffrey. *Rewriting the Torah*. Heidelberg: Mohr Siebeck, 2007.

Staerk, Willy. *Beiträge zur Kritik des Deuteronomiums*. Leipzig: A. Pries, 1894.

Steiner, George. *Real Presences: Is There Anything in What We Say?* London: Faber & Faber, 1989.

Stern, Philip D. "The Origins and Significance of the 'Land Flowing with Milk and Honey.'" *Vetus Testamentum* XLII (1992): 554–57.

Steuernagel, Carl. *Das Deuteronomium*. Göttingen: Vandenhoek & Ruprecht, 1898.

Stratton, Valerie N., and Annette H. Zalanowski. "Affective Impact of Music vs. Lyrics." *Empirical Studies of the Arts* 12 (1994): 173–84.

Suddendorf, Thomas. *Discovery of the Fourth Dimension: Mental Time Travel and Human Evolution*. Master's thesis: University of Waikato, 1994.

Suddendorf, Thomas, and Michael Corballis. "Mental Time Travel and the Evolution of the Human Mind." *Genetic Social and General Psychology Monographs* 123 (1997):133–67.

Sutton, David E. *Remembrance of Repasts*. 2nd ed. Oxford: Berg, 2001.

Sutton, John. "Between Individual and Collective Memory: Coordination, Interaction, Distribution." *Social Research* 75, no. 1 (2008): 23–48.

Sutton, John, Celia B. Harris, Paul G. Keil, and Amanda J. Barnier. "The Psychology of Memory, Extended Cognition, and Socially Distributed Remembering." *Phenomenology and the Cognitive Sciences* 9 (2010): 521–60.

Tai, Hue-Tam Ho. "Remembered Realms: Pierre Nora and French National Memory." *The American Historical Review* 106, no. 3 (2001): 906–22.

Talarico, J. M., and D. C. Rubin. "Confidence, not Consistency, Characterizes Flashbulb Memories." *Psychological Science* 14, no. 5 (2003): 455–61.

Talstra, Eep. "Deuteronomy 31: Confusion or Conclusion? The Story of Moses' Threefold Succession." In *Deuteronomy and Deuteronomic Literature*, edited by Marc Vervenne and Johan Lust, 87–110. Leuven: Leuven University Press, 1997.
———. "Texts for Recitation: Deuteronomy 6:7; 11:19." In *Unless Someone Guide Me*, edited by J. W. Dyk, 67–76. Maastricht: Shaker Publishing, 2001.
Tamplin, Jeanette. "Singing for Respiratory Muscle Training: Using Therapeutic Singing and Vocal Interventions to Improve Respiratory Function and Voice Projection for People with a Spinal Cord Injury." In *Voicework in Music Therapy*, edited by F. Baker and Sylka Uhlig, 155. London: Jessica Kingsley Publishers, 2011.
Taschner, Johannes. *Die Mosereden im Deuteronomium*. Heidelberg: Mohr Siebeck, 2008.
Tate, Marvin E. "Deuteronomic Philosophy of History." *Review and Expositor* 61 (1964): 311–19.
Terdiman, Richard. *Present Past*. New York: Cornell University Press, 1993.
Terrien, Samuel. *The Elusive Presence*. Eugene, OR: Wipf & Stock, 2000.
Thomas, Ayanna K., and Elizabeth F. Loftus. "Creating Bizarre False Memories Through Imagination." *Memory and Cognition* 30 (2002): 423–31.
Thomas, Ayanna K., John B. Bulevich, and Elizabeth F. Loftus. "Exploring the Role of Repetition and Sensory Elaboration in the Imagination Inflation Effect." *Memory and Cognition* 31 (2003): 63–640.
Thompson, John Arthur. *Deuteronomy*. Downers Grove, IL: InterVarsity, 1974.
Thompson, Richard, and Stephen Madigan. *Memory*. Princeton, New Jersey: Princeton University Press, 2007.
Tigay, Jeffrey. *Deuteronomy*. Philadelphia, PA: The Jewish Publication Society, 1996.
———. "On the Meaning of T(W)TPT." *Journal of Biblical Literature* 101 (1982): 321–23.
Treier, Daniel. *Introducing Theological Interpretation of Scripture: Recovering a Christian Practice*. Grand Rapids, MI: Baker, 2008.
Truc, Gérôme. "Memory of Places and Places of Memory: For a Halbwachsian Socio-ethnography of Collective Memory." *International Social Science Journal* 62 (2012): 147–59.
Tulving, Endel. "Does Memory Encoding Exist?" In *Perspectives on Human Memory and Cognitive Aging: Essays in Honor of Fergus Craik*, edited by Moshe Naveh-Benjamin, Morris Moscovitch, and Henry L. Roediger III, 6–27. Philadelphia: Psychology Press, 2002.
———. *Elements of Episodic Memory*. Oxford: Clarendon Press, 1983.
———. "Episodic and Semantic Memory." In *Organization of Memory*, edited by Endel Tulving and Wayne Donaldson, 381–402. Cambridge, MA: Academic Press, 1972.
———. "Episodic Memory: From Mind to Brain." *Annual Review of Psychology* 53 (2002): 1–25.
———. "Origin of Autonoesis in Episodic Memory." In *The Nature of Remembering: Essays in Honor of Robert G. Crowder*, edited by Henry L. Roediger III,

James S. Nairne, Ian Neath, and Aimée M. Surprenant, 17–34. Washington, DC: American Psychological Association, 2001.

Tulving, Endel, and Donald M. Thomson. "Encoding Specificity and Retrieval Processes in Episodic Memory." *Psychological Review* 80 (1973): 352–73.

Turner, Victor. *The Ritual Process: Structure and Anti-Structure*. London: Aldine-Transaction, 2008 (1969).

University of Copenhagen. Faculty of Theology. "The Dissemination of the Centre." Accessed January 13, 2014. http://www.teol.ku.dk/english/dept/bicum/projects/.

Van der Kooij, Arie. "The Public Reading of Scriptures at Feasts." In *Feasts and Festivals*, edited by Christopher Tuckett, 27–44. Leuven: Peeters, 2009.

Vanhoozer, Kevin. *Biblical Narrative in the Philosophy of Paul Ricoeur*. Cambridge: Cambridge University Press, 1990.

———. *First Theology*. Downers Grove, IL: InterVarsity Press, 2002.

———. "Introduction." In *Dictionary for Theological Interpretation of the Bible*, edited by Kevin Vanhoozer, 22. Grand Rapids, MI: Baker, 2005.

Van Houten, Christiana. *Alien in Israelite Law*. Sheffield: Sheffield Academic Press.

Veijola, Timo. "The History of Passover in Light of Deuteronomy 16, 1–8." *Zeitschrift für Altorientalische und Biblische Rechtsgeschichte* 2 (1996): 53–75.

Vogt, Peter. *Deuteronomic Theology and the Significance of Torah*. University Park, PA: Eisenbrauns, 2006.

Volf, Miroslav. *The End of Memory*. Grand Rapids, MI: Eerdmans, 2006.

Von Rooy, H. F. "Deuteronomy 28:69—Superscript or Subscript?" *Journal of Northwest Semitic Languages* 14 (1988): 215–22.

Vriezen, Theodore Christiaan, and Adam Simon van der Woude. *Ancient Israelite and Early Jewish Literature*. Translated by Brian Doyle. Leiden: Brill, 2005.

Waaler, Erik. "A Revised Date for Pentateuchal Texts? Evidence from Ketef Hinnom." *Tyndale Bulletin* 53 (2002): 29–55.

Wagenaar, Jan. *Origin and Transformation of the Ancient Israelite Festival Calendar*. Leipzig: Harrassowitz Verlag, 2005.

Waltke, Bruce, and M. O'Connor. *An Introduction to Biblical Hebrew Syntax*. University Park, PA: Eisenbrauns, 1990.

Waterhouse, S. Douglas. "A Land Flowing with Milk and Honey." *Andrews University Seminary Studies* 1 (1961): 152–66.

Watts, James W. *Psalm and Story*. Sheffield: Sheffield Academic Press, 1992.

Watts, John D. W. "The Deuteronomic Theology." *Review and Expositor* 74 (1977): 326.

Weinfeld, Moshe. *Deuteronomy 1–11: A New Translation with Introduction and Commentary*. New York: Doubleday, 1991.

———. *Deuteronomy and the Deuteronomic School*. Oxford: Oxford University Press, 1972.

———. *The Place of the Law in the Religion of Ancient Israel*. Leiden: Brill, 2004.

Weitzman, Steven. "Sensory Reform in Deuteronomy." In *Religion and the Self in Antiquity*, edited by David Brakke, Michael L. Satlow, and Steven Weitzman, 123–39. Bloomington, IN: Indiana University Press, 2005.

———. *Song and Story in Biblical Narrative*. Bloomington, IN: Indiana University Press, 1997.

Wenham, Gordon. *The Psalter Reclaimed*. Wheaton, IL: Crossway, 2013.
Wevers, John. *Notes on the Greek Text of Deuteronomy*. Atlanta, GA: Scholars Press, 1995.
Weyde, Karl. *The Appointed Festivals of Yahweh*. Heidelberg: Mohr Siebeck, 2004.
Wheeler, Mark A. "Episodic Memory and Autonoetic Awareness." In *The Oxford Handbook of Memory*, edited by Endel Tulving and Fergus I. M. Craik, 597–608. Oxford: Oxford University Press, 2000.
Whitehead, Anne. *Memory*. Abingdon, UK: Taylor & Francis, 2009.
Whitehouse, Andrew J. O., Murray T. Maybery, and Kevin Durkin. "The Development of the Picture-Superiority Effect." *British Journal of Developmental Psychology* 24 (2010): 767–73.
Whybray, R. Norman. *Introduction to the Pentateuch*. Grand Rapids: Eerdmans, 1995.
Williams, Helen, Martin Conway, and Gillian Cohen. "Autobiographical Memory." In *Memory in the Real World*, edited by Gillian Cohen and Martin Conway, 21–90. London: Psychology Press, 2008.
Wilson, Ian. *Out of the Midst of the Fire*. Atlanta, GA: Scholars Press, 1995.
Wolff, Hans Walter. *Anthropology of the Old Testament*. Philadelphia: Westminster, 1974.
Wood, Nancy. "Memory's Remains: *Les Lieux de mémoire*." *History and Memory* 6 (1994): 123–51.
———. *Vectors of Memory: Legacies of Trauma in Postwar Europe*. Oxford: Berg, 1999.
Wright, Christopher J. H. *God's People in God's Land*. Milton Keynes, UK: Paternoster, 1990.
Wright, George Ernest. "The Lawsuit of God: A Form-Critical Study of Deuteronomy 32." In *Israel's Prophetic Heritage*, edited by Bernhard W. Anderson and Walter J. Harrelson, 26–67. New York: Harper, 1962.
Wright, Lawrence. *Remembering Satan*. New York: Alfred A. Knopf, 1994.
Yamasaki, Gary. *Watching a Biblical Narrative*. London: T. & T. Clark, 2007.
Yates, Frances A. *The Art of Memory*. 2nd ed. Chicago, IL: University of Chicago Press, 1966.
Yerushalmi, Yosef Hayim. *Zakhor: Jewish History and Jewish Memory*. University of Washington Press, 1982.
Zelizer, Barbie. *Remembering to Forget*. Chicago, IL: University of Chicago Press, 1998.
Zerubavel, Eviatar. *Social Mindscapes*. Cambridge, MA: Harvard University Press, 1997.
———. *Time Maps*. Chicago, IL: University of Chicago Press, 2003.

Index

Note: Page numbers followed by "n" refer to notes.

actualization (*Vergegenwärtigung*), 8–11, 14, 23, 25, 27n11, 36, 37, 54n33, 163;
   cultic, 184;
   historical, 54n33;
   mnemonic, 139n120;
   ritual, 72
AKB. *See* autobiographical knowledge base (AKB)
Altmann, Peter, 142, 165n15, 170n119
Amos 9:11, 179
AM. *See* autobiographical memory (AM)
analogous events, 69
anamnesis, 129
anchoring events, 69
Ancien Régime, 100
aniconic worship/aniconism, 22–23, 44–46, 50, 51, 60n98, 79
Antiquities of the Jews, 175
appropriation, 194
ars memorativa, 103, 111n29
assertive speech act, 24
Assmann, Aleida, 107
Assmann, Jan, 33–34, 52n5, 52n6, 65, 72, 73, 85n1, 94n104, 105, 106, 112n39, 112n48

autobiographical knowledge base (AKB), 67–70;
   event-specific knowledge, 68–69;
   general events, 68;
   lifetime periods, 68
autobiographical memory (AM), 3, 66, 72, 73, 126
autonoetic consciousness, 66

Bartholomew, Craig, 196–97
benevolence, 10, 27n18, 131, 149, 150, 156, 198
Ben Zvi, Ehud, 18–19
biblical scholars, overgrown path of, 16–19
BiCuM. *See* The Centre for Bible and Cultural Memory (BiCuM)
blurring of generations, 35–37
bodily wisdom, 125
body memory, 112n42
Braulik, Georg, 19, 127, 151, 167n58, 167n62

calendrical repetition, 4, 159, 160
Canaanite worship, 106–8
canonization, 105–6

Carasik, Michael, 24–25, 46–48, 54n33, 60n107, 93n91
Carlson, R. A., 176
Carr, David, 123
CC. *See* Covenant Code (CC)
The Centre for Bible and Cultural Memory (BiCuM), 16
"Chewing the Cud" (MacDonald), 25
Childs, Brevard, 8–12, 14, 22, 25, 26n2, 26n3, 27n11, 54n33
The Chronicles of Narnia (Lewis), 1
Cody, Aelred, 129
collective memory (*mémoire collective*), 3, 12, 13, 15, 20, 28n39, 52n4, 70, 72, 73, 83, 84, 99, 101, 104, 107;
  Deuteronomy as, 33–62
"command admonition" (*Gebotsmahnung*), 10
commemoration, 4, 100–104, 108, 111n25, 112n42, 116n86, 116n93, 141, 154, 157–63, 167n62, 171n124, 172n154, 172n156, 173n170;
  exodus, 145–47, 159, 162, 166n51, 167n58;
  liturgical, 129;
  rehearsed, 129
communal memory, 198
communicative memory, 112n39
community memory, 7, 104
Connerton, Paul, 25, 124, 158, 159, 172n156
consolidation, 65
continuity, establishing, 9
Conway, Martin, 67, 70
counterfactual agent, 34
counter-memory, 52n7
Couroyer, Bernard, 127
covenantal devotion, 11
covenantal memory, 2, 4, 82–83
  shape of, Deuteronomy and, 72–83
Covenant Code (CC), 141, 142
Craigie, Peter, 22–23, 25
cultural memory, 16, 52n4, 112n48, 182

DC. *See* Deuteronomic Code (DC)
deep encoding, 181
Deut:
  1:1, 133n5;
  1:1, 19, 31, 40, 97n138;
  1:2, 46, 38;
  1–3, 59n83, 82, 97n139;
  1–4, 41;
  1:19, 82;
  1:28, 82, 83;
  1:30, 58n76, 81;
  1:30–31, 81, 82;
  1:31, 81, 83;
  2:1, 38;
  2:1, 7, 8, 26, 97n138;
  2:7, 82;
  2:14–15, 36, 53n15;
  2:16, 38;
  2:16–3:20, 38;
  3, 38;
  4, 23, 39, 43–50, 45–50, 57n73, 59n83, 71, 79, 157;
  4:2, 133n5;
  4:3, 44, 81;
  4:3, 9, 58n76;
  4:3, 34, 58n76;
  4:9, 58n76, 79;
  4:9–10a, 49;
  4:9–12, 50;
  4:9–14, 32–40, 157;
  4:10, 53n26, 55n54, 156;
  4:10, 13, 36, 133n6;
  4:10–14, 20;
  4:11, 79;
  4:20, 77;
  4:32, 179;
  4:34, 58n76, 77;
  4:43, 97n138;
  4:45, 138n97;
  5, 44;
  5:5, 22, 133n6;
  5:6, 77;
  5–11, 41;
  5:15, 9, 153;

5:30, 144, 166n40;
6, 23, 123, 138n112, 184;
6:2, 77;
6:4, 117–18;
6:4–5, 21, 117, 118, 123, 197;
6:4–9, 25, 83, 136n59;
6:6, 119;
6:6–9, 105, 117–28, 132, 132n1, 134n19, 157;
6:7, 119, 120, 128, 135n34;
6:7–9, 121;
6:8–12, 75, 76, 121, 122;
6:9, 123;
6:9a, 122;
6:9b, 122;
6–11, 11, 41;
6:12, 76;
6:17, 138n97;
6:20–24, 77, 127–28;
6:20–25, 21, 50, 120, 126–30, 132, 157;
6:22, 58n76;
6:22–23, 43;
7, 106;
7:5, 25, 106;
7:8, 77;
7:8–13, 73;
7:9, 119;
7:18, 8;
7:19, 58n76;
8, 82, 179;
8:2, 8;
8:2, 15, 16, 97n138;
8:2–5, 34, 83;
8:2–18, 50;
8:5, 81, 83;
8:7–9, 34, 75–76, 180;
8:11–18, 76;
8:12–14, 180;
8:14, 77;
8:15–1, 180;
8:19, 180;
9, 58n76;
9:7, 8, 44, 80, 83, 97n139;
9:7, 28, 97n138;

9:7–10:11, 97n139;
9:7–29, 50;
9:10, 133n6;
9:17, 58n76, 79, 80;
9:22–24, 83;
10:2, 4, 133n6;
10:21, 58n76;
11, 23, 44, 138n112;
11:2–4, 19–21, 77;
11:2–7, 50;
11:2–9, 157;
11:5, 24, 97n138;
11:6, 81;
11:7, 58n76, 81, 83;
11:9–11, 75;
11:13–21, 136n59;
11:18, 133n8;
11:18–20, 105;
11:18–21, 120, 132n1, 134n19;
11:19, 119;
11:29–32, 115n78;
12, 106, 142;
12:2–3, 106;
12:3, 106;
12:5, 11, 21, 106, 108;
12–26, 41;
12:28, 133n7;
13:1, 133n5;
13:5, 10, 77;
14:1, 81;
14:21, 155;
15:15, 9, 133n7;
16, 23, 142, 148, 159, 165n22;
16:1–2, 143;
16:1–8, 78, 143, 145, 146, 161;
16:1–17, 25, 141–58, 163n1, 165n17;
16:3, 77;
16:6b, 146;
16:7, 144, 145, 154;
16:7b, 144;
16:8, 144;
16:9, 148;
16:9–12, 147;
16:10, 149;
16:11, 150;

16:11–12, 153;
16:12, 9, 152, 153;
16:13, 153, 154;
16:13–15, 153;
19:18, 96n120;
20:18, 96n120;
24:9, 8;
24:18, 9;
24:18, 22, 133n7;
24:22, 9;
25:17, 8;
26, 21–22, 149, 173n160;
26:1–11, 149;
26:5–9, 128;
26:6–8, 78;
26:8, 77;
27:1–8, 107, 115n78;
27:1–10, 115n78;
27:3, 108;
27–34, 23, 41;
28:1–14, 76;
28:15–68, 76;
29, 41–42, 57n72;
29:1, 42;
29:2, 3, 58n76;
29:2–3, 43;
29:5, 97n138;
29:10–11, 171n134;
29:11, 156;
30, 42, 57n73;
30:6, 94n103;
31, 176;
31:6, 78, 95n116;
31:9–13, 42, 154–56, 162, 171n140;
31:10–13, 11;
31:12, 156;
31:19, 189n66;
31:19, 22, 133n8, 183, 189n62;
31:19–13, 176;
31:19–30, 182;
31:30, 189n62;
31–32, 155;
32, 4, 5, 42, 159, 175, 177;
32:1–43, 42, 155, 157, 175–80;
32:5–6, 81;
32:10, 51, 97n138;
32:19, 79;
32:41, 119;
32:44–47, 183–84;
32:45–47, 177;
33, 184n5;
34, 44;
36b, 44

Deutehorizont, 130, 131
Deuteronomic Code (DC), 142
Deuteronomy:
  as collective memory, 33–62;
  as memory maker, 33–35;
  as memory-producing agent, 5;
  memory vectors in, 105–9;
  overgrown path of, 19–25;
  and shape of covenantal memory, 72–83;
  See also individual entries
Deuteronomy and the Meaning of "Monotheism" (MacDonald), 25
dialectic negation, 131
Dickens, Charles, 53n15
distanciation, 193, 199n20
distribution, 103–4
Doan, William, 180–82
Durkheim, Emile, 28n34

ecphory, 65, 66
Edelman, Diana, 19
Ehlich, Konrad, 105–6
emotive repetition, 4, 159
emphatic contemporaneity, 36, 39, 43, 57n72
emplotment, 4, 117–40, 192
encoding specificity principle, 65
engram, 64, 66, 71
engraphy, 64–65, 66
episodic memory, 66–67, 84, 88n27, 194, 195
ESK. *See* event-specific knowledge (ESK)
Eucharist, 13
event renewal, 9
event-specific knowledge (ESK), 73, 78, 80

Exod:
   12, 142;
   12:7, 122;
   12:48–49, 171n169;
   13:3–10, 142;
   13:6, 144;
   13:9, 121;
   13:14, 127;
   19:1, 171n170;
   20–23, 141;
   23, 148, 166n29;
   23:15, 143, 146;
   23:16, 148–50, 153;
   23:17, 143;
   28, 122;
   28:29–30, 119;
   28:30, 118, 119;
   34, 166n29;
   34:18, 146;
   34:18–26, 142
exodus, 77–78:
   commemoration, 145–47, 159, 162, 166n51, 167n58;
   generation, 3, 4, 13, 35–37, 43, 51, 56n62, 61n115, 72, 74, 75, 78, 95n119, 131, 140n131, 161, 179, 182;
   journey, 4, 10, 51;
   and Pesach-Massot, mnemonic relationship between, 19
explicit or declarative memory, 88n27
extended mind, 111n35
extraterritoriality, 34
"eyes" motif, 3, 33–62, 73, 77, 82, 195:
   blurring of generations, 35–37;
   drawn into the journey, 37–43;
   remembering, 43–50
Ezek 9:4–6, 122
Ezek 33:30, 135n34

false memory. *See* imagination inflation
fathers, 56n33;
   See also patriarchs

Feast of Booths, 153–57
Feast of Ingathering, 153
feast of Passover-Unleavened Bread, 142–47
Feasts of Weeks, 147–53
festivals, 105
festive calendar, 4, 25, 142, 143, 147, 148, 151, 153–55, 158, 159, 161, 163, 165n25, 166n29, 167n54, 168n69
figurative interpretation, 121
Finsterbusch, Karin, 112n48, 120, 128, 131, 132
Firstfruits, 149, 173n160
Fisch, Harold, 180
Fisch, Max H., 187n45
Fischer, Georg, 120
flashbulb memory, 87n16
Fletcher, Andrew, 184
forgetting, 20, 106–7;
   active, 107, 114n67, 114n68;
   passive, 107
frequency of use, 73

Gedenken im Alten Orient und im Alten Testament (Schottroff), 8
Geller, Stephen A., 45, 46
Gen:
   10–11, 179;
   17:8, 74–75;
   31:48, 186n22;
   33:18–20, 115n78;
   35:2–4, 115n78
gestural repetition, 4, 159, 160
Gesundheit, Shimon, 146, 147, 149, 165n22
Gibeonites, 156
Giles, Terry, 180–82
goal-orientation, 70
Goff, Lyn M., 71
group memory, 12, 14, 15, 28n27;
   as personal identity, 66–72
Groves, Joseph, 36, 37
guarding, 49

228   Index

habitus, 117–24, 158, 183, 184;
   in memory-making, 124–26
Halbwachs, Maurice, 12–16, 28n34,
   28n35, 28n39, 33, 99, 101, 102
Hartenstein, Friedhelm, 19
hearing and seeing, relationship
   between, 45–50, 126
Hebrew Bible, 24
Heilsgeschichte, 72–73, 78, 85
Hendel, Ronald, 17
hermeneutic arc, 199n18
hermeneutic of self-involvement,
   196
Hervieu–Léger, Danièle, 13, 51
Hinnom, Ketef, 119, 121
historical actualization, 54n33
historical justification, 59–60n92
hologram, 64, 65
Horeb-actualizing imagery, 23
How Societies Remember (Connerton),
   158
Hwang, Jerry, 23–24

imagination conflation, 84, 131
imagination inflation, 70–71
imaginative speech-acts, 24
incorporated memory, 25, 124,
   172n156
individual memory, 3, 12, 63, 65–67
inscribed memory, 25, 124, 172n156
intentionality, 101–3, 110n19,
   110n20
Isa 44:5, 121–22
Isa 57:8, 122

Johnson, Luke Timothy, 5, 191
Josh 4:6–7, 127
Josh 8:30–35, 115n78
Josh 22:27, 28, 34, 186n22
Josh 24, 115n78

Kadesh Barnea, 38, 82, 83, 85, 195
Kaufman, Gordon, 62n140
Keel, Othmar, 77, 122
Koch, Klaus, 145

Landy, Francis, 19
Lavisse, Ernest, 100
legato time, 140n131
Lemaire, André, 136n66
Lev 23, 154
Lev 23:42–43, 154, 161
Leveen, Adriane, 17–18
levels-of-processing effect, 64
Levin, Christoph, 19
Levinson, Bernard, 141–47, 165n29
Lewis, C. S., 1–2, 5, 69
Lohfink, Norbert, 37, 40, 57n72, 72,
   120, 127, 150–51
long-term memory, 64, 66, 88n27, 194
Ludwig Maximilians University, 18

MacDonald, Nathan, 25–26, 44, 59n83,
   59n92, 72, 118, 119, 121, 122,
   145, 151, 158, 167n58, 187n27
Mann, Thomas, 21–23, 25, 33, 44
materials memory, 110n20
mazzot, 160–62
McClintock Fulkerson, Mary, 124–25
McConville, J. G., 38, 59n89, 76,
   96n132, 96n136, 113n60, 144,
   145, 149, 167n58
McCormack, Jo, 100, 101, 110n8
The Memoirs of God (Smith), 17, 20
memorization command, 73
memory:
   autobiographical, 3, 66, 72, 73,
      126;
   body, 112n42;
   collective, 3, 12, 13, 15, 20, 28n39,
      52n4, 70, 72, 73, 83, 84, 99, 101,
      107;
   communal, 198;
   communicative, 112n39;
   community, 7, 104;
   of conversion, 52n5;
   counter-memory, 52n7;
   covenantal, 2, 4, 82–83;
   cultural, 16, 52n4, 112n48, 182;
   episodic, 66–67, 84, 88n27, 194,
      195;

explicit or declarative, 88n27;
false. *See* imagination inflation;
flashbulb, 87n16;
group, 12, 14, 15, 28n27;
incorporated, 25, 124;
individual, 3, 12, 63, 65;
inscribed, 25, 124;
intentional *versus* unintentional, 101–2;
long-term, 64, 66, 88n27, 194;
maker, Deuteronomy as, 33–35;
materials, 110n20;
normative, 34–35;
physical workings of, 86n5;
place, 112n42;
poetics of, 19;
as portal into divine presence, 191–200;
producer, Scripture as, 7–31;
psychology of, 3;
repressed, 52n6;
semantic, 66, 74, 84, 88n27, 155, 194;
sensory, 68;
short-term or working, 64;
social, 3, 12–16, 28n31, 52n4;
theory, 2–5, 16–19, 24, 35, 83
"memory admonition" (*Erinnerungsmahnung*), 10–11
Memory and Tradition in Ancient Israel (Childs), 8
Memory and Tradition in the Book of Numbers (Leveen), 17
memory-making, 99–116;
  habitus in, 124–26;
  ritual in, 158–63;
  song in, 180–84;
  storytelling in, 130–32
memory vector(s), 3;
  in Deuteronomy, 105–9;
  identification of, 99–116;
  ritual as, 4, 141–73;
  in society, 99–104;
  song as, 4–5, 175–89;
  story as, 4, 117–40

Mic 7:14, 179
Millar, J. G., 37–43, 51, 75, 79
Miller, Patrick, 44
mnemohistory, 52n5
Mnemosyne Atlas, 14
mnemotechnique, 105
Moab, 5, 38–42;
  covenant, 43, 57n72
monotheism, 20, 52n6
monotheistic worship, 25
mood congruency, 4, 160
mood facilitation, 160
Morrow, William, 19
Mount Ebal/Mt Ebal, 41, 42, 107–9, 115n76, 155
Mount Gerizim, 41, 42, 107, 155
Mount Horeb/Mt Horeb, 38–41, 79–81, 95n119, 130, 194, 195;
  revelation at, 39, 41, 45, 55n47, 72, 78, 161, 171n31, 173n170;
  theophany play, 50
Mount Sinai, 20–21

name theology, 113n61
Neh 8:1–9:37, 156
Nora, Pierre, 100–102
normative memory, 34–35
Not Bread Alone (MacDonald), 25
"Now Print" mechanism, 87n16
Num 6:24–26, 119, 121
Num 13:27–29, 82
Num 16:32, 81
Numeruswechsel (number change), 36, 40, 43, 56n62

O'Dowd, Ryan, 23
Olick, Jeffrey, 85n2, 99–101
1 Kgs 18:34, 119
1 Sam 27:8, 179
1 Sam 1, 150
originating events, 69
overgrown path, 2, 7–31, 191;
  of biblical scholars, 16–19;

clearing, 26;
of Deuteronomy, 19–25;
of social memory, 12–16

patriarchal promises, 73–76, 84, 93n91, 129–31, 194
patriarchs, 56n33;
See also fathers
performativity, 102, 110n20
personal identity, group memory as, 66–72
personal memory, nature of, 63–66
physical workings of memory, 86n5
Picture-Superiority Effect, 71, 84
Pillemer, David, 92n73
Pitkänen, Pekka, 111n26
place memory, 112n42
Pleydell-Pearce, Christopher, 67, 70
poetics of memory, 19
Pribram, Karl, 64
promised land, 1, 4, 21, 22, 25, 34, 38, 41, 42, 51, 73–76, 82, 84, 88n24, 93n88, 94n103, 107, 129–31, 142, 147, 158, 161, 194
Proverbs, 24, 60n107, 121;
Prov 3:3, 121
Ps 64:4, 119
Psalms, 2
psychology of memory, 3

Reading Genesis (Hendel), 17
reading event, 194–96
Realms of Memory (McCormack), 100
recycled songs, 180–81
relational epistemology, 23
remembering, 18, 20, 64, 72, 161;
covenant relationship, 8;
"eyes" motif, 43–50;
Deut 4, 43–45;renew the past, 9
Remembering Abraham (Hendel), 17
Remembering and Forgetting in Early Second Temple Judah (Levin), 18

repressed memory, 52n6
Rev 15:3, 175
The Rhetoric of Remembrance (Hwang), 23–24
Richter, Sandra, 107–8, 115–16n80, 115n79, 116n81
Ricoeur, Paul, 5, 192–95, 199n18
ritual, as memory vector, 4, 141–73;
Deut 16:1–17, 141–58;
memory-making, 158–63
ritual reenactment, 9
rock motif, 178
Roediger, Henry L., 71
Römer, Thomas, 36, 40

Schacter, Daniel, 64, 65, 86n3, 86n5, 86n7
Schottroff, Willy, 8, 10–12, 14, 22, 26n2, 27n16
Scripture, 5;
as memory producer, 7–31
Searle, 24
seeing and hearing, relationship between, 45–50, 126
semantic autonomy, 193
semantic memory, 66, 74, 84, 88n27, 155, 194
Semon, Richard, 86n7
sensory memory, 68
Sentilles, Sarah, 62n140
Shema, 21, 25, 117–19, 123–28, 130, 133n10, 138n94, 158, 183, 197
short-term or working memory, 64
The Silver Chair (Lewis), 1
situational competence, 125
Smith, Mark, 17, 20
social frameworks (*cadres sociaux*) of memory, 101
social memory, 3, 28n31, 52n4;
overgrown paths of, 12–16
sociomental topography, 4, 130
song, as memory vector, 4–5, 175–89;
Deut 32:1–43, 175–80;

memory-making, 180–84
song, transportive power of, 5
Song of Moses, 4, 5, 42, 175, 181, 182
source monitoring, 71
space allocation, 73
speech act theory, 24, 196
staccato time, 140n131
Steiner, George, 197
Stern, P. D., 75
story, as memory vector, 4, 117–40;
   habitus, 117–24;
   habitus, in memory-making, 124–26
storytelling, 126–30;
   in memory-making, 130–32
Struktursignal, 127
Sutton, David, 25
Sutton, John, 85–86n2
symbolic typography, 167n60

Talstra, Eep, 120
temporal knowledge, 68
tents, 144, 145
texts:
   as agents of cultural memory making, 3;
   as extended contexts, 105–6;
   as memory producers, 52n5;
   as memory-producing agents, 2;
   as memory products, 2, 52n5, 191;
   and real presence, 196–98;
   as world-projecting agents, 5;
   and world projection, 192–95
thematic knowledge, 68
theological interpretation, 196
Thomson, Donald M., 65
Tigay, Jeffrey H., 135–36n53, 138n95, 170–71n124, 178
Tulving, Endel, 65

turning points, 69
Twice Used Songs (Giles and Doan), 180
2 Kgs 23, 156, 171n139

University of Alberta, 18
University of Copenhagen, 16

Vanhoozer, Kevin, 192, 196
verbal repetition, 159
visual language, 3, 23, 49, 51, 80, 84, 146, 194, 195, 198
visual presentation, 123
von Rad, Gerhard, 10, 36–37, 51, 54n33, 59n92, 72, 74–75, 128–29, 139n114
Vorlagen, 141, 142, 146, 165n22

Warburg, Aby, 14–15
Watts, J. D. W., 74
Weinfeld, Moshe, 43, 50, 148
Weitzman, Steven, 47–48, 61n120, 61n121
Wenham, Gordon, 2
Weyde, Karl, 142, 144, 166n29
Wiederholung, 36
wilderness, 1, 4, 17, 34, 35, 38, 51, 72–74, 78, 81–85, 92n78, 95n119, 97n139, 129, 131, 140n131, 144, 145, 147, 154, 158, 160–62, 170n124, 179–80, 182, 194, 195
Wood, Nancy, 101–3, 110n19, 110n21
working self, 67, 69–70

Yahwistic worship, 46, 106, 113n60

Zelizer, Barbie, 104
Zerubavel, Eviatar, 130, 140n131

About the Author

A.J. Culp is lecturer in Old Testament and Biblical Languages at Malyon Theological College, an affiliated institution of the Australian College of Theology, and honorary research fellow at the University of Queensland. His work has appeared in various publications and focuses especially on how the Bible works as a "world-building" text—as a text that creates a world in which readers encounter the divine.

www.ingramcontent.com/pod-product-compliance
Lightning Source LLC
Chambersburg PA
CBHW021848300426
44115CB00005B/65